T0322030

ALGORITHMS FOR
BIG DATA

ALGORITHMS FOR
BIG DATA

Moran Feldman

The Open University of Israel, Israel

World Scientific

NEW JERSEY · LONDON · SINGAPORE · BEIJING · SHANGHAI · HONG KONG · TAIPEI · CHENNAI · TOKYO

Published by

World Scientific Publishing Co. Pte. Ltd.

5 Toh Tuck Link, Singapore 596224

USA office: 27 Warren Street, Suite 401-402, Hackensack, NJ 07601

UK office: 57 Shelton Street, Covent Garden, London WC2H 9HE

Library of Congress Cataloging-in-Publication Data
Names: Feldman, Moran, author.
Title: Algorithms for big data / Moran Feldman, The Open University of Israel, Israel.
Description: New Jersey : World Scientific, 2020.
Identifiers: LCCN 2020011810| ISBN 9789811204739 (hardcover) |
    ISBN 9789811204746 (ebook for institutions) | ISBN 9789811204753 (ebook for individuals)
Subjects: LCSH: Algorithms.
Classification: LCC QA9.58 .F45 2020 | DDC 005.701/5181--dc23
LC record available at https://lccn.loc.gov/2020011810

British Library Cataloguing-in-Publication Data
A catalogue record for this book is available from the British Library.

For any available supplementary material, please visit
https://www.worldscientific.com/worldscibooks/10.1142/11398#t=suppl

Desk Editors: Anthony Alexander/Steven Patt

Typeset by Stallion Press
Email: enquiries@stallionpress.com

Printed in Singapore

Preface

The emergence of the Internet has allowed people, for the first time, to access huge amounts of data. Think, for example, of the graph of friendships in the social network Facebook and the graph of links between Internet websites. Both these graphs contain more than one billion nodes, and thus, represent huge datasets. To use these datasets, they must be processed and analyzed. However, their mere size makes such processing very challenging. In particular, classical algorithms and techniques, that were developed to handle datasets of a more moderate size, often require unreasonable amounts of time and space when faced with such large datasets. Moreover, in some cases it is not even feasible to store the entire dataset, and thus, one has to process the parts of the dataset as they arrive and discard each part shortly afterwards.

The above challenges have motivated the development of new tools and techniques adequate for handling and processing "big data" (very large amounts of data). In this book, we take a theoretical computer science view on this work. In particular, we will study computational models that aim to capture the challenges raised by computing over "big data" and the properties of practical solutions developed to answer these challenges. We will get to know each one of these computational models by surveying a few classic algorithmic results, including many state-of-the-art results.

This book was designed with two contradicting objectives in mind, which are as follows:

(i) on the one hand, we try to give a wide overview of the work done in theoretical computer science in the context of "big data" and

(ii) on the other hand, we strive to do so with sufficient detail to allow the reader to participate in research work on the topics covered.

While we did our best to meet both goals, we had to compromise in some aspects. In particular, we had to omit some important "big data" subjects such as dimension reduction and compressed sensing. To make the book accessible to a broader population, we also omitted some classical algorithmic results that involve tedious calculations or very advanced mathematics. In most cases, the important aspects of these results can be demonstrated by other, more accessible, results.

About the Author

 **Moran Feldman** is a faculty member at the Computer Science Department of the University of Haifa. He obtained his B.A. and M.Sc. degrees from the Open University of Israel, and his Ph.D. from the Technion. Additionally, he spent time, as an intern, post-doctoral follow and a faculty member, in Yahoo! Research, Google, Microsoft Research, EPFL and the Open University of Israel. Moran was a fellow of the Alon Scholarship and the Google European Fellowship in Market Algorithms. He was also awarded the Cisco Prize, the Rothblum Award and the SIAM Outstanding Paper Prize. Moran's main research interests lie in the theory of algorithms. Many of his works are in the fields of submodular optimization, streaming algorithms and online computation.

Contents

Part I: Data Stream Algorithms

Chapter 1

Introduction to Data Stream Algorithms

Modern computer networks often include monitoring elements which constantly analyze the network's traffic. These monitoring elements can serve various purposes such as studying changes in the network's use over time or detecting malicious network activity. The algorithms employed by the monitoring elements have to process all the network traffic they receive, and then extract out of this traffic the information they are looking for. The task faced by these algorithms is made more complicated by the fact that a monitoring element typically receives a huge amount of traffic, and it is only possible for it to store a small fraction of this traffic. In other words, an algorithm used by the monitoring element views the traffic received by the element packet by packet. The algorithm can, then, store in memory some of these packets for future reference; however, the size of the memory available to the algorithm is relatively small, and thus, at every given time it can keep in memory only a small fraction of the packets it has viewed. Intuitively, this memory restriction means that in order to produce a meaningful output, the algorithm must find a way to "guess" the important packets that should be kept in memory, and filter them out of the rest of the traffic.

Consider now a very different scenario which leads to similar algorithmic obstacles. Magnetic tapes are viewed by most people as a technology of the past. Surprisingly, however, this is not really the case. Despite the many types of storage devices available today, magnetic tapes are still often used by organizations that store very large amounts of data when it is not necessary to have a quick access to this information (prime examples are archives and cold backups). Magnetic tapes are an appealing storage option for such uses since they are very cost effective, and allow the storage of huge amounts of data for a relatively cheap price. Unfortunately, reading of data from a magnetic tape is only efficient when the data is read sequentially, i.e., the data is read in the order in which it is written on the tape. If a user requests a piece of information from a magnetic tape which is not physically close to the piece of information read before, then the tape must be rewound to the location of the requested information, which is a very slow operation (on the order of multiple seconds). In view of this issue, algorithms processing the data of a magnetic tape often read it sequentially. Just like in the network monitoring scenario, the algorithm can store some of the information it gets from the tape in the computer's main memory. However, typically this memory is large enough to contain only a small fraction of the tape's data, and thus, the algorithm has to "guess" the important parts of the data that should be kept in memory.

1.1 The Data Stream Model

The two above scenarios, as well as other similar scenarios involving big data systems, motivate a computational model, named the *data stream model*, which attempts to capture the algorithmic issues demonstrated by these scenarios. An algorithm for the data stream model receives a stream of "tokens" as its input. To make things concrete, one can think of these tokens, in light of the above scenarios, as network packets or records on a magnetic tape. Like non-data stream algorithms, the objective of a data stream algorithm is to compute some output based on its input stream of tokens. However, the data stream algorithm is only allowed a sequential access to its input stream. In other words, the algorithm must read its input tokens one after the other in the order they appear in the stream, and can never read again tokens that have already been read before.

A mock example of a data stream algorithm is given as Algorithm 1. This algorithm simply calculates the length (in tokens) of its input stream. It is customary to denote this length by n, and we will use this notation throughout this book when considering the data stream model (except when explicitly stated otherwise).

Exercise 1 asks you to write your first data stream algorithm. At this point, our objective is simply to get you accustomed to the data stream model, so there is no need to worry too much about the quality of the algorithm you write. In fact, this will be the case until Section 1.1.2, in which we will have a detailed discussion about ways to evaluate data stream

---

Algorithm 1: Count Stream Length

1. $n \leftarrow 0$.
2. **while** there are more tokens **do**
3.   Read the next token.
4. $n \leftarrow n + 1$.
5. **return** n.

---

algorithms and the properties that we expect from a good data stream algorithm.

Exercise 1. Write a data stream algorithm that checks whether all the tokens in its input stream are identical. The algorithm should output TRUE if this is the case, and FALSE if the input stream contains at least two different tokens.

As defined above, a data stream algorithm is allowed to read its input stream only once. This fits very well with the above network monitoring scenario, where the monitoring element can see each packet only once. However, an algorithm processing a magnetic tape can read the tape multiple times by rewinding the tape to its beginning after each complete read. Reading the tape multiple times is, of course, slower than reading it only once; however, an algorithm doing a small number of tape reads is often still practical. In light of this observation, it is common to allow a data stream algorithm multiple passes over its input stream. During each pass, the algorithm reads the tokens of the input stream one after the other in the order they appear in the stream.

An example of a 2-passes data stream algorithm is given as Algorithm 3. The objective of this algorithm is to find the tokens that appear often in its input stream. More specifically, the algorithm has a parameter k, and it finds the tokens that appear more than n/k times in the stream (recall that n is the length of the stream in tokens). For example, given the input stream "*ababcbca*" and the parameter $k = 3$, the algorithm will output the tokens "*a*" and "*b*" which appear more than $8/3 \approx 2.666$ times in this input stream.

Before getting to the pseudocode of Algorithm 3, it is useful to look at the following simple data stream algorithm that obtains the same goal using a single pass.

Algorithm 2: Frequent Elements Algorithm — One Pass (k)

1. $n \leftarrow 0$.
2. **while** there are more tokens **do**
3.   Let t be the next token.
4. $n \leftarrow n + 1$.
5.   Increase the counter of t by 1.
6. **return** the list of tokens whose counters are larger than n/k.

This algorithm maintains a counter for every token it views, and these counters are implicitly assumed to be initially zero. The counter of every token counts the number of appearances of this token, and the algorithm can then check which tokens have more than n/k appearance by simply checking the values of all the counters.

While this algorithm is very simple, it is not very useful in practice because it might need to keep very many counters if there are many distinct tokens in the stream. Our 2-passes algorithm (Algorithm 3) avoids this issue by using one pass to filter out most of the tokens that do not appear many times in the stream. More specifically, in its first pass, Algorithm 3 produces a small set F of tokens that includes all the tokens that *might* appear many times in the stream. Then, in its second pass, Algorithm 3 mimics Algorithm 2, but only for the tokens of F. Thus, as long as F is small, the number of counters maintained by Algorithm 3 is kept small, even when there are many unique tokens in the stream (technically, Algorithm 3 still maintains a counter for every token in the stream. However, most of these counters are zeros at every given time point, so a good implementation does not require much space for storing all of them).

Let us now explain the pseudocode of Algorithm 3 in more detail. Like Algorithm 2, Algorithm 3 also implicitly assumes that the counter of each token is initially zero. During the first pass of this algorithm over the input stream, it processes each token t by doing two things as follows:

- It increases the counter of t by 1.
- If after this increase there are at least k counters with non-zero values, then every such counter is decreased by 1.

To make this more concrete, let us consider the behavior of Algorithm 3 during its first pass when given the above input example (i.e., the input stream "*ababcbca*" and $k = 3$). While reading the first 4 tokens of the input stream, the algorithm increases both the counters of "*a*" and "*b*" to 2. Then,

---

Algorithm 3: Frequent Elements Algorithm (k)

1. **while** there are more tokens **do**
2.   Let t be the next token.
3.   Increase the counter of t by one.
4.   **if** there are at least k non-zero counters **then**
5.   Decrease *all* the non-zero counters by 1.
6. Let F be the set of tokens currently having a non-zero counter.
7. Reset all the counters to zero.

8. Start the *second pass* over the input stream.
9. $n \leftarrow 0$.
10. **while** there are more tokens **do**
11.   Let t be the next token.
12. $n \leftarrow n + 1$.
13.   **If** $t \in F$ **then** increase the counter of t by 1.
14. **return** the list of tokens whose counters are larger than n/k.

---

the algorithm gets to the first occurrence of the token "c", which makes it increase the counter of "c" to 1 momentarily. However, as the number of non-zero counters is now equal to k, all these counters are decreased by 1, which sets the counter of "c" back to zero and also decreases the counters of "a" and "b" to 1.

Exercise 2. Manually simulate the remaining part of the first pass of Algorithm 3 on the input example. Write down the values of the counters immediately after the algorithm processes each token of the input stream.

After Algorithm 3 completes its first pass, it stores in F the set of tokens whose counters end up with a non-zero value at the end of the first pass. Recall that in the intuitive description of Algorithm 3, we claimed that F is a small set that includes every token that might have many appearances in the stream. Lemma 1 shows that this is indeed the case. We will prove this lemma soon.

Lemma 1. *During the first pass of Algorithm 3 at most k counters have non-zero values at every given time, and thus, the size of the set F is at most k. Additionally, F contains every element which appears more than n/k times in the input stream.*

During its second pass, Algorithm 3 determines the total length of the input stream and counts the number of times each token of F appears. Then, it outputs the list of tokens in F that appear more than n/k times in the input stream. Given Lemma 1, it is easy to see from this description that Algorithm 3 fulfills its objective, i.e., it outputs exactly the tokens that appear more than n/k times in the input stream. Thus, Lemma 1 remains to be proved.

Proof of Lemma 1. During the first pass of Algorithm 3, the processing of each arriving token consists of two steps: increasing the counter of the token, and then decreasing all the counters if the number of non-zero counters reached k. The first step might increase the number of non-zero counters when the counter of the arriving token increases from zero to one. However, if the number of counters reaches k following this increase, then the second step will decrease the counter of the arriving token back to zero; which will make the number of non-zero counters smaller than k again. Hence, the number of counters remains smaller than k following the processing of each input token, and is not larger than k at any given time.[1]

To prove the second part of the lemma, we observe that during the first pass of Algorithm 3 the total number of counter increases is equal to the number of tokens in the input stream, i.e., n. On the other hand, each time that the algorithm decreases counters (i.e., executes the line 5) it decreases k different counters. As no counter ever becomes negative, this means that the algorithm decreases counters at most n/k times. In particular, every given counter is decreased by at most n/k throughout the entire first pass. Hence, the counter of a token with more than n/k appearances in the input stream will remain positive at the end of the first pass, and thus, will end up in F. □

Exercise 3. The second pass of Algorithm 3 is used to differentiate between the tokens of F which really appear more than n/k times in the input stream and the tokens of F which do not appear so many times. In order to avoid the need for this second pass, a student suggested using the values of the counters at the end of the first pass to determine which tokens of F appear more than n/k times in the input stream. Prove that this cannot be done by finding an input stream for Algorithm 3 and value k which make the algorithm produce a set F such that:

---

[1]This can be proved more formally by induction on the number of tokens already processed.

1. F contains exactly two tokens.
2. One of the tokens in F appears more than n/k times in the input stream, while the other does not.
3. At the end of the first pass, the counters of the two tokens have the same values.

1.2 Evaluating Data Stream Algorithms

There are many different criteria which are used to evaluate the quality of a data stream algorithm. Often, the criterion that is considered to be the most important is the space complexity of the algorithm (the amount of memory used by the algorithm). The space complexity is usually given in terms of the length n of the input stream (in tokens) and the number m of different possible tokens. For example, Algorithm 1 maintains a single variable which counts the number of tokens viewed by the algorithm so far. Since this variable never exceeds the value n, it requires $O(\log n)$ bits, and this is also the space complexity of the algorithm.

Exercise 4. Recall that m is the number of different possible tokens. Show that the space complexity of Algorithm 3 is $O(k(\log n + \log m))$. **Hint:** Lemma 1 implies that only a few of the counters used by Algorithm 3 are non-zero at any given time. Suggest an implementation for Algorithm 3 which takes advantage of this observation.

Note that it is possible to store the entire input stream using a space complexity of $O(n \log m)$. Therefore, a data stream algorithm is only interesting when its space complexity is smaller than that. In particular, people are especially interested in data stream algorithms whose space complexity is poly-logarithmic in n and m (i.e., it is polynomial in log n and log m). Such algorithms are called *streaming algorithms*, and they are interesting because their memory requirement remains relatively small even when the input stream is very large. Observe that Algorithm 1 is a streaming algorithm, and Algorithm 3 is a streaming algorithm when k is considered to be a constant.

A few other criterions, beside the space complexity, that are used to evaluate data stream algorithms are given by the following list:

- *Number of passes* — A data stream algorithm is better when it makes fewer passes. In particular, algorithms with only a single pass are especially important since many real-world scenarios, like the above network monitoring scenario, do not allow for multiple passes. Accordingly, most of the data stream algorithms we will see in this book use only a single pass. Algorithms using more passes are also considered interesting, but only as long as the number of passes is relatively small (usually at most logarithmic in n and m).

- *Time complexity and token processing time* — A data stream algorithm is better when its time complexity is smaller, i.e., it runs faster. In addition to the time complexity of the entire algorithm, it is also important that the time it takes for the algorithm to process every given token is relatively short. This requirement is quantified by the token processing time of the algorithm, which is defined as the maximum number of basic operations the algorithm might perform from the moment it reads a token of the stream which is not the last one until it reads the next token. To see why it is important for an algorithm to have a short token processing time, recall the above network monitoring scenario. In this scenario, the monitoring element receives packets and has to process them as they arrive. Since the monitoring element does not control the arrival times of the packets, it must process each packet quickly, and be ready for the next packet when it arrives.

- *The quality of the solution* — The data stream algorithms presented in this chapter produce exact answers. However, such algorithms are rare in this book, and most of the algorithms we will see in the subsequent chapters produce only approximate answers. For such algorithms, the quality of the answer it produces (i.e., how well does it approximate the real answer) is an important criterion for evaluating the quality of the algorithm.

To illustrate the token processing time criterion, let us consider Algorithm 1. After reading each token, this algorithm performs only a single operation, which is to increase its variable n. Hence, its token processing time is $O(1)$.[2]

‖ **Exercise 5.** Determine the token processing time of Algorithm 3.

---

[2]Note that we assume here that standard operations on numbers such as addition and multiplication can be done using a single basic operation. A more accurate analysis of the token processing time should take into account the time required for these operations (which is often logarithmic in the number of bits necessary to represent the numbers). However, in the interest of simplicity we ignore, throughout this book, this extra complication and assume standard operations on numbers require only a single basic operation.

1.3 Bibliographic Notes

The data stream model was studied in one form or another by various works already in the 1970s and 1980s (see, for example, Flajolet and Martin, 1985; Morris, 1978; Munro and Paterson, 1980). However, it only became popular after the publication of a paper by Alon *et al.* (1999) which introduced many important techniques often used in modern data stream algorithms. For this paper, the authors won the Gödel Prize in 2005.

The first pass of Algorithm 3 is known as the Misra–Gries algorithm (Misra and Gries, 1982) for estimating the frequencies vector. This algorithm outputs for every token t an estimate $\tilde{f}_t$ of the number of its appearances in the data stream. The estimate $\tilde{f}_t$ can never overestimate the real number of appearances f_t and can underestimate it by at most n/k. More formally,

$$f_t - \frac{n}{k} \leq \tilde{f}_t \leq f_t.$$

N. Alon, Y. Matias and M. Szegedy. The Space Complexity of Approximating the Frequency Moments. *Journal of Computer and System Sciences*, 58(1): 137–147, 1999.

P. Flajolet and G. N. Martin. Probabilistic Counting Algorithms for Data Base Aplications. *Journal of Computer and System Sciences*, 31(2): 182–209, 1985.

J. Misra and D. Gries. Finding Repeated Elements. *Science of Computer Programming*, 2(2): 143–152, 1982.

R. Morris. Counting Large Number of Events in Small Registers. *Communications of the ACM*, 21(10): 840–842, 1978.

J. I. Munro and M. S. Paterson. Selection and Sorting with Limited Storage. *Theoretical Computer Science*, 12: 315–323, 1980.

Exercise Solutions

Solution 1

One possible solution is given as Algorithm 4.

Algorithm 4: Input Stream Uniform

1. **if** there are no tokens **then return** TRUE.
2. Let t_1 be the first token.
3. **while** there are more tokens **do**
4.   Let t be the next token.
5.   **If** $t \neq t_1$ **then return** FALSE.
6. **return** TRUE.

The first line of the algorithm handles the case in which the input stream is empty (and outputs TRUE in this case). The rest of the algorithm compares all the tokens of the stream to the first token. If the algorithm finds any token in the stream which is different from the first token, then it outputs FALSE. Otherwise, all the tokens of the stream must be identical, and thus, the algorithm outputs TRUE.

Solution 2

Recall that, after reading the first 5 tokens of the input stream, the counters of the tokens "a", "b" and "c" in Algorithm 3 have the values 1, 1 and 0, respectively. The next token that the algorithm reads is "b", which causes the algorithm to increase the counter of "b" to 2. Then, the algorithm reads the second occurrence of the token "c", which momentarily increases the counter of "c" to 1. However, the number of non-zero counters is now equal to k again, which makes the algorithm decrease all the non-zero counters by 1. This sets the value of the counter of "c" back to zero, and decreases the counters of "a" and "b" to 0 and 1, respectively. The final token that the algorithm reads is "a", which increases the counter of "a" back to 1.

The following table summarizes the values of the counters after the algorithm processes each one of the input stream tokens. Each column of the table corresponds to one token of the input stream, and gives the values of the counters after this token is processed by the algorithm. Note that the rightmost column of the table corresponds to the last token of the input stream, and thus, gives the values of the counters at the end of the first pass of the algorithm.

Token Processed:	"a"	"b"	"a"	"b"	"c"	"b"	"c"	"a"
Counter of "a":	1	1	2	2	1	1	0	1
Counter of "b":	0	1	1	2	1	2	1	1
Counter of "c":	0	0	0	0	0	0	0	0

Solution 3

Consider the input stream "$abcabcad$" and $k = 3$. One can verify, by simulating the algorithm, that when Algorithm 3 gets this input stream and value of k, it produces the set $F = \{a, d\}$. Moreover, the values of the counters of "a" and "d" are both 1 at the end of the first pass of the algorithm. It can also be observed that "a" appears $3 > n/k$ times in the above input stream, while "d" appears only once in this input stream.

Solution 4

Algorithm 3 maintains a counter for every token. However, by Lemma 1 only k of these counters can be non-zero at every given time. Hence, it is enough to keep in memory only these (up to) k non-zero counters. For each such counter, we need to maintain the token it is associated with and its value. Since there are m possible tokens, each token can be specified using $O(\log m)$ bits. Similarly, since the value of each counter is upper bounded by the length n of the stream, it requires only $O(\log n)$ bits. Combining these bounds we get that maintaining the counters of Algorithm 3 requires only $O(k(\log n + \log m))$ bits.

In addition to its counters, Algorithm 3 uses two additional variables: n — which counts the number of input tokens, and thus, can be represented using $O(\log n)$ bits, and F — which is a set of up to k tokens, and thus, can be represented using $O(k \log m)$ bits. One can observe, however, that the space requirements of these two variables are dominated by the space requirement $O(k(\log n + \log m))$ of the counters, and thus, can be ignored.

Solution 5

We assume throughout this solution that Algorithm 3 maintains explicitly only the values of its non-zero counters. Note that Lemma 1 guarantees that there are at most k non-zero counters during the first pass of Algorithm 3. Additionally, Lemma 1 also guarantees $|F| \leq k$, which implies that Algorithm 3 has at most k non-zero counters during its second pass as well. Since only the non-zero counters are explicitly maintained by Algorithm 3, these observations imply that it is possible for Algorithm 3 to find the counter of every given token in $O(k)$ time.

During its first pass, Algorithm 3 performs three steps after reading each token. First, it finds the counter of the read token, then it increases this counter, and finally, if there are at least k non-zero counters, it decreases all the non-zero counters. By the above discussion, steps one and two can be done in $O(k)$ time. Similarly, the third step can be implemented by scanning the list of non-zero counters and decreasing each one of them (when necessary), and thus, also requires only $O(k)$ time.

During its second pass, Algorithm 3 performs a few steps after reading each token. First, it increases the variable n used to determine the length of the input stream. Then, if the read token belongs to F, it finds its counter and increases it. Again, the above discussion implies that these steps can be done in $O(k)$ time.

In conclusion, after reading each token Algorithm 3 performs $O(k)$ operations in both passes, and thus, this is its token processing time.

Chapter 2

Basic Probability and Tail Bounds

In this chapter, we take a short break from the data stream model and study some tools from probability theory that we will use throughout the rest of the book. The chapter will begin with a review of the basic probability theory. This review will be quite quick as we assume that the reader already took a basic probability course at some point and, thus, is familiar with the reviewed material. After the review, we will study the topic of *tail bounds*, which is an essential tool for many of the results we will see in this book, but is not covered very well by most basic probability courses.

2.1 Discrete Probability Spaces

Probability theory studies random processes such as the toss of a coin or the roll of a dice. In this book, we are only interested in discrete random processes. Such processes are modeled in probability theory by *discrete probability spaces*. Formally, a discrete probability space is a pair (Ω, P), where Ω is the set of all possible outcomes of the random process we would like to model and P is a function from Ω to $[0, 1]$ assigning to each outcome in Ω the probability of this outcome to realize. The set Ω and the function P should also have the following properties:

- The set Ω of outcomes should be of countable size.
- The sum of the probabilities assigned by P to the outcomes should be 1.

To exemplify the above definition, consider the toss of a fair coin. This random process has two possible outcomes: "head" and "tail". Since these two outcomes have equal probabilities of being realized (for a fair coin), each one of them is realized with a probability of $1/2$. Thus, the discrete probability space corresponding to this random process is (Ω, P) for

$$\Omega = \{\text{head, tail}\} \quad \text{and} \quad P(x) = 1/2 \quad \forall x \in \Omega.$$

Exercise 1. Define the discrete probability space corresponding to

(a) the roll of a fair dice,
(b) the toss of a biased coin that falls on "head" with probability $2/3$,
(c) tossing both a fair dice and the biased coin from (b).

In most of the cases we will study in this book, the set Ω is not only countable but also finite. Accordingly, while all the results we mention in this chapter apply to general countable Ω, the proofs we give for some of them work only for the case of a finite Ω.

Consider now the roll of a fair dice. Such a roll has six possible outcomes: $\{1, 2, 3, 4, 5, 6\}$, and the discrete probability space corresponding to the roll assigns a probability to each one of these outcomes. However, often we are interested in probabilities of things that are not outcomes. For example, we might be interested in the probability that the outcome is even or that it is larger than 4. To study such probabilities formally, we need to define the notion of events. Every subset of $E \subseteq \Omega$ is called an *event*, and the probability of an event is the sum of the probabilities of the outcomes in it.

To exemplify the notion of events, assume that we would like to determine the probability that the dice shows an even number. To calculate this probability, we first note that the event that the dice shows an even number is the set of even possible outcomes, i.e., $\{2, 4, 6\}$. The probability of this event is

$$\Pr\left[\left\{\begin{array}{c} \text{dice shows} \\ \text{an even number} \end{array}\right\}\right] = \Pr[\{2, 4, 6\}] = P(2) + P(4) + P(6)$$

$$= 3 \cdot \frac{1}{6} = \frac{1}{2},$$

where the penultimate equality holds since the outcomes 2, 4 and 6 are realized with probability $1/6$ each.[1]

---

[1] The function P was defined as function over outcomes, and thus, we use it only when referring to probabilities of individual outcomes. For probabilities of events, we use the notation $\Pr[\cdot]$.

Exercise 2. Consider a biased dice whose probability to show each one of its sides is given by the following table. What is the probability of the event that this dice shows a number larger than or equal to 4?

Shown Number	1	2	3	4	5	6
Probability	0.05	0.2	0.15	0.25	0.25	0.1

In many random processes, all the outcomes have equal probabilities. It is not difficult to verify that for such processes the probability of an event E is equal to $|E|/|\Omega|$, i.e., the fraction of the possible outcomes that belong to E. While this observation is useful, it can also be very confusing because people often apply it intuitively also in situations in which the outcomes do not have equal probabilities to realize. The solution of Exercise 2 demonstrates one example of an event E whose probability is not equal to $|E|/|\Omega|$.

Given two events E_1, $E_2 \subseteq \Omega$, the expression $\Pr[E_1|E_2]$ is used to denote the *conditional probability* of E_1 given E_2, i.e., the probability of event E_1 conditioned on the fact that event E_2 happened. Intuitively, $\Pr[E_1|E_2]$ need not be equal to $\Pr[E_1]$ because the fact that E_2 happened gives us some information about the outcome that is realized. The value of $\Pr[E_1|E_2]$ is given by the formula

$$\Pr[E_1|E_2] = \frac{\Pr[E_1 \cap E_2]}{\Pr[E_2]}.$$

To better understand this formula, observe that E_2 is the set of outcomes that can still happen given the fact that E_2 happened, and $E_1 \cap E_2$ is the set of such outcomes that also belong to E_1. Thus, $\Pr[E_1|E_2]$ is the ratio between the total probability of the outcomes that can still happen and belong to E_1 and the total probability of all the outcomes that can still happen. It is important to observe that the formula used to define $\Pr[E_1|E_2]$ can be used only when the event E_2 has a non-zero probability because otherwise it results in a division by zero. Thus, the conditional probability $\Pr[E_1|E_2]$ is defined only when the event E_2 has a non-zero probability.

Let us now consider an example. Let E_1 be the event that a fair dice shows an even number, and let E_2 be the event that the dice shows a number no larger than 3. We already know from the discussion before Exercise 2 that $\Pr[E_1] = 1/2$, and let us calculate now the conditional probability $\Pr[E_1|E_2]$. Observe that $E_1 = \{2, 4, 6\}$ and $E_2 = \{1, 2, 3\}$. Thus, using the formula given above, we get

$$\Pr[E_1 | E_2] = \frac{\Pr[E_1 \cap E_2]}{\Pr[E_2]} = \frac{\Pr[\{2,4,6\} \cap \{1,2,3\}]}{\Pr[\{1,2,3\}]}$$

$$= \frac{\Pr[\{2\}]}{\Pr[\{1,2,3\}]} = \frac{1/6}{3/6} = \frac{1}{3}.$$

In other words, the last series of equalities shows that the probability that the dice shows an even number given that it shows a number no larger than 3 is $1/3$, which intuitively makes sense since only one out of the three numbers on the dice of value at most 3 is even.

Some pairs of events do not convey any information about each other. For example, if we toss a coin twice, then the result of one toss does not affect the result of the other toss. Thus, the event that the coin fell on "head" in the first toss does not tell us anything about the event that the coin fell on "head" in the second toss, and vice versa. Such pairs of events are called *independent* events, and mathematically, we say that two events E_1 and E_2 are independent if

$$\Pr[E_1] \cdot \Pr[E_2] = \Pr[E_1 \cap E_2].$$

To make sense out of this definition, note that if the probabilities of E_1 and E_2 are both non-zero, then for two independent events E_1 and E_2, we have

$$\Pr[E_1 | E_2] = \frac{\Pr[E_1 \cap E_2]}{\Pr[E_2]} = \Pr[E_1] \quad \text{and}$$

$$\Pr[E_2 | E_1] = \frac{\Pr[E_1 \cap E_2]}{\Pr[E_1]} = \Pr[E_2].$$

Hence, the probability of E_1 happening is unchanged when conditioned on E_2, and vice versa, which is exactly the intuitive behavior we expect from a pair of independent events that do not convey any information about each other.

Another kind of relationship that can exist between pairs of events is disjointness. We say that two events E_1 and E_2 are *disjoint* if their intersection is empty (formally, $E_1 \cap E_2 = \varnothing$). One can observe that for such events

$$\Pr[E_1 \cup E_2] = \sum_{o \in E_1 \cup E_2} P(o) = \sum_{o \in E_1} P(o) + \sum_{o \in E_2} P(o) = \Pr[E_1] + \Pr[E_2].$$

Occasionally, people mix up between disjointness and independence. Thus, it is important to keep in mind that these are two different notions. In fact, it is almost impossible for two events to be both independent and disjoint because, for two disjoint events E_1 and E_2, the fact that one of them happened necessarily implies that the other did not happen. The following exercise asks you to formally prove this (almost) contradiction between disjointness and independence.

Exercise 3. Prove that if E_1 and E_2 are a pair of disjoint and independent events, then at least one of them must have zero probability.

At this point, we already have enough tools to calculate the probabilities of some non-trivial events. The following exercises give you an opportunity to practice a few such calculations.

Exercise 4. Consider two tosses of a coin which falls on "head" with probability 2/3. Calculate the probability that both tosses result in the same output (i.e., the coin either falls on "head" in both tosses or falls on "tail" in both of them).

Exercise 5. Consider two rolls of a fair dice. Calculate the probability that the dice shows either five or six in at least one of the rolls. How does your answer change if the dice is rolled k times (for some positive integer k) rather than two times?

The tools described above can also be used to prove the following very useful lemma, which is known as the *law of total probability*.

Lemma 1 (law of total probability). *Let $A_1, A_2, \ldots, A_k$ be a set of k disjoint events such that their union includes all the possible outcomes and the probability of each individual event A_i is non-zero. Then, for every event E, it holds that*

$$\Pr[E] = \sum_{i=1}^{k} \Pr[A_i] \cdot \Pr[E|A_i].$$

Exercise 6. Prove the law of total probability (Lemma 1).

The law of total probability is very useful when one has to calculate the probability of an event E through a case analysis that distinguishes between multiple disjoint cases. The reader will be asked to apply this technique in Exercise 7.

Exercise 7. Consider a roll of two fair dices. Calculate the probability that the sum of the numbers shown by the two dices is even. **Hint:** For every integer i between 1 and 6, let A_i be the event that the first dice shows the value of i. Use the law of total probability with the disjoint events $A_1, A_2, \ldots, A_6$.

In the above discussions, we defined independence for pairs of events. We now would like to extend this notion to larger collections of events. Given a set of h events $E_1, E_2, \ldots, E_h$, we say that they are independent if knowing that some of these events happened or did not happen does not give us any information about the other events.[2] Formally, the events $E_1, E_2, \ldots, E_h$ are independent if

$$\Pr\left[\bigcap_{i \in I} E_i\right] = \prod_{i \in I} \Pr[E_i] \quad \forall I \subseteq \{1, 2, \ldots, h\}.$$

Independence is a very strong property, so we sometimes have to settle for a weaker property. We say that the events $E_1, E_2, \ldots, E_h$ are *pairwise independent* if every pair of them is independent, i.e.,

$$\Pr[E_i \cap E_j] = \Pr[E_i] \cdot \Pr[E_j] \quad \forall 1 \leqslant i < j \leqslant k.$$

Exercise 8 demonstrates that pairwise independence is strictly weaker than independence by giving an example of a set of events that are pairwise independent but not independent.

Exercise 8. Consider three tosses of a fair coin. For every two distinct values $i, j \in \{1, 2, 3\}$, let E_{ij} be the event that tosses i and j have the same outcome.

(a) Prove that the events E_{12}, E_{23} and E_{13} are pairwise independent.
(b) Prove that the above three events are not independent.

Let us now introduce a third notion of independence that generalizes pairwise independence. We say that the events $E_1, E_2, \ldots, E_h$ are k-wise *independent* for some integer $k \geqslant 2$ if every subset of k out of these events

---

[2]This kind of independence is formally known as mutual independence. However, the word "mutual" is often omitted, and in this book we follow this practice of omission.

is independent, i.e.,

$$\Pr\left[\bigcap_{i \in I} E_i\right] = \prod_{i \in I} \Pr[E_i] \quad \forall I \subseteq \{1, 2, \ldots, h\}, |I| \leqslant k.$$

To see why k-wise independence is a generalization of pairwise independence, note that for $k = 2$, the two notions are identical. Observation 1 gives additional relationships between the different notions of independence mentioned above. Make sure that you understand why this observation is true.

Observation 1. Given h events $E_1, E_2, \ldots, E_h$,

1. If these events are k-wise independent, then they are also k'-wise independent for every $2 \leqslant k' < k$. Thus, the property of k-wise independence is stronger for larger values of k, and it is always at least as strong as pairwise independence.
2. If these events are independent, then they are k-wise independent for every $k \geqslant 2$. Thus, independence is a stronger property than k-wise independence (and pairwise independence).

In the rest of the chapters of the book, we will analyze many randomized algorithms. Such algorithms often have bad cases, and it is necessary to upper bound the probability that any of these bad cases happens. More formally, there are events $B_1, B_2, \ldots, B_k$ that are bad for the algorithm, and it is necessary to upper bound the probability of their union. We already know that if the events $B_1, B_2, \ldots, B_k$ are disjoint, then

$$\Pr\left[\bigcup_{i=1}^{k} B_i\right] = \sum_{i=1}^{k} \Pr[B_i].$$

However, it turns out that the requirement that the events $B_1, B_2, \ldots, B_k$ are disjoint can be dropped if we only need an upper bound on the probability of the union rather than an exact expression for it. Lemma 2, which is known as the *union bound*, makes this more formal.

Lemma 2 (union bound). *For every two events E_1 and E_2, $\Pr[E_1 \cup E_2] \leqslant \Pr[E_1] + \Pr[E_2]$.*

Proof. Since the probability of every individual outcome is non-negative,

$$\Pr[E_1 \cup E_2] = \sum_{o \in E_1 \cup E_2} P(o) \leqslant \sum_{o \in E_1} P(o) + \sum_{o \in E_2} P(o) = \Pr[E_1] + \Pr[E_2].$$

$\square$

Using the union bound (Lemma 2) and induction, it is not difficult to prove that for any k (not necessarily disjoint) bad events $B_1, B_2, \ldots, B_k$, we have that

$$\Pr\left[\bigcup_{i=1}^{k} B_i\right] \leqslant \sum_{i=1}^{k} \Pr[B_i].$$

2.2 Random Variables

A *random variable* is a value (usually numerical) that can be calculated based on the outcome of a random process (formally, it is a function from Ω to some range). For example, if we consider the roll of two dices, then the sum of the numbers that they show is a random variable taking integer values between 2 and 12.

One of the most important properties of a numerical random variable is its *expectation*. Given a numerical random variable X taking values from a range R, the expectation $\mathrm{E}[X]$ of X is defined as

$$\mathrm{E}[X] = \sum_{r \in R} r \cdot \Pr[X = r].^3$$

In other words, the expectation $\mathrm{E}[X]$ is a weighted average of the values that X can take, where the weight of every possible value $r \in R$ is the probability of X to take this value.

Exercise 9. Consider a roll of two fair dices, and let X be the sum of the values they show. Calculate X.

As is evident by the solution for Exercise 9, calculating expectations directly via their definition is often a tedious work. Lemma 3, known as the *linearity of expectation*, can sometimes make these calculations much simpler. It should be noted that this lemma involves the expectations of mathematical expressions involving random variables. Such expectations make sense because any mathematical expression involving random variables can be viewed as a random variable on its own right.

---

[3] When Ω is infinite, this might be the sum of an infinite series, in which case the expectation is defined only if the series converges absolutely.

Lemma 3. *Let X and Y be two numerical variables with finite expectations, and let c be a real number. Then,*

1. $\mathrm{E}[X + Y] = \mathrm{E}[X] + \mathrm{E}[Y]$,
2. $\mathrm{E}[c \cdot X] = c \cdot \mathrm{E}[X]$.

Proof.

(1) Let R be the set of values that either X, Y or $X + Y$ can take. For every $r \in R$, we have

$$\Pr[X + Y = r] = \sum_{\substack{r_X, r_Y \in R \\ r_X + r_Y = r}} \Pr[X = r_X \wedge Y = r_Y]$$

since the events $\{X = r_X$ and $Y = r_Y\}$ are disjoint for different values of r_X and r_Y. For the same reason, for every value $r_X \in R$, we have

$$\Pr[X = r_X] = \sum_{r_Y \in R} \Pr[X = r_X \wedge Y = r_Y],$$

and for every value $r_Y \in R$, we have

$$\Pr[Y = r_Y] = \sum_{r_X \in R} \Pr[X = r_X \wedge Y = r_Y].$$

Using these three equalities and the definition of expectation, we get

$$\begin{aligned}
\mathrm{E}[X + Y] &= \sum_{r \in R} r \cdot \Pr[X + Y = r] \\
&= \sum_{r_X \in R} \sum_{r_Y \in R} (r_X + r_Y) \cdot \Pr[X = r_X \wedge Y = r_Y] \\
&= \sum_{r_X \in R} \sum_{r_Y \in R} r_X \cdot \Pr[X = r_X \wedge Y = r_Y] \\
&\quad + \sum_{r_X \in R} \sum_{r_Y \in R} r_Y \cdot \Pr[X = r_X \wedge Y = r_Y] \\
&= \sum_{r_X \in R} r_X \cdot \Pr[X = r_X] \\
&\quad + \sum_{r_Y \in R} r_Y \cdot \Pr[Y = r_Y] = \mathrm{E}[X] + \mathrm{E}[Y].
\end{aligned}$$

(2) It is not difficult to verify that $\mathrm{E}[c \cdot X] = c \cdot \mathrm{E}[X] = 0$ when $c = 0$. Thus, in the rest of the proof, let us assume $c \neq 0$. Let R be the set of values that either X or $c \cdot X$ takes. Then, by the definition of expectation, we have

$$\mathrm{E}[c \cdot X] = \sum_{r \in R} r \cdot \Pr[c \cdot X = r] = c \cdot \sum_{r \in R} \frac{r}{c} \cdot \Pr\left[X = \frac{r}{c}\right]$$

$$= c \cdot \sum_{r \in R} r \cdot \Pr[X = r] = c \cdot \mathrm{E}[X]. \qquad \square$$

Exercise 10. Use the linearity of expectation to get a simpler solution for Exercise 9.

Given a numerical random variable X, the linearity of expectation allows us to give an expression for $\mathrm{E}[f(X)]$ when f is a linear function. This naturally raises the question of what can be said about $\mathrm{E}[f(x)]$ for more general functions f. One answer for this question is given by the following lemma, which is known as *Jensen's inequality.*

Lemma 4 (Jensen's inequality). *Let X be a numeric random variable with a finite expectation whose value is always within some range C, and let f be a function from the reals to themselves. Then,*

(1) *if f is convex within C, then $f(\mathrm{E}[X]) \leqslant \mathrm{E}[f(X)]$,*
(2) *if f is concave within C, then $f(\mathrm{E}[X]) \geqslant \mathrm{E}[f(X)]$.*

Proof. We prove the lemma only for the case in which f is a convex within C. The proof for the other case is analogous. We begin by proving by induction on k that for every set of non-negative numbers $\lambda_1, \lambda_2, \ldots, \lambda_k$ whose sum is 1 and arbitrary numbers $y_1, y_2, \ldots, y_k \in C$, we have that

$$f\left(\sum_{i=1}^{k} \lambda_i y_i\right) \leqslant \sum_{i=1}^{k} \lambda_i \cdot f(y_i). \tag{2.1}$$

For $k = 1, \lambda_1$ must be equal 1, and thus, Inequality (2.1) holds as equality. Assume now that Inequality (2.1) holds for $k - 1 \geqslant 1$, and let us prove it for k. If $\lambda_1 = 1$, then Inequality (2.1) again holds as equality, and thus, we can assume $\lambda_1 < 1$. Since f is convex within C, this implies

$$f\left(\sum_{i=1}^{k} \lambda_i y_i\right) \leqslant \lambda_1 \cdot f(y_i) + (1 - \lambda_1) \cdot f\left(\sum_{i=2}^{k} \frac{\lambda_i}{1 - \lambda_1} \cdot y_i\right)$$

$$\leqslant \lambda_1 \cdot f(y_i) + (1 - \lambda_1) \cdot \sum_{i=2}^{k} \frac{\lambda_i}{1 - \lambda_1} \cdot f(y_i) = \sum_{i=1}^{k} \lambda_i \cdot f(y_i),$$

where the second inequality holds by the induction hypothesis. This completes the proof by induction of Inequality (2.1). Using Inequality (2.1) we can now prove the lemma as follows. Let R be the set of values that X takes with a positive probability. Then, since $\sum_{r \in R} \Pr[X = r] = 1$,

$$\mathrm{E}[f(X)] = \sum_{r \in R} f(r) \cdot \Pr[X = r] \geqslant f\left(\sum_{r \in R} r \cdot \Pr[X = r]\right) = f(\mathrm{E}[X]). \quad \square$$

One consequence of Jensen's inequality (Lemma 4) is that if X is a random variable taking only positive numeric values whose expectation is finite, then

$$\mathrm{E}\left[\frac{1}{X}\right] \geqslant \frac{1}{\mathrm{E}[X]}. \tag{2.2}$$

Exercise 11. Find an example of a random variable for which Inequality (2.2) holds as equality and an example for which this inequality does not hold as equality.

Given a numeric random variable X and an event A with a non-zero probability, we denote by $\mathrm{E}[X|A]$ the *conditional expectation* of X given A. Intuitively, $\mathrm{E}[X|A]$ is the expected value of X under the assumption that only outcomes from A can realize; and formally, the value of $\mathrm{E}[X|A]$ is given by the following formula. Let R be the set of values X can take, then we have

$$\mathrm{E}[X|A] = \sum_{r \in R} r \cdot \Pr[X = r|A].$$

Exercise 12. Let X be the value obtained by rolling a fair dice, let O be the event that this number is odd and let E be the event that it is even.

(a) Calculate $\mathrm{E}[X|O]$ and $\mathrm{E}[X|E]$,
(b) intuitively explain why $\mathrm{E}[X|O] < \mathrm{E}[X|E]$.

Using the notation of conditional expectation, we can now give the law of total expectation, which is an analogue of the law of total probability (Lemma 1) that we have seen before.

Lemma 5 (Law of total expectation). *Let $A_1, A_2, \ldots, A_k$ be a set of k disjoint events such that their union includes all the possible outcomes and the probability of each individual event A_i is non-zero. Then, for every random variable X, we have that*

$$E[X] = \sum_{i=1}^{k} \Pr[A_i] \cdot E[X|A_i].$$

Proof. Let us denote by R the set of values that X can take, then

$$
\begin{aligned}
\sum_{i=1}^{k} \Pr[A_i] \cdot E[X|A_i] &= \sum_{i=1}^{k} \Pr[A_i] \cdot \sum_{r \in R} (r \cdot \Pr[X = r|A_i]) \\
&= \sum_{r \in R} \left(r \cdot \sum_{i=1}^{k} \Pr[A_i] \cdot \Pr[X = r|A_i] \right) \\
&= \sum_{r \in R} r \cdot \Pr[X = r] = E[X],
\end{aligned}
$$

where the second equality follows by changing the order of summation, and the penultimate equality holds by the law of total probability. □

Recall that the law of total probability is useful for calculating probabilities using a case analysis. The law of total expectation can be used in a similar way to calculate expectations.

Exercise 13. Consider the following game. A player rolls a dice and gets a number d. She then rolls the dice d more times. The sum of the values shown by the dice in these d rolls is the number of points that the player gets in the game. Calculate the expectation of this sum.

We say that two random variables X and Y are independent if for every value r_X that X can take and value r_Y that Y can take, the events $X = r_X$ and $Y = r_Y$ are independent. Intuitively, two random variables are independent if and only if knowing the value of one of them gives us no information about the value of the other. Lemma 6 states a useful property of independent numerical random variables.

Lemma 6. *If X and Y be two independent numerical random variables with finite expectations, then $E[X \cdot Y] = E[X] \cdot E[Y]$.*

Proof. Let R be the set of values that X, Y or $X \cdot Y$ can take. Then,

$$
E[X \cdot Y] = \sum_{r \in R} r \cdot \Pr[X \cdot Y = r] = \sum_{\substack{r_X \in R \\ r_Y \in R}} (r_X r_Y) \cdot \Pr[X = r_X \wedge Y = r_Y]
$$

$$
= \sum_{\substack{r_X \in R \\ r_Y \in R}} (r_X r_Y) \cdot \Pr[X = r_X] \cdot \Pr[Y = r_Y]
$$

$$
= \left(\sum_{r_X \in R} r_X \cdot \Pr[X = r_X] \right) \cdot \left(\sum_{r_Y \in R} r_Y \cdot \Pr[X = r_Y] \right)
$$

$$
= E[X] \cdot E[Y],
$$

where the second equality holds since the events $\{X = r_X \wedge Y = r_Y\}$ are disjoint for different values of r_X and r_Y, and the third equality holds since X and Y are independent. $\qquad\square$

Exercise 14. Show that Lemma 6 does not necessarily hold when X and Y are not independent.

The notion of independence can be extended to many pairs of random variables. There are multiple ways to do that, paralleling the different ways described above to define independence for collections of more than two events.

Definition 1. Consider h random variables $X_1, X_2, \ldots, X_h$, and let R_i be the set of values X_i can take.

(1) The above variables are independent if the events $X_1 = r_1$, $X_2 = r_2, \ldots, X_h = r_h$ are independent for any choice of values $r_1 \in R_1$, $r_2 \in R_2, \ldots, r_h \in R_h$.
(2) The above variables are k-wise independent if the events $X_1 = r_1$, $X_2 = r_2, \ldots, X_h = r_h$ are k-wise independent for any choice of values $r_1 \in R_1$, $r_2 \in R_2, \ldots, r_h \in R_h$.
(3) The above variables are pairwise independent if every pair of them is independent. One can verify that this definition is equivalent to 2-wise independence.

At this point, we would like to present another important property of numerical random variables known as the variance. The variance of a random variable measures its tendency to be far from its expectation. Formally, the *variance* of a numerical random variable X is given by the formula

$$\text{Var}[X] = \text{E}[(X - \text{E}[X])^2].$$

In other words, the variance is the expectation of the squared distance of the value of X from its expectation. Lemma 7 gives an alternative formula for the variance that is often easier to use than the above definition.

Lemma 7. *For every variable X whose variance exists,*[4] $\text{Var}[X] = \text{E}[X^2] - (\text{E}[X])^2$.

Proof. Note that

$$\text{Var}[X] = \text{E}[(X - \text{E}[X])^2] = \text{E}[X^2 - 2X \cdot \text{E}[X] + (\text{E}[X])^2]$$
$$= \text{E}[X^2] - 2\text{E}[X] \cdot \text{E}[X] + (\text{E}[X])^2 = \text{E}[X^2] - (\text{E}[X])^2,$$

where the penultimate equality holds by the linearity of expectation (in particular, note that $\text{E}[X]$ is a constant, and thus, the linearity of expectation implies $\text{E}[X \cdot \text{E}[X]] = \text{E}[X] \cdot \text{E}[X]$). $\qquad\square$

In general, the variance does not have nice linear properties like the expectation. Nevertheless, it does have some properties that resemble linearity. Two such properties are listed in Lemma 8.

Lemma 8. *Given two numerical random variables X and Y whose variances exist and two constant numbers c and c', we have*

(a) $\text{Var}[c \cdot X + c'] = c^2 \cdot \text{Var}[X]$,
(b) *if X and Y are independent, then* $\text{Var}[X + Y] = \text{Var}[X] + \text{Var}[Y]$.

The proof of Lemma 8 is based on the linearity of expectation, and we leave it as an exercise.

---

[4] We do not encounter in this book any examples of random variables whose variances do not exist (such variables can be defined only in the context of infinite probability spaces, which we rarely consider). However, for completeness, we include the technical requirement that the variance exists in the necessary places.

‖ **Exercise 15.** Prove Lemma 8.

One consequence of Lemma 8 is that if $X_1, X_2, \ldots, X_h$ are h independent numerical random variables whose variances exist, then

$$\mathrm{Var}\left[\sum_{i=1}^{h} X_i\right] = \sum_{i=1}^{h} \mathrm{Var}[X_i].$$

Lemma 9 strengthens this observation by showing that the same equality holds even if we are only guaranteed that the variables $X_1, X_2, \ldots, X_h$ are pairwise independent (as opposed to independent).

Lemma 9. *Let $X_1, X_2, \ldots, X_h$ be h pairwise independent numerical random variables whose variances exist. Then, we have* $\mathrm{Var}[\sum_{i=1}^{h} X_i] = \sum_{i=1}^{h} \mathrm{Var}[X_i]$.

Proof. Since the variables $X_1, X_2, \ldots, X_h$ are pairwise independent, for every two distinct values $1 \leqslant i, j \leqslant h$, we get by Lemma 6 that $\mathrm{E}[X_i X_j] = \mathrm{E}[X_i] \cdot \mathrm{E}[X_j]$. Thus,

$$\mathrm{Var}\left[\sum_{i=1}^{h} X_i\right] = \mathrm{E}\left[\left(\sum_{i=1}^{h} X_i\right)^2\right] - \left(\mathrm{E}\left[\sum_{i=1}^{h} X_i\right]\right)^2$$

$$= \mathrm{E}\left[\sum_{i=1}^{h} X_i^2 + 2\sum_{i=1}^{h}\sum_{j=i+1}^{h} X_i X_j\right] - \left(\sum_{i=1}^{h} \mathrm{E}[X_i]\right)^2$$

$$= \sum_{i=1}^{h} \mathrm{E}[X_i^2] + 2\sum_{i=1}^{h}\sum_{j=i+1}^{h} \mathrm{E}[X_i] \cdot \mathrm{E}[X_j]$$

$$- \sum_{i=1}^{h} (\mathrm{E}[X_i])^2 - 2\sum_{i=1}^{h}\sum_{j=i+1}^{h} \mathrm{E}[X_i] \cdot \mathrm{E}[X_j]$$

$$= \sum_{i=1}^{h} \{\mathrm{E}[X_i^2] - (\mathrm{E}[X_i])^2\} = \sum_{i=1}^{h} \mathrm{Var}[X_i],$$

where the second and third equalities hold by the linearity of expectation. $\qquad\square$

2.3 Indicators and the Binomial Distribution

There are many standard types of random variables that are defined and analyzed in every basic course on probability theory. In this section, we review a few of these types that we will use later in this book.

Given an event E, an *indicator* for this event is a random variable that takes the value of 1 when the event E happens and the value of 0 otherwise. Observation 2 states some useful properties of indicators.

Observation 2. Given an event E and an indicator X for E,

(1) $E[X] = \Pr[E]$,
(2) $\text{Var}[X] = \Pr[E] \cdot (1 - \Pr[E])$.

Proof. By the definition of expectation, since X takes only the values of 0 and 1,

$$E[X] = 0 \cdot \Pr[X = 0] + 1 \cdot \Pr[X = 1] = \Pr[X = 1] = \Pr[E].$$

We now observe that since X takes only the values 0 and 1, $X = X^2$. Thus,

$$\text{Var}[X] = E[X^2] - (E[X])^2 = E[X] - (E[X])^2$$
$$= \Pr[E] - (\Pr[E])^2 = \Pr[E] \cdot (1 - \Pr[E]). \qquad \square$$

Indicators are often used in combination with the linearity of expectation to calculate the expectations of the involved random variables. Exercise 16 gives the reader an opportunity to practice this method.

Exercise 16. Consider a uniformly random permutation π of the integers $1, 2, \ldots, n$ (i.e., π has equal probability to be each one of the $n!$ possible permutations of these integers). We say that a pair of distinct numbers $i, j \in \{1, 2, \ldots, n\}$ is reversed in π if $\min\{i, j\}$ appears in π after $\max\{i, j\}$. Let X be a random variable denoting the number of pairs of distinct numbers $i, j \in \{1, 2, \ldots, n\}$ which are reversed in π. Calculate the expectation of X. **Hint:** Define for every pair of distinct numbers $i, j \in \{1, 2, \ldots, n\}$ an indicator X_{ij} for the event that this pair is reversed in π.

A *Bernoulli trial* is an experiment that succeeds with some probability p and fails with probability $q = 1 - p$. A *Bernoulli random variable* is an indicator for the success of a Bernoulli trial, i.e., a random variable taking the value of 1 with probability p and the value 0 with probability q. One can note that, by Observation 2, the expectation and variance of a Bernoulli random variable are p and pq, respectively.

Consider now n independent Bernoulli trials with a success probability of p for each trial. The distribution of the total number of successes in these trials is denoted by $B(n, p)$ and is called a *binomial distribution*.

Lemma 10. *Consider a variable X with a binomial distribution $B(n, p)$ for some positive integer n and $p \in [0, 1]$. Then, we have*

(1) $\mathrm{E}[X] = np$,
(2) $\mathrm{Var}[X] = npq$.

Proof. By definition, X is the number of successes in n independent Bernoulli trials. Let us denote by X_i an indicator for success in the ith trail. Observe that X_i is a Bernoulli variable, and moreover,

$$X = \sum_{i=1}^{n} X_i.$$

Using the linearity of expectation, we now get

$$\mathrm{E}[X] = \sum_{i=1}^{n} \mathrm{E}[X_i] = \sum_{i=1}^{n} p = np.$$

To determine the variance of X, we recall that the n Bernoulli trials used to define X are independent. Hence, the variables $X_1, X_2, \ldots, X_n$ are also independent, which yields (by either Lemma 8 or Lemma 9)

$$\mathrm{Var}[X] = \sum_{i=1}^{n} \mathrm{Var}[X_i] = \sum_{i=1}^{n} pq = npq. \qquad \square$$

2.4 Tail Bounds

It is often desirable to prove that a random variable is *concentrated* around its expectation, i.e., that it is likely to take a value close to its expectation. In this section, we study inequalities that allow us to show that some classes of random variables exhibit such concentration. Such inequalities are usually called tail bounds (see Figure 2.1 for an intuitive explanation for this name).

We begin the section with an example showing that a general random variable need not concentrate at all around its expectation. Consider a random variable X taking the value $M > 0$ with probability $1/2$ and the value $-M$ otherwise. Clearly, the expected value of X is 0. However, if M is large, then X is always very far from its expectation and does not exhibit any kind of concentration around it. In light of this example, it is clear that one needs to assume something about the random variable to get any tail bounds. One of the simplest assumptions is that the random variable takes

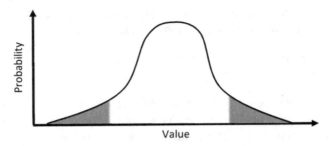

Figure 2.1. A schematic picture of the distribution of a characteristic random variable. The x-axis corresponds to the values that the random variable can take, and the height of the curve above each such value represents the probability that the random variable takes this value. For many useful random variables, the curve obtained this way has a "bell" shape having a bulge near the expected value of the random variable. On both sides of the bulge, the curve has "tails" in which the probability gradually approaches 0 as the values go further and further from the expected value. The tails are shaped gray in the above figure. To show that the random variable is concentrated around its expectation, one should bound the size of the tails and show that they are small compared to the bulge. This is the reason that inequalities showing concentration are called tail bounds.

only non-negative values. This assumption leads to a very basic tail bound known as *Markov's inequality.*

Lemma 11 (Markov's inequality). *If X is a numeric random variable with a finite expectation taking only non-negative values, then $\Pr[X \geqslant t] \leqslant E[X]/t$ for every value $t > 0$.*

Proof. Looking back at the above example of a random variable with no concentration, we can observe that the random variable from this example could combine extreme values with an expectation of 0 because the positive extreme values canceled the negative ones. Since we assume in this proof that X is non-negative, this cannot happen for X. In other words, if X takes large values often, then this should result in a large expectation since these large values cannot be canceled by negative values. If we think of values of at least t as large, then we can use this logic to get the following lower bound on the expectation of X. Let r be the set of values that X can take. Then, we have

$$E[X] = \sum_{r \in R} r \cdot \Pr[X = r] \geqslant \sum_{\substack{r \in R \\ r \geqslant t}} r \cdot \Pr[X = r] \geqslant \sum_{\substack{r \in R \\ r \geqslant t}} t \cdot \Pr[X = r]$$

$$= t \cdot \Pr[X \geqslant t].$$

Dividing the above inequality by t completes the proof of the lemma.   □

The following is an alternative form of Markov's inequality that is often used. It is not difficult to verify that the two forms are equivalent whenever $E[X] > 0$ (because $E[X]$ is simply some constant value).

Corollary 1. *If X is a numeric random variable with a finite positive expectation taking only non-negative values, then $\Pr[X \geqslant t \cdot E[X]] \leqslant 1/t$ for every value $t > 0$.*

As mentioned in its proof, Markov's inequality allows us to bound the probability of very high values to appear because we assume that X does not take very low values, and thus, the very high values cannot be canceled in the calculation of X's expectation. Markov's inequality combines this principle with a lower bound of 0 on X, but in general, this principle can be combined with an arbitrary upper or lower bound on X. In Exercise 17 to reader is directed to determine the tail bounds that can be obtained in this way in general.

Exercise 17. Let X be a numeric random variable with a finite expectation.

(a) Prove using Markov's inequality that if X is always lower bounded by a, then $\Pr[X \geqslant t] \leqslant (E[X] - a)/(t - a)$ for every $t > a$.
(b) Prove using Markov's inequality that if X is always upper bounded by b, then $\Pr[X \leqslant t] \leqslant (b - E[X])/(b - t)$ for every $t < b$.
(c) Prove (a) and (b) again without using Markov's inequality.

The bound given by Markov's inequality (and its variants discussed in Exercise 17) depends only on the range of values taken by the random variable and the expectation of the random variable. The use of so little information about the random variable in the bound is both an advantage and a disadvantage. The advantage is that Markov's inequality can be used even with random variables on which we know very little, and the disadvantage is that the bound given by this inequality tends to be weak.

In general, having more information about the random variable should allow us to get stronger tail bounds because the bounds can use the extra information to yield a guarantee that is better tailored for the specific random variable at hand. One piece of information that is natural to use for this purpose is the variance of the random variable. Lemma 12 states a tail bound, known as *Chebyshev's inequality*, that employs this piece of information.

Lemma 12 (Chebyshev's inequality). *If X is a numeric random variable whose variance exists, then $\Pr[|X - \mathrm{E}[X]| \geqslant t] \leqslant \mathrm{Var}[X]/t^2$ for every $t > 0$.*

Proof. Consider the random variable $(X - \mathrm{E}[X])^2$. Since this random variable is non-negative, by Markov's inequality we get

$$\Pr[(X - \mathrm{E}[X])^2 \geqslant t^2] \leqslant \frac{\mathrm{E}[(X - \mathrm{E}[X])^2]}{t^2}.$$

Recalling now that $\mathrm{Var}[X]$ was defined as $\mathrm{E}[(X - \mathrm{E}[X])^2]$, we get

$$\Pr[(X - \mathrm{E}[X])^2 \geqslant t^2] \leqslant \frac{\mathrm{Var}[X]}{t^2},$$

which is equivalent to the inequality that we want to prove.   □

Like Markov's inequality, Chebyshev's inequality also has an alternative form given by Corollary 2. The two forms are equivalent unless X has a variance of zero.

Corollary 2. *If X is a numeric random variable whose variance exists and is non-zero, then for every value $t > 0$, we have that*

$$\Pr\left[|X - \mathrm{E}[X]| \geqslant t \cdot \sqrt{\mathrm{Var}[X]}\right] \leqslant \frac{1}{t^2}.$$

The expression $\sqrt{\mathrm{Var}[X]}$ is known as the *standard deviation* of X. To better understand Markov's and Chebyshev's inequalities, in Exercise 18 the reader is encouraged to use them to bound the concentration of the binomial distribution.

Exercise 18. Consider a random variable X with a binomial distribution $B(n, p)$ for some positive integer n and probability $p \in (0, 1)$. Recall that the expectation of the binomial distribution is np. We would like to upper bound the probability that the value of X is much larger than that.

(a) Use Markov's inequality to show that $\Pr[X \geqslant 2np] \leqslant 1/2$.
(b) Use Chebyshev's inequality to show that $\Pr[X \geqslant 2np] \leqslant 1/(np)$.

One can observe that the bound obtained in Exercise 18 via Chebyshev's inequality is much stronger than the bound obtained via Markov's inequality unless the expectation of X is small. This is consistent with our intuitive expectation that bounds obtained via Chebyshev's inequality will usually outperform bounds obtained via Markov's inequality because the former inequality uses more information about the variable X. Nevertheless, it turns out that Chebyshev's inequality is still not powerful enough to fully capture the strong concentration properties of the binomial distribution. To better capture these properties, we now present another tail bound, known as the *Chernoff bound*.

Lemma 13 (Chernoff bound). *Let $X_1, X_2, \ldots, X_n$ be n independent numeric random variables taking only values from the range $[0, 1]$. Then, the random variable $X = \sum_{i=1}^{n} X_i$ obeys*

$$\Pr[X \geqslant (1 + \delta) \cdot \mathrm{E}[X]] \leqslant \left(\frac{e^{\delta}}{(1 + \delta)^{1+\delta}} \right)^{\mathrm{E}[X]} \quad \text{for every } \delta > 0,$$

and

$$\Pr[X \geqslant (1 - \delta) \cdot \mathrm{E}[X]] \leqslant \left(\frac{e^{-\delta}}{(1 - \delta)^{1-\delta}} \right)^{\mathrm{E}[X]} \quad \text{for every } \delta \in (0, 1).$$

Proof. Observe that the lemma is trivial when $\mathrm{E}[X] = 0$. Thus, we may assume in the rest of the proof that this is not the case. Let us now denote by p_i the expectation of X_i for every $1 \leqslant i \leqslant n$ and by R_i the set of values that X_i can take. Fix an arbitrary value $t \neq 0$ and consider the random variable e^{tX}. Since the variables $X_1, X_2, \ldots, X_n$ are independent, we have

$$\mathrm{E}[e^{tX}] = \mathrm{E}\left[e^{t \cdot \sum_{i=1}^{n} X_i} \right] = \mathrm{E}\left[\prod_{i=1}^{n} e^{tX_i} \right]$$

$$= \prod_{i=1}^{n} \mathrm{E}[e^{tX_i}] = \prod_{i=1}^{n} \sum_{r \in R_i} e^{tr} \cdot \Pr[X_i = r]$$

$$\leqslant \prod_{i=1}^{n} \left\{ \sum_{r \in R_i} [r \cdot e^{t} + (1 - r) \cdot e^{0}] \cdot \Pr[X_i = r] \right\}$$

$$= \prod_{i=1}^{n} [E[X_i] \cdot e^{t} + (1 - E[X_i]) \cdot e^{0}]$$

$$= \prod_{i=1}^{n} [p_i e^t + (1 - p_i)e^0] = \prod_{i=1}^{n} [p_i(e^t - 1) + 1]$$

$$\leqslant \prod_{i=1}^{n} e^{p_i(e^t - 1)} = e^{(e^t - 1) \cdot E[X]},$$

where the first inequality follows from the convexity of the function e^x and the last inequality holds since $e^x \geqslant x + 1$ for every real value x.

We now observe that e^{tX} is a non-negative function, and thus, we can use Markov's inequality to obtain for every $t > 0$

$$\Pr[X \geqslant (1 + \delta) \cdot E[X]] = \Pr[e^{tX} \geqslant e^{(1+\delta)t \cdot E[X]}] \leqslant \frac{E[e^{tx}]}{e^{(1+\delta)t \cdot E[X]}}$$

$$\leqslant \frac{e^{(e^t - 1) \cdot E[X]}}{e^{(1+\delta)t \cdot E[X]}} = \left(\frac{e^{e^t - 1}}{e^{(1+\delta)t}} \right)^{E[X]}.$$

We now need to find the right value of t to plug into the above inequality. One can observe that for $\delta > 0$ we can choose $t = \ln(1 + \delta)$ because this value is positive, and moreover, plugging this value into the above inequality yields the first part of the lemma. To prove the other part of the lemma, we use Markov's inequality again to get the following equation for every $t < 0$:

$$\Pr[X \leqslant (1 - \delta) \cdot E[X]] = \Pr[e^{tX} \geqslant e^{(1-\delta)t \cdot E[X]}]$$

$$\leqslant \frac{E[e^{tx}]}{e^{(1-\delta)t \cdot E[X]}} \leqslant \frac{e^{(e^t - 1) \cdot E[X]}}{e^{(1-\delta)t \cdot E[X]}} = \left(\frac{e^{e^t - 1}}{e^{(1-\delta)t}} \right)^{E[X]}.$$

For $\delta \in (0, 1)$, we can plug $t = \ln(1 - \delta) < 0$ into the above inequality, which completes the proof of the lemma. $\square$

The bounds given by Lemma 13 are quite complicated expressions, and thus, the Chernoff bound is rarely used in its basic form given by this lemma. Instead, people usually use the much simpler, but slightly weaker, bounds given by Corollary 3. The proof of this corollary and the solution for the exercise following it (Exercise 19) are mostly technical, and readers who want to skip them can feel free to do so. No detail from these proofs is necessary for other parts of this book.

Corollary 3 (Useful form of the Chernoff bound). *Let* X_1, $X_2, \ldots, X_n$ *be* n *independent numeric random variables taking only values* *from the range* $[0,1]$. *Then, the random variable* $X = \sum_{i=1}^{n} X_i$ *obeys*

$$\Pr[X \geqslant (1+\delta) \cdot \mathrm{E}[X]] \leqslant e^{-\frac{\delta^2 \cdot \mathrm{E}[X]}{2+\delta}} \leqslant e^{-\frac{\min\{\delta, \delta^2\} \cdot \mathrm{E}[X]}{3}} \quad \textit{for every } \delta > 0,$$

and

$$\Pr[X \geqslant (1-\delta) \cdot \mathrm{E}[X]] \leqslant e^{-\frac{\delta^2 \cdot \mathrm{E}[X]}{2}} \quad \textit{for every } \delta \in (0,1).$$

Proof. By Lemma 13, to prove the first part of the corollary, it suffices to show that for every $\delta > 0$, we have

$$\left(\frac{e^{\delta}}{(1+\delta)^{1+\delta}} \right)^{\mathrm{E}[X]} \leqslant e^{-\frac{\delta^2 \cdot \mathrm{E}[X]}{2+\delta}}.$$

Since the expectation of X is non-negative, to show that this inequality is true, it suffices to prove

$$\frac{e^{\delta}}{(1+\delta)^{1+\delta}} \leqslant e^{-\frac{\delta^2}{2+\delta}} \Leftrightarrow \delta - (1+\delta)\ln(1+\delta) \leqslant -\frac{\delta^2}{2+\delta}$$

$$\Leftrightarrow \frac{2\delta + 2\delta^2}{2+\delta} \leqslant (1+\delta)\ln(1+\delta) \Leftrightarrow \frac{2\delta}{2+\delta} \leqslant \ln(1+\delta),$$

where the first equivalence can be shown by taking the ln of both sides of the first inequality. It is not difficult to verify using basic calculus that the last of the above inequalities holds for every $\delta > 0$, which completes the proof of the first part of the corollary. Similarly, to prove the second part of the corollary, we need to show that

$$\left(\frac{e^{-\delta}}{(1-\delta)^{1-\delta}} \right)^{\mathrm{E}[X]} \leqslant e^{-\frac{\delta^2 \cdot \mathrm{E}[X]}{2}},$$

and since the expectation of X is non-negative, to show that this inequality is true, it suffices to prove

$$\frac{e^{-\delta}}{(1-\delta)^{1-\delta}} \leqslant e^{-\frac{\delta^2}{2}} \Leftrightarrow -\delta - (1-\delta)\ln(1-\delta) \leqslant -\frac{\delta^2}{2}$$

$$\Leftrightarrow \frac{\delta^2 - 2\delta}{2} \leqslant (1-\delta)\ln(1-\delta) \Leftrightarrow \frac{\delta^2 - 2\delta}{2 - 2\delta} \leqslant \ln(1-\delta).$$

The rightmost of these inequalities can again be proved using basic calculus to hold for every $\delta \in (0,1)$. $\qquad\square$

Exercise 19. Prove the inequalities used by the proof of Corollary 3. Specifically prove

(a) $\frac{2\delta}{2+\delta} \leqslant \ln(1 + \delta)$ for every $\delta > 0$.

(b) $\frac{\delta^2 - 2\delta}{2 - 2\delta} \leqslant \ln(1 - \delta)$ for every $\delta \in (0, 1)$.

Before presenting the Chernoff bound, we claimed that it can be used to get better concentration results for the binomial distribution. To see an example for that, let us consider again the variable X from Exercise 18. Since this variable has a binomial distribution, using Chernoff bound we get

$$\Pr[X \geqslant 2np] = \Pr[X \geqslant 2 \cdot \mathrm{E}[X]] \leqslant e^{-\frac{\mathrm{E}[X]}{3}} = e^{-np/3}.$$

This upper bound on $\Pr[X \geqslant 2np]$ decreases exponentially in np, which is much faster than the upper bound of $1/(np)$ that was obtained in Exercise 18 via Chebyshev's inequality and decreases only linearly in np.

We conclude this chapter with the following exercise, which gives another demonstration of the power of the Chernoff bound.

Exercise 20. Let X be a random variable following the binomial distribution $B(n, 1/2)$ for some integer $n > 100$. Prove using the Chernoff bound that

$$\Pr\left[\left|X - \frac{n}{2}\right| \geqslant 5\sqrt{n}\right] \leqslant 10^{-7}.$$

Exercise Solutions

Solution 1

(a) The roll of a dice has 6 possible outcomes: 1, 2, 3, 4, 5 and 6. Each one of these outcomes has an equal probability to be realized in a fair dice and, is thus, realized with a probability of $1/6$. Hence, the discrete probability space corresponding to the roll of a fair dice is

$$\Omega_1 = \{1, 2, 3, 4, 5, 6\} \quad \text{and} \quad P_1(x) = 1/6 \quad \forall x \in \Omega_1.$$

(b) Like in the case of a toss of a fair coin, the toss of a biased coin (like the one we consider here) has two possible outcomes: "head" and "tail". In the exercise, it is specified that $P(\text{head}) = 2/3$. Since the sum of $P(\text{head})$ and $P(\text{tail})$ should be 1, this implies that $P(\text{tail}) = 1/3$. Thus, the discrete probability space corresponding to the toss of this biased coin is

$$\Omega_2 = \{\text{head, tail}\} \quad \text{and} \quad P_2(x) = \begin{cases} 2/3 & x = \text{head}, \\ 1/3 & x = \text{tail}. \end{cases}$$

(c) Every outcome of the random process specified in the exercise consists of an outcome for the dice and an outcome for the coin. Hence, the set Ω_3 of the discrete probability space corresponding to this random process is

$$\Omega_3 = \Omega_1 \times \Omega_2 = \{(i, j) | i \in \{1, 2, 3, 4, 5, 6\} \quad \text{and} \quad j \in \{\text{head, tail}\}\}.$$

To determine the probability of each outcome in Ω_3, we note that the fair dice has equal probability to fall on each one of its six sides regardless of the behavior of the coin. Thus, the outcomes (1, head), (2, head), (3, head), (4, head), (5, head) and (6, head) should equally split the probability of the biased coin to fall on "head", which means that they should have a probability of $(2/3)/6 = 1/9$ each. Similarly, the other 6 outcomes of Ω_3 should equally split the $1/3$ probability of the biased coin to fall on "tail" and, thus, should have a probability of $(1/3)/6 = 1/18$ each.

Solution 2

We need to determine the probability of the event that the biased dice falls on a number which is at least 4. This event is formally denoted by the set $\{4, 5, 6\}$ because these are the three possible outcomes that are at least 4. The probability of this event is

$$\Pr[\{4, 5, 6\}] = P(4) + P(5) + P(6) = 0.25 + 0.25 + 0.1 = 0.6.$$

Solution 3

By the inclusion–exclusion principle,

$$\Pr[E_1 \cup E_2] + \Pr[E_1 \cap E_2] = \sum_{o \in E_1 \cup E_2} P(o) + \sum_{o \in E_1 \cap E_2} P(o)$$
$$= \sum_{o \in E_1} P(o) + \sum_{o \in E_2} P(o) = \Pr[E_1] + \Pr[E_2].$$

Additionally, since E_1 and E_2 are both disjoint and independent, we get

$$\Pr[E_1 \cup E_2] = \Pr[E_1] + \Pr[E_2] \quad \text{and} \quad \Pr[E_1 \cap E_2] = \Pr[E_1] \cdot \Pr[E_2].$$

Combining all the above equalities, we get

$$\Pr[E_1] + \Pr[E_2] + \Pr[E_1] \cdot \Pr[E_2] = \Pr[E_1] + \Pr[E_2] \Rightarrow \Pr[E_1] \cdot \Pr[E_2] = 0,$$

and this can happen only when at least one of the probabilities $\Pr[E_1]$ or $\Pr[E_2]$ is zero.

Solution 4

Let H_i be the event that the coin falls on "head" in toss number i, and let T_i be the event that the coin falls on "tail" in toss number i. Using this notation, we can write down the probability that we are required to calculate in the exercise as

$$\Pr[(H_1 \cap H_2) \cup (T_1 \cap T_2)] = \Pr[H_1 \cap H_2] + \Pr[T_1 \cap T_2],$$

where the equality holds since the event $H_1 \cap H_2$ (the event that the coin falls twice on "head") is disjoint from the event $T_1 \cap T_2$ (the event that the coin falls twice on "tail"). We now observe that the event H_1 contains only information about the first toss of the coin, and the event H_2 contains only information about the second toss of the coin. Since the two tosses are independent, so are the events H_1 and H_2, which implies

$$\Pr[H_1 \cap H_2] = \Pr[H_1] \cdot \Pr[H_2] = \left(\frac{2}{3}\right)^2 = \frac{4}{9}.$$

A similar argument yields

$$\Pr[T_1 \cap T_2] = \Pr[T_1] \cdot \Pr[T_2] = \left(\frac{1}{3}\right)^2 = \frac{1}{9}.$$

Combining all the above equalities, we get that the probability that we need to calculate is

$$\Pr[(H_1 \cap H_2) \cup (T_1 \cap T_2)] = \Pr[H_1 \cap H_2] + \Pr[T_1 \cap T_2] = \frac{4}{9} + \frac{1}{9} = \frac{5}{9}.$$

Solution 5

Let E_i be the event that the dice shows a number other than 5 or 6 in roll number i. Since the dice has an equal probability to show every number, $\Pr[E_i] = |\{1, 2, 3, 4\}|/6 = 2/3$. Additionally, since the two rolls of the dice are independent, $\Pr[E_1 \cap E_2] = \Pr[E_1] \cdot \Pr[E_2] = (2/3)^2 = 4/9$.

At this point it is important to observe that $E_1 \cap E_2$ is the complement of the event whose probability we would like to calculate. In other words, we want to calculate the probability that in at least one of the two rolls the dice shows 5 or 6, and $E_1 \cap E_2$ is the event that neither roll of the dice shows 5 or 6. This observation implies that the probability that we want to calculate is

$$\Pr[\Omega \backslash (E_1 \cap E_2)] = \Pr[\Omega] - \Pr[E_1 \cap E_2] = 1 - \frac{4}{9},$$

where the first equality holds since $E_1 \cap E_2$ and $\Omega \backslash (E_1 \cap E_2)$ are disjoint.

Let us consider now the change if the number of rolls is k rather than 2. In this case, we need to calculate the probability of the event complementing $E_1 \cap E_2 \cap \cdots \cap E_k$, which is

$$\Pr\left[\Omega \backslash \left(\bigcap_{i=1}^{k} E_i\right)\right] = 1 - \Pr\left[\bigcap_{i=1}^{k} E_i\right] = 1 - \prod_{i=1}^{k} \Pr[E_i] = 1 - \left(\frac{2}{3}\right)^k,$$

where the second equality holds since every roll of the dice is independent of all the other rolls.

Solution 6

By plugging in the definition of conditional probability, we get

$$\sum_{i=1}^{k} \Pr[A_i] \cdot \Pr[E|A_i] = \sum_{i=1}^{k} \Pr[A_i] \cdot \frac{\Pr[E \cap A_i]}{\Pr[A_i]} = \sum_{i=1}^{k} \Pr[E \cap A_i]$$

$$= \Pr\left[E \cap \left(\bigcup_{i=1}^{k} A_i\right)\right] = \Pr[E],$$

where the penultimate equality holds since the disjointness of $A_1, A_2, \ldots, A_k$ implies that the events $E \cap A_1, E \cap A_2, \ldots, E \cap A_k$ are also disjoint, and the last equality holds since the union of all the sets $A_1, A_2, \ldots, A_k$ is Ω, which is a superset of any event (including E).

Solution 7

As suggested by the hint, let A_i be the event that the first dice shows the number i. Additionally, let E be the event that the sum of the two numbers shown by the dices is even. We observe that if the first dice shows an even number i, then the sum of the two numbers is even if and only if the second dice shows one of the numbers 2, 4 or 6. Thus, for any even i we have

$$\Pr[E|A_i] = \frac{|\{2,4,6\}|}{6} = \frac{1}{2}.$$

Similarly, if the first dice shows an odd number i, then the sum of the two numbers is even if and only if the second dice shows one of the numbers 1, 3 or 5. Thus, for any odd i, we have

$$\Pr[E|A_i] = \frac{|\{1,3,5\}|}{6} = \frac{1}{2}.$$

Since the events $A_1, A_2, \ldots, A_6$ are disjoint, and their union includes all the possible outcomes, we get by the law of total probability

$$\Pr[E] = \sum_{i=1}^{6} \Pr[A_i] \cdot \Pr[E|A_i] = \sum_{i=1}^{6} \frac{\Pr[A_i]}{2} = \frac{1}{2} \cdot \sum_{i=1}^{6} \Pr[A_i] = \frac{1}{2}.$$

Solution 8

(a) Due to symmetry, to show that E_{12}, E_{23} and E_{13} are pairwise independent, it suffices to prove that E_{12} and E_{23} are independent. The event E_{12} is the event that coin tosses 1 and 2 either both produce heads or both produce tails. Since these are two of the four possible outcomes for a pair of tosses, we get $\Pr[E_{12}] = 2/4 = 1/2$. Similarly, we also get $\Pr[E_{23}] = 1/2$ and $\Pr[E_{13}] = 1/2$.

Let us now consider the event $E_{12} \cap E_{23}$. One can observe that this is the event that all three coin tosses result in the same outcome, i.e., either they all produce heads or they all produce tails. Since these are two out of the eight possible outcomes for three coin tosses, we get $\Pr[E_{12} \cap E_{23}] = 2/8 = 1/4$. To verify that E_{12} and E_{23} are independent, it remains to be observed that

$$\Pr[E_{12}] \cdot \Pr[E_{23}] = \frac{1}{2} \cdot \frac{1}{2} = \frac{1}{4} = \Pr[E_{12} \cap E_{23}].$$

(b) Consider the event $E_{12} \cap E_{23} \cap E_{13}$. One can verify that this event is again the event that all three coin tosses resulted in the same outcomes, and thus, it is equal to the event $E_{12} \cap E_{23}$. Thus, we get

$$\Pr[E_{12}] \cdot \Pr[E_{23}] \cdot \Pr[E_{13}] = \frac{1}{2} \cdot \frac{1}{2} \cdot \frac{1}{2} = \frac{1}{8} \neq \frac{1}{4} = \Pr[E_{12} \cap E_{23} \cap E_{13}],$$

which implies that the three events E_{12}, E_{23} and E_{13} are not independent. To understand on a more intuitive level why that is the case, note that knowing that any two of these events happened implies that all three coin tosses produced the same outcome and, thus, guarantees that the third event happened as well.

Solution 9

Let us denote by (i, j) the outcome in which the first dice shows the number i and the second dice shows the number j. There are 36 such possible outcomes, each having a probability of 1/36. We note that there is only a single outcome (namely $(1, 1)$) for which $X = 2$, and thus, $\Pr[X = 2] = 1/36$. Similarly, there are two outcomes ($(2, 1)$ and $(1, 2)$) for which $X = 3$, and thus, $\Pr[X = 3] = 2/36 = 1/18$. Continuing in the same way, we get the following probabilities for all the possible values of X.

X	2	3	4	5	6	7	8	9	10	11	12
Prob.	1/36	1/18	1/12	1/9	5/36	1/6	5/36	1/9	1/12	1/18	1/36

Using the definition of expectation, we now get

$$\mathrm{E}[X] = \sum_{i=2}^{12} i \cdot \Pr[X = i]$$

$$= 2 \cdot \frac{1}{36} + 3 \cdot \frac{1}{18} + 4 \cdot \frac{1}{12} + 5 \cdot \frac{1}{9} + 6 \cdot \frac{5}{36} + 7 \cdot \frac{1}{6} + 8 \cdot \frac{5}{36} + 9 \cdot \frac{1}{9}$$

$$+ 10 \cdot \frac{1}{12} + 11 \cdot \frac{1}{18} + 12 \cdot \frac{1}{36}$$

$$= \frac{1}{18} + \frac{1}{6} + \frac{1}{3} + \frac{5}{9} + \frac{5}{6} + \frac{7}{6} + \frac{10}{9} + 1 + \frac{5}{6} + \frac{11}{18} + \frac{1}{3} = 7.$$

Solution 10

Let X and Y be the values shown by the first and second dice, respectively. Since a dice shows every value between 1 and 6 with equal probability, the expectations of X and Y are

$$\frac{1+2+3+4+5+6}{6} = 3.5.$$

Exercise 9 asks for the expectation of $X + Y$, which by the linearity of expectation is $E[X + Y] = E[X] + E[Y] = 3.5 + 3.5 = 7$.

Solution 11

If X takes only a single value c with a positive probability, then

$$E\left[\frac{1}{X}\right] = \frac{1}{c} = \frac{1}{E[X]}.$$

It can be shown that this is the only case in which Inequality (2) holds as equality. Thus, to give an example for which it does not hold as an equality, we can take an arbitrary non-constant random variable. In particular, if we choose as X a random variable that takes the value 2 with probability $1/2$ and the value 4 otherwise, then

$$E[X] = \frac{1}{2} \cdot 2 + \frac{1}{2} \cdot 4 = 1 + 2 = 3$$

and

$$E\left[\frac{1}{X}\right] = \frac{1}{2} \cdot \frac{1}{2} + \frac{1}{2} \cdot \frac{1}{4} = \frac{1}{4} + \frac{1}{8} = \frac{3}{8},$$

which together imply

$$E\left[\frac{1}{X}\right] = \frac{3}{8} > \frac{1}{3} = \frac{1}{E[X]}.$$

Solution 12

(a) Consider a number $r \in \{1, 2, 3, 4, 5, 6\}$. If r is even, then $\Pr[X = r|O] = 0$ because the event O implies that X takes an odd value, and $\Pr[X = r|E] = 1/3$ because under the event E the variable X has equal probability to take each one of the three even numbers 2, 4 or 6. Similarly, if r is odd, then $\Pr[X = r|O] = 1/3$ and $\Pr[X = r|E] = 0$.

Using these observations, we get

$$E[X|O] = \sum_{r=1}^{6} r \cdot \Pr[X = r|O] = \frac{1 + 3 + 5}{3} = 3,$$

and

$$E[X|E] = \sum_{r=1}^{6} r \cdot \Pr[X = r|E] = \frac{2 + 4 + 6}{3} = 4.$$

(b) Since X is a uniformly random number from the set $\{1, 2, 3, 4, 5, 6\}$, $E[X]$ is the average of the numbers in this set. Similarly, $E[X|O]$ and $E[X|E]$ are the averages of the even and odd numbers in this set, respectively. Thus, the inequality $E[X|O] < E[X|E]$ holds simply because the average of the even numbers in $\{1, 2, 3, 4, 5, 6\}$ happens to be larger than the average of the odd numbers in this set.

Solution 13

Let X be a random variable of the number of points earned by the player, and let D be a random variable representing the result in the first roll of the dice (i.e., the value of d). Since the expected value of the number shown on the dice in a single roll is 3.5 (see the solution for Exercise 10), by the linearity of expectation we get that the expected sum of the values shown by the dice in d rolls is $3.5d$. Thus, $E[X|D = d] = 3.5d$. Using the law of total expectation, we now get

$$E[X] = \sum_{d=1}^{6} \Pr[D = d] \cdot E[X|D = d] = \frac{\sum_{d=1}^{6} 3.5d}{6} = \frac{3.5 \cdot 21}{6} = 12.25.$$

Solution 14

Let X be a random variable taking the values 1 and 3 with probability $1/2$ each, and let $Y = X + 1$. Clearly, X and Y are not independent since knowing the value of one of them suffices for calculating the value of the other. Now, note that

$$E[X] = 1 \cdot \Pr[X = 1] + 3 \cdot \Pr[X = 3] = \frac{1 + 3}{2} = 2,$$

$$E[Y] = 2 \cdot \Pr[Y = 2] + 4 \cdot \Pr[Y = 4] = \frac{2 + 4}{2} = 3,$$

and

$$E[X \cdot Y] = 2 \cdot \Pr[X = 1, Y = 2] + 12 \cdot \Pr[X = 3, Y = 4] = \frac{2 + 12}{2} = 7.$$

Thus, Lemma 6 does not apply to these X and Y because

$$E[X \cdot Y] = 7 \neq 2 \cdot 3 = E[X] \cdot E[Y].$$

Solution 15

Using the linearity of expectation, we get

$$\text{Var}[c \cdot X + c'] = E[(c \cdot X + c' - E[c \cdot X + c'])^2] = E[(c \cdot X - c \cdot E[X])^2]$$
$$= E[c^2 \cdot (X - E[X])^2] = c^2 \cdot E[(X - E[X])^2] = c^2 \cdot \text{Var}[X].$$

If X and Y are independent (and thus, $E[XY] = E[X] \cdot E[Y]$), then we also get

$$\text{Var}[X + Y] = E[(X + Y)^2] - (E[X + Y])^2$$
$$= E[X^2 + 2XY + Y^2] - (E[X] + E[Y])^2$$
$$= (E[X^2] + 2E[X] \cdot E[Y] + E[Y^2])$$
$$\quad - [(E[X])^2 + 2E[X] \cdot E[Y] + (E[Y])^2]$$
$$= E[X^2] - (E[X])^2 + E[Y^2] - (E[Y])^2 = \text{Var}[X] + \text{Var}[Y].$$

Solution 16

As suggested by the hint, let us define for every pair of distinct numbers $i, j \in \{1, 2, \ldots, n\}$ an indicator X_{ij} for the event that this pair is reversed in π. Since X is the number of reversed pairs in π, we get

$$X = \sum_{i=1}^{n} \sum_{j=i+1}^{n} X_{ij}.$$

Using now the linearity of expectation, the last equality implies

$$E[X] = \sum_{i=1}^{n} \sum_{j=i+1}^{n} E[X_{ij}] = \sum_{i=1}^{n} \sum_{j=i+1}^{n} \Pr[\text{the pair of } i \text{ and } j \text{ is reversed}],$$

where the second equality holds by Observation 2. It remains now to be observed that due to symmetry, the probability that $\min\{i, j\}$ appears before $\max\{i, j\}$ in π is identical to the probability of the reverse order to appear, and thus, both probabilities are equal to half. Plugging this into the previous equality yields

$$
\mathrm{E}[X] = \sum_{i=1}^{n} \sum_{j=i+1}^{n} \Pr[\text{the pair of } i \text{ and } j \text{ is reversed}]
$$

$$
= \sum_{i=1}^{n} \sum_{j=i+1}^{n} \frac{1}{2} = \frac{n(n-1)/2}{2} = \frac{n(n-1)}{4}.
$$

Solution 17

(a) Consider the random variable $Y = X - a$. Since Y is always non-negative, using Markov's inequality, we get

$$
\Pr[X \geqslant t] = \Pr[Y \geqslant t - a] \leqslant \frac{\mathrm{E}[Y]}{t - a} = \frac{\mathrm{E}[X] - a}{t - a}.
$$

(b) Consider the random variable $Z = b - X$. Since Z is always non-negative, using Markov's inequality, we get

$$
\Pr[X \leqslant t] = \Pr[Z \geqslant b - t] \leqslant \frac{\mathrm{E}[Z]}{b - t} = \frac{b - \mathrm{E}[X]}{b - t}.
$$

(c) To prove (a) without using Markov's inequality, we will lower bound the expectation of X. Like in the proof of Markov's inequality, we need to distinguish between high and low values of X. The high values of X are the values larger than t. We will lower bound these values by t. Values of X smaller than t are considered low values, and we will lower bound them by a. Let R be the set of values that X can take, i.e.,

$$
\mathrm{E}[X] = \sum_{r \in R} r \cdot \Pr[X = r] = \sum_{\substack{r \in R \\ r \geqslant t}} r \cdot \Pr[X = r] + \sum_{\substack{r \in R \\ r < t}} r \cdot \Pr[X = r]
$$

$$
\geqslant \sum_{\substack{r \in R \\ r \geqslant t}} t \cdot \Pr[X = r] + \sum_{\substack{r \in R \\ r < t}} a \cdot \Pr[X = r]
$$

$$
= t \cdot \Pr[X \geqslant t] + a \cdot \Pr[X < t].
$$

We now note that the two probabilities on the rightmost side of the last inequality add up to 1. Using this observation, we get from the last inequality

$$E[X] \geqslant a + (t - a) \cdot \Pr[X \geqslant t],$$

and the inequality that we need to prove follows by rearranging this inequality.

We omit the proof of (b) because it is very similar, except that now we need to lower bound the expectation of X rather than upper bound it.

Solution 18

(a) Since X counts the number of successes in n independent Bernoulli trials, it takes only non-negative values, thus, we can apply Markov's inequality to it. Choosing $t = 2$ in the alternative form of Markov's inequality given by Corollary 1, we get

$$\Pr[X \geqslant 2np] = \Pr[X \geqslant t \cdot E[X]] \leqslant \frac{1}{t} = \frac{1}{2}.$$

(b) Recall that the variance of a variable X distributed according to the binomial distribution $B(n, p)$ is npq, where $q = 1 - p$. Thus, by Chebyshev's inequality, we have

$$\Pr[X \geqslant 2np] \leqslant \Pr[|X - np| \geqslant np] \leqslant \frac{\text{Var}[X]}{(np)^2} = \frac{q}{np} \leqslant \frac{1}{np}.$$

Solution 19

(a) For $\delta = 0$, the two sides of the inequality

$$\frac{2\delta}{2 + \delta} \leqslant \ln(1 + \delta)$$

are equal to 0. Thus, to prove that the inequality holds for $\delta \geqslant 0$, it suffices to show that for every $\delta \geqslant 0$ the derivative of the left-hand side of the inequality with respect to δ is upper bounded by the derivative with respect to δ of the right-hand side. The derivative of the left-hand side is

$$\frac{2(2 + \delta) - 2\delta \cdot 1}{(2 + \delta)^2} = \frac{4}{(2 + \delta)^2},$$

and the derivative of the right-hand side is

$$\frac{1}{1+\delta}.$$

The first of these derivatives is indeed upper bounded by the second one because

$$\frac{4}{(2+\delta)^2} \leqslant \frac{1}{1+\delta} \Leftrightarrow 4 + 4\delta \leqslant 4 + 4\delta + \delta^2 \Leftrightarrow 0 \leqslant \delta^2.$$

(b) For $\delta = 0$, the two sides of the inequality

$$\frac{\delta^2 - 2\delta}{2 - 2\delta} \leqslant \ln(1-\delta)$$

are again equal to 0. Thus, to prove that the inequality holds for $\delta \in [0,1)$, it suffices to show that for every δ in this range the derivative of the left-hand side of the inequality with respect to δ is upper bounded by the derivative with respect to δ of the right-hand side. The derivative of the left-hand side is

$$\frac{(2\delta - 2)(2 - 2\delta) + 2(\delta^2 - 2\delta)}{(2 - 2\delta)^2} = \frac{(8\delta - 4\delta^2 - 4) + (2\delta^2 - 4\delta)}{(2 - 2\delta)^2}$$

$$= \frac{4\delta - 2\delta^2 - 4}{(2 - 2\delta)^2},$$

and the derivative of the right-hand side is

$$-\frac{1}{1-\delta}.$$

The first of these derivatives is indeed upper bounded by the second one when $\delta \in [0,1)$ because

$$\frac{4\delta - 2\delta^2 - 4}{(2 - 2\delta)^2} \leqslant -\frac{1}{1-\delta} \Leftrightarrow (4\delta - 2\delta^2 - 4)(1-\delta) \leqslant -(2 - 2\delta)^2$$

$$\Leftrightarrow 8\delta - 2\delta^3 - 6\delta^2 - 4 \leqslant -4 + 8\delta - 4\delta^2 \Leftrightarrow 0 \leqslant 2\delta^2 + 2\delta^3.$$

Solution 20

Observe that the assumption in the exercise about n implies $10/\sqrt{n} \in (0,1)$. Using this observation and the fact that $E[X] = n/2$, we get using the

Chernoff bound that

$$\Pr\left[X \geqslant \frac{n}{2} + 5\sqrt{n}\right] = \Pr\left[X \geqslant \left(1 + \frac{10}{\sqrt{n}}\right) \cdot \mathrm{E}[X]\right]$$

$$\leqslant e^{-\left(\frac{10}{\sqrt{n}}\right)^2 \cdot \frac{\mathrm{E}[X]}{3}} = e^{-\frac{100}{n} \cdot \frac{n}{6}} = e^{-\frac{50}{3}} \leqslant 6 \cdot 10^{-8}$$

and

$$\Pr\left[X \geqslant \frac{n}{2} - 5\sqrt{n}\right] = \Pr\left[X \geqslant \left(1 - \frac{10}{\sqrt{n}}\right) \cdot \mathrm{E}[X]\right]$$

$$\leqslant e^{-\left(\frac{10}{\sqrt{n}}\right)^2 \cdot \frac{\mathrm{E}[X]}{2}} = e^{-\frac{100}{n} \cdot \frac{n}{4}} = e^{-25} \leqslant 2 \cdot 10^{-11}.$$

We can combine the above two bounds using the union bound, which gives us

$$\Pr\left[\left|X - \frac{n}{2}\right| \geqslant 5\sqrt{n}\right] \leqslant \Pr\left[X \geqslant \frac{n}{2} + 5\sqrt{n}\right] + \Pr\left[X \leqslant \frac{n}{2} - 5\sqrt{n}\right]$$

$$\leqslant 6 \cdot 10^{-8} + 2 \cdot 10^{-11} \leqslant 10^{-7}.$$

Chapter 3

Estimation Algorithms

In Chapter 1, we saw the data stream model, and studied a few algorithms for this model; all of which produced exact solutions. Unfortunately, producing exact solutions often requires a large space complexity, and thus, most of the algorithms we will see in this book will be estimation and approximation algorithms. An *estimation algorithm* is an algorithm which produces an estimate for some value (such as the length of the stream). Similarly, an *approximation algorithm* is an algorithm which given an optimization problem finds a solution which approximately optimizes the objective function of the problem. For example, an approximation algorithm for the minimum weight spanning tree problem produces a spanning tree whose weight is approximately minimal.

In this chapter, we will see our first examples of estimation algorithms for the data stream model, and will learn how to quantify the quality of the estimate produced by these algorithms. Further discussion and examples of approximation algorithms can be found in Chapter 8.

3.1 Morris's Algorithm for Estimating the Length of the Stream

In Chapter 1, we saw a simple streaming algorithm for exact calculation of the length n of the stream using a space complexity of $O(\log n)$. Exercise 1 proves that this cannot be improved significantly as long as the algorithm is required to output an exact answer.

Exercise 1. Prove that every algorithm outputting the exact length of its input stream must have space complexity $\Omega(\log n)$. **Hint:** Consider the internal

51

state of the algorithm, and argue that it must encode the number of tokens read so far by the algorithm.

Exercise 1 shows that if we want to have an algorithm for calculating the length of the stream with a space complexity of $O(\log n)$, then we must resort to an estimation algorithm. Indeed, we give below an estimation algorithm named Morris's Algorithm which manages to estimate the length of the stream using an expected space complexity of about $O(\log \log n)$ bits. Before getting to the formal presentation of this algorithm, let us describe the intuitive idea underlying it.

Think of the algorithm as a worker climbing a ladder. The worker starts at bar 0 of the ladder, and reads the tokens of the stream one after the other. Every time he reads a token from the stream, the worker tries to climb to the next bar of the ladder, and succeeds with probability 0.01. Intuitively, we expect the worker to end up around bar $0.01n$ after reading the entire stream. Thus, if we denote by X the random variable representing the bar at which the worker ended up, then $100 \cdot X$ can be used to estimate the length n of the stream. The important observation now is that X tends to be smaller by a factor of 100 compared to the number of tokens seen so far, and thus, storing it requires fewer bits.

Unfortunately, the above idea suffers from two main drawbacks. The first drawback is that the random variable X used to estimate n tends to be smaller than n only by a constant factor (100), and thus, storing it instead of n reduces the space complexity only by a constant number of bits. The second drawback is that each bar of the ladder "represents" about 100 stream tokens, and thus, we expect the estimation error of the algorithm to be on the order of 100 regardless of the value of n.[1] This is problematic since it is usually desirable for the estimation error of an estimation algorithm to be small compared to the real value it estimates. For example, consider two cases. In one case, the stream contains 10 tokens and the algorithm claims that it contains only a single token, while in the other case the stream contains 1000 tokens and the algorithm claims that it contains 991 tokens. In both cases, the error in the estimation of the algorithm is 9 tokens, however, the estimation in the second case is usually considered to be much better than the estimation in the first case.

---

[1] In fact, the expected estimation error of the algorithm described increases with n since the deviation of X from its expectation increases as n becomes larger. However, this increase is very slow compared to the increase in n itself.

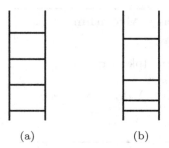

(a)   (b)

Figure 3.1. A graphical representation of the ladder on which the worker climbs. The space above each bar represents the number of stream tokens "represented" by this bar, which is inversely proportional to the probability to climb from this bar to the next (the larger the space, the lower this probability). Ladder (a) represents the basic setting in which the probability to move from each bar to the next one is identical. Ladder (b) represents the more advanced setting in which this probability decreases as we get higher on the ladder. One can observe that in ladder (b) the space above each bar of the ladder is proportional to the height of the bar in the ladder, which intuitively means that the estimation error increases roughly in proportion to n.

One solution for the above drawbacks is to make the probability that the worker moves from one bar to the next different for different bars. Specifically, we want this probability to be large for the first bar, and then decrease gradually as we get to higher and higher bars. Since the low bars are associated with relatively high probabilities, each such bar "represents" only a few stream tokens, and thus, we expect the estimation error to be small when n is small; which solves the second drawback presented above. Moreover, as the worker gets higher, the probability of him climbing to the next bar with each token decreases, which also decreases his expected climbing speed. Hence, the worker is not expected to climb very high even when n is large, and this should allow us to keep track of the bar where the worker is currently present using a relatively small space complexity (solving the first drawback). A graphical explanation of this approach is given in Figure 3.1.

Morris's algorithm, the algorithm we promised above, is based on the last idea, and is given as Algorithm 1. One can think of the variable X used by this algorithm as representing the current bar of the worker.

Exercise 2. To get a feeling of Algorithm 1, run it manually a few times with a stream of length 10. As humans are very bad at simulating randomness, we recommend making the random decisions of the algorithm during the manual runs using coin flips. **Hint:** Executing Algorithm 1 requires the implementation

---

Algorithm 1: Morris's Algorithm

1. $X \leftarrow 0$.
2. **while** there are more tokens **do**
3.   Read the next token.
4.   **with** probability 2^{-X} **do**
5. $X \leftarrow X + 1$.
6. **return** $2^X - 1$.

---

of a random variable which takes the value 1 with probability 2^{-X}, and the value 0 otherwise. The solutions section describes one way in which this can be done using a fair coin.

In order to analyze Algorithm 1, we need to define some notation. For every $0 \leqslant i \leqslant n$, we denote by X_i the value of X after Algorithm 1 reads i tokens from its input stream. Additionally, let $Y_i = 2^{X_i}$. Observe that the output of Algorithm 1 can be written as $Y_n - 1$. Lemma 1 shows that the expected value of this expression is n, i.e., Algorithm 1 outputs a random value which in expectation is equal to the value it tries to estimate.

Lemma 1. *For every $0 \leqslant i \leqslant n$, $E[Y_i] = i + 1$.*

Proof. We prove the lemma by induction on i. First, observe that X_0 is deterministically 0, which proves the base case of the induction since

$$E[Y_0] = E[2^{X_0}] = 1 = 0 + 1.$$

Next, assume that the lemma holds for some $i \geqslant 0$, and let us prove it for $i + 1$. By the law of total probability, for every $2 \leqslant j \leqslant i$, we get

$$\Pr[X_{i+1} = j] = \Pr[X_i = j] \cdot \Pr[X_{i+1} = j | X_i = j]$$

$$+ \Pr[X_i = j - 1] \cdot \Pr[X_{i+1} = j | X_i = j - 1]$$

$$= \Pr[X_i = j] \cdot (1 - 2^{-j}) + \Pr[X_i = j - 1] \cdot 2^{-(j-1)}$$

$$= \Pr[X_i = j] + 2^{-j}(2\Pr[X_i = j - 1] - \Pr[X_i = j]).$$

Moreover, one can verify that the equality

$$\Pr[X_{i+1} = j] = \Pr[X_i = j] + 2^{-j}(2\Pr[X_i = j - 1] - \Pr[X_i = j])$$

holds also when $j = 0$, $j = 1$ or $j = i + 1$.[2] Using the last equality, we can now calculate the expectation of Y_{i+1}.

$$E[Y_{i+1}] = E[2^{X_{i+1}}] = \sum_{j=0}^{i+1} 2^j \cdot \Pr[X_{i+1} = j] = \sum_{j=0}^{i+1} 2^j \cdot \Pr[X_i = j]$$

$$+ \sum_{j=0}^{i+1} (2\Pr[X_i = j - 1] - \Pr[X_i = j]).$$

Consider the two sums on the rightmost side of the last equality. By observing that X_i takes with a positive probability only values within the range 0 to i, the first sum becomes

$$\sum_{j=0}^{i+1} 2^j \cdot \Pr[X_i = j] = \sum_{j=0}^{i} 2^j \cdot \Pr[X_i = j] = E[2^{X_i}] = E[Y_i]$$

and the second sum becomes

$$\sum_{j=0}^{i+1} (2\Pr[X_i = j - 1] - \Pr[X_i = j]) = 2 \cdot \sum_{j=1}^{i+1} \Pr[X_i = j - 1]$$

$$- \sum_{j=0}^{i} \Pr[X_i = j] = \sum_{j=0}^{i} \Pr[X_i = j] = 1.$$

Combining all of the above yields

$$E[Y_{i+1}] = \sum_{j=0}^{i+1} 2^j \cdot \Pr[X_i = j] + \sum_{j=0}^{i+1} (2\Pr[X_i = j - 1] - \Pr[X_i = j])$$

$$= E[Y_i] + 1 = i + 2,$$

where the last equality holds by the induction hypothesis. □

The fact that the expected output of Algorithm 1 is equal to the length of the stream can already be used to prove the following weak guarantee on the quality of the estimation given by this value.

---

[2]These cases require a slightly different proof. For the cases of $j = 0$ and $j = 1$, such a proof is required since the conditional probability $\Pr[X_{i+1} = j | X_i = j - 1]$ might not be defined because the event it conditions on may have zero probability. Similarly, in the case of $j = i + 1$, the conditional probability $\Pr[X_{i+1} = j | X_i = j]$ is not defined for the same reason.

Corollary 1. *For every $\varepsilon \geqslant 1$, $\Pr[|(Y_n - 1) - n| > \varepsilon n] \leqslant \frac{1}{1+\varepsilon}$.*

Proof. Note that $Y_n - 1$ is always positive. Since $\varepsilon \geqslant 1$, this implies $(Y_n - 1) - n \geqslant -n \geqslant -\varepsilon n$. Thus,

$$\Pr[|(Y_n - 1) - n| > \varepsilon n] = \Pr[(Y_n - 1) - n > \varepsilon n]$$
$$= \Pr[Y_n - 1 > (1 + \varepsilon)n] \leqslant \frac{1}{1 + \varepsilon},$$

where the inequality holds due to Markov's inequality. $\square$

Guarantees of a similar form to the one given by Corollary 1 appear often in this book. Definition 1 will allow us to state them in a clearer way.

Definition 1. Given $\varepsilon > 0$, we say that an algorithm estimates a value A up to a *relative error* of ε if the value V produced by it obeys $|V - A| \leqslant \varepsilon A$.

Using Definition 1, Corollary 1 can be restated as follows:

Corollary 1 (rephrased). *For every $\varepsilon \geqslant 1$, Algorithm 1 estimates the length of the stream up to a relative error of ε with probability at least $1 - (1 + \varepsilon)^{-1}$.*

Clearly, the guarantee of Corollary 1 is very weak. In particular, Corollary 1 gives no guarantee when $\varepsilon < 1$, i.e., when one is interested in the probability that Algorithm 1 makes an error smaller than the value it tries to estimate. Unfortunately, as is shown by Exercise 3, proving a guarantee for $\varepsilon < 1$ requires more information besides the expected value of the algorithm's output.

Exercise 3. Find an example of a non-negative random variable X whose value always falls outside the range $(0, 2\mathrm{E}[X])$. In other words, if one used X to estimate $\mathrm{E}[X]$, then one would always get an estimation error which is at least as large as the value one tries to estimate.

In Section 3.2, we will see techniques that can be used to bypass the above issue and get an estimation guarantee also for $\varepsilon < 1$. However, before getting there, we prove Lemma 2 which analyzes the space complexity of Algorithm 1.

Lemma 2. *The expected space complexity of Algorithm 1 is $O(\log \log n)$.*

Proof. Algorithm 1 maintains a single variable X whose value can only increase over time. Thus, it can be implemented using a space complexity of $O(\log X_n)$. In the worst case, X_n can be as large as n, which results in a space complexity of $O(\log n)$. However, usually X_n is much smaller than n. More specifically, by Jensen's inequality and Lemma 1, we obtain

$$E[\log_2 X_n] = E[\log_2 \log_2 Y_n] \leqslant \log_2 \log_2 E[Y_n] = \log_2 \log_2(n+1).^3 \qquad \square$$

3.2 Improving the Estimation

In Section 3.1 we have seen that, when $\varepsilon \geqslant 1$, Algorithm 1 estimates the length of the stream up to a relative error of ε with probability at least $1 - (1 + \varepsilon)^{-1}$. In this section, we will see how to get a better estimation guarantee. In particular, we are interested in getting an estimation guarantee for smaller ε values.

The first step toward the above goal is bounding the variance of the output of Algorithm 1. This is done by Lemma 3.

Lemma 3. $\mathrm{Var}[Y_n] = n(n-1)/2$.

Proof. Recall that $\mathrm{Var}[Y_n] = E[Y_n^2] - E[Y_n]^2$. We already know that $E[Y_n] = n + 1$ from Lemma 1. Thus, to prove the lemma, it is enough to show that $E[Y_n^2] = \frac{3}{2}n^2 + \frac{3}{2}n + 1$. We will prove by induction the stronger claim that $E[Y_i^2] = \frac{3}{2}i^2 + \frac{3}{2}i + 1$ for every $0 \leqslant i \leqslant n$.

First, observe that X_0 is deterministically 0, which proves the base case of the induction since

$$E[Y_0^2] = E[2^{2X_0}] = 1 = \frac{3}{2} \cdot 0^2 + \frac{3}{2} \cdot 0 + 1.$$

Next, assume that the lemma holds for some $i \geqslant 0$, and let us prove it for $i + 1$. We already know, from the proof of Lemma 1, that for every $0 \leqslant j \leqslant i + 1$,

$$\Pr[X_{i+1} = j] = \Pr[X_i = j] + 2^{-j}(2\Pr[X_i = j - 1] - \Pr[X_i = j]).$$

---

[3] Inside the big O notation, the base of a log function is not stated (as long as it is constant) because changing the base from one constant to another is equivalent to multiplying the log by a constant. This is the reason we can assume, for simplicity, in this calculation that the base of the log is 2.

Using the last equality, we can now calculate the expectation of Y_{i+1}^2.

$$E[Y_{i+1}^2] = E[2^{2X_{i+1}}] = \sum_{j=0}^{i+1} 2^{2j} \cdot \Pr[X_{i+1} = j]$$

$$= \sum_{j=0}^{i+1} 2^{2j} \cdot \Pr[X_i = j] + \sum_{j=0}^{i+1} (2^j \cdot 2\Pr[X_i = j-1] - 2^j \cdot \Pr[X_i = j]).$$

Consider the two sums on the rightmost side of the last equation. Since X_i takes with a positive probability only values within the range 0 to i, the first sum is equal to

$$\sum_{j=0}^{i+1} 2^{2j} \cdot \Pr[X_i = j] = \sum_{j=0}^{i} 2^{2j} \cdot \Pr[X_i = j] = E[2^{2X_i}] = E[Y_i^2]$$

and the second sum is equal to

$$\sum_{j=0}^{i+1} (2^j \cdot 2\Pr[X_i = j-1] - 2^j \cdot \Pr[X_i = j])$$

$$= 4 \cdot \sum_{j=1}^{i+1} 2^{j-1} \cdot \Pr[X_i = j-1] - \sum_{j=0}^{i} 2^j \cdot \Pr[X_i = j]$$

$$= 3 \cdot \sum_{j=0}^{i} 2^j \cdot \Pr[X_i = j] = 3 \cdot E[Y_i].$$

Combining the last three equalities gives

$$E[Y_{i+1}^2] = \sum_{j=0}^{i+1} 2^{2j} \cdot \Pr[X_i = j] + \sum_{j=0}^{i+1} (2^j \cdot 2\Pr[X_i = j-1]$$

$$- 2^j \cdot \Pr[X_i = j]) = E[Y_i^2] + 3 \cdot E[Y_i]$$

$$= \left(\frac{3}{2}i^2 + \frac{3}{2}i + 1\right) + 3(i+1) = \frac{3}{2}(i+1)^2 + \frac{3}{2}(i+1) + 1,$$

where the penultimate equality holds by the induction hypothesis.   □

The expression for the variance given by Lemma 3 can be used to derive an estimation guarantee for Algorithm 1 which is slightly better than the guarantee given by Corollary 1.

Exercise 4. Use Chebyshev's inequality and Lemma 3 to show that, for every $\varepsilon > 0$, Algorithm 1 estimates the length of the stream up to a relative error of ε with probability at least $1 - \varepsilon^{-2}/2$.

Unfortunately, the improved estimation guarantee given by Exercise 4 is not much better than the guarantee proved by Corollary 1. In particular, observe that the new guarantee is meaningless when $\varepsilon \leqslant 1/\sqrt{2}$ (because in this case the guarantee only shows that the probability of attaining a good estimate is larger than some non-positive value, which is trivial). To get a much stronger estimation guarantee, we need to consider a modification of Algorithm 1.

Consider an algorithm that maintains $h = \lceil 2/\varepsilon^2 \rceil$ copies of Algorithm 1, runs them in parallel on the input stream and then averages the estimations produced by the copies. The pseudocode of this algorithm is given as Algorithm 2. Intuitively, if the different copies of Algorithm 1 are independent, then we expect the average of their outputs to be closer to its expected value than the outputs themselves; and thus, it is likely to be a better estimate for the length of the stream.

Algorithm 2: Averaging Multiple Copies of Algorithm 1 (ε)

1. Initialize $h = \lceil 2/\varepsilon^2 \rceil$ copies of Algorithm 1, each using independent randomness.
2. Each time that a token of the input stream arrives, forward it to all the copies of Algorithm 1.
3. For every $1 \leqslant i \leqslant h$, let Z_i be the output of the i-th copy (i.e., $Z_i = Y_n - 1$, where Y_n is the variable Y_n corresponding to the i-th copy).
4. Return $\bar{Z} = \frac{1}{h} \sum_{i=1}^{h} Z_i$.

We begin the analysis of Algorithm 2 by calculating the expectation and variance of its output.

Lemma 4. $E[\bar{Z}] = E[Y_n - 1] = n$ and $\text{Var}[\bar{Z}] = \text{Var}[Y_n]/h = n(n-1)/(2h)$.

Proof. For every $1 \leqslant i \leqslant h$, the random variable Z_i is distributed like $Y_n - 1$. Thus, by the linearity of the expectation, we get

$$E[\bar{Z}] = E\left[\frac{1}{h} \sum_{i=1}^{h} Z_i\right] = \frac{1}{h} \sum_{i=1}^{h} E[Z_i] = \frac{1}{h} \sum_{i=1}^{h} E[Y_n - 1] = E[Y_n - 1] = n,$$

where the last equality holds by Lemma 1.

Next, we recall that each copy of Algorithm 1 used by Algorithm 2 uses independent randomness, and thus, the variance of the sum $\sum_{i=1}^{h} Z_i$ is equal to the sum of the variances of the individual variables in the sum. Thus, we get

$$\text{Var}[\bar{Z}] = \text{Var}\left[\frac{1}{h}\sum_{i=1}^{h} Z_i\right] = \frac{1}{h^2} \cdot \text{Var}\left[\sum_{i=1}^{h} Z_i\right] = \frac{1}{h^2}\sum_{i=1}^{h} \text{Var}[Z_i],$$

where the second equality holds since $1/h$ is a constant. As the addition of a constant to a random variable does not change its variance, we also have

$$\frac{1}{h^2}\sum_{i=1}^{h} \text{Var}[Z_i] = \frac{1}{h^2}\sum_{i=1}^{h} \text{Var}[Y_n - 1] = \frac{1}{h^2}\sum_{i=1}^{h} \text{Var}[Y_n]$$

$$= \frac{\text{Var}[Y_n]}{h} = \frac{n(n-1)}{2h},$$

where the last equality holds by Lemma 3. The lemma now follows by combining the above equalities. $\qquad\square$

Using Chebyshev's inequality, we can now get an estimation guarantee for Algorithm 2 which is much stronger than what we have for Algorithm 1.

Corollary 2. *For every $\varepsilon > 0$, Algorithm 2 estimates the length of the stream up to a relative error of ε with probability at least $3/4$.*

Proof. By Chebyshev's inequality,

$$\Pr[|\bar{Z} - n| \geqslant \varepsilon n] \leqslant \frac{\text{Var}[\bar{Z}]}{(\varepsilon n)^2} = \frac{n(n-1)/(2h)}{(\varepsilon n)^2} < \frac{1}{2h\varepsilon^2} \leqslant \frac{1}{4}. \qquad\square$$

Corollary 2 shows that Algorithm 2 estimates n up to a relative error of ε with a constant probability. Usually, however, we want the probability that the estimation produced by the algorithm is poor (i.e., that the relative error is more than ε) to be very small. Exercise 5 shows that this can be done by averaging the outputs of more copies of Algorithm 1.

Exercise 5. Show that, for every $\varepsilon, \delta > 0$, changing the number h of copies of Algorithm 1 used by Algorithm 2 to $h = \lceil \varepsilon^{-2}\delta^{-1}/2 \rceil$ makes Algorithm 2 estimate the length of the stream up to a relative error ε with probability at least $1 - \delta$.

Recall that we showed in Lemma 2 that the expected space complexity of a single copy of Algorithm 1 is $O(\log \log n)$. By the linearity of

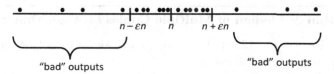

Figure 3.2. A typical distribution of the outputs of multiple executions of Algorithm 2. The majority of the outputs fall within the range $[n - \varepsilon n, n + \varepsilon n]$, while a minority of "bad" outputs fall outside this range. Note, however, that the "bad" outputs might have extreme values, i.e., they might fall quite far from the above range.

expectation, h copies of Algorithm 1 require $O(h \cdot \log\log n)$ space in expectation. Thus, the estimation algorithm suggested by Exercise 5 has an expected space complexity $O(\varepsilon^{-2}\delta^{-1} \cdot \log\log n)$. However, it is possible to get an estimation algorithm with the same estimation guarantee whose space complexity has a better dependence on δ. In the next few paragraphs, we explain how this better dependence can be achieved.

Algorithm 2 uses an "averaging technique" to get the probability that the estimation error is larger than εn down to a constant smaller than $1/2$. This means that if we execute Algorithm 2 multiple times, then we can expect the majority of these executions to produce a good estimation for the length of the stream. In other words, the majority of the outputs of these executions should be quite similar to each other (and to the real value of n), while the remaining outputs might be "bad" and have values which are either much smaller or much larger than n (see Figure 3.2 for a graphic illustration). Intuitively, the extreme values of these "bad" outputs are the reason that getting a relative error of ε with probability at least $1 - \delta$ using the averaging technique alone requires a space complexity which is linear in δ^{-1}.

One way to decrease the impact of the "bad" outputs on the space complexity is to replace the average with the median,[4] which is much less sensitive to extreme values. This idea is used in Algorithm 3.

Theorem 1. *Algorithm 3 estimates the length of the stream up to a relative error of ε with probability at least $1 - \delta$, and its expected space complexity is $O(\varepsilon^{-2} \cdot \log \delta^{-1} \cdot \log\log n)$.*

---

[4]Recall that the median of a list of numbers is any number that is smaller than or equal to 50% of the numbers in the list and larger than or equal to the other 50%.

Algorithm 3: Median of Multiple Copies of Algorithm 2 (ε, δ)

1. Initialize $k = \lceil 12 \cdot \ln \delta^{-1} \rceil$ copies of Algorithm 2, each using independent randomness.
2. Each time that a token of the input stream arrives, forward it to all the copies of Algorithm 2.
3. For every $1 \leqslant i \leqslant k$, let W_i be the output of the i-th copy (i.e., $W_i = \bar{Z}$, where $\bar{Z}$ is the variable $\bar{Z}$ corresponding to the i-th copy).
4. Return the median of the values $W_1, W_2, \ldots, W_k$.[5]

Proof. Algorithm 3 uses $k = \lceil 12 \cdot \ln \delta^{-1} \rceil$ copies of Algorithm 2, which in turn each use $h = \lceil 2/\varepsilon^2 \rceil$ copies of Algorithm 1. Moreover, each copy of Algorithm 1 has an expected space complexity of $O(\log \log n)$. Thus, by the linearity of expectation, Algorithm 3 has an expected space complexity of

$$O(hk \cdot \log \log n) = O(\varepsilon^{-2} \cdot \log \delta^{-1} \cdot \log \log n).$$

It remains to be seen that with probability at least $1 - \delta$, the relative error of the estimation produced by Algorithm 3 is at most ε. In other words, we need to show that Algorithm 3 outputs a value outside the range $[n - \varepsilon n, n + \varepsilon n]$ with probability at most δ. Note that if more than half of the values $W_1, W_2, \ldots, W_k$ fall within this range, then their median must also fall within this range. Thus, it is enough to prove that the probability that at least $k/2$ values out of $W_1, W_2, \ldots, W_k$ fall outside the above range is at most δ.

To make the last claim more formal, we need some notation. For every $1 \leqslant i \leqslant k$, let Q_i be an indicator for the event that W_i falls outside the range $[n - \varepsilon n, n + \varepsilon n]$. Additionally, let $Q = \sum_{i=1}^{k} Q_i$. Based on the above discussion, we need to prove that

$$\Pr[Q \geqslant k/2] \leqslant \delta.$$

Observe that the indicators $Q_1, Q_2, \ldots, Q_k$ are independent indicators having identical distributions (i.e., they all take the value 1 with same probability). Moreover, by Corollary 2 the probability that each one of these indicators takes the value 1 is at most $1/4$. Thus, Q is a random

---

[5]If k is even, there might be multiple possible median values. We allow Algorithm 2 to return any one of these values.

variable with a binomial distribution $B(k, p)$ for some value $p \in [0, 1/4]$. By the Chernoff bound, we now get

$$\Pr[Q \geqslant k/2] = \Pr\left[Q \geqslant \left(1 + \frac{1-2p}{2p}\right) \cdot pk\right]$$

$$= \Pr\left[Q \geqslant \left(1 + \frac{1-2p}{2p}\right) \cdot E[Q]\right]$$

$$\leqslant e^{-\frac{1-2p}{2p} \cdot E[Q]/3} = e^{\frac{2p-1}{6} \cdot k} \leqslant e^{-k/12} \leqslant e^{-\ln \delta^{-1}} = \delta. \qquad \square$$

Note that Algorithm 3 uses both a "median technique" and an "averaging technique". The median technique is used directly by Algorithm 3, while the averaging technique is used by Algorithm 2, which is used in its turn by Algorithm 3. Theorem 1 shows that the combination of these techniques allows us to improve the dependence of the expected space complexity to be logarithmic in δ^{-1}. In contrast, using the averaging technique alone we were not able to get a better than linear dependence on δ^{-1}. This might give the impression that the median technique is better than the averaging technique, and thus, can replace the averaging technique altogether. Exercise 6 shows that this is not the case.

Exercise 6. The only information about Algorithm 1 that we used in the analysis of Algorithms 2 and 3 is that its output $Y_n - 1$ has an expectation of n and a variance of $n(n-1)/2$. For $n \geqslant 3$, describe a random variable X having these expectation and variance such that the median of k independent copies of X is never within the range $[n/2, 3n/2]$ for any k.

Algorithm 3 exhibits a tradeoff between the quality of the estimation and the space complexity, i.e., to get a better estimation guarantee, the algorithm requires more space. Exercise 7 studies the tradeoff between the quality of the estimation of Algorithm 3 and its token processing time.

Exercise 7. Recall that the token processing time of a data stream algorithm is the maximum number of basic operations that the algorithm might perform from the moment it reads a token of its input stream (which is not the last token in the stream) until the moment it reads the next token. Determine the token processing time of Algorithm 3. Is there a tradeoff between the token processing time and the quality of the estimation guaranteed by the algorithm?

3.3 Concluding Remarks

In this section, we have seen the first examples in this book of estimation algorithms. The quality of the estimation obtained by the first algorithm we studied (Algorithm 1) was quite poor. However, by applying the averaging and median techniques to the algorithm we were able to improve the quality of the estimation at the cost of increasing the algorithm's space complexity.

The averaging and median techniques are quite general, and can be applied to many randomized estimation algorithms.[6] Exercise 8 describes an alternative way to trade space complexity for an improved estimation guarantee which is specifically tailored to Morris's Algorithm. Note that by using this tailored way, we are able to get a better tradeoff than what we managed to get using the general averaging and median techniques.

Exercise 8. Show that Algorithm 4 estimates the length of the stream up to a relative error of ε with probability at least $1 - \delta$, and its expected space complexity is $O(\log \log n + \log \varepsilon^{-1} + \log \delta^{-1})$. **Hint:** For calculating the expected space complexity of Algorithm 4, use the inequality $\ln(1 + x) \geqslant \frac{2x}{2+x}$, which is true for every $x \geqslant 0$.

Algorithm 4: Morris's Improved Algorithm (ε, δ)

1. Let $X \leftarrow 0$ and $a \leftarrow 1 + 2\varepsilon^2\delta$.
2. **while** there are more tokens **do**
3.   **with** probability a^{-X} **do**
4. $X \leftarrow X + 1$.
5. **return** $(a^X - 1)/(a - 1)$.

3.4 Bibliographic Notes

Morris's algorithm and a generalization of it similar to Algorithm 4 was originally suggested by Morris (1978). Interestingly, the work of

---

[6]Note that these techniques can never be used to improve deterministic algorithms because running multiple copies of a deterministic algorithm in parallel is useless — the outputs of all the copies will always be identical.

Robert Morris was motivated by a real-world problem. In this problem, a computer received a stream of events of various types, and was required to (approximately) keep track of the number of events of each type. Unfortunately, the size of the computer's memory was so small that it only allowed for a single byte counter per event type. Morris's algorithm allowed the above computer to deal correctly with more than 255 events of each type. A more detailed mathematical analysis of Morris's algorithm was later given by Flajolet (1985).

P. Flajolet. Approximate Counting: A Detailed Analysis. *BIT Numerical Math.*, 25(1): 113–134, 1985.

R. Morris. Counting Large Number of Events in Small Registers. *Communications of the ACM*, 21(10): 840–842, 1978.

Exercise Solutions

Solution 1

Consider an algorithm outputting the exact length of the input stream. The algorithm reads the tokens of the stream sequentially, and updates its internal state after every read. Note that, from the point of view of the algorithm, every token might be the last token of the stream, and thus, the algorithm must be ready at every given point to output the number of tokens read so far based on its internal state. In other words, the internal state of the algorithm must encode in some way the number of tokens read so far by the algorithm. This means that the internal state must be able to encode at least n different values, and therefore, it cannot be represented using $o(\log n)$ bits.

Solution 2

Here, we explain one way to implement, using a fair coin, a random variable which takes the value 1 with probability 2^{-X}, and the value 0 otherwise. Let us flip a fair coin X times, and consider a random variable Z which takes the value 1 if and only if all the coin flips resulted in "heads" (and the value 0 otherwise).

Let us prove that Z is distributed like the random variable we want to implement. The probability that a given coin flip results in a "head" is $1/2$. Since the coin flips are independent, the probability that they all result in "heads" is simply the product of the probabilities that the individual coin flips result in "heads". Thus,

$$\Pr[Z = 1] = \Pr[\text{All the coin flips result in "heads"}]$$

$$= \prod_{i=1}^{X} \Pr[\text{Coin flip } i \text{ resulted in a "head"}] = \prod_{i=1}^{X} \frac{1}{2} = 2^{-X}.$$

Solution 3

Consider a random variable X which takes the value 0 with probability $1/2$, and the value 2 otherwise. The expected value of X is

$$\frac{1}{2} \cdot 0 + \frac{1}{2} \cdot 2 = 1.$$

Thus, X, which only takes the values 0 and 2, never falls within the range $(0, 2E[X]) = (0, 2)$.

Solution 4

Recall that adding a constant to a random variable does not change its variance. Hence, by Chebyshev's inequality,

$$\Pr[|(Y_n - 1) - n| \geqslant \varepsilon n] \leqslant \frac{\mathrm{Var}[Y_n - 1]}{(\varepsilon n)^2} = \frac{\mathrm{Var}[Y_n]}{(\varepsilon n)^2} = \frac{n(n-1)/2}{(\varepsilon n)^2} < \frac{1}{2\varepsilon^2}.$$

Solution 5

Observe that Lemma 4 holds for any value of h. Thus, by choosing $h = \lceil \varepsilon^{-2} \delta^{-1}/2 \rceil$, we get, by Chebyshev's inequality,

$$\Pr[|\bar{Z} - n| \geqslant \varepsilon n] \leqslant \frac{\mathrm{Var}[\bar{Z}]}{(\varepsilon n)^2} = \frac{n(n-1)/(2h)}{(\varepsilon n)^2} < \frac{1}{2h\varepsilon^2} \leqslant \delta.$$

Solution 6

The only way to guarantee that the median of k independent copies of X never falls within the range $[n/2, 3n/2]$ is to construct a variable X which never takes values within this range. Thus, our objective is to construct a random variable X with expectation n and variance $n(n-1)/2$ which never takes values within the above range.

To make the construction of X simple, we allow it to take only two values a and b with a non-zero probability. Moreover, we set the probability of both these values to $1/2$. Given these choices, the expectation and variance of X are given by

$$\mathrm{E}[X] = \frac{a+b}{2} \text{ and } \mathrm{Var}[X] = \frac{(a - E[X])^2 + (b - E[X])^2}{2}.$$

Plugging into the above formulas the values we have for the desired expectation and variance of X, we get two equations as follows:

$$n = \frac{a+b}{2} \text{ and } \frac{n(n-1)}{2} = \frac{(a-n)^2 + (b-n)^2}{2}.$$

Solving these equations yields

$$a = n - \sqrt{\frac{n(n-1)}{2}} \text{ and } b = n + \sqrt{\frac{n(n-1)}{2}} \text{ (or the other way around)}.$$

That a and b are outside the range $[n/2, 3n/2]$ remains to be proven, which is equivalent to proving

$$\sqrt{\frac{n(n-1)}{2}} > \frac{n}{2}.$$

The last inequality is true for $n \geqslant 3$ because

$$\sqrt{\frac{n(n-1)}{2}} > \frac{n}{2} \Leftrightarrow \frac{n(n-1)}{2} > \frac{n^2}{4} \Leftrightarrow n(n-2) > 0.$$

Solution 7

The only thing Algorithm 3 does from the moment it reads a token from its input stream which is not the last token until it reads the next token is passing this token to k copies of Algorithm 2. Similarly, the only thing Algorithm 2 does from the moment it reads a token from its input stream which is not the last token until it reads the next token is passing this token to h copies of Algorithm 1. Thus, the token processing time of Algorithm 3 is simply $k \cdot h$ times the token processing time of Algorithm 1.

Consider now Algorithm 1. After reading a non-last token from its input stream, Algorithm 1 does only two things until it reads the next token from the input stream. First, it makes a random decision. Second, based on the result of the random decision, it might increase X by 1. Hence, the token processing time of Algorithm 1 is $O(1)$.

The above discussion implies that the token processing time of Algorithm 3 is

$$k \cdot h \cdot O(1) = O(k \cdot h) = O(\varepsilon^{-2} \cdot \log \delta^{-1}).$$

Observe that there is indeed a tradeoff between the token processing time of Algorithm 3 and its estimation guarantee. More specifically, the token processing time increases as the estimation guarantee improves (i.e., ε and δ become smaller).

Solution 8

The analysis of Algorithm 4 we present here is very similar to the analysis of Algorithm 1. In particular, we define for every $0 \leqslant i \leqslant n$ the random variable X_i in the same way it is defined in the analysis of Algorithm 1. Recall that this means that X_i is the value of X after Algorithm 4 reads i tokens from its input stream. Additionally, let $Y_i = a^{X_i}$. Observe that the output of Algorithm 4 can be written as $(Y_n - 1)/(a - 1)$. Lemma 5 is analogous to Lemma 1. In particular, it shows that the expected output of Algorithm 4 is equal to the length n of the stream.

Lemma 5. *For every* $0 \leqslant i \leqslant n$, $\mathrm{E}[Y_i] = (a - 1)i + 1$.

Proof. We prove the lemma by induction on i. First, observe that X_0 is deterministically 0, which proves the base case of the induction since

$$\mathrm{E}[Y_0] = \mathrm{E}[a^{X_0}] = 1 = (a - 1) \cdot 0 + 1.$$

Next, assume that the lemma holds for some $i \geqslant 0$, and let us prove it for $i + 1$. By the law of total probability, for every $2 \leqslant j \leqslant i$, we get

$$\Pr[X_{i+1} = j] = \Pr[X_i = j] \cdot \Pr[X_{i+1} = j | X_i = j]$$
$$+ \Pr[X_i = j - 1] \cdot \Pr[X_{i+1} = j | X_i = j - 1]$$
$$= \Pr[X_i = j] \cdot (1 - a^{-j}) + \Pr[X_i = j - 1] \cdot a^{-(j-1)}$$
$$= \Pr[X_i = j] + a^{-j}(a \cdot \Pr[X_i = j - 1] - \Pr[X_i = j]).$$

Moreover, one can verify that the equality

$$\Pr[X_{i+1} = j] = \Pr[X_i = j] + a^{-j}(a \cdot \Pr[X_i = j - 1] - \Pr[X_i = j])$$

holds also when $j = 0$, $j = 1$ or $j = i + 1$. Using the last equality, we can now calculate the expectation of Y_{i+1}.

$$E[Y_{i+1}] = E[a^{X_{i+1}}] = \sum_{j=0}^{i+1} a^j \cdot \Pr[X_{i+1} = j] = \sum_{j=0}^{i+1} a^j \cdot \Pr[X_i = j]$$

$$+ \sum_{j=0}^{i+1} (a \cdot \Pr[X_i = j - 1] - \Pr[X_i = j]).$$

Consider the two sums on the rightmost side of the last equality. By observing that X_i takes with a positive probability only values within the range 0 to i, the first sum becomes

$$\sum_{j=0}^{i+1} a^j \cdot \Pr[X_i = j] = \sum_{j=0}^{i} a^j \cdot \Pr[X_i = j] = \mathrm{E}[a^{X_i}] = \mathrm{E}[Y_i]$$

and the second sum becomes

$$\sum_{j=0}^{i+1} (a \Pr[X_i = j - 1] - \Pr[X_i = j]) = a \cdot \sum_{j=1}^{i+1} \Pr[X_i = j - 1] - \sum_{j=0}^{i} \Pr[X_i = j]$$

$$= (a - 1) \cdot \sum_{j=0}^{i} \Pr[X_i = j] = a - 1.$$

Combining all of the above yields

$$E[Y_{i+1}] = \sum_{j=0}^{i+1} a^j \cdot \Pr[X_i = j] + \sum_{j=0}^{i+1} (a \cdot \Pr[X_i = j - 1] - \Pr[X_i = j])$$

$$= \mathrm{E}[Y_i] + (a - 1)$$

$$= [(a - 1)i + 1] + (a - 1) = (a - 1)(i + 1) + 1,$$

where the penultimate equality holds by the induction hypothesis. □

Using the last lemma, we can now analyze the expected space complexity of Algorithm 4.

Corollary 3. *The expected space complexity of Algorithm 4 is* $O(\log \log n + \log \varepsilon^{-1} + \log \delta^{-1})$.

Proof. Algorithm 4 can be implemented using a space complexity of $O(\log X_n)$. For $n \geqslant 1$, by Jensen's inequality and Lemma 5, we get

$$
\begin{aligned}
E[\log_2 X_n] = E[\log_2 \log_a Y_n] &\leqslant \log_2 \log_a E[Y_n] = \log_2 \log_a[(a-1) \cdot n + 1] \\
&= \log_2 \log_a(2\varepsilon^2 \delta \cdot n + 1) \\
&= \log_2 \frac{\log_2(2\varepsilon^2\delta \cdot n + 1)}{\log_2 a} \leqslant \log_2 \frac{\log_2(3n)}{\log_2 a} \\
&= \log_2 \log_2(3n) - \log_2 \log_2 a.
\end{aligned}
$$

According to the hint of the exercise, $\ln(1+x) \geqslant \frac{2x}{2+x}$. Thus,

$$
-\log_2 \log_2 a = -\log_2 \log_2(1 + 2\varepsilon^2\delta) \leqslant -\log_2 \frac{4\varepsilon^2\delta}{2 + 2\varepsilon^2\delta} \leqslant -\log_2(\varepsilon^2\delta)
$$

$$
= 2\log_2 \varepsilon^{-1} + \log_2 \delta^{-1}.
$$

The corollary now follows by combining all the above inequalities. $\qquad\square$

Next, we prove an analog of Lemma 3 which gives an expression for the variance of Y_n.

Lemma 6. $\mathrm{Var}[Y_n] = (a-1)^3 n(n-1)/2 = (a-1)^3 n^2/2 - (a-1)^3 n/2$.

Proof. Recall that $\mathrm{Var}[Y_n] = E[Y_n^2] - E[Y_n]^2$. We already know that $E[Y_n] = (a-1)n+1$ from Lemma 5. Thus, to prove the lemma, it is enough to show that

$$
\begin{aligned}
E[Y_n^2] &= \left[\frac{(a-1)^3 n^2}{2} - \frac{(a-1)^3 n}{2}\right] + [(a-1)n+1]^2 \\
&= \frac{[(a-1)^3 + 2(a-1)^2] \cdot n^2}{2} + \frac{[-(a-1)^3 + 4(a-1)] \cdot n}{2} + 1 \\
&= \frac{(a^2-1)(a-1)}{2} \cdot n^2 + \frac{(a^2-1)(3-a)}{2} \cdot n + 1.
\end{aligned}
$$

We will prove by induction the stronger claim that, for every $0 \leqslant i \leqslant n$,

$$
E[Y_i^2] = \frac{(a^2-1)(a-1)}{2} \cdot i^2 + \frac{(a^2-1)(3-a)}{2} \cdot i + 1.
$$

First, observe that X_0 is deterministically 0, which proves the base case of the induction since

$$
E[Y_0^2] = E[a^{2X_0}] = 1 = \frac{(a^2-1)(a-1)}{2} \cdot 0^2 + \frac{(a^2-1)(3-a)}{2} \cdot 0 + 1.
$$

Next, assume that the lemma holds for some $i \geqslant 0$, and let us prove it for $i + 1$. We already know, from the proof of Lemma 5, that for every $0 \leqslant j \leqslant i + 1$,

$$\Pr[X_{i+1} = j] = \Pr[X_i = j] + a^{-j}(a \cdot \Pr[X_i = j - 1] - \Pr[X_i = j]).$$

Using the last equality, we can now calculate the expectation of Y_{i+1}^2.

$$E[Y_{i+1}^2] = E[2^{2X_{i+1}}] = \sum_{j=0}^{i+1} a^{2j} \cdot \Pr[X_{i+1} = j]$$

$$= \sum_{j=0}^{i+1} a^{2j} \cdot \Pr[X_i = j] + \sum_{j=0}^{i+1} (a^j \cdot a \cdot \Pr[X_i = j - 1] - a^j \cdot \Pr[X_i = j]).$$

Consider the two sums on the rightmost side of the last equation. Since X_i takes with a positive probability only values within the range 0 to i, the first sum is equal to

$$\sum_{j=0}^{i+1} a^{2j} \cdot \Pr[X_i = j] = \sum_{j=0}^{i} a^{2j} \cdot \Pr[X_i = j] = E[a^{2X_i}] = E[Y_i^2]$$

and the second sum is equal to

$$\sum_{j=0}^{i+1} (a^j \cdot a \cdot \Pr[X_i = j - 1] - a^j \cdot \Pr[X_i = j])$$

$$= a^2 \cdot \sum_{j=1}^{i+1} a^{j-1} \cdot \Pr[X_i = j - 1] - \sum_{j=0}^{i} a^j \cdot \Pr[X_i = j]$$

$$= (a^2 - 1) \cdot \sum_{j=0}^{i} a^j \cdot \Pr[X_i = j] = (a^2 - 1) \cdot E[Y_i].$$

Combining the last three equalities gives

$$E[Y_{i+1}^2] = \sum_{j=0}^{i+1} a^{2j} \cdot \Pr[X_i = j] + \sum_{j=0}^{i+1} (a^j \cdot a \cdot \Pr[X_i = j - 1]$$

$$- a^j \cdot \Pr[X_i = j]) = E[Y_i^2] + (a^2 - 1) \cdot E[Y_i]$$

$$= \left[\frac{(a^2 - 1)(a - 1)}{2} i^2 + \frac{(a^2 - 1)(3 - a)}{2} i + 1 \right]$$

$$+ (a^2 - 1) \cdot [(a - 1)i + 1]$$

$$= \frac{(a^2 - 1)(a - 1)}{2}(i + 1)^2 + \frac{(a^2 - 1)(3 - a)}{2}(i + 1) + 1,$$

where the penultimate equality holds by the induction hypothesis. □

We are now ready to prove the estimation guarantee of Algorithm 4.

Corollary 4. *For every ε, $\delta > 0$, Algorithm 4 estimates the length of the stream up to a relative error of ε with probability at least $1 - \delta$.*

Proof. By Chebyshev's inequality, we get

$$\Pr\left[\left| \frac{Y_n - 1}{a - 1} - n \right| \geqslant \varepsilon n \right] = \Pr[|Y_n - 1 - (a - 1)n| \geqslant (a - 1)\varepsilon n]$$

$$= \Pr[|Y_n - E[Y_n]| \geqslant (a - 1)\varepsilon n]$$

$$\leqslant \frac{\mathrm{Var}[Y_n]}{[(a - 1)\varepsilon n]^2} = \frac{(a - 1)^3 n(n - 1)/2}{(a - 1)^2 \varepsilon^2 n^2} < \frac{a - 1}{2\varepsilon^2}$$

$$= \frac{2\varepsilon^2 \delta}{2\varepsilon^2} = \delta.$$

□

Chapter 4

Reservoir Sampling

Many data stream algorithms work in two steps. In the first step, the algorithm reads its input stream and produces a summary of this stream, while in the second step the algorithm processes the summary and produces an output. The summary used by such an algorithm should satisfy two seemingly contradicting requirements. On the one hand, it should be short so as to keep the space complexity of the algorithm small. On the other hand, the summary should capture enough information from the original stream to allow the algorithm to produce an (approximately) correct answer based on the summary alone. In many cases, it turns out that a summary achieving a good balance between these requirements can be produced by simply taking a random sample of tokens out of the algorithm's input stream. In this chapter, we study data stream algorithms for extracting random samples of tokens from the stream, and present one application of these algorithms.

4.1 Uniform Sampling

The simplest kind of random sampling from a stream is sampling a uniformly random single token. In other words, we want to pick one token from the stream, and we want each token of the stream to be this picked token with probability $1/n$ (recall that n is the length of the stream). A two-pass data stream algorithm can produce a sample of this kind using the following simple strategy. In the first pass, the algorithm determines the length n of the stream, and chooses a uniformly random position from the range 1 to n. Then, in its second pass, the algorithm picks from the stream the token appearing at this randomly chosen position. Unfortunately, however, a single-pass data stream algorithm cannot use this simple strategy because it cannot deduce n before viewing the last token of the stream. A more involved strategy for sampling a uniformly random single token from a stream, which can be implemented by a single-pass data stream algorithm, is given as Algorithm 1.

Algorithm 1: Sampling a Uniformly Random Token

1. $n \leftarrow 0$.
2. **while** there are more tokens **do**
3. $n \leftarrow n + 1$.
4.   Let t_n be the next token.
5.   **with** probability $1/n$ **do**
6.   Update $c \leftarrow t_n$.
7. **return** c.

Algorithm 1 maintains a candidate output token c which it updates over time. More specifically, whenever the algorithm reads a new token, it replaces the current candidate with the new token with a probability of one over the number of tokens read so far (and keeps the existing candidate token with the remaining probability). When the algorithm reaches the end of its input stream, the final candidate token becomes the algorithm's output.

Exercise 1. Prove that Algorithm 1 outputs a uniformly random token from its input stream. **Hint:** Prove by induction that after Algorithm 1 has read n' tokens, every one of the tokens it has read is the candidate c with probability $1/n'$.

Let us now consider a generalization of the above sampling problem in which we want to uniformly sample k tokens from the stream. There are two natural ways to understand uniform sampling of k tokens. The first way is to define such a sample as a list of k tokens, where each token in the list is an independent uniformly random token from the stream. The standard name for this kind of uniform sampling is *uniform sampling with replacement*.[1] Observe that the independence of the k tokens in a uniform

---

[1] Let us explain the intuition behind the name. Assume that we have a hat with n balls, and we conduct the following procedure: draw a random ball from the hat, note which ball it is, and then replace the ball in the hat. One can observe that by repeating this procedure k times, we get a uniform sample of k balls with replacement.

sample of k tokens from the stream with replacement means that one can get such a sample by simply running k copies of Algorithm 1 and combining their outputs.

The other natural way to understand uniform sampling of k tokens from the stream is *uniform sampling without replacement*.[2] Here, we want to pick a set of k distinct tokens from the stream, and we want each such set to be picked with equal probability. It is important to note that in the context of uniform sampling without replacement, we treat each one of the n tokens of the stream as unique. This means that if a token appears in multiple positions in the stream, then these appearances are considered different from each other, and thus, can appear together in a sample without replacement. To make it easier to handle this technical point, whenever we discuss sampling from this point on we implicitly assume that the tokens of the stream are all distinct.

Exercise 2 shows that in some cases sampling without replacement can be reduced to sampling with replacement (which we already know how to do).

Exercise 2. Let S be a uniform sample of k tokens from a stream of n tokens with replacement, and let E be the event that S does not contain any repetitions (i.e., every token appears in S at most once):

(a) Prove that $\Pr[E] \geqslant 1 - k^2/n$. Note that this implies that E happens with high probability (a probability approaching 1 when n approaches infinity) when $k = o(\sqrt{n})$.

(b) Recall that S is a list of tokens, and let $\hat{S}$ be the set of tokens appearing in S. Prove that conditioned on E, the distribution of $\hat{S}$ is identical to the distribution of a uniform sample of k tokens from the stream without replacement.

(c) Explain how the above observations can be used to get a data stream algorithm that given a value $k = o(\sqrt{n})$ outputs, with high probability, a uniform sample of k tokens out of its data stream without replacement.

A different method for sampling k tokens without replacement is demonstrated by Algorithm 2. Note that Algorithm 2 implicitly assumes $k \leqslant n$. If necessary, code can be added to this algorithm to handle the case

---

[2]Again, the intuition for the name comes from a hat with n balls. Given such a hat, one can get a uniform sample of k balls without replacement by repeatedly drawing a ball from the hat, noting which ball it is and then throwing the ball away (so that it cannot be drawn again later).

Algorithm 2: Uniform Sampling without Replacement (k)

1. Let R be the set of the first k tokens.
2. $n \leftarrow k$.
3. **while** there are more tokens **do**
4. $n \leftarrow n + 1$.
5.   Let t_n be the next token.
6.   **with** probability k/n **do**
7.   Let t'_n be a uniformly random token from R.
8.   Update R by removing t'_n from it and adding t_n instead.
9. **return** R.

$k > n$ in an appropriate manner (for example, by returning in this case a sample consisting of all the tokens of the stream).

Algorithm 2 maintains a reservoir R of tokens from the stream. Originally, the reservoir contains the first k tokens of the stream. Then, the algorithm reads the remaining $n - k$ tokens of the stream one after the other, and updates the reservoir occasionally while doing so. Specifically, after reading each one of these $n - k$ tokens, the algorithm makes a random decision, and with some probability replaces a token that currently appears in the reservoir with the newly read token. When Algorithm 2 eventually reaches the end of its input stream, the final content of the reservoir becomes the algorithm's output.

Algorithm 2 belongs to a class of sampling algorithms called *reservoir sampling algorithms*. Any algorithm in this class maintains a reservoir of tokens. Every time the algorithm reads a new token, it can add this token to the reservoir, and can also remove from the reservoir some of the tokens currently appearing in it. Finally, when the reservoir sampling algorithm reaches the end of its input stream, the output of the algorithm is a subset of the tokens existing in the reservoir at this point.

As it turns out, not only Algorithm 2, but all the sampling algorithms presented in this chapter are reservoir sampling algorithms. For example, Algorithm 1 is a reservoir sampling algorithm because the candidate token it maintains can be viewed as a reservoir whose size is always equal to 1.

Exercise 3. Prove that when $k \leqslant n$, Algorithm 2 outputs a uniform sample of k tokens from its input stream without replacement. **Hint:** Prove by induction that after Algorithm 2 has read $n' \geqslant k$ tokens, the reservoir R is a uniform sample of k tokens without replacement from the set of the first n' tokens of the input stream.

4.2 Approximate Median and Quantiles

In this section, we assume that the tokens of the stream come from a set whose elements have some natural order. For example, the tokens of the stream can be natural numbers. Note that given this assumption, it is possible to sort the tokens of the stream. Let us define the *rank* of every token to be its position in this hypothetical sorted stream. For example, if the stream consists of the tokens 5, 100, 3 and 2, then the rank of the token 5 is 3 because 5 appears in the third place when these tokens are sorted. To define the rank uniquely, we assume in this section that the tokens of the stream are all distinct.

It is convenient to denote the rank of a token t by $\text{rank}(t)$. Additionally, we also use the *relative rank* of t, which is defined as

$$\text{relrank}(t) = \frac{\text{rank}(t) - 1}{n - 1}.$$

Note that the relative rank is always a number between 0 and 1, and it is equal to the fraction of the other tokens that appear before t in the sorted stream. For example, if n is odd, then the token with the relative rank of $1/2$ is the median of the stream.

Finding the token with a given relative rank has many applications (for example, in database programming). For most of these applications, however, it is sufficient to find a token whose relative rank is close to a given relative rank. For example, many applications that use the median can in fact work with any token whose relative rank is within the range $[1/2 - \varepsilon, 1/2 + \varepsilon]$ for some small constant $\varepsilon > 0$. Such tokens are called *approximate medians*. More generally, given a token t, if $\text{relrank}(t) \in [r - \varepsilon, r + \varepsilon]$, then we say that t's relative rank is ε-*close* to r and call t an *approximate r-quantile*.

In this section, we will present algorithms based on sampling that, given a relative rank r and an accuracy parameter $\varepsilon > 0$, find a token whose relative rank is ε-close to r. The first algorithm of this kind is given as Algorithm 3. Aside from r and ε, this algorithm gets an additional parameter $\delta \in (0, 1]$, which controls the probability that the algorithm succeeds to find a token whose relative rank is ε-close to r.

Note that the space complexity of Algorithm 3 is independent of n, and thus, Algorithm 3 is a streaming algorithm when ε and δ are considered to be constants. In the next paragraphs, we analyze Algorithm 3. However, before doing so, it is important to note that the type of guarantee we want to prove for Algorithm 3 is very different from the estimation guarantees

---

Algorithm 3: Approximate Quantile (r, ε, δ)

1. Run $k = \lceil 24\varepsilon^{-2} \cdot \ln(2/\delta) \rceil$ independent copies of Algorithm 1 in parallel to get a uniform sample S of k tokens from the input stream with replacement.
2. Let S' be a sorted copy of S, i.e., S' contains the same tokens as S, but they appear in S' in a sorted order.
3. **return** the token at position $\lceil rk \rceil$ in S'.

---

we saw in Chapter 3. Specifically, the algorithms in Chapter 3 outputted a value which was close, in some sense, to the value of the exact solution. On the other hand, Algorithm 3 attempts to output a token whose relative rank is ε-close to r, but the token itself can be very different from the token whose relative rank is exactly r. To illustrate this point, consider the (sorted) list of tokens as follows:

$$1, \ 2, \ 3, \ 4, \ 5, \ 1000, \ 1001, \ 1002, \ 1003, \ 1004, \ 1005.$$

The token 5 has a relative rank which is ε-close to $1/2$ when $\varepsilon = 0.1$, however, its value is very different from the value of the true median (which is 1000).

We now begin the analysis of Algorithm 3 by upper bounding the probability that the token selected by Algorithm 3 has a relative rank smaller than $r - \varepsilon$. Note that, since Algorithm 3 picks token number $\lceil rk \rceil$ in the sorted version S' of S, this is equivalent to upper bounding the probability that S contains at least $\lceil rk \rceil$ tokens of relative ranks smaller than $r - \varepsilon$ (see Figure 4.1 for a graphical explanation).

Lemma 1. *Assuming $\varepsilon \geqslant 2/n$, the probability that S contains at least $\lceil rk \rceil$ tokens of relative ranks smaller than $r - \varepsilon$ is at most $\delta/2$.*

Proof. If $r < \varepsilon$, then the lemma is trivial since the relative rank of every token is non-negative. Thus, we may assume $r \geqslant \varepsilon$ in the rest of the proof.

For every $1 \leqslant i \leqslant k$, let X_i be an indicator for the event that the ith token in S is of a relative rank smaller than $r - \varepsilon$. Recall that S is a uniform sample with replacement, and thus, every token of S is an independent uniform token from the stream. Hence, the indicators $X_1, X_2, \ldots, X_k$ are independent. Moreover, since the number of tokens in the stream having a relative rank smaller than $r - \varepsilon$ is $\lceil (r - \varepsilon) \cdot (n - 1) \rceil$, each indicator X_i

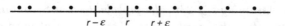

Figure 4.1. A graphical explanation of the analysis of Algorithm 3. The dots represent the k tokens of S, and each dot appears at a position representing its relative rank. The objective of the algorithm is to select a dot between the lines labeled $r - \varepsilon$ and $r + \varepsilon$. The algorithm tries to do this by selecting dot number $\lceil rk \rceil$ when counting from the left. Note that the selected dot has a relative rank at least $r - \varepsilon$ if and only if the number of dots to the left of the line marked by $r - \varepsilon$ is less than $\lceil rk \rceil$. Similarly, the selected dot has a relative rank at most $r + \varepsilon$ if and only if the number of dots to the right of the line marked by $r + \varepsilon$ is at most $k - \lceil rk \rceil$.

takes the value 1 with probability

$$\frac{\lceil (r - \varepsilon) \cdot (n - 1) \rceil}{n} \leqslant \frac{(r - \varepsilon) \cdot (n - 1) + 1}{n} = r - \varepsilon + \frac{\varepsilon - r + 1}{n} \leqslant r - \frac{\varepsilon}{2}.$$

Let us now define X as the sum of the indicators $X_1, X_2, \ldots, X_k$. Using this notation, the claim that we need to prove can be rewritten as

$$\Pr[X \geqslant \lceil rk \rceil] \leqslant \frac{\delta}{2}.$$

Clearly, the probability $\Pr[X \geqslant \lceil rk \rceil]$ is a function of the probabilities of the individual indicators $X_1, X_2, \ldots, X_k$ to take the value 1; and moreover, this probability is maximized when the probabilities of the indicators $X_1, X_2, \ldots, X_k$ to take the value 1 are as large as they can be. Thus, for the sake of the proof let us assume from now on that each one of these indicators take the value 1 with probability exactly $r - \varepsilon/2$. Since the indicators $X_1, X_2, \ldots, X_k$ are independent, by the Chernoff bound we get

$$\Pr[X \geqslant \lceil rk \rceil] \leqslant \Pr\left[X \geqslant rk - \frac{k\varepsilon^2}{4r}\right] = \Pr\left[X \geqslant \left(r - \frac{\varepsilon}{2}\right) \cdot k \cdot \left(1 + \frac{\varepsilon}{2r}\right)\right]$$

$$\leqslant e^{-\frac{(\varepsilon/2r)^2}{3} \cdot E[X]} = e^{-\frac{\varepsilon^2}{12r^2} \cdot k \cdot \left(r - \frac{\varepsilon}{2}\right)} \leqslant e^{-\frac{\varepsilon^2}{12r^2} \cdot (24\varepsilon^{-2} \cdot \ln(2/\delta)) \cdot \frac{r}{2}}$$

$$\leqslant e^{-\ln(2/\delta)} = \frac{\delta}{2}. \qquad \qquad \square$$

The next step in the analysis of Algorithm 3 is upper bounding the probability that the token selected by it has a relative rank larger than $r + \varepsilon$. Since Algorithm 3 picks token number $\lceil rk \rceil$ in the sorted version S' of S, this is equivalent to upper bounding the probability that S contains more than $k - \lceil rk \rceil$ tokens of relative ranks larger than $r + \varepsilon$ (again, see Figure 4.1 for a graphical explanation).

Lemma 2. *Assuming $\varepsilon \geqslant 2/n$, the probability that S contains more than $k - \lceil rk \rceil$ tokens of relative ranks larger than $r + \varepsilon$ is at most $\delta/2$.*

The proof of Lemma 2 is very similar to the proof of Lemma 1, and thus, we leave it as an exercise.

‖ **Exercise 4.** Prove Lemma 2.

Lemmata 1 and 2 together imply Theorem 1.

Theorem 1. *Assuming $\varepsilon \geqslant 2/n$, Algorithm 1 outputs a token whose relative rank is ε-close to r with probability at least $1 - \delta$.*

Proof. As discussed above, Lemma 1 proves that the probability that the token outputted by Algorithm 1 has a relative rank smaller than $r - \varepsilon$ is at most $\delta/2$. Additionally, Lemma 2 proves that the probability that the token outputted by Algorithm 1 has a relative rank larger than $r + \varepsilon$ is at most $\delta/2$. By the union bound, we now get that the probability that the token outputted by Algorithm 1 has a relative rank which is either smaller than $r - \varepsilon$ or larger than $r + \varepsilon$ is at most δ. $\qquad\square$

‖ **Exercise 5.** Theorem 1 proves a guarantee on the output of Algorithm 1, which holds as long as $\varepsilon \geqslant 2/n$. Prove that this cannot be improved significantly, i.e., show that no algorithm can output a token whose relative rank is ε-close to r with a constant probability for $\varepsilon \leqslant 1/(2n)$.

Algorithm 3 has an interesting property. It constructs S' without referring to r at all, and then uses r and S' in Line 3 to get a token whose relative rank is ε-close to r. In other words, S' can be viewed as a summary of the stream which Algorithm 3 creates while reading the stream, and then this summary is used to produce an answer for a given value of r. This raises the following natural question. Suppose we are given h relative ranks $r_1, r_2, \ldots, r_h$, and we want to find h tokens $t_1, t_2, \ldots, t_h$ such that t_i's relative rank is ε-close to r_i for every $1 \leqslant i \leqslant h$. Can we use the summary S' to get all the tokens $t_1, t_2, \ldots, t_h$?

In some sense, the answer to the above question is positive. Theorem 1 guarantees that, for every given $1 \leqslant i \leqslant h$, if t_i is selected as the token at location $\lceil r_i k \rceil$ in S', then t_i's relative rank is ε-close to r_i with probability at least $1 - \delta$. However, we often want a stronger property, namely, we want the relative rank of the token t_i to be ε-close to r_i for *all* $1 \leqslant i \leqslant h$ at

---

Algorithm 4: Multiple Approximate Quantiles $(r_1, r_2, \ldots, r_h, \varepsilon, \delta)$

1. Run Algorithm 1 $k = \lceil 24\varepsilon^{-2} \cdot \ln(2h/\delta) \rceil$ times independently to get a uniform sample S of k tokens from the input stream with replacement.
2. Let S' be a sorted copy of S, i.e., S' contains the same tokens as S, but they appear in S' in a sorted order.
3. **for** $i = 1$ to h **do**
4.   Let t_i be the token at position $\lceil r_i k \rceil$ in S'.
5. **return** $(t_1, t_2, \ldots, t_h)$.

---

the same time with probability at least $1 - \delta$. Exercise 6 shows that this property can be made true by making the size of S' dependent on h.

Exercise 6. Algorithm 4 is a variant of Algorithm 3 which uses a larger sample S, gets h numbers $r_1, r_2, \ldots, r_h \in [0, 1]$ rather than only one such number as in Algorithm 3 and outputs h tokens $t_1, t_2, \ldots, t_h$. Prove that with probability at least $1 - \delta$, the relative rank of the token t_i found by this algorithm is ε-close to r_i for *all* $1 \leqslant i \leqslant h$ at the same time.

4.3 Weighted Sampling

In Section 4.1, we studied uniform sampling of tokens from the stream, i.e., sampling processes whose behavior is symmetric with respect to all the tokens of the stream. For example, in a uniform sample of a single token from the stream, the sampled token is equal to each one of the tokens of the stream with equal probability. Sometimes it is interesting to consider also sampling processes which do not treat all the tokens of the stream symmetrically. In particular, in this section we consider *weighted sampling*.

In weighted sampling, we assume that each token t of the stream is accompanied by a positive weight $w(t)$, and tokens with larger weights should be more likely (in some sense) to be in the sample. The simplest form of weighted sampling is weighted sampling of a single token from the stream. In this kind of sampling we want to pick a single token from the stream, and the probability of each token to be this picked token should be proportional to its weight. In other words, if W is the total weight of all the tokens in the stream, then the probability of a token t to be the picked token should be $w(t)/W$.

Exercise 7. If the weights of the tokens are all integral, then it is possible to reduce weighted sampling of a single token from the stream to *uniform* sampling of a single token. Describe a way to construct this reduction, i.e., explain how an algorithm for uniform sampling of a single token, such as Algorithm 1, can be used for weighted sampling of a single token when all weights are integral.

The reduction described by Exercise 7 works only when the weights of the tokens are integral, and it is also quite slow (it results in an algorithm with a quasi-polynomial time complexity, i.e., a time complexity which is polynomial in the weights rather than in the size of their representations). Thus, it is interesting to find an algorithm that directly implements weighted sampling of a single token. One such algorithm is given as Algorithm 5.

Algorithm 5: Weighted Sampling of a Single Token

1. $n \leftarrow 0$, $W \leftarrow 0$.
2. **while** there are more tokens **do**
3. $\quad n \leftarrow n + 1$.
4. $\quad$ Let t_n be the next token.
5. $\quad W \leftarrow W + w(t_n)$.
6. $\quad$ **with** probability $w(t_n)/W$ **do**
7. $\quad\quad$ Update $c \leftarrow t_n$.
8. **return** c.

Like Algorithm 1, Algorithm 5 also maintains a candidate output token c which is updated occasionally and becomes the output of the algorithm once the algorithm reaches the end of its input stream. The main difference between Algorithms 1 and 5 is the way in which they decide whether a newly arriving token should replace the existing candidate token. In Algorithm 1, an arriving token becomes the candidate token with a probability equal to 1 over the number of tokens viewed so far, while in Algorithm 5 it becomes the candidate token with a probability equal to its weight over the total weight of the tokens seen so far.

Theorem 2. *Algorithm 5 produces a weighted sample of a single token from its input stream.*

Proof. Let $W(i)$ be the total weight of the first i tokens of the input stream. We prove by induction that after Algorithm 1 has read n' tokens, every token t that it reads is the candidate c with probability $w(t)/W(n')$. Note that this implies that after the algorithm reads all n tokens of the stream, each token t of the stream is the candidate c with probability $w(t)/W$, which is what we want to prove.

The base case of the induction is the case $n' = 1$. To see why the claim we want to prove holds in this case, observe that when Algorithm 5 reads the first token t_1, it updates the candidate c to be equal to t_1 with probability $w(t_1)/W(1) = 1$. In other words, after Algorithm 1 reads a single token, its candidate c is always equal to this token. Assume now that the claim we want to prove holds after Algorithm 5 has read $n' - 1$ tokens (for some $n' > 1$), and let us prove it holds also after the algorithm reads the next token. Note that when Algorithm 5 reads the token $t_{n'}$, it updates the candidate c to be this token with probability $w(t_{n'})/W(n')$. Thus, it only remains to prove that the probability of every previous token t is the candidate c at this point is $w(t)/W(n')$.

Fix some token t which is one of the first $n' - 1$ tokens of the stream. In order for t to be the candidate c after Algorithm 5 has read n' tokens, two events must happen. First, t has to be the candidate c after the algorithm has read $n' - 1$ tokens, and second, Algorithm 5 must not change its candidate after viewing $t_{n'}$. Since these events are independent,

$$\Pr\begin{bmatrix} t \text{ is the candidate after} \\ n' \text{ tokens are read} \end{bmatrix} = \Pr\begin{bmatrix} t \text{ is the candidate after} \\ n' - 1 \text{ tokens are read} \end{bmatrix}$$

$$\cdot \Pr\begin{bmatrix} \text{Reading token } t_{n'} \text{does not make} \\ \text{the algorithm change its candidate} \end{bmatrix}$$

$$= \frac{w(t)}{W(n' - 1)} \cdot \left(1 - \frac{w(t_{n'})}{W(n')}\right) = \frac{w(t)}{W(n') - w(t_{n'})} \cdot \left(1 - \frac{w(t_{n'})}{W(n')}\right)$$

$$= \frac{w(t)}{W(n')},$$

where the second equality holds by the induction hypothesis and the above observation that Algorithm 5 changes its candidate after reading $t_{n'}$ with probability $w(t_{n'})/W(n')$. □

Like uniform sampling, weighted sampling can also be generalized to samples of k tokens from the stream. However, there are multiple natural ways to do that, and the sampling algorithms implementing these natural ways tend to be quite involved. For these reasons, we do not study weighted sampling of multiple tokens in this book. However, interested readers can find references to papers studying this kind of sampling in Section 4.4.

4.4 Bibliographic Notes

The term "reservoir sampling" was first coined by Vitter (1985) who studied algorithms for uniform sampling from a file using a single pass, and described Algorithm 2. One can observe that Algorithm 2 has the interesting property that it often dismisses tokens immediately after reading them, i.e., most tokens never become the candidate token of the algorithm. Vitter observed that in the context of a file, unlike in a streaming algorithm, one can use this property to speed up the algorithm. Specifically, if the algorithm detects a portion of the file whose tokens are going to be dismissed immediately (regardless of their identity), then the implementation of the algorithm can simply pretend that this portion was read and skip the actual reading of it from the file, which is a slow operation. Accordingly, the main focus of Vitter (1985) is on efficient methods for determining the portions of the file that can be safely skipped.

Two natural interpretations of weighted sampling of k tokens from the stream were studied by Min-Te Chao (1982) and Efraimidis and Spirakis (2006). Min-Te Chao (1982) studied weighted sampling in which the probability of every token to be among the k tokens of the sample is proportional to the weight of this token (up to a small technical issue with elements of large weight). Efraimidis and Spirakis (2006) studied a different kind of weighted sampling which is similar in spirit to uniform sampling without replacement. In this kind of weighted sampling, one can think of the tokens as balls in a hat. To get a sample, one draws k balls from the hat in k rounds. In each such round, a single ball is drawn from the hat without replacement, and the probability of each ball in the hat to be this drawn ball is equal to the weight of the ball over the total weight of the balls that are still in the hat (i.e., were not drawn in the previous rounds).

The problem of finding a token which is ε-*close* to a given relative rank and the related problem of estimating the rank of a given token have been both studied extensively. The interested reader is referred to the work of Karnin *et al.* (2016) (and the references therein) for more information about these problems.

P. S. Efraimidis and P. G. Spirakis. Weighted Random Sampling with a Reservoir. *Information Processing Letters*, 97(5): 181–185, 2006.

Min-Te Chao. A General Purpose Unequal Probability Sampling Plan. *Biometrika*, 69(3): 653–656, 1982.

Z. S. Karnin, K. Lang and E. Liberty. Optimal Quantile Approximation in streams. In *Proceedings of the IEEE 57th Annual Symposium on Foundations of Computer Science (FOCS)*, 71–78, 2016.

J. S. Vitter. Random Sampling with a Reservoir. *ACM Transactions on Mathematical Software*, 11(1): 37–57, 1985.

Exercise Solutions

Solution 1

Following the hint, we prove by induction that after Algorithm 1 has read n' tokens, every one of the tokens it has read is the candidate c with probability $1/n'$. Note that this implies that after the algorithm reads all n tokens of the stream, the candidate c is a uniformly random token out of the n tokens of the stream, which is what we want to prove.

The base case of the induction is the case $n' = 1$. To see why the claim we want to prove holds in this case, observe that when Algorithm 1 reads the first token t_1, it updates the candidate c to be equal to t_1 with probability $1/n' = 1$. In other words, after Algorithm 1 reads a single token, its candidate c is always equal to this token. Assume now that the claim we want to prove holds after Algorithm 1 has read $n' - 1$ tokens (for some $n' > 1$), and let us prove it holds also after the algorithm reads the next token. Note that when Algorithm 1 reads the token $t_{n'}$, it updates the candidate c to be this token with probability $1/n'$. Thus, it only remains to be proved that the probability of every previous token to be the candidate c at this point is also $1/n'$.

Fix some $1 \leqslant i < n'$. In order for t_i to be the candidate c after Algorithm 1 has read n' tokens, two events must happen. First, t_i has to be the candidate c after the algorithm has read $n' - 1$ tokens, and second, Algorithm 1 must not change its candidate after viewing $t_{n'}$. Since these events are independent,

$$
\Pr\begin{bmatrix} t_i \text{ is the candidate after} \\ n' \text{ tokens are read} \end{bmatrix} = \Pr\begin{bmatrix} t_i \text{ is the candidate after} \\ n' - 1 \text{ tokens are read} \end{bmatrix}
$$

$$
\cdot \Pr\begin{bmatrix} \text{Reading token } t_{n'} \text{ does not make} \\ \text{the algorithm change its candidate} \end{bmatrix}
$$

$$
= \frac{1}{n' - 1} \cdot \left(1 - \frac{1}{n'} \right) = \frac{1}{n'},
$$

where the second equality holds by the induction hypothesis and the above observation that Algorithm 1 changes its candidate after reading $t_{n'}$ with probability $1/n'$.

Solution 2

(a) Let us name the k tokens of the sample S by $s_1, s_2, \ldots, s_k$, and for every $1 \leqslant i \leqslant k$, let us denote by E_i the event that the tokens $s_1, s_2, \ldots, s_i$ are all distinct. Clearly, $\Pr[E_1] = 1$. Moreover, since each one of the tokens $s_1, s_2, \ldots, s_k$ is a uniformly random token from the stream which is independent of the other tokens of the sample S, we get, for every $1 < i \leqslant k$,

$$\Pr[E_i | E_{i-1}] = 1 - \frac{i-1}{n}.$$

Note that the event E_i implies the event E_{i-1} for every $1 < i \leqslant k$. Thus, the conditional probabilities calculated above can be combined to give

$$\Pr[E_k] = \Pr[E_1] \cdot \prod_{i=2}^{k} \frac{\Pr[E_i]}{\Pr[E_{i-1}]} = \Pr[E_1] \cdot \prod_{i=2}^{k} \frac{\Pr[E_{i-1} \cap E_i]}{\Pr[E_{i-1}]}$$

$$= \Pr[E_1] \cdot \prod_{i=2}^{k} \Pr[E_i | E_{i-1}]$$

$$= \prod_{i=2}^{k} \left(1 - \frac{i-1}{n}\right) \geqslant \prod_{i=2}^{k} \left(1 - \frac{k}{n}\right) \geqslant 1 - \frac{k^2}{n}.$$

It remains to observe now that the event E, whose probability we want to lower bound, is in fact equal to the event E_k.

(b) We need to prove that conditioned on E, the set $\hat{S}$ has the same distribution as a uniformly random sample of k tokens from the stream without replacement. In other words, if K is the collection of sets of k distinct tokens from the stream, then we need to prove that conditioned on E the set $\hat{S}$ is a uniformly random set out of K. There are two ways to prove this.

Let us begin with the first way, which is based on a symmetry argument. The definition of E guarantees that conditioned on E the set $\hat{S}$ contains k distinct tokens from the stream, and thus, belongs to K. Moreover, the definitions of $\hat{S}$, E and K are completely symmetric with respect to the different tokens of the stream, and thus, $\hat{S}$ must have an equal probability to be each one of the sets of K.

The other way to prove that $\hat{S}$ is a uniformly random set from K is more explicit. Fix some set $S' \in K$. Since S is a uniform sample of k tokens from the stream with replacement, we get

$$\Pr[\hat{S} = S'] = \frac{k!}{n^k}.$$

Observe that the event $\hat{S} = S'$ implies the event E, and thus,

$$\Pr[S = S'|E] = \frac{\Pr[S = S' \wedge E]}{\Pr[E]} = \frac{k!/n^k}{\prod_{i=2}^{k}\left(1 - \frac{i-1}{n}\right)}$$

$$= \frac{k!}{n \cdot \prod_{i=2}^{k}\left(n - i + 1\right)} = \frac{k! \cdot (n - k)!}{n!} = \binom{n}{k}^{-1}.$$

In conclusion, we got that conditioned on E the probability that $\hat{S}$ is equal to the set S' is equal to 1 over the number of sets in K. Since S' is an arbitrary set of K, we get that $\hat{S}$ is a uniformly random set out of K.

(c) Consider the data stream algorithm given as Algorithm 6.

Algorithm 6: Uniform Sampling without Replacement with High Probability (k)

1. Run in parallel k independent copies of Algorithm 1 to get a uniform sample S of k tokens from the input stream with replacement.
2. **if** S contains repetitions **then**
3.   **declare** failure.
4. **else**
5.   **return** the set of tokens in S.

Part (a) of the exercise guarantees that Algorithm 6 returns an output with high probability when $k = o(\sqrt{n})$. Moreover, part (b) of the exercise guarantees that, conditioned on not declaring a failure, Algorithm 6 produces an output set having the same distribution as a uniformly random sample of k tokens from its input stream without replacement.

Solution 3

Following the hint, we prove by induction that after Algorithm 2 has read $n' \geqslant k$ tokens, the reservoir R is a uniform sample of k tokens without replacement from the set of the first n' tokens of the input stream. Note that this implies that after the algorithm reads all n tokens of the stream, the reservoir is a uniform sample of k tokens without replacement from the algorithm's input stream, which is what we want to prove.

The base case of the induction is the case $n' = k$. In this case, after Algorithm 2 reads n' tokens, its reservoir contains the first k tokens of the input stream. This is consistent with the claim we want to prove since a uniform sample of k tokens without replacement from a set of size k always contains all the tokens of the set. Assume now that the claim we want to prove holds after Algorithm 2 has read $n' - 1$ tokens (for some $n' > k$), and let us prove it holds also after the algorithm reads the next token.

Let N' be the set of the first n' tokens of the stream, (i.e., $N' = \{t_1, t_2, \ldots, t_{n'}\}$), and let $R(i)$ denote the reservoir R after Algorithm 2 has read i tokens. We need to prove that for every given set $S \subseteq N'$ of k tokens, we obtain

$$\Pr[S = R(n')] = \binom{n'}{k}^{-1} .$$

There are two cases to consider. The first case is when $t_{n'} \notin S$. In this case, we can have $R(n') = S$ only if Algorithm 2 did not change its reservoir after reading $t_{n'}$. Since the decision to make a change in the reservoir after reading $t_{n'}$ is independent of the content of the reservoir, this implies

$$\Pr[S = R(n')] = \Pr[S = R(n' - 1)]$$
$$\cdot \Pr\left[\begin{matrix} \text{The algorithm does not make a change} \\ \text{in its reservoir after reading } t_{n'} \end{matrix}\right]$$
$$= \binom{n' - 1}{k}^{-1} \cdot \left(1 - \frac{k}{n'}\right)$$
$$= \frac{k! \cdot (n' - k - 1)!}{(n' - 1)!} \cdot \frac{n' - k}{n'} = \binom{n'}{k}^{-1} ,$$

where the second equality holds by the induction hypothesis.

The other case we need to consider is when $t_{n'} \in S$. In this case, we can get $R(n') = S$ if and only if the following conditions hold:

- $R(n' - 1)$ is equal to $(S \cup \{t\}) \setminus \{t_{n'}\}$ for some token $t \in N' \setminus S$. Since $|N' \setminus S| = n' - k$, the induction hypothesis guarantees that this condition holds with probability

$$(n' - k) \cdot \binom{n' - 1}{k}^{-1}.$$

- Given that the previous condition holds, Algorithm 2 decides to add $t_{n'}$ to its reservoir instead of the token t. The probability that this condition holds, given that the previous one holds, is

$$\frac{k}{n'} \cdot \frac{1}{k} = \frac{1}{n'}.$$

It now remains to be observed that the probability that both conditions hold at the same time is

$$\left[(n' - k) \cdot \binom{n' - 1}{k}^{-1} \right] \cdot \frac{1}{n'} = \frac{n' - k}{n'} \cdot \frac{k! \cdot (n - k - 1)!}{(n' - 1)!} = \binom{n'}{k}^{-1}.$$

Solution 4

If $r + \varepsilon > 1$, then Lemma 2 is trivial since the relative rank of every token is at most 1. Thus, we may assume $r + \varepsilon \leqslant 1$ in the rest of the proof.

For every $1 \leqslant i \leqslant k$, let X_i be an indicator for the event that the ith token in S is of relative rank larger than $r + \varepsilon$. Recall that S is a uniform sample with replacement, and thus, every token of S is an independent uniform token from the stream. Hence, the indicators $X_1, X_2, \ldots, X_k$ are independent. Moreover, since the number of tokens in the stream having a relative rank larger than $r + \varepsilon$ is $\lceil (1 - r - \varepsilon) \cdot (n - 1) \rceil$, each indicator X_i takes the value 1 with probability

$$\frac{\lceil (1 - r - \varepsilon) \cdot (n - 1) \rceil}{n} \leqslant \frac{(1 - r - \varepsilon) \cdot (n - 1) + 1}{n}$$

$$= 1 - r - \varepsilon + \frac{1 - (1 - r - \varepsilon)}{n} \leqslant 1 - r - \frac{\varepsilon}{2}.$$

Let us now define X as the sum of the indicators $X_1, X_2, \dots, X_k$. Using this notation, the claim that we need to prove can be rewritten as follows:

$$\Pr[X > k - \lceil rk \rceil] \leqslant \frac{\delta}{2}.$$

Clearly, the probability $\Pr[X > k - \lceil rk \rceil]$ can only increase if the probability of the indicators $X_1, X_2, \dots, X_k$ to take the value 1 is increased. Thus, for the sake of the proof let us assume from now on that each one of these indicators takes the value 1 with probability exactly $1 - r - \varepsilon/2$. Since the indicators $X_1, X_2, \dots, X_k$ are independent, by the Chernoff bound we get

$$\Pr[X > k - \lceil rk \rceil] \leqslant \Pr[X \geqslant k - rk] \leqslant \Pr\left[X \geqslant k - rk - \frac{\varepsilon^2 k}{4(1-r)}\right]$$

$$= \Pr\left[X \geqslant \left(1 - r - \frac{\varepsilon}{2}\right) \cdot k \cdot \left(1 + \frac{\varepsilon}{2(1-r)}\right)\right]$$

$$\leqslant e^{-\frac{(\varepsilon/2(1-r))^2}{3} \cdot E[X]}$$

$$= e^{-\frac{\varepsilon^2}{12(1-r)^2} \cdot k \cdot \left(1 - r - \frac{\varepsilon}{2}\right)} \leqslant e^{-\frac{\varepsilon^2}{12(1-r)^2} \cdot (24\varepsilon^{-2} \cdot \ln(2/\delta)) \cdot \frac{1-r}{2}}$$

$$\leqslant e^{-\ln(2/\delta)} = \frac{\delta}{2},$$

where the first inequality holds since X takes only integer values.

Solution 5

Intuitively, a small value for ε reduces the number of tokens whose relative rank is ε-close to r, and thus, makes life more difficult for an algorithm that needs to find such a token. We will show that when ε becomes too small (i.e., $\varepsilon \leqslant 1/(2n)$), there might be no tokens at all whose relative rank is ε-close to r, which means that the algorithm cannot find such a token.

The relative rank of every token is of the form $i/(n-1)$ for some integer $0 \leqslant i < n$. This means that for every $1 \leqslant i < n$, the range

$$\left(\frac{i-1}{n-1}, \frac{i}{n-1}\right)$$

does not contain the relative rank of any token. Since the size of this range is $(n-1)^{-1} > 1/n$, this means that the range

$$\left[\frac{i-1/2}{n-1} - \frac{1}{2n}, \frac{i-1/2}{n-1} + \frac{1}{2n}\right]$$

also does not contain the relative rank of any token. Thus, for $\varepsilon \leqslant 1/(2n)$, there is no token whose relative rank is ε-close to $(i - 1/2)/(n - 1)$.

Solution 6

Assume that Algorithm 4 is executed with some values ε' and δ' for the parameters ε and δ, respectively. Then, the size of the sample S it uses is $\lceil 24\varepsilon'^2 \cdot \ln(2h/\delta') \rceil$. Note that Algorithm 3 uses a sample S of that size when its parameters ε and δ are set to ε' and δ'/h, respectively. Thus, one can repeat the proof of Theorem 1 and get that, for every $1 \leqslant i \leqslant h$, t_i's relative rank is ε'-close to r_i with probability at least $1 - \delta'/h$. In other words, the probability that the relative rank of t_i is not ε'-close to r_i is at most δ'/h. By the union bound, we now get that the probability that for some $1 \leqslant i \leqslant h$ the relative rank of the token t_i is not ε'-close to r_i is at most δ', which is what we want to prove.

Solution 7

Let ALG be an arbitrary algorithm for uniform sampling of a single token from the stream, such as Algorithm 1, and consider Algorithm 7. This algorithm applies ALG to a stream which contains $w(t)$ copies of every token t in the stream of Algorithm 7, and then returns the output of ALG. Note that this is possible since $w(t)$ is integral by the assumption of the exercise.

Algorithm 7: Weighted Sampling by Uniform Sampling

1. Create an instance of ALG.
2. **while** there are more tokens **do**
3.   Let t be the next token.
4.   Add to the stream of ALG $w(t)$ copies of the token t.
5. **return** the output of ALG.

Consider an arbitrary token t from the stream of Algorithm 7. Clearly, the length of the stream faced by ALG is equal to the total weight of all the tokens in the stream of Algorithm 7, i.e., it is equal to W. Thus, every copy of t in the stream of ALG is selected by ALG (and thus, also by Algorithm 7) with probability W^{-1}. Since there are $w(t)$ copies of t in the stream of ALG, and the selection of each one of them is a disjoint event, we get that the probability that any copy of t is selected by ALG is $w(t)/W$.

Recall that t was chosen as an arbitrary token from the stream of Algorithm 7. Thus, we have proven that Algorithm 7 performs weighted sampling of a single token from its stream using an algorithm ALG for uniform sampling of a single token.

Chapter 5

Pairwise Independent Hashing

In many settings, it is desirable to have access to a random function. Unfortunately, to store such a function one must keep a table mapping every possible element to its image, which is often infeasible. A popular workaround for this problem is to use hash functions, which are functions that behave as random functions (in some sense), but can be stored using a small amount of space. This workaround is especially important for data stream algorithms, which are often required to have very low space complexities. In this chapter, we present one particularly useful kind of hash functions. These hash functions will come into use in many of the data stream algorithms that we will see in the following chapters.

5.1 Pairwise Hash Functions Families

To be useful, a *hash function* should behave like a random function. However, every particular function is deterministic, and thus, cannot exhibit random properties. Thus, to get provable random properties, one must consider a function chosen at random from some set of possible options. More formally, given a domain D and a range R, a *hash functions family* F is a set of functions from D to R. Such a family is considered useful when a function f chosen uniformly at random from F exhibits properties that we expect a random function to have, such as

$$\Pr\left[f\left(d_1\right) = f\left(d_2\right)\right] = \frac{1}{|R|} \quad \text{for every two distinct } d_1, d_2 \in D.$$

A hash family having the above property is called a *universal family*.

Exercise 1. Consider the four functions from the domain $\{a, b, c, d\}$ to the range $\{0, 1\}$ that are specified by the following tables, and let F be the set of the four functions represented by these tables. Verify that F is a universal hash functions family.

Element	Image
a	0
b	0
c	0
d	0

Element	Image
a	1
b	0
c	1
d	0

Element	Image
a	0
b	1
c	1
d	0

Element	Image
a	1
b	1
c	0
d	0

The definition of a universal hash functions family is very weak. This is demonstrated, for example, by the fact that all the functions of the universal family F from Exercise 1 map the element d to the value 0, which is clearly not something that one would expect from a random function. To remedy this problem, stronger kinds of hash functions families have been suggested. In this chapter, we are interested in two such kinds of functions known as *pairwise independent families* and *k-wise independent families*.

Definition 1. A family F of hash functions from a domain D to a range R is called pairwise independent (or 2-wise independent) if for a uniformly random function $f \in F$ and any fixed choice of two distinct d_1, $d_2 \in D$ and two r_1, $r_2 \in R$ it holds that

$$\Pr[f(d_1) = r_1 \text{ and } f(d_2) = r_2] = \frac{1}{|R|^2}.$$

More generally, it is called k-wise independent if for a uniformly random function $f \in F$ and any fixed choice of k distinct $d_1, d_2, \ldots, d_k \in D$ and k elements $r_1, r_2, \ldots, r_k \in R$ it holds that

$$\Pr[\forall_{1 \leqslant i \leqslant k} f(d_i) = r_i] = \frac{1}{|R|^k}.$$

Exercise 2. Let F be the set of four functions from Exercise 1 restricted to the domain $\{a, b, c\}$ (in other words, we remove the row of d from the four tables in Exercise 1, and the functions corresponding to the tables after this removal are the functions of F). Verify that F is a 2-wise independent hash functions family.

Exercise 3 suggests an alternative equivalent definition of k-wise independent families. This definition explicitly states the properties that make k-wise independent families useful in applications.

Exercise 3. Consider a hash functions family F from domain D of size at least k to range R, and let f be a uniformly random function from F. Prove that F is k-wise independent if and only if the following two claims hold:

(1) For every $d \in D$, the expression $f(d)$ has a probability of $1/|R|$ to be equal to each element of the range R.
(2) The random variables in the set $\{f(d)|d \in D\}$ are k-wise independent (note that for any fixed $d \in D$, the expression $f(d)$ is a random variable taking values from R).

The rest of this chapter is devoted to the presentation of various constructions of pairwise and k-wise independent hash functions families.

5.2 Simple Construction of a Pairwise Independent Hash Family

Recall that $\{0, 1\}^m$ is the set of all strings of m bits. Given a string $x \in \{0, 1\}^m$, we denote by $x^{(i)}$ the bit at the ith position in it. Using this notation we can now define, for every positive integer m, a family F_X of hash functions from the domain $\{0, 1\}^m$ to the range $\{0, 1\}$. The family F_X contains a function $f_{b,S}$ for every bit $b \in \{0, 1\}$ and set $S \subseteq \{1, 2, \ldots, m\}$ which is defined by

$$f_{b,S}(x) = b \oplus (\oplus_{i \in S} x^{(i)}) \quad \forall x \in \{0, 1\}^m,$$

where the operator $\oplus$ represents here the XOR operation. In other words, the value of $f_{b,S}(x)$ is the XOR of b with all the bits of x at the positions specified by S.

Exercise 4. For $m = 2$, write down for every function $f_{b,S} \in F_X$ a table specifying the image corresponding to each input according to $f_{b,S}$.

Lemma 1 proves that the F_X hash functions family is pairwise independent.

Lemma 1. *For every two distinct strings $x, y \in \{0,1\}^m$, two bits b_x, $b_y \in \{0,1\}$ and a hash function f drawn uniformly at random from F_X, it holds that $\Pr[f(x) = b_x \wedge f(y) = b_y] = 1/4$.*

Proof. Since x and y are distinct, there must be a position in which they do not agree. In other words, there is an integer $1 \leqslant i \leqslant m$ such that $x^{(i)} \neq y^{(i)}$, and let us assume without loss of generality $x^{(i)} = 0$ and $y^{(i)} = 1$. Consider now an arbitrary set $S \subseteq \{1, 2, \ldots, m\}\backslash\{i\}$, then

$$f_{0,S}(x) = \oplus_{j \in S} x^{(j)} \qquad\qquad f_{0,S}(y) = \oplus_{j \in S} y^{(j)}$$

$$f_{0,S\cup\{i\}}(x) = x^{(i)} \oplus (\oplus_{j \in S} x^{(j)}) \qquad f_{0,S\cup\{i\}}(y) = y^{(i)} \oplus (\oplus_{j \in S} y^{(j)})$$

$$= \oplus_{j \in S} x^{(j)} \qquad\qquad\qquad = 1 \oplus (\oplus_{j \in S} y^{(j)})$$

$$f_{1,S}(x) = 1 \oplus (\oplus_{j \in S} x^{(j)}) \qquad\qquad f_{1,S}(y) = 1 \oplus (\oplus_{j \in S} y^{(j)})$$

$$f_{1,S\cup\{i\}}(x) = 1 \oplus x^{(i)} \oplus (\oplus_{j \in S} x^{(j)}) \quad f_{1,S\cup\{i\}}(y) = 1 \oplus y^{(i)} \oplus (\oplus_{j \in S} y^{(j)})$$

$$= 1 \oplus (\oplus_{j \in S} x^{(j)}) \qquad\qquad\qquad = \oplus_{j \in S} y^{(j)}$$

Looking at these equations, one can observe that regardless of the values that $\oplus_{j \in S} x^{(j)}$ and $\oplus_{j \in S} y^{(j)}$ happen to have, exactly one of the four pairs $(f_{0,S}(x), f_{0,S}(y))$, $(f_{0,S\cup\{i\}}(x), f_{0,S\cup\{i\}}(y))$, $(f_{1,S}(x), f_{1,S}(y))$ or $(f_{1,S\cup\{i\}}(x), f_{1,S\cup\{i\}}(y))$ is equal to (b_x, b_y). Thus, out of the four functions $f_{0,S}$, $f_{0,S\cup\{i\}}$, $f_{1,S}$ and $f_{1,S\cup\{i\}}$, exactly one is an option for f which makes the event $\{f(x) = b_x \wedge f(y) = b_y\}$ hold, which implies

$$\Pr\left[f(x) = b_x \wedge f(y) = b_y | f \in \{f_{0,S}, f_{0,S\cup\{i\}}, f_{1,S}, f_{1,S\cup\{i\}}\}\right] = \frac{1}{4}.$$

To complete the proof of the lemma, it remains to be observed that the sets $\{f_{0,S}, f_{0,S\cup\{i\}}, f_{1,S}, f_{1,S\cup\{i\}}\}$ obtained for the various choices of $S \subseteq \{1, 2, \ldots, r\}\backslash\{i\}$ are disjoint and that their union is the entire family F_X. Thus, by the law of total probability,

$$\Pr[f(x) = b_x \wedge f(y) = b_y]$$

$$= \sum_{S \subseteq \{1,2,\ldots,m\}\backslash\{i\}} \Pr\left[f \in \{f_{0,S}, f_{0,S\cup\{i\}}, f_{1,S}, f_{1,S\cup\{i\}}\}\right] \cdot \frac{1}{4} = \frac{1}{4}. \quad \square$$

The hash functions family F_X is the first construction of a pairwise independent family that we have. We recall that our motivation to study hash functions was to find functions that behave like random functions but have a small representation. Thus, to determine whether the F_X family is good, we need to determine the number of bits necessary for representing a hash function in this family. Every function $f_{S,b} \in F_X$ is determined by the bit b and the set $S \subseteq \{1, 2, \ldots, m\}$ that can be represented (in the natural way) using m bits. Thus, $m + 1$ bits are enough for representing $f_{S,b}$. One can observe that this number of bits is much smaller than the 2^m bits necessary for representing a general function from the domain $\{0, 1\}^m$ to the range $\{0, 1\}$, which is what we expect from a good hash functions family. Theorem 1 summarizes the properties that we have proved for the hash functions family F_X.

Theorem 1. *For every positive integer m, there is a pairwise independent hash functions family F_X from $\{0, 1\}^m$ to $\{0, 1\}$ whose functions can be represented using $m + 1$ bits.*

The domain of F_X can be made as large as necessary by increasing the parameter m. In contrast, the range of F_X is of size 2, and there is no immediate parameter that can be modified to make it larger; which is problematic in some applications. Exercise 5 explores a simple technique that can solve this problem, and more generally can be used to extend the range of any pairwise independent hash functions family.

Exercise 5. Consider a pairwise independent hash functions family F from a domain D to a range R. For every positive integer n, one can construct a new hash functions family G from D to R^n as follows. For every n (not necessarily distinct) hash functions $f_1, f_2, \ldots, f_n \in F$, the family G includes a function $g_{f_1, f_2, \ldots f_n}$ defined as

$$g_{f_1, f_2, \ldots f_n}(d) = (f_1(d), f_2(d), \ldots, f_n(d)) \quad \forall d \in D.$$

Informally, $g_{f_1, f_2, \ldots f_n}$ maps every element d of the domain to a tuple containing the value of every one of the functions $f_1, f_2, \ldots, f_n$ for d.

(a) Prove that G is a pairwise independent hash functions family from D to R^n.

(b) Show that a function of G can be represented using $n b_F$ bits, where b_F is the number of bits necessary for representing a function of F.

Combining Theorem 1 with Exercise 5, we immediately get Corollary 1.

Corollary 1. *For every two positive integers m and n, there is a pairwise independent hash functions family F from $\{0,1\}^m$ to $\{0,1\}^n$ whose functions can be represented using $n(m+1)$ bits.*

Corollary 1 improves over Theorem 1 by allowing the range of the hash functions to be as large as necessary. Nevertheless, we would like to further improve over Corollary 1 by reducing the number of bits necessary for representing a function of the hash functions family. We note that the basic reason that the size of the representation in Corollary 1 involves the product of n and m is that this corollary was derived by a two-step process (i.e., first, we got a hash functions family for a range of constant size, and then we used the general technique from Exercise 5 to increase the size of the range). Thus, to get significantly smaller representation size, it seems necessary to avoid this two-step process. In Section 5.3 we do just that. In other words, we present there a construction of a pairwise independent (and k-wise independent) hash functions family that natively supports large ranges, and then we show that this allows for a representation size which is significantly smaller than the size guaranteed by Corollary 1.

5.3 Advanced Constructions of Pairwise and k-wise Independent Hash Families

Our objective in this section is to prove Theorem 2.

Theorem 2. *For every three positive integers m, n and $k \geqslant 2$, there exists a k-wise independent hash functions family F from $\{0,1\}^m$ to $\{0,1\}^n$ whose functions can be represented using $k \cdot \max\{m,n\} = O(k(m+n))$ bits.*

Since "pairwise independent hash functions family" is just another name for the "2-wise independent hash functions family", Theorem 2 implies for $k = 2$ the following Corollary 2.

Corollary 2. *For every two positive integers m and n, there exists a pairwise independent hash functions family F from $\{0,1\}^m$ to $\{0,1\}^n$ whose functions can be represented using $2 \cdot \max\{m,n\} = O(m+n)$ bits.*

It is important to note that the construction from Corollary 2 can be converted into a pairwise independent hash functions family from any domain D whose size is a power of 2 to any range R whose size is also a power of 2, as long as there is an efficient way to map the elements of D and R to strings of bits from $\{0,1\}^{\log|D|}$ and $\{0,1\}^{\log|R|}$, respectively. Finding such a mapping is often easy, and thus, in the subsequent chapters we will refer to the guarantee of Corollary 2 under the assumption that it works for any domain and range whose sizes are powers of two.

The proof of Theorem 2 is not very difficult, but it requires prior knowledge that is in general not assumed in this book. Since the rest of this book does not use the ideas presented in this proof, readers who lack the necessary prior knowledge can freely skip the rest of this section (which is devoted to this proof). Nevertheless, most readers should be familiar with the necessary prior knowledge from their bachelor degree studies, and to those readers we recommend reading the proof since it is quite elegant.

As a first step towards proving Theorem 2, let us consider the following claim.

Lemma 2. *For every two positive integers r and $k \geqslant 2$, there exists a k-wise independent hash functions family F_P from $\{0,1\}^r$ to $\{0,1\}^r$ whose functions can be represented using kr bits.*

It is not difficult to see that Lemma 2 is implied by Theorem 2 by setting $m = n = r$. More surprisingly, however, the reverse is also true. Exercise 6 asks you to prove this.

> **Exercise 6.** Prove Theorem 2 under the assumption that Lemma 2 is true. **Hint:** Start with the hash functions family guaranteed by Lemma 2 for $r = \max\{m,n\}$, and then add either pre-processing or post-processing to each hash function in the family.

The equivalence proved by the last exercise between Lemma 2 and Theorem 2 implies that to prove the theorem it will suffice to prove the lemma, which is what we concentrate on from now on. As a warmup, we first prove the lemma for $k = 2$.

Proof of Lemma 2 for $k = 2$. In this proof, we unify $\{0,1\}^r$ with some field of size 2^r (the match between strings of $\{0,1\}^r$ and the field elements can be done in an arbitrary way). Using this unification, we can define for every two strings $a, b \in \{0,1\}^r$ a function $f_{a,b}(x) = ax + b$ from $\{0,1\}^r$ to itself. Additionally, we define a hash functions family

$F_P = \{f_{a,b}|a, b \in \{0, 1\}^r\}$. In the rest of the proof, we show that this family obeys all properties guaranteed for it by Lemma 2.

Every function $f_{a,b}$ in F_P is defined by the strings a and b. Since these two strings each consist of r bits, the representation of the function $f_{a,b}$ using these strings requires only $2r$ bits, as guaranteed. Let us now prove that F_P is pairwise independent. Consider two distinct strings $d_1, d_2 \in \{0, 1\}^r$ and two arbitrary strings $r_1, r_2 \in \{0, 1\}^r$. We are interested in determining the number of (a, b) pairs for which it holds that $f_{a,b}(d_1) = r_1$ and $f_{a,b}(d_2) = r_2$. To do this, we observe that the last two equalities are equivalent to the following two equations:

$$ad_1 + b = r_1 \quad \text{and} \quad ad_2 + b = r_2.$$

Since we fixed a value for r_1, r_2, d_1 and d_2, these two equations are a pair of linear equations in two variables a and b. Moreover, these linear equations must have exactly one solution since the fact $d_1 \neq d_2$ implies that the coefficients matrix corresponding to these equations is non-singular. Thus, there is a single pair (a, b) for which $f_{a,b}(d_1) = r_1$ and $f_{a,b}(d_2) = r_2$, which implies that for a uniformly random function $f_{a,b} \in F_P$, we have

$$\Pr\left[f_{a,b}(d_1) = r_1 \wedge f_{a,b}(d_2) = r_2\right]$$
$$= \frac{1}{|\{(a, b)\,|a, b \in \{0, 1\}^r\}|} = \frac{1}{|\{0, 1\}^r|^2}. \qquad \square$$

The proof of Lemma 2 for general k values follows roughly the same line of argument as the proof for the case of $k = 2$, but invokes well-known properties of polynomials instead of well-known properties of linear equations.

Proof of Lemma 2 for general k. Like in the proof for $k = 2$, we unify $\{0, 1\}^r$ with a field $\mathbb{F}$ of size 2^r. Using this unification, we can define for every k strings $a_0, a_1, \ldots, a_{k-1} \in \{0, 1\}^r$ a function $f_{a_0, a_1, \ldots, a_{k-1}}(x) = \sum_{i=0}^{k-1} a_i x^i$ from $\{0, 1\}^r$ to itself. Additionally, we define a hash functions family $F_P = \{f_{a_0, a_1, \ldots, a_{k-1}}|a_0, a_1, \ldots, a_{k-1} \in \{0, 1\}^r\}$. In the rest of the proof, we show that this family obeys all properties guaranteed for it by Lemma 2.

Every function $f_{a_0, a_1, \ldots, a_{k-1}}$ in F_P is defined by the strings $a_0, a_1, \ldots, a_{k-1}$. Since these k strings each consist of r bits, the representation of the function $f_{a_0, a_1, \ldots, a_{k-1}}$ using them requires kr bits, as guaranteed by the lemma. Let us now prove that F_P is k-wise independent. Consider k distinct strings $d_1, d_2, \ldots, d_k \in \{0, 1\}^r$ and k arbitrary strings

$r_1, r_2, \ldots, r_k \in \{0,1\}^r$. We are interested in determining the number of k-tuples $(a_0, a_1, \ldots, a_{k-1})$ for which it holds that $f_{a_0,a_1,\ldots,a_{k-1}}(d_i) = r_i$ for every integer $1 \leqslant i \leqslant k$. Towards this goal, consider the polynomial

$$P(x) = \sum_{i=1}^{k} \left(r_i \cdot \frac{\prod_{\substack{1 \leqslant j \leqslant k \\ i \neq j}} (x - d_j)}{\prod_{\substack{1 \leqslant j \leqslant k \\ i \neq j}} (d_i - d_j)} \right).$$

Note that the definition of $P(x)$ does not involve a division by zero because the strings $d_1, d_2, \ldots, d_k$ are all distinct by definition. Additionally, $P(x)$ is a polynomial of degree at most $k - 1$ over the field $\mathbb{F}$ and thus, it is equal to $f_{a_0,a_1,\ldots,a_{k-1}}$ for some k-tuple $(a_0, a_1, \ldots, a_{k-1})$. One can observe that $P(d_i) = r_i$ for every integer $1 \leqslant i \leqslant k$, and thus, the function $f_{a_0,a_1,\ldots,a_{k-1}}$ equal to $P(x)$ must also obey $f_{a_0,a_1,\ldots,a_{k-1}}(d_i) = r_i$ for every integer $1 \leqslant i \leqslant k$. Hence, there exists at least one k-tuple $(a_0, a_1, \ldots, a_{k-1})$ for which these equalities hold.

Assume now toward a contradiction that there exist distinct k-tuples $(a_0, a_1, \ldots, a_{k-1})$ and $(b_0, b_1, \ldots, b_{k-1})$ such that $f_{a_0,a_1,\ldots,a_{k-1}}(d_i) = f_{b_0,b_1,\ldots,b_{k-1}}(d_i) = r_i$ for every integer $1 \leqslant i \leqslant k$. This assumption implies that the polynomial

$$Q(x) = f_{a_0,a_1,\ldots,a_{k-1}}(x) - f_{b_0,b_1,\ldots,b_{k-1}}(x) = \sum_{i=0}^{k-1} (a_i - b_i)x^i$$

is a non-zero polynomial of degree at most $k - 1$ with at least k roots r_1, $r_2, \ldots, r_k$, which is a contradiction. Hence, there must be exactly one k-tuple $(a_0, a_1, \ldots, a_{k-1})$ for which it holds that $f_{a_0,a_1,\ldots,a_{k-1}}(d_i) = r_i$ for every integer $1 \leqslant i \leqslant k$.

Using this result, we get that for a uniformly random function $f_{a_0,a_1,\ldots,a_{k-1}} \in F_P$

$$\Pr\left[\forall_{1 \leqslant i \leqslant k} \, f_{a_0,a_1,\ldots,a_{k-1}}(d_i) = r_i\right]$$
$$= \frac{1}{|\{(a_0, a_1, \ldots, a_{k-1}) \,|\, a_0, a_1, \ldots, a_{k-1} \in \{0,1\}^r\}|} = \frac{1}{|\{0,1\}^r|^k},$$

which completes the proof that F_P is k-wise independent. $\qquad\square$

5.4 Bibliographic Notes

The concept of universal hashing was introduced by Carter and Wegman (1979), and the stronger notion of k-wise independent hashing was introduced a few years after that by the same authors under the name *strongly universal$_k$* (Wegman and Carter, 1981). The same two papers also introduced the constructions of hash functions families used above for proving Theorems 1 and 2.

J. L. Carter and M. N. Wegman. Universal Classes of Hash Functions. *Journal of Computer and System Sciences*, 18(2): 143–154, 1979.

M. N. Wegman and J. L. Carter. New Hash Functions and Their Use in Authentication and Set Equality. *Journal of Computer and System Sciences*, 22(3): 265–279, 1981.

Exercise Solutions

Solution 1

To solve this exercise, one should verify that for every pair of distinct elements $x, y \in \{a, b, c, d\}$, exactly two out of the four tables map x and y to the same number. We do this here only for two pairs as a demonstration, but it is not difficult to verify that this is the case for all the pairs.

- The elements b and c are mapped to the same image by the first and third tables, and to different images by the two other tables.
- The elements b and d are mapped to the same image by the first two tables, and to different images by the two other tables.

Solution 2

We need to verify that for every pair of distinct elements $x, y \in \{a, b, c\}$, a function f chosen uniformly at random from F has an equal probability (of $1/|R|^2 = 1/4$) to map x and y to every possible pair of range items r_1, $r_2 \in R$. There are six possible assignments to x and y, however, it turns out that in order to verify this claim it suffices to consider only three out of these assignments because the roles of x and y are symmetric. In other words, we need to verify the claim only for the assignments $(x, y) = (a, b)$, $(x, y) = (a, c)$ and $(x, y) = (b, c)$, and this will imply that the claim also holds for the three other possible assignments. Furthermore, in this solution, we only verify the claim for the assignment $(x, y) = (a, b)$ because the verification for the two other assignments that we need to consider is very similar, and we leave it as an exercise for the reader.

Consider now the four tables from Exercise 1 restricted to the lines of $x = a$ and $y = b$. These restricted tables are as follows:

Element	Image
a	0
b	0

Element	Image
a	1
b	0

Element	Image
a	0
b	1

Element	Image
a	1
b	1

Observe now that every one of these tables contains a distinct combination of images for the elements a and b. Thus, if we pick a uniformly random table (or equivalently, a uniformly random function from F), we will get a uniformly random combination of images for a and b out of the $|R|^2 = 4$ possible combinations, which is what we wanted to prove.

Solution 3

We begin by proving that if F is a k-wise independent family, then the properties stated in the exercise hold. The first property holds because for every k distinct $d, d_1, d_2, \ldots, d_{k-1} \in D$ and an element $r \in R$, we have

$$\Pr[f(d) = r]$$

$$= \sum_{r_1 \in R} \sum_{r_2 \in R} \cdots \sum_{r_{k-1} \in R} \Pr[f(d) = r \text{ and } \forall_{1 \leqslant i \leqslant k-1} f(d_i) = r_i]$$

$$= \sum_{r_1 \in R} \sum_{r_2 \in R} \cdots \sum_{r_{k-1} \in R} \frac{1}{|R|^k} = \frac{1}{|R|},$$

where the first equality holds since the events $\{\forall_{1 \leqslant i \leqslant k-1} f(d_i) = r_i\}$ are disjoint for every fixed choice of $r_1, r_2, \ldots, r_{k-1}$. One consequence of the property that we have proved is that for every k distinct $d_1, d_2, \ldots, d_k \in D$ and k element $r_1, r_2, \ldots, r_k \in R$, it holds that

$$\Pr\left[\forall_{1 \leqslant i \leqslant k} f(d_i) = r_i\right] = \frac{1}{|R|^k} = \prod_{i=1}^{k} \Pr\left[f(d_i) = r_i\right],$$

which is the second property stated in the exercise (the first equality holds since F is k-wise independent).

The other direction remains to be proved, namely that if F obeys the properties stated in the exercise, then it is a k-wise independent family. Fix k distinct $d_1, d_2, \ldots, d_k \in D$ and k elements $r_1, r_2, \ldots, r_k \in R$. Then, we get

$$\Pr\left[\forall_{1 \leqslant i \leqslant k} \; f(d_i) = r_i\right] = \prod_{i=1}^{k} \Pr\left[f(d_i) = r_i\right] = \frac{1}{|R|^k},$$

where the first equality holds since the first property in the exercise asserts that the variables in $\{f(d_i) \mid 1 \leqslant i \leqslant k\}$ are k-wise independent, and the second equality holds since the second property in the exercise asserts that $f(d_i)$ has equal probability to be any element of R (including r_i).

Solution 4

For $m = 2$, there are 8 functions in F_X since there are two options for b and $2^m = 4$ options for S. The tables corresponding to these functions are as follows:

$f_{0,\varnothing}$		$f_{0,\{1\}}$		$f_{0,\{2\}}$	
Input	Image	Input	Image	Input	Image
00	0	00	0	00	0
01	0	01	0	01	1
10	0	10	1	10	0
11	0	11	1	11	1

$f_{0,\{1,2\}}$		$f_{1,\varnothing}$		$f_{1,\{1\}}$	
Input	Image	Input	Image	Input	Image
00	0	00	1	00	1
01	1	01	1	01	1
10	1	10	1	10	0
11	0	11	1	11	0

$f_{1,\{2\}}$		$f_{1,\{1,2\}}$	
Input	Image	Input	Image
00	1	00	1
01	0	01	0
10	1	10	0
11	0	11	1

Solution 5

(a) Since G contains a function $g_{f_1,f_2,\ldots,f_n}$ for every possible choice of n (not necessarily distinct) functions $f_1, f_2, \ldots, f_n$ from F, choosing a function g from G uniformly at random is equivalent to choosing n functions $f_1, f_2, \ldots, f_n$ from F uniformly and independently at random. Thus, assuming $g, f_1, f_2, \ldots, f_n$ are distributed this way, for every two distinct elements $d_1, d_2 \in D$ and two tuples $(r_{1,1}, r_{1,2}, \ldots, r_{1,n})$, $(r_{2,1}, r_{2,2}, \ldots, r_{2,n}) \in D^n$ it holds that

$$\Pr\left[g(d_1) = (r_{1,1}, r_{1,2}, \ldots, r_{1,n}) \wedge g(d_2) = (r_{2,1}, r_{2,2}, \ldots, r_{2,n})\right]$$
$$= \Pr\left[\forall_{1 \leqslant i \leqslant n} \; f_i(d_1) = r_{1,i} \wedge f_i(d_2) = r_{2,i}\right]$$
$$= \prod_{i=1}^{n} \Pr\left[f_i(d_1) = r_{1,i} \wedge f_i(d_2) = r_{2,i}\right] = \left(\frac{1}{|R|^2}\right)^n = \frac{1}{|R^n|^2},$$

where the second equality holds since the functions $f_1, f_2, \ldots, f_n$ are chosen independently out of F, and the third equality holds since F is pairwise independent.

(b) A function of g is defined by n functions $f_1, f_2, \ldots, f_n$ from F. Thus, to represent g, it suffices to represent the n functions $f_1, f_2, \ldots, f_n$, which can be done in nb_F space since each one of these functions can be represented using b_F bits by definition.

Solution 6

As suggested by the hint, let F_P be the hash functions family whose existence is guaranteed by Lemma 2 when setting $r = \max\{m, n\}$. Note that every function in F_P is a function from the domain $\{0,1\}^{\max\{n,m\}}$ to the range $\{0,1\}^{\max\{n,m\}}$, and to solve the exercise, we need to convert it into a function from the domain $\{0,1\}^m$ to the range $\{0,1\}^n$. More formally, we need to construct using F_P a k-wise independent hash functions family F from the domain $\{0,1\}^m$ to the range $\{0,1\}^n$. In the following paragraphs, we do this by considering two cases distinguished by the relationship they assume between m and n.

- The first case we consider is the case, of $m \geqslant n$. In this case, the domain of the functions of F_P is already $\{0,1\}^m$ because $\max\{m, n\} = m$. However, to make the range of these functions $\{0,1\}^n$, we need to shorten the images they produce by $m - n$ bits, which we can do (for example) by removing the rightmost $m - n$ bits of every such image. More formally, we define a function s from $\{0,1\}^m$ to $\{0,1\}^n$ as follows:

$$s(x) = x^{(1)}x^{(2)}\cdots x^{(n)} \quad \forall x \in \{0,1\}^m.$$

Using s, we can now define a new hash functions family $F = \{s \circ f | f \in F_P\}$, where $\circ$ is the concatenation operation of functions. One can observe that every function in F is from the domain $\{0,1\}^m$ to the range $\{0,1\}^n$. Additionally, F is k-wise independent because for every k distinct domain elements $d_1, d_2, \ldots, d_k \in \{0,1\}^m$, k range elements $r_1, r_2, \ldots, r_k \in \{0,1\}^n$, a uniformly random function $f \in F$ and a uniformly random function $f_P \in F_P$, it holds that

$$\Pr\left[\forall_{1 \leqslant i \leqslant k} f(d_i) = r_i\right] = \Pr\left[\forall_{1 \leqslant i \leqslant k} s(f_P(d_i)) = r_i\right]$$

$$= \Pr\left[\forall_{1 \leqslant i \leqslant k} \exists_{x \in \{0,1\}^{m-n}} f_P(d_i) = r_i x\right]$$

$$= \sum_{x_1 \in \{0,1\}^{m-n}} \sum_{x_2 \in \{0,1\}^{m-n}} \cdots \sum_{x_k \in \{0,1\}^{m-n}} \Pr[\forall_{1 \leqslant i \leqslant k} f_P(d_i) = r_i x_i]$$

$$= \sum_{x_1 \in \{0,1\}^{m-n}} \sum_{x_2 \in \{0,1\}^{m-n}} \cdots \sum_{x_k \in \{0,1\}^{m-n}} \frac{1}{|\{0,1\}^m|^k}$$

$$= \left|\{0,1\}^{m-n}\right|^k \cdot \frac{1}{|\{0,1\}^m|^k} = \frac{1}{|\{0,1\}^n|^k},$$

where the third equality holds since the events $\{\forall_{1 \leqslant i \leqslant k} f_P(d_i) = r_i x_i\}$ obtained for different choices of $x_1, x_2, \ldots, x_k \in \{0,1\}^{m-n}$ are disjoint, and the penultimate equality holds because F_P is k-wise independent.

The second case we consider is the case of $m \leqslant n$. In this case, the range of the functions of F_P is already $\{0,1\}^n$ because $\max\{m,n\} = n$. However, to make the domain of these functions $\{0,1\}^m$, we need to extend input strings from $\{0,1\}^m$ to strings of $\{0,1\}^n$, which we can do (for example) by adding $n - m$ trailing zeros to the end of the input string. More formally, we define a function t from $\{0,1\}^m$ to $\{0,1\}^n$ as follows:

$$t(x) = x0^{n-m} \quad \forall x \in \{0,1\}^m.$$

Using t, we can now define a new hash functions family $F = \{f \circ t | f \in F_P\}$. One can again observe that every function in F is from the domain $\{0,1\}^m$ to the range $\{0,1\}^n$. Additionally, F is k-wise independent because for every k distinct domain elements $d_1, d_2, \ldots, d_k \in \{0,1\}^m$, k range elements $r_1, r_2, \ldots, r_k \in \{0,1\}^n$, a uniformly random function $f \in F$ and a uniformly random function $f_P \in F_P$ it holds that

$$\Pr\left[\forall_{1 \leqslant i \leqslant k} \ f(d_i) = r_i\right] = \Pr\left[\forall_{1 \leqslant i \leqslant k} \ f_P(t(d_i)) = r_i\right] = \frac{1}{|\{0,1\}^n|^k},$$

where the second equality holds because F_P is k-wise independent and the definition of t guarantees that the strings $t(d_1), t(d_2), \ldots, t(d_k)$ are distinct strings of $\{0,1\}^n$ whenever $d_1, d_2, \ldots, d_k$ are distinct strings of $\{0,1\}^m$.

Chapter 6

Counting Distinct Tokens

Counting the distinct tokens in a data stream is an important problem having many real-world applications. For example, a router often tracks statistics such as the number of distinct IPs appearing in the packets that have passed through it, or the number of distinct URLs that have been requested. A more juicy application of this problem is detection of Denial of Service attacks on servers. Such attacks are often characterized by a large amount of traffic originating from a relatively limited number of computers or sub-networks, and thus, can sometimes be detected by simply counting the distinct traffic sources.

In this chapter, we will study two classic streaming algorithms for estimating the number of distinct tokens. Both algorithms are randomized, and the better one among them can estimate the number of distinct tokens to any desirable accuracy. We will complement these algorithms by showing that this cannot be done by a deterministic algorithm. In other words, we will show that there exists some level of accuracy such that no deterministic streaming algorithm can produce an estimation for the number of distinct tokens with this level of accuracy.

6.1 The AMS Algorithm

The two algorithms we present in this chapter assume that the tokens of the stream are integers from the range 1 to m, where m is some value known to the algorithm. Furthermore, we also assume for simplicity that m is a power of 2. These assumptions are usually not problematic because in many applications the tokens that we need to count can be easily represented by integers of a bounded size. For example, the size of an IP address is only 32 bits, and thus, an IP address can be naturally represented as a number between 1 and 2^{32}.

We are now ready to describe the intuitive idea underlying the first algorithm we study. Consider a set D of d random tokens from the set $[m] = \{1, 2, \ldots, m\}$. If d is small, then we are unlikely to find in D a token whose binary representation has many trailing zeros. However, as d becomes larger, it gets more and more likely to find in D a token having many trailing zeros in its binary representation. Thus, the maximum number of trailing zeros in the binary representation of any token in D can be used to estimate the number d of random tokens in D. Moreover, one can observe that this method for estimating d can be used even if the tokens of D are given to us in the form of a data stream, and even if the stream may contain multiple copies of each token of D. In other words, this method gives us a way to estimate the number of distinct tokens in a data stream when the distinct tokens are chosen at random from the set of the m possible tokens.

It remains to deal with the fact that the distinct tokens of the stream may not be random. To solve this issue, we pass the tokens through a hash function. In other words, we pick a hash function h, and for every token t we look at the number of trailing zeros in the binary representation of $h(t)$ rather than the number of trailing zeros in the binary representation of t itself. If h is a good hash function, the images it produces for the tokens should look like random values even though the original tokens themselves were not selected at random.

An algorithm implementing the above intuitive idea is given as Algorithm 1. This algorithm is often referred to as the "AMS Algorithm".[1] In the pseudocode of this algorithm, we denote by zeros(v) the number of trailing zeros in the binary representation of a token v. Furthermore, in this algorithm and in some of the other algorithms presented in this chapter, we implicitly assume that the data stream contains at least one token. The case of an empty data stream can be easily handled using additional logic, and we ignore it for simplicity.

---

[1] The algorithm got this name since AMS are the initials of the authors of the paper in which this algorithm was first published. This paper presented also other algorithms, and unfortunately, these algorithms are also often called the "AMS Algorithm". Thus, it is more accurate to refer to the algorithm we study here as the AMS algorithm for counting distinct tokens.

Algorithm 1: AMS Algorithm

1. Choose a random hash function $h: [m] \rightarrow [m]$ from a pairwise independent hash functions family H.
2. $z \leftarrow 0$.
3. **while** there are more tokens **do**
4.   Let t be the next token.
5. $z \leftarrow \max\{z, \text{zeros}(h(t))\}$.
6. **return** $2^{z+1/2}$.

Observation 1 shows that the space complexity of Algorithm 1 is poly-logarithmic in m, and thus, it is a streaming algorithm.

Observation 1. The space complexity of Algorithm 1 is $O(\log m)$.

Proof. The space complexity of Algorithm 1 is the space necessary for storing the variables t and z plus the space required for representing the random hash function h. Recall that we assume that m is a power of 2. Hence, as we saw in Chapter 5, the hash function h can be represented using only $O(\log m)$ bits for an appropriate choice of a pairwise independent hash functions family H. Moreover, since the largest values that can appear in the variables t and z are m and $\log_2 m$, respectively, both these variables can also be represented using $O(\log m)$ bits. $\qquad\square$

Let us now begin the analysis of the quality of the estimation obtained by Algorithm 1. This analysis requires some additional notation. Let D be the set of distinct tokens in the stream, and let d be their number. Additionally, for every value $0 \leq i \leq \log_2 m$, let Z_i be the number of tokens in D whose hash images have at least i trailing zeros. More formally,

$$Z_i = |\{t \in D|\text{zeros}(h(t)) \geq i\}|.$$

Note that the final value of the variable z of Algorithm 1 is the maximum value of i for which Z_i is non-zero. Thus, to get a guarantee on the quality of the answer produced by Algorithm 1, we need to show that Z_i is likely to be 0 when 2^i is significantly larger than d, and unlikely to be 0 when 2^i is significantly smaller than d. Corollary 1 shows that this indeed is the case. Lemma 1 is a first step toward proving this corollary.

Lemma 1. *For every $0 \leq i \leq \log_2 m$, $\mathrm{E}[Z_i] = d/2^i$ and $Var[Z_i] < d/2^i$.*

Proof. For every $0 \leq i \leq \log_2 m$ and token $t \in D$, let $W_{i,t}$ be an indicator for the event that $h(t)$ has at least i trailing zeros. Since $h(t)$ is a random value from $[m]$, the probability that $W_{i,t}$ takes the value 1 is 2^{-i}. Moreover, by definition,

$$Z_i = \sum_{t \in D} W_{i,t}. \tag{6.1}$$

Hence, by the linearity of expectation, we obtain

$$E[Z_i] = \sum_{t \in D} E[W_{i,t}] = \sum_{t \in D} 2^{-i} = \frac{|D|}{2^i} = \frac{d}{2^i}.$$

At this point we need to use the pairwise independence of the hash functions family H. Note that this pairwise independence means that the random variables in the sum (6.1) are also pairwise independent as each one of them depends on a different single value of h. Thus,

$$\text{Var}[Z_i] = \sum_{t \in D} \text{Var}[W_{i,t}] = \sum_{t \in D} 2^{-i}\left(1 - 2^{-i}\right) < \sum_{t \in D} 2^{-i} = \frac{|D|}{2^i} = \frac{d}{2^i}. \qquad \square$$

Corollary 1. *For every constant $c \geq 1$ and integer $0 \leq i \leq \log_2 m$,*

(a) $\Pr[Z_i \neq 0] \leq 1/c$ *if* $2^i \geq c \cdot d$, *and*
(b) $\Pr[Z_i = 0] \leq 1/c$ *if* $2^i \leq d/c$.

Proof. Let us first consider the case $2^i \geq c \cdot d$. In this case, Markov's inequality implies

$$\Pr[Z_i \neq 0] = \Pr\left[Z_i \geq \frac{c \cdot d}{2^i}\right] = \Pr[Z_i \geq c \cdot E[Z_i]] \leq \frac{1}{c}.$$

Consider now the case $2^i \leq d/c$. In this case, Chebyshev's inequality implies

$$\Pr[Z_i = 0] = \Pr\left[Z_i \leq E[Z_i] - \frac{d}{2^i}\right] \leq \Pr\left[|Z_i - E[Z_i]| \geq \frac{d}{2^i}\right]$$

$$\leq \frac{\text{Var}[Z_i]}{(d/2^i)^2} < \frac{2^i}{d} \leq \frac{1}{c}. \qquad \square$$

We are now ready to prove a guarantee for the quality of the answer produced by Algorithm 1.

Theorem 1. *For every $c \geq 2$, with probability at least $1 - 2/c$, Algorithm 1 estimates the number d of distinct elements in its data stream up to* *a multiplicative factor of $\sqrt{2} \cdot c$ (i.e., its output is within the range $[d/(\sqrt{2} \cdot c), \sqrt{2} \cdot cd]$).*

Proof. Recall that the output of Algorithm 1 is $2^{z+1/2}$, where z is the largest value for which Z_i is non-zero. Let ℓ be the smallest integer such that $2^\ell > c \cdot d$. If $\ell \leq \log_2 m$, then Corollary 1 states that with probability at least $1 - 1/c$, the value of Z_ℓ is 0, which implies that $Z_i = 0$ for every $i \geq \ell$, and thus, also

$$2^{z+1/2} \leq \sqrt{2} \cdot 2^{\ell-1} \leq \sqrt{2} \cdot cd.$$

Additionally, note that the inequality $2^{z+1/2} \leq \sqrt{2} \cdot cd$ always holds when $\ell > \log_2 m$ because in this case $cd \geq m$, while $2^{z+1/2}$ is always at most $\sqrt{2} \cdot m$ since z cannot take a value larger than $\log_2 m$.

Similarly, let us now define ℓ' to be the largest integer such that $2^{\ell'} < d/c$. If $\ell' \geq 0$, then Corollary 1 states that with probability at least $1 - 1/c$, the value of $Z_{\ell'}$ is non-zero, which implies

$$2^{z+1/2} \geq 2^{\ell'+1/2} = 2^{\ell'+1}/\sqrt{2} \geq d/(\sqrt{2} \cdot c).$$

Again, the inequality $2^{z+1/2} \geq d/(\sqrt{2} \cdot c)$ always holds when $\ell' < 0$ because in this case $d/c \leq 1$, while $2^{z+1/2}$ is always at least $\sqrt{2}$ since z cannot take a value smaller than 0.

By the union bound we now get that with probability at least $1 - 2/c$, the two above inequalities hold at the same time. $\square$

Theorem 1 shows that with a constant probability, the estimate produced by Algorithm 1 is correct up to a constant multiplicative factor. Unfortunately, this guarantee is quite weak, in the sense that if one wants the probability that the algorithm succeeds to estimate d up to this multiplicative factor to be close to 1, then the multiplicative factor itself must be very large. This weakness can be somewhat alleviated using the median technique we have seen in Chapter 3.

Exercise 1. Explain how the median technique can be applied to Algorithm 1 to get an algorithm that, given parameters $\varepsilon, \delta \in (0, 1]$, estimates the number d of distinct tokens up to a multiplicative factor of $(4 + \varepsilon)\sqrt{2}$ with probability at least $1 - \delta$. What is the space complexity of the algorithm you obtained?

In Section 6.2, we give a second algorithm for estimating the number d of distinct tokens which has a better estimation guarantee than the one given in Exercise 1. However, before presenting this second algorithm,

---

Algorithm 2: Alternative Rareness Measure

1. Choose a random hash function h: $[m] \rightarrow [m]$ from a pairwise independent hash functions family H.
2. $u \leftarrow m$.
3. **while** there are more tokens **do**
4.   Let t be the next token.
5. $u \leftarrow \min \{u, h(t)\}$.
6. **return** m/u.

---

we would like to end this section with two exercises which further study Algorithm 1.

Exercise 2. Recall that we assume that m is a power of 2. In Algorithm 1, this assumption is necessary to guarantee that the hash function h has a compact representation. Explain how Algorithm 1 can be modified to avoid this assumption.

Exercise 3. Intuitively, Algorithm 1 works by defining a measure of how "rare" a number is — the more zeros a number has in its binary representation, the rarer it is considered. The algorithm then uses the rareness of the rarest hash image it encounters as a signal giving information about the number d of distinct tokens. As it turns out, this idea can also be used with other measures of rareness. For example, Algorithm 2 treats a number as rare if it is small.

Prove that, for every $c \geq 3$, with probability $1 - 2/(c - 1)$ Algorithm 2 estimates the number d of distinct elements in its data stream up to a multiplicative factor of c (i.e., its output is within the range $[d/c, cd]$).

6.2 An Improved Algorithm

In section 6.1, we have seen Algorithm 1, and proved a weak estimation guarantee for it. Intuitively, the reason that we were only able to prove such a weak guarantee is that Algorithm 1 keeps track of only one token — the one with the largest number of trailing zeros in the binary representation of its hash image. This means that Algorithm 1 can be completely fooled by a single token whose hash representation happens to have, by chance, many trailing zeros. One way to handle this issue (at the cost of increasing

---

Algorithm 3: Multi-tokens Memory Algorithm (ε)

1. Choose a random hash function h: $[m] \rightarrow [m]$ from a pairwise independent hash functions family H.
2. $z \leftarrow 0$, $B \leftarrow \varnothing$.
3. **while** there are more tokens **do**
4. Let t be the next token.
5. **if** zeros($h(t)$) $\geq z$ **then**
6.   Add t to B if it is not already there.
7. **while** $B > c/\varepsilon^2$ **do**
8. $z \leftarrow z + 1$.
9.   Remove from B every token t' such that zeros($h(t')$) $< z$.
10. **return** $|B| \cdot 2^z$.

---

the space complexity a bit) is to store more than one token, i.e., store the set of tokens whose hash images have the largest numbers of trailing zeros. This intuitive idea is implemented by Algorithm 3. We note that Algorithm 3 gets a parameter $\varepsilon > 0$ controlling the accuracy of its output.

The set of tokens that Algorithm 3 stores is denoted by B. The algorithm also has a threshold z such that a token is stored in B if and only if the binary representation of its hash image has at least z trailing zeros. To keep its space complexity reasonable, the algorithm cannot let the set B become too large. Thus, whenever the size of B exceeds a threshold of c/ε^2 (c is a constant whose value we later set to 576), the algorithm increases z and accordingly removes tokens from B.

We begin the study of Algorithm 3 by analyzing its space complexity.

Exercise 4. Prove that the space complexity of Algorithm 3 is $O(\varepsilon^{-2} \cdot \log m)$, and thus, it is a streaming algorithm when ε is considered to be a constant.

Our next objective is to prove an estimation guarantee for Algorithm 3. For that purpose, we once again need the random variables Z_i defined above. Recall that Z_i is the number of tokens from D whose hash image has at least i trailing zeros. More formally, we get

$$Z_i = |\{t \in D | zeros(h(t)) \geq i\}|.$$

Let r represent the final value of the variable z of Algorithm 3, then the output of Algorithm 3 is $2^r \cdot Z_r$. Thus, we need to show that with a significant probability this expression is close to d. We note that according to Lemma 1, for every $0 \leq i \leq \log_2 m$, the expected value of Z_i is $d/2^i$, and thus, the expected value of $2^i \cdot Z_i$ is d. Hence, if there were a significant probability that the expression $2^i \cdot Z_i$ is close to its expectation for all the relevant values of i, then we would be done. Unfortunately, we are not able to prove such a strong claim. The source of the difficulty is that for large values of i the variable Z_i tends to be very small, and thus, does not concentrate very well.

Observation 2 solves the above issue by showing that r (the final value of z) is unlikely to take a large value, which means that for a large i the value of Z_i rarely affects the output of Algorithm 3. The observation is given using a value s, which is defined as the unique integer such that

$$\frac{12}{\varepsilon^2} \leq \frac{d}{2^s} < \frac{24}{\varepsilon^2}.$$

Observation 2. If $s \geq 1$, then $\Pr[r \geq s] \leq 48/c$. Hence, for $c = 576$ we get $\Pr[r \geq s] \leq 1/12$.

Proof. By Markov's inequality, we get

$$\Pr[r \geq s] = \Pr\left[Z_{s-1} > c/\varepsilon^2\right] = \Pr\left[Z_{s-1} > \frac{c2^{s-1}}{\varepsilon^2 d} \cdot \mathrm{E}\left[Z_{s-1}\right]\right]$$

$$\leq \frac{\varepsilon^2 d}{c2^{s-1}} = \frac{2\varepsilon^2}{c} \cdot \frac{d}{2^s} < \frac{2\varepsilon^2}{c} \cdot \frac{24}{\varepsilon^2} = \frac{48}{c},$$

where the last inequality holds by the definition of s. $\qquad \square$

We now show that for $i < s$, the variables Z_i concentrate strongly enough so that, for such i values, there is a significant probability that the expressions $2^i \cdot Z_i$ are all close to their expectation at the same time.

Lemma 2. *With probability at least* $11/12$, $|2^i \cdot Z_i - d| < \varepsilon d$ *for every* $0 \leq i < s$.

Proof. Recall that, by Lemma 1, $\mathrm{Var}[Z_i] < d/2^i$. Hence, by Chebyshev's inequality, for every $0 \leq i < s$, we get

$$\Pr\left[\left|2^i \cdot Z_i - d\right| \geq \varepsilon d\right] = \Pr\left[\left|2^i \cdot Z_i - E[2^i \cdot Z]\right| \geq \varepsilon d\right]$$

$$\leq \frac{\mathrm{Var}\left[2^i \cdot Z_i\right]}{(\varepsilon d)^2} = \frac{2^{2i} \cdot \mathrm{Var}\left[Z_i\right]}{(\varepsilon d)^2} < \frac{2^i}{\varepsilon^2 d}.$$

Hence, by the union bound, the probability that $|2^i \cdot Z_i - d| \geq \varepsilon d$ for any $0 \leq i < s$ is at most

$$\sum_{i=0}^{s-1} \frac{2^i}{\varepsilon^2 d} < \frac{2^s}{\varepsilon^2 d} = \varepsilon^{-2} \cdot \left(\frac{d}{2^s}\right)^{-1} \leq \varepsilon^{-2} \cdot \left(\frac{12}{\varepsilon^2}\right)^{-1} = \frac{1}{12},$$

where the last inequality holds by the definition of s. □

We can now conclude the analysis of Algorithm 3.

Theorem 2. *Algorithm 3 estimates d up to a relative error of ε with probability at least $5/6$.*

Proof. Our objective is to prove $\Pr[|2^r \cdot Z_r - d| \leq \varepsilon d] \geq 5/6$. There are two cases to consider based on the value of s. If $s \leq 0$, then, by the definition of s and the value of c, we obtain

$$d < \frac{24}{\varepsilon^2} \cdot 2^s \leq \frac{c}{\varepsilon^2}.$$

This means that during the execution of Algorithm 3, the size of B can never become larger than c/ε^2, and thus, the variable z is never increased from its initial value of 0. Hence, the final value of z, which is denoted by r, is also 0. Moreover, observe that Z_0 counts the number of tokens from D whose hash images have at least 0 trailing zeros. Clearly, all the tokens of D obey this criterion, and thus, $Z_0 = |D| = d$. Combining the above observations, we get that when $s \leq 0$, the expression $2^r \cdot Z_r$ is deterministically equal to d.

The case of $s \geq 1$ remains to be considered. Note that in this case, by the law of total probability, we have

$$\begin{aligned}
\Pr\left[|2^r \cdot Z_r - d| > \varepsilon d\right] &= \Pr\left[r < s\right] \cdot \Pr\left[|2^r \cdot Z_r - d| > \varepsilon d | r < s\right] \\
&\quad + \Pr\left[r \geq s\right] \cdot \Pr\left[|2^r \cdot Z_r - d| > \varepsilon d | r \geq s\right] \\
&\leq \Pr\left[|2^r \cdot Z_r - d| > \varepsilon d \wedge r < s\right] + \Pr\left[r \geq s\right] \\
&\leq \Pr\left[\exists_{0 \leq i < s} |2^i \cdot Z_i - d| > \varepsilon d\right] + \Pr\left[r \geq s\right] \leq \left(1 - \frac{11}{12}\right) + \frac{1}{12} = \frac{1}{6},
\end{aligned}$$

where the last inequality follows from Observation 2 and Lemma 2. □

Algorithm 4: Alternative Rareness Measure (ε)

1. Choose a random hash function $h: [m] \rightarrow [m]$ from a pairwise independent hash functions family H.
2. $B \leftarrow \emptyset$.
3. **while** there are more tokens **do**
4.   Let t be the next token.
5.   Add t to B if it is not already there.
6.   **if** $|B| > c/\varepsilon^2$ **then**
7.   Remove from B a token t' maximizing $h(t')$.
8. Let u be a token in B maximizing $h(u)$.
9. **if** $|B| \geq c/\varepsilon^2$ **then**
10.   **return** $mc/(\varepsilon^2 \cdot h(u))$.
11. **else**
12.   **return** $|B|$.

Exercise 5. Recall that one can intuitively view Algorithm 1 as an algorithm storing the rarest token it encounters, where the rareness of a token is defined as the number of trailing zeros in the binary representation of its hash image. Given this point of view, Algorithm 3 uses the same definition of rareness, but differs from Algorithm 1 by storing a set of rare tokens rather than only the rarest one. In this exercise, we will see that this idea of storing multiple rare tokens can also be used for other measures of rareness. Specifically, we study Algorithm 4 which applies this idea to the notation of rareness used by Algorithm 2 (here a token is considered rare if its hash image is a small number).

Algorithm 4 gets an accuracy parameter $\varepsilon > 0$, and maintains a set B containing the c/ε^2 tokens whose hash images are the smallest (where c is some constant, and we assume for simplicity that c/ε^2 is an integer). If the algorithm does not manage to fill B (i.e., there are less than c/ε^2 tokens), then it returns the size of the set B. Otherwise, it returns the value $mc/(\varepsilon^2 h(u))$, where $h(u)$ is the maximum hash image of any token in B. Prove that for $c = 12$ and $\varepsilon \in (0, 1)$, Algorithm 4 estimates the number d of distinct tokens up to a relative error of ε with probability at least $2/3$.

We conclude this section we two remarks as follows:

- Observe that both Algorithms 3 and 4 estimate the number d of distinct tokens up to a relative error of ε with a constant probability larger than $1/2$. Using the median technique it is possible to increase this probability to be $1 - \delta$, for every $\delta \in (0,1)$, at the cost of increasing their space complexity by a factor of $O(\log \delta^{-1})$. If you are not sure why that is the case, revisit the solution of Exercise 1.

- The space complexity of Algorithm 3 can be improved by storing in set B the compressed versions of the original tokens. The compressed version of every token t consists of two parts: the value of $\text{zero}(h(t))$ (which requires only $O(\log \log m)$ bits), and the value of $g(t)$ for a second hash function g mapping the tokens from $[m]$ into a smaller space. If the range of g is small enough, then the compressed versions of the tokens can be represented using significantly fewer bits than the original tokens, which decreases the algorithm's space complexity. Observe that the value of $\text{zero}(h(t))$ has to be part of the compressed version because Algorithm 3 uses it. The reason $g(t)$ is also part of the compressed version is more subtle. The analysis of Algorithm 3 fails if two distinct tokens that are added to B have identical compressed versions since this means that the algorithm cannot determine how many distinct tokens have been added to B. Thus, the role of $g(t)$ is to make the probability of such a collision small enough. Formally analyzing this possible modification of Algorithm 3 is outside the scope of this book. However, we note that, by choosing g at random from an appropriate hash functions family, one can get an algorithm which estimates the number d of distinct tokens up to a relative error of ε, for every $\varepsilon \in (0, 1)$, with a probability at least $2/3$ using a space complexity of $O(\log m + \varepsilon^{-2}(\log \varepsilon^{-1} + \log \log m))$.

6.3 Impossibility Result

In the previous sections we have seen two randomized algorithms for estimating the number d of distinct tokens, the better of which can produce an estimate up to a relative error of ε for ε which is arbitrarily close to 0. In this section, we complement these algorithms by showing that any deterministic algorithm with the same kind of guarantee must use $\Omega(m)$ memory. We begin with the following easier to prove claim.

Theorem 3. *Every deterministic data stream algorithm for calculating the exact number of d distinct tokens must have a space complexity of at least m.*

Proof. Assume by way of contradiction that there exists a deterministic data stream algorithm ALG which exactly calculates the number d of distinct tokens in its stream using less than m bits of memory. Let $2^{[m]}$ be the collection of all subsets of $[m]$, and for every set $S \in 2^{[m]}$ let us denote by σ_S a data stream consisting of the elements of S in an arbitrary (but fixed) order and by M_S the state of the memory of ALG after it has received σ_S.

The important point to observe is that the size of $2^{[m]}$ is 2^m, but M_S can be represented by less than m bits by our assumption, and thus, can take less than 2^m different values. By the pigeon hole principle, we now get that there must exist at least two sets $S, T \in 2^{[m]}$ such that $S \neq T$ but $M_S = M_T$. Let us also assume, without loss of generality, that $T \not\subseteq S$ (otherwise, we can just exchange the roles of S and T). Consider now two data streams. Data stream σ_1 is obtained by concatenating two copies of σ_S, while data stream σ_2 is obtained by concatenating σ_T and σ_S (in that order). Since the memory content of ALG is the same after it reads either σ_S or σ_T, it cannot distinguish between the data streams σ_1 and σ_2, and must output the same output for both streams.

To see why that is a contradiction, note that σ_1 contains only tokens of S, and thus, has fewer distinct tokens compared to σ_2 which contains all the tokens of $S \cup T$ (which is a strict superset of S since $T \not\subseteq S$). $\quad\square$

Observe that Theorem 3 applies only to deterministic algorithms which calculate the number d of distinct tokens exactly, and does not imply anything for algorithms that only estimate d. Intuitively, the reason for that is that the sets S and T between which the algorithm cannot distinguish might be very similar to each other. Thus, to get a result similar to Theorem 3 for algorithms which produce an estimation of d we must find a large collection of sets such that the size of the intersection of every two sets in the collection is much smaller than the sets themselves. Lemma 3 proves the existence of such a collection.

Lemma 3. *For every integer constant $c \geq 1$ and a large enough value m dividable by c, there exists a collection $C_m \subseteq 2^{[m]}$ of size at least $2^{m/c'}$, where c' is a positive constant depending only on c, such that:*

- *every set in C_m is of size m/c,*
- *the intersection of every two sets in C_m is of size at most $2m/c^2$.*

Exercise 6. Prove that, for every $\varepsilon \in (0, \sqrt{2} - 1)$, every deterministic data stream algorithm for estimating the number d of distinct tokens up to a multiplicative factor of $\sqrt{2} - \varepsilon$ must have a space complexity of at least $\Omega(m)$. **Hint:** The proof is very similar to the proof of Theorem 3, but uses the collection whose existence is promised by Lemma 3 instead of the collection $2^{[m]}$.

It remains to prove Lemma 3.

Proof. Let us partition the tokens of $[m]$ in an arbitrary way into m/c buckets of size c each. We can now define a random set R which contains a uniformly random single token from each bucket. One can observe that the size of R is always m/c.

Consider now two independent random sets R_1 and R_2 having the same distribution as R, and let X_i be an indicator for the event that R_1 and R_2 contain the same token of bucket i for $1 \leq i \leq m/c$. Note that

$$|R_1 \cap R_2| = \sum_{i=1}^{m/c} X_i.$$

Moreover, the variables $X_1, X_2, \ldots, X_{m/c}$ all the take the value 1 with probability $1/c$, independently. Thus, by the Chernoff bound,

$$\Pr\left[|R_1 \cap R_2| \geq \frac{2m}{c^2}\right] = \Pr\left[\sum_{i=1}^{m/c} X_i \geq \frac{2m}{c^2}\right]$$

$$= \left[\sum_{i=1}^{m/c} X_i \geq 2 \cdot \mathrm{E}\left[\sum_{i=1}^{m/c} X_i\right]\right] \leq e^{-\mathrm{E}\left[\sum_{i=1}^{m/c} X_i\right]/3} = e^{-m/(3c^2)}.$$

If we now take a collection C of $\lceil 2^{m/(7c^2)} \rceil$ independent random sets such that each one of them is distributed like R, then by the last inequality and the union bound we get

$$\Pr\left[\exists_{R_1, R_2 \in C} R_1 \cap R_2 \geq \frac{2m}{c^2}\right] \leq \binom{|C|}{2} \cdot e^{-m/(3c^2)}$$

$$\leq \frac{\left(\lceil 2^{m/(7c^2)} \rceil\right)^2}{2} \cdot e^{-m/(3c^2)} \leq \frac{\left(2^{m/(6c^2)}\right)^2}{2} \cdot e^{-m/(3c^2)}$$

$$\leq 2^{m/(3c^2)} \cdot e^{-m/(3c^2)} < 1,$$

where the third and last inequalities hold for a large enough m.

Observe that we have proved that with a probability larger than 0 the collection C has all the properties we require C_m to have (for $c' = 7c^2$). Hence, there must exist a collection having all the properties required from C_m.[2] $\square$

6.4 Bibliographic Notes

The intuitive idea of storing the token whose hash image is the rarest can be traced back to the work of Flajolet and Martin (1985). However, the work of Flajolet and Martin (1985) assumes access to a hash functions family with very strong properties, and there is no known construction of such a hash functions family allowing a small size representation for the individual hash functions. This has motivated the work of Alon *et al.* (1999), who came up with Algorithm 1 (or, more correctly, with a small variant of Algorithm 1 having roughly the same guarantee).

The guarantee of Algorithm 1 has been improved in a series of works, of which we mention only two. Bar-Yossef *et al.* (2004) came up with three algorithms for counting the number of distinct tokens, the best of which is a variant of Algorithm 3 compressing the tokens in the set B. It is also worth mentioning that Algorithm 4 is a variant of another algorithm presented by Bar-Yossef *et al.* (2004). The best known algorithm for estimating the number of distinct elements was given by Kane *et al.* (2010). This algorithm estimates this number up to a relative error of ε, for every $\varepsilon > 0$, with probability $2/3$ using a space complexity of only $O(\varepsilon^{-2} + \log m)$. As usual, the median trick can be used to increase the probability of a successful estimation to be $1 - \delta$ for every $\delta \in (0, 1)$ at the cost of increasing the space complexity by a factor of $O(\log \delta^{-1})$.

The algorithm of Kane *et al.* (2010) is known to be optimal in a very strong sense due to two lower bounds. On the one hand, Alon *et al.* (1999) showed that estimating the number of distinct tokens up to a relative error of 0.1 requires $\Omega(\log m)$ space. On the other hand, Woodruff (2004) showed

---

[2]This is an example of a more general method, known as the probabilistic method, for proving the existence of various objects. In this method, the prover gives a distribution and shows that an object drawn from this distribution has some properties with a non-zero probability, and this implies to the existence of an object having these properties. Note that in the proof given here the random object in fact has the required properties with high probability (because $2^{m/(3c^2)} \cdot e^{-m/(3c^2)}$ approaches 0 as m increases). However, in general, the probabilistic method works even when the random object has the required properties only with a very low probability.

that estimating the number of distinct tokens up to a relative error of ε for $\varepsilon = \Omega(m^{-1/2})$ requires $\Omega(\varepsilon^2)$ space.

N. Alon, Y. Matias and M. Szegedy. The Space Complexity of Approximating the Frequency Moments. *Journal of Computer and System Sciences*, 58(1): 137–147, 1999.

Z. Bar-Yossef, T. S. Jayram, R. Kumar, D. Sivakumar and L. Trevisan. Counting Distinct Elements in a Data Stream. In *Proceedings of the 6th International Workshop on Randomization and Approximation Techniques in Computer Science (RANDOM)*, 128–137, 2004.

P. Flajolet and G. N. Martin. Probabilistic Counting Algorithms for Data Base Applications. *Journal of Computer and System Sciences*, 31: 182–209, 1985.

D. M. Kane, J. Nelson and D. P. Woodruff. An Optimal Algorithm for the Distinct Elements Problem. In *Proceeding of the 29th ACM SIGMOD-SIGACT-SIGART Symposium on Principles of Database Systems (PODS)*, 41–52, 2010.

D. P. Woodruff. Optimal Space Lower Bounds for all Frequency Moments. In *Proceedings of the 15th Annual ACM-SIAM Symposium on Discrete Algorithms (SODA)*, 167–175, 2004.

Exercise Solutions

Solution 1

To apply the median technique we run multiple parallel copies of Algorithm 1, and output the median of the results produced by these copies. Formally, the algorithm we get by applying the median technique to Algorithm 1 is Algorithm 5. We will later choose the value of the parameter C based on the values of ε and δ.

Algorithm 5: Median of Multiple Copies Algorithm 1 (C)

1. Initialize C copies of Algorithm 1, each using independent randomness.
2. Each time that a token of the input stream arrives, forward it to all the copies of Algorithm 1.
3. For every $1 \leq i \leq C$, let d_i be the output of the i-th copy.
4. Return the median of the values $d_1, d_2, \ldots, d_C$.

Recall that the median technique works when each copy has a probability of more than $1/2$ to output an estimate with the required accuracy. In our case, we want the estimation to be correct up to a multiplicative factor of $(4 + \varepsilon)\sqrt{2}$, and by Theorem 1, the probability that each copy of Algorithm 1 produces an estimate which is correct up to this factor is at least

$$1 - \frac{2}{4+\varepsilon} = \frac{2+\varepsilon}{4+\varepsilon} = \frac{1}{2} + \frac{\varepsilon/2}{4+\varepsilon} = \frac{1}{2} + \frac{\varepsilon}{2(4+\varepsilon)} \geq \frac{1}{2} + \frac{\varepsilon}{10},$$

where the inequality holds since $\varepsilon \leq 1$. Hence, we can indeed apply the median technique in this case.

For every $1 \leq i \leq C$, let X_i be an indicator for the event that copy number i of Algorithm 1 produced an estimate d_i of d which is not correct up to a multiplicative factor of $(4+\varepsilon)\sqrt{2}$, i.e., d_i falls outside the range

$$\left[\frac{d}{(4+\varepsilon)\sqrt{2}}, d \cdot (4+\varepsilon)\sqrt{2}\right]. \tag{6.2}$$

Note that if more than half of the values $d_1, d_2, \ldots, d_C$ fall within this range, then their median must also fall within this range. Thus, the probability that the output of Algorithm 5 does not belong to this range is upper bounded by

$$\Pr\left[\sum_{i=1}^{C} X_i \geq C/2\right]. \tag{6.3}$$

Observe that the indicators $X_1, X_2, \ldots, X_C$ are independent indicators having identical distributions (i.e., they all take value 1 with the same probability). Moreover, by the above discussion, the probability that each one of these indicators takes the value 1 is at most $1/2 - \varepsilon/10$. Thus, their sum is a random variable with a binomial distribution $B(C, p)$ for some value $p \in [0, 1/2 - \varepsilon/10]$. Clearly, probability (6.3) is maximized when p is equal to the upper bound, of its range. Thus, we may assume that this is the case in the rest of the proof. By the Chernoff bound, we now get

$$\Pr\left[\sum_{i=1}^{C} X_i \geq C/2\right] = \Pr\left[\sum_{i=1}^{C} X_i \geq \frac{1}{2p} \cdot pC\right]$$

$$= \Pr\left[\sum_{i=1}^{C} X_i \geq \frac{1}{1-\varepsilon/5} \cdot pC\right] \leq \Pr\left[\sum_{i=1}^{C} X_i \geq \left(1+\frac{\varepsilon}{5}\right) \cdot pC\right]$$

$$= \Pr\left[\sum_{i=1}^{C} X_i \geq \left(1+\frac{\varepsilon}{5}\right) \cdot E\left[\sum_{i=1}^{C} X_i\right]\right]$$

$$\leq e^{-\left(\frac{\varepsilon}{5}\right)^2 E\left[\sum_{i=1}^{C} X_i\right]/3} = e^{-\frac{\varepsilon^2}{75} \cdot pC} \leq e^{-2\varepsilon^2 C/375}.$$

In other words, we see that with probability at least $1 - e^{-2\varepsilon^2 C/375}$, Algorithm 5 outputs a correct estimate for d up to a multiplicative factor of $(4 + \varepsilon)\sqrt{2}$ (i.e., a value within the range (6.2)). Recall that we want this probability to be at least $1 - \delta$, which can be guaranteed by choosing $C = \lceil 188 \cdot \varepsilon^{-2} \cdot \ln \delta^{-1} \rceil$.

The space complexity of Algorithm 5 remains to be analyzed. Algorithm 5 uses $O(\varepsilon^{-2} \cdot \log \delta^{-1})$ copies of Algorithm 1, and each one of these copies uses $O(\log m)$ space by Observation 1. Thus, the total space complexity of Algorithm 5 is $O(\varepsilon^{-2} \cdot \log \delta^{-1} \cdot \log m)$. Note that for any fixed value for ε this space complexity is larger than the space complexity of Algorithm 1 by a factor of $O(\log \delta^{-1})$.

Solution 2

Algorithm 1 requires the integer m to have two properties. First, it needs to be a power of 2, and second, every token of the stream should belong to the range 1 to m. Note that m has the second property by definition. However, it might violate the first property. To solve this issue, let us define m' as the smallest power of 2 larger than m. Clearly, m' has both the above properties, and thus, the guarantee of Theorem 1 for Algorithm 1 will still hold if we replace every reference to m in Algorithm 1 with a reference to m'.

In conclusion, by making the above replacement we get a modified version of Algorithm 1 which has the same guarantee as the original version, but does not need to assume that m is a power of 2. The space complexity of this modified version is

$$O(\log m') = O(\log m),$$

where the equality holds since $m' \leq 2m$.

Solution 3

For every value $x \in [0, m]$, let U_x be the number of tokens in D whose hash images are smaller than or equal to x. Additionally, for every token $t \in D$, let $W_{x,t}$ be an indicator for the event that $h(t) \leq x$. One can observe that

$$U_x = \sum_{t \in D} W_{x,t}.$$

Each one of the indicators in the last sum takes the value 1 with probability $\lfloor x \rfloor / m$. Thus, by the linearity of expectation, we get $\mathrm{E}[U_x] = d \lfloor x \rfloor / m$.

Moreover, the pairwise independence of the hash functions family H implies that the indicators in the last sum are pairwise independent as each one of them depends on a different single value of h. Thus,

$$\text{Var}[U_x] = \sum_{t \in D} \text{Var}[W_{x,t}] = \sum_{t \in D} \frac{\lfloor x \rfloor}{m}\left(1 - \frac{\lfloor x \rfloor}{m}\right) \leq \sum_{t \in D} \frac{\lfloor x \rfloor}{m} = \frac{d\lfloor x \rfloor}{m}.$$

We are now ready to upper bound the probability that Algorithm 2 makes a large estimation error. First, let us upper bound the probability that the algorithm outputs a number larger than cd. If $cd > m$, then this cannot happen since the variable u can never take a value smaller than 1. In contrast, if $cd \leq m$, then Algorithm 2 can output a number larger than cd only when $U_{m/(cd)}$ is non-zero, and thus, it is enough to upper bound the probability of this event. By Markov's inequality, we get

$$\Pr\left[U_{m/(cd)} > 0\right] = \Pr\left[U_{m/(cd)} \geq 1\right]$$

$$= \Pr\left[U_{m/(cd)} \geq \frac{m}{d\lfloor m/(cd) \rfloor} \cdot \text{E}\left[U_{m/(cd)}\right]\right]$$

$$\leq \frac{d\lfloor m/(cd) \rfloor}{m} \leq \frac{dm/(cd)}{m} = \frac{1}{c}.$$

Next, let us upper bound the probability that the algorithm outputs a number smaller than d/c. If $d/c < 1$, then this cannot happen since the variable u can never take a value larger than m. In contrast, if $d/c \geq 1$, then Algorithm 2 can output a number larger than d/c only when $U_{mc/d} = 0$. Hence, it is again enough to upper bound the probability of this event. By Chebyshev's inequality, we obtain

$$\Pr\left[U_{mc/d} = 0\right] = \Pr\left[U_{mc/d} \leq \text{E}\left[S_{mc/d}\right] - \frac{d\lfloor mc/d \rfloor}{m}\right]$$

$$\leq \Pr\left[\left|U_{mc/d} - \text{E}\left[U_{mc/d}\right]\right| \geq \frac{d\lfloor mc/d \rfloor}{m}\right]$$

$$\leq \frac{\text{Var}\left[U_{mc/d}\right]}{(d\lfloor mc/d \rfloor /m)^2} \leq \frac{d\lfloor mc/d \rfloor /m}{(d\lfloor mc/d \rfloor /m)^2}$$

$$= \frac{m}{d\lfloor mc/d \rfloor} \leq \frac{m}{d(mc/d - 1)} = \frac{1}{c - d/m} \leq \frac{1}{c - 1}.$$

Using the union bound we now get that the probability that the output of Algorithm 2 is outside the range $[d/c, cd]$ is at most $2/(c-1)$.

Solution 4

The space complexity of Algorithm 3 is the space necessary for storing the variables t and z plus the space required for representing the random hash function h and the set B. Recall that we assume that m is a power of 2. Hence, as we saw in Chapter 5, the hash function h can be represented using only $O(\log m)$ bits for an appropriate choice of a pairwise independent hash functions family H. Moreover, since the largest values that can appear in the variables t and z are m and $\log_2 m$, respectively, both these variables can also be represented using $O(\log m)$ bits. It remains to bound the space required for representing the set B. The size of this set is never larger than $c/\varepsilon^2 + 1$, and each element in it is a number between 1 and m (and thus, can be represented using $O(\log m)$ bits). Hence, representing the set B requires $O(\varepsilon^{-2} \cdot \log m)$ bits, and this term dominates the space complexity of the entire algorithm.

Solution 5

If $d < c/\varepsilon^2$, then Algorithm 4 stores all the tokens of D in the set B (since this set never reaches its maximum size c/ε^2), and then returns the size of this set as its output. Thus, Algorithm 4 always outputs the correct value for d when $d < c/\varepsilon^2$. In the rest of the proof we consider the case $d \geq c/\varepsilon^2$. Note that in this case the output of Algorithm 4 is $mc/(\varepsilon^2 \cdot h(u))$, where $h(u)$ is the maximum hash image of any token appearing in B when the algorithm terminates.

We now need two lemmata.

Lemma 4. $\Pr[mc/(\varepsilon^2 \cdot h(u)) > (1 + \varepsilon)d] \leq 1/6$.

Proof. Observe that the lemma is equivalent to proving that

$$\Pr\left[h(u) < \frac{mc}{\varepsilon^2(1 + \varepsilon)d}\right] \leq \frac{1}{6}.$$

Let X be a random variable denoting the number of tokens from D whose hash images are smaller than $mc/[\varepsilon^2(1 + \varepsilon)d]$. Note that $h(u)$ is smaller than $mc/[\varepsilon^2(1 + \varepsilon)d]$ if and only if there are at least c/ε^2 tokens in D whose hash images are smaller than this value. Thus, we can use X to rewrite the last inequality as

$$\Pr\left[X \geq \frac{c}{\varepsilon^2}\right] \leq \frac{1}{6}.$$

Hence, we need to prove a concentration bound for X. For every token $t \in D$, let X_t be an indicator for the event that $h(t) < mc/[\varepsilon^2(1+\varepsilon)d]$, then we get, by definition,

$$X = \sum_{t \in D} X_t.$$

Additionally, the indicators X_t are pairwise independent because of the pairwise independence of the hash functions family H, and each one of them takes the value 1 with probability

$$p = \frac{\left\lceil mc/\left[\varepsilon^2(1+\varepsilon)d\right]\right\rceil - 1}{m} \leq \frac{c}{\varepsilon^2(1+\varepsilon)d}. \tag{6.4}$$

Thus, the expectation and variance of X are

$$\mathrm{E}[X] = \sum_{t \in D} \mathrm{E}[X_t] = \sum_{t \in D} p = dp \quad \text{and} \quad \mathrm{Var}[X] = \sum_{t \in D} \mathrm{Var}[X_t]$$

$$= \sum_{t \in D} p(1-p) \leq dp.$$

By Chebyshev's inequality we now get

$$\Pr\left[X \geq \frac{c}{\varepsilon^2}\right] = \Pr\left[X \geq (\mathrm{E}[X] - dp) + \frac{c}{\varepsilon^2}\right]$$

$$\leq \Pr\left[|X - \mathrm{E}[X]| \geq \frac{c}{\varepsilon^2} - dp\right] \leq \frac{\mathrm{Var}[X]}{(c/\varepsilon^2 - dp)^2}$$

$$\leq \frac{dp}{(c/\varepsilon^2 - dp)^2} \leq \frac{dc/\left[\varepsilon^2(1+\varepsilon)d\right]}{(c/\varepsilon^2 - dc/\left[\varepsilon^2(1+\varepsilon)d\right])^2}$$

$$= \frac{\varepsilon^2(1+\varepsilon)}{c((1+\varepsilon)-1)^2} = \frac{(1+\varepsilon)}{c} \leq \frac{1}{6},$$

where the penultimate inequality follows by plugging in the upper bound on p given by (6.4), and the last inequality follows from the value of c and the fact that $\varepsilon < 1$. $\qquad \square$

Lemma 5. $\Pr[mc/(\varepsilon^2 \cdot h(u)) > (1-\varepsilon)d] \leq 1/6.$

Proof. Observe that the lemma is equivalent to proving that

$$\Pr\left[h(u) > \frac{mc}{\varepsilon^2(1-\varepsilon)d}\right] \leq \frac{1}{6}.$$

If $mc/[\varepsilon^2(1-\varepsilon)d] \geq m$ then this is trivial since $h(u)$ only takes values between 1 and m. Thus, we may assume in the rest of the proof

$mc/[\varepsilon^2(1-\varepsilon)d] < m$. Let X be a random variable denoting the number of tokens from D whose hash images are smaller or equal to $mc/[\varepsilon^2(1-\varepsilon)d]$. Note that $h(u)$ is larger than $mc/[\varepsilon^2(1-\varepsilon)d]$ if and only if there are less than c/ε^2 tokens in D whose hash images are smaller or equal to this value. Thus, we can use X to rewrite the last inequality as

$$\Pr\left[X < \frac{c}{\varepsilon^2}\right] \leq \frac{1}{6}.$$

Thus, we need to prove a concentration bound for X. For every token $t \in D$, let X_t be an indicator for the event that $h(t) \leq mc/[\varepsilon^2(1-\varepsilon)d]$, then we get, by definition,

$$X = \sum_{t \in D} X_t.$$

Additionally, the indicators X_t are pairwise independent because of the pairwise independence of the hash functions family H, and each one of them takes the value 1 with probability

$$p = \frac{\lfloor mc/\left[\varepsilon^2(1-\varepsilon)d\right]\rfloor}{m} \geq \frac{c}{\varepsilon^2(1-\varepsilon)d} - \frac{1}{m}$$

$$\geq \frac{c-\varepsilon^2}{\varepsilon^2(1-\varepsilon)d} \geq \frac{c(1-\varepsilon^2)}{\varepsilon^2(1-\varepsilon)d} = \frac{c(1+\varepsilon)}{\varepsilon^2 d}, \tag{6.5}$$

where the penultimate inequality holds since $m \geq d \geq (1-\varepsilon)d$, and the last inequality holds since $c \geq 1$. Like in the proof of Lemma 4, we can now bound the expectation and variance of X by

$$\mathrm{E}[X] = \sum_{t \in D} \mathrm{E}[X_t] = \sum_{t \in D} p = dp \quad \text{and} \quad \mathrm{Var}[X]$$

$$= \sum_{t \in D} \mathrm{Var}[X_t] = \sum_{t \in D} p(1-p) \leq dp.$$

By Chebyshev's inequality, we now get

$$\Pr\left[X < \frac{c}{\varepsilon^2}\right] = \Pr\left[X < (E[X] - dp) + \frac{c}{\varepsilon^2}\right]$$

$$\leq \Pr\left[|X - E[X]| \geq dp - \frac{c}{\varepsilon^2}\right] \leq \frac{\mathrm{Var}[X]}{(dp - c/\varepsilon^2)^2}$$

$$\leq \frac{dp}{(dp - c/\varepsilon^2)^2} = \frac{1}{dp(1 - c/(\varepsilon^2 dp))^2}.$$

Using the lower bound on p given by (6.5), we can lower bound the denominator of the rightmost side of the last inequality by

$$dp\left(1 - \frac{c}{\varepsilon^2 dp}\right)^2 \geq \frac{c(1+\varepsilon)}{\varepsilon^2} \cdot \left(1 - \frac{1}{1+\varepsilon}\right)^2$$

$$= \frac{c(1+\varepsilon)}{\varepsilon^2} \cdot \left(\frac{\varepsilon}{1+\varepsilon}\right)^2 = \frac{c}{1+\varepsilon} \; .$$

Combining the last two inequalities, we get

$$\Pr\left[X < \frac{c}{\varepsilon^2}\right] \leq \frac{1}{dp(1 - c/(\varepsilon^2 dp))^2} \leq \frac{1+\varepsilon}{c} \leq \frac{1}{6},$$

where the last inequality follows again from the value of c and the fact that $\varepsilon < 1$. $\square$

To complete the solution of the exercise, it remains to be observed that the last two lemmata imply, by the union bound, that the probability that the output $mc/(\varepsilon^2 \cdot h(u))$ of Algorithm 4 deviates from the value d by more than εd is at most $1/3$.

Solution 6

Let c be a constant depending on ε to be determined later. Additionally, let c' be the positive constant whose existence is guaranteed by Lemma 3 for that value of c, and let m_0 be a large enough constant so that Lemma 3 holds for every $m \geq m_0$ which is dividable by c. Assume by way of contradiction that the claim we need to prove is incorrect. In other words, we assume that there exists a deterministic data stream algorithm ALG which estimates the number d of distinct tokens up to a multiplicative factor of $\sqrt{2}-\varepsilon$ whose space complexity is not $\Omega(m)$. In particular, this means that there exists a value $m_1 \geq m_0 + 2c$ such that the space complexity of ALG is less than $m_1/2c'$) bits when $m = m_1$. In the rest of the proof we assume $m = m_1$.

Let m' be the largest integer which is not larger than m_1 and is divisible by c. Clearly, $m' \geq m_0$, and thus, by Lemma 3, there exists a collection $C_{m'}$ of size at least $2^{m'/c'}$ such that every set in $C_{m'}$ is of size m'/c and the intersection of every two sets in this collection is of size at most $2m'/c^2$. For every set $S \in C_{m'}$ we denote by σ_S a data stream consisting of the elements of S in an arbitrary (but fixed) order and by M_S the state of the memory of ALG after it has received σ_S.

Since the memory used by ALG is less than $m_1/(2c')$ bits, we get that the number of different values this memory can take is less than $2^{m_1/(2c')} \leq 2^{m'/c'}$, where the inequality follows since $m' > m_1 - c$ and $m_1 \geq 2c$. Thus, by the pigeon hole principle, there must exist at least two sets $S, T \in C_{m'}$ such that $S \neq T$ but $M_S = M_T$. Consider now two data streams. Data stream σ_1 is obtained by concatenating two copies of σ_S, while data stream σ_2 is obtained by concatenating σ_T and σ_S (in that order). Since the memory content of ALG is the same after it reads either σ_S or σ_T, it cannot distinguish between the data streams σ_1 and σ_2, and must output the same output for both streams.

We now observe that σ_1 contains only tokens of S, and thus, the number of distinct tokens in it is m'/c. On the other hand, since the definition of $C_{m'}$ implies that the intersection of S and T is of size at most $2m'/c^2$, the number of distinct tokens in σ_2 is at least

$$2 \cdot \frac{m'}{c} - \frac{2m'}{c^2} = \frac{2m'}{c}\left(1 - \frac{1}{c}\right).$$

Hence, the ratio between the number of distinct tokens in σ_1 and σ_2 is at least $2(1 - 1/c)$, which means that the single value that ALG outputs given either σ_1 or σ_2 cannot estimate the number of distinct tokens in both streams up a multiplicative factor of $\sqrt{2} - \varepsilon$, unless

$$\left(\sqrt{2} - \varepsilon\right)^2 \geq 2\left(1 - 1/c\right) \Leftrightarrow \left(1 - \frac{\varepsilon}{\sqrt{2}}\right)^2 \geq 1 - 1/c$$

$$\Leftrightarrow c \leq \frac{1}{1 - \left(1 - \varepsilon/\sqrt{2}\right)^2} = \frac{1}{\sqrt{2} \cdot \varepsilon - \varepsilon^2/2}.$$

By choosing c to be large enough so that it violates this inequality, we get the contradiction that we seek. In particular, choosing $c = \sqrt{2} \cdot \varepsilon^{-1}$ does the job.

Chapter 7

Sketches

As discussed in Chapter 4, many data stream algorithms work by first constructing a short summary of their input data stream, and then extracting their answer from this summary. This mode of operation naturally suggests the following question. Suppose we would like to speed up a calculation by using multiple machines, and suppose that we use each machine to construct a summary of a different part of the data stream. Then, is it possible to efficiently combine the summaries we get for the different parts of the stream into a new summary for the entire stream?

In this chapter, we will study summaries that allow for this kind of combination. Such summaries are called *sketches*. In addition to allowing a speed up through the use of multiple machines as explained above, sketches also have other applications, and we will discuss one such application later in this chapter. Furthermore, the sketches that we will study also apply to a few generalizations of the data stream model, and we will use this as an opportunity to introduce these important generalizations.

7.1 Generalizations of the Data Stream Model

The *frequency* of a token is the number of times it has appeared in the data stream so far. Furthermore, the *frequency vector* f is a vector summarizing the frequencies of all the possible tokens. In other words, f has an entry for every possible token, and the entry corresponding to a token t (we denote this entry by f_t) contains its frequency. Given these definitions, one can think of the arrival of a token t as an *update event* which updates the frequency vector f by increasing f_t by 1 (note that the initial frequencies of the tokens are all 0).

The data stream model that we have studied so far is sometimes called the *plain vanilla data stream model* because it only allows for the very simple type of update events as mentioned above.[1] Allowing more interesting kinds of update events gives rise to various important generalizations of the data stream model. We will consider here update events which, rather than changing the frequency of a single token by exactly 1, like in the plain vanilla data stream model, can change it by an arbitrary integer amount. More formally, each update event corresponds to the arrival of an ordered pair (t, c), where t is a token and c is the integer change in the frequency of t caused by this update event.

Often there are constraints on the change in the frequency that an update event may cause, and each choice of these constraints results in a different model. For example, if the value of c must be 1 in every update event (t, c), then we get back the plain vanilla data stream model. Below we present a few other common models that can be obtained by choosing different constraints.

- In the *cash register (data stream) model*, the frequency change in each update event must be positive. In other words, one can think of each update event (t, c) as an arrival of c copies of token t. This model is called the cash register model because update events in it can increase the frequencies of tokens, but these frequencies can never decrease; which is similar to the behavior of a cash register in a shop, which usually registers only incoming payments.

- In the *turnstile (data stream) model*, the frequency change in each update event can be an arbitrary (possibly negative) integer. One can think of each update event (t, c) with a positive c value as the arrival of c copies of token t, and of each such event with a negative c value as the departure of $|c|$ copies of token t. Thus, the frequency of a token t is equal to the number of its copies that have arrived minus the number of its copies that have departed.

  This point of view gave the turnstile model its name as turnstiles are often used to count the number of people who are currently inside a given area. This is done as follows: Every time that a person enters

---

[1] A vanilla model is a model which is relatively simple and clean.

the area he must rotate the turnstile in one direction, which causes the turnstile to increase its count by one. In contrast, when a person leaves the area he rotates the turnstile in the other direction, which makes the turnstile decrease its count accordingly.

• In many settings it does not make sense to have a negative frequency for tokens. In other words, at every given point the number of copies of a token that departed can be at most equal to the number of copies of that token that have arrived so far. The *strict turnstile model* is a special case of the turnstile model in which we are guaranteed that the updates obey this requirement (i.e., that at every given point the frequencies of the tokens are all non-negative).

In the above models, it is natural to change the role of the parameter n. So far we have used this parameter to denote the length of the stream, i.e., the number of update events. This definition made sense because the length of the stream was equal to the sum of the frequencies of the tokens in the plain vanilla data stream model. However, when a single update event can change the frequency of a token significantly, the length of the stream might be much smaller than the sum of the frequencies. We denote by $\|f\|_1$ the sum of the absolute values of the frequencies of all the tokens. More formally, if we denote by M the set of all possible tokens, then

$$\|f\|_1 = \sum_{t \in M} |f_t|.$$

The quantity $\|f\|_1$ is usually called the ℓ^1 *norm* of the vector f. Using this notation, we redefine n to be the maximum value that $\|f\|_1$ takes at any given time. One can observe that this new definition of n is consistent with the way we defined it so far for the plain vanilla data stream model, i.e., in the special case of the plain vanilla data stream model the new definition of n is equivalent to defining n as equal to the length of the data stream. We also would like to point out that in the context of the above models, a data stream algorithm is considered a streaming algorithm if its space complexity is poly-logarithmic in n and in m (recall that m is the number of possible tokens). Again, this definition is consistent with the way streaming algorithms are defined in the plain vanilla data stream model.

To demonstrate the above models, we now give as Algorithm 1 a simple data stream algorithm that calculates $\|f\|_1$ in the cash register and strict turnstile model.

Algorithm 1: ℓ^1 Norm Calculation

1. $\ell^1 \leftarrow 0$.
2. **while** there are more update events **do**
3.   Let $(t,\, c)$ be the next update event.
4. $\ell^1 \leftarrow \ell^1 + c$.
5. **return** ℓ^1.

Exercise 1. Prove that Algorithm 1 calculates $\|f\|_1$ in the cash register and strict turnstile model, and show that it might fail to do so in the general turnstile model.

Observation 1. Algorithm 1 is a streaming algorithm.

Proof. Let us upper bound the space complexity necessary for the three variables used by Algorithm 1. The variable t contains a single token, and thus, requires only $O(\log m)$ bits.[2] Next, we observe that the variable ℓ^1 is equal at every given point to the sum of the frequencies of all the tokens at this point. More formally, if M is the set of all possible tokens, then

$$|\ell^1| = \left| \sum_{t \in M} f_t \right| \leqslant \sum_{t \in M} |f_t| = \|f\|_1.$$

As n is the maximum value that $\|f\|_1$ takes, the absolute value of ℓ^1 is always upper bounded by n, and thus, it can be represented using $O(\log n)$ bits. Finally, c is the change in ℓ^1, and thus, its absolute value is upper bounded by either twice the absolute value of ℓ^1 before the change, or twice this absolute value after the change. Since the absolute value of ℓ^1 both before and after the change is upper bounded by n, we get that $|c| \leqslant 2n$, and thus, the representation of c also requires only $O(\log n)$ bits.

Combining all the above, we get that the space complexity of Algorithm 1 is upper bounded by $O(\log n + \log m)$. $\qquad \square$

We conclude this section with one more exercise. Recall that in Chapter 1 we described an algorithm for the plain vanilla data stream model that uses two passes over the data stream to find the tokens that

---

[2]In fact, the variable t can be dropped altogether from the description of Algorithm 1 as its value is never used.

Algorithm 2: Frequent Elements Algorithm (k)

1. **while** there are more tokens **do**
2.   Let t be the next token.
3.   Increase the counter of t by one.
4.   **if** there are at least k non-zero counters **then**
5.   Decrease all the non-zero counters by 1.
6. Let F be the set of tokens currently having a non-zero counter.
7. Reset all the counters to zero.

8. Start the second pass over the input stream.
9. $n \leftarrow 0$.
10. **while** there are more tokens **do**
11.   Let t be the next token.
12. $n \leftarrow n + 1$.
13.   **If** $t \in F$ **then** increase the counter of t by 1.
14. **return** the list of tokens whose counters are larger than n/k.

---

appear more than n/k times in the data stream (where k is a parameter of the algorithm). For ease of reading, we repeat this algorithm here as Algorithm 2. We remind the reader that the pseudocode of this algorithm assumes that for every possible token there exists a counter whose initial value is zero.

Using the notation defined in this chapter, we can restate the objective of Algorithm 2 as finding the tokens whose frequency is larger than $k^{-1} \cdot \|f\|_1$. Restated this way, this objective makes sense also in the context of the more general models presented in this chapter.

Exercise 2. Give a variant of Algorithm 2 achieving the above goal in the cash register model. Explain why your variant indeed returns exactly the set of tokens whose frequency is larger than $k^{-1} \cdot \|f\|_1$, and analyze its space complexity.

7.2 The Count-Min Sketch

We begin this section with a formal definition of the sketch notion. In this definition, and in the rest of this chapter, given two streams σ_1 and σ_2, we use the notation $\sigma_1 \cdot \sigma_2$ to denote their concatenation. In other words, $\sigma_1 \cdot \sigma_2$ is a stream which contains the update events of σ_1 followed by the update events of σ_2. For example, if the stream σ_1 consists of the update events ($"a"$, 1), ($"b"$, 2), ($"a"$, -1) and the stream σ_2 consists of the update events ($"b"$, 2), ($"c"$, -1), ($"a"$, 1), then the concatenated stream $\sigma_1 \cdot \sigma_2$ is

$$("a", 1), ("b", 2), ("a", -1), ("b", 2), ("c", -1), ("a", 1).$$

Definition 1. A data structure $DS(\sigma)$ computed by a data stream algorithm ALG based on an input stream σ is called a *sketch* if there exists an algorithm $COMB$ such that, for every two streams σ_1 and σ_2,

$$COMB(DS(\sigma_1), DS(\sigma_2)) = DS(\sigma_1 \cdot \sigma_2).$$

Ideally, both the data stream algorithm ALG and the combination algorithm $COMB$ should be space efficient, but this is not required by the formal definition. Exercise 3 gives a mock example of a sketch.

Exercise 3. Explain why the ℓ^1 norm is a sketch in the cash register and strict turnstile models.

In the last exercise, the sketch consisted of the ℓ^1 norm, which is an interesting value, and thus, it might be the value that we are interested in calculating. However, this is not often the case. In other words, usually the value that we are interested in calculating cannot be used as a sketch. Thus, most sketches are data structures which are not interesting directly, but it is possible to calculate from them interesting information about the stream. The next sketch that we present belongs to this kind.

The Count-Min sketch is used for estimating the frequencies of tokens in the strict turnstile model. A basic version of this sketch is given as Algorithm 3 (the full Count-Min sketch appears later in this chapter). We note that Algorithm 3 gets an accuracy parameter $\varepsilon \in (0, 1]$. Additionally, it assumes that the tokens of the stream are integers between 1 and m. We make this assumption throughout the rest of this chapter.

Lines 1–5 of Algorithm 3 process its input stream and update an array C while doing so. This array and the hash function h together form the sketch created by the algorithm, as is explained by Line 6 of the algorithm. Once the sketch is created, it is possible to query it on any given token t and get an estimate for the frequency of t. Line 7 of the algorithm explains how this querying is done.

Algorithm 3: Count-Min (Basic Version) (ε)

1. Let k be the least power of two such that $k \geqslant 2/\varepsilon$, and let C be an array of size k whose cells are all initially zero.
2. Choose a random hash function $h : [m] \rightarrow [k]$ from a pairwise independent hash functions family H.
3. **while** there are more update events **do**
4.   Let (t, c) be the next update event.
5. $C[h(t)] \leftarrow C[h(t)] + c$.
6. **sketch:** the sketch consists of C and h.
7. **query:** given a token t, output $C[h(t)]$ as an estimate for f_t.

Observation 2. For any fixed choice of a hash function h, Algorithm 3 produces a sketch.

Proof. Consider two streams σ_1 and σ_2, and let C^1, C^2 and C^{12} denote the content of the array C after Algorithm 3 processes σ_1, σ_2 and $\sigma_1 \cdot \sigma_2$, respectively. To prove the observation, we need to show that Algorithm 3 has the properties guaranteed by Definition 1 for ALG. In other words, we need to show that C^{12} can be calculated based on C^1 and C^2 alone (by some algorithm $COMB$). We do that in the next paragraph.

Observe that each cell of C contains the total frequency of all the tokens mapped to this cell by the hash function h. Hence, each cell of C^{12} is equal to the sum of the corresponding cells of C^1 and C^2, and thus, can be calculated using the values of these cells alone. $\square$

Note that the algorithm $COMB$ implicitly described by Observation 2 can only combine sketches produced by Algorithm 3 when they use the same hash function h. Technically speaking, this property is not enough to make them "real" sketches because the formal definition of sketches requires that it must always be possible to combine sketches. This is the reason that Observation 2 only claims that Algorithm 3 produces a sketch once h is fixed. However, for most applications this technical issue is not important, and thus, we refer to the product of Algorithm 3 as a sketch. A similar issue applies to most other sketches that appear in this chapter.

Lemma 1 bounds the quality of the frequency estimations which can be obtained from the sketch produced by Algorithm 3.

Lemma 1. *When queried on a token t, Algorithm 3 outputs a value $\tilde{f}_t$ such that, with probability at least $1/2$,*

$$f_t \leqslant \tilde{f}_t \leqslant f_t + \varepsilon \cdot \|f\|_1.$$

Moreover, the first inequality always holds.

Proof.   Observe that when queried on token t, Algorithm 3 outputs the cell $C[h(t)]$ of the array C. This cell contains the total frequency of all the tokens mapped to this cell by the hash function h. More formally,

$$\tilde{f}_t = C[h(t)] = \sum_{\substack{t' \in [m] \\ h(t)=h(t')}} f_{t'} = f_t + \sum_{\substack{t' \in [m]\setminus\{t\} \\ h(t)=h(t')}} f_{t'}.$$

Since we are in the strict turnstile model, all the frequencies are non-negative, and thus, the last equality implies $\tilde{f}_t \geqslant f_t$. It remains to be shown that with probability at least $1/2$, we also have

$$\sum_{\substack{t' \in [m]\setminus\{t\} \\ h(t)=h(t')}} f_{t'} \leqslant \varepsilon \cdot \|f\|_1. \qquad (7.1)$$

For every token $t' \in [m]\setminus\{t\}$, let us define an indicator $X_{t'}$ for the event that $h(t) = h(t')$. Since h is selected from a pairwise independent hash functions family, the probability that $X_{t'}$ takes the value 1 must be k^{-1}. Using this notation, we can now rewrite the left-hand side of Inequality (7.1) as

$$\sum_{t' \in [m]\setminus\{t\}} X_{t'} \cdot f_{t'},$$

and its expectation can be upper bounded, using the linearity of expectation, by

$$\sum_{t' \in [m]\setminus\{t\}} \mathrm{E}[X_{t'}] \cdot f_{t'} = k^{-1} \cdot \sum_{t' \in [m]\setminus\{t\}} f_{t'} \leqslant k^{-1} \cdot \|f\|_1 \leqslant \frac{\varepsilon \cdot \|f\|_1}{2}.$$

The lemma now follows since the last inequality and Markov's inequality together imply that Inequality (7.1) holds with probability at least $1/2$. $\square$

According to Lemma 1, Algorithm 3 produces a good estimation for f_t with probability at least $1/2$. Naturally, we want to increase this probability, and we will later present algorithms that do that by employing multiple independent copies of Algorithm 3. However, before getting to these algorithms, we would like to end our study of Algorithm 3 with

Observation 3, which upper bounds the size of the sketch created by this algorithm. We note that this observation works only when ε is not too small (namely, it must be at least $(mn)^{-1}$). For smaller values of ε, the size of the sketch is larger than the size required for storing the entire data stream, and thus, using such small values for ε does not make sense.

Observation 3. The size of the sketch created by Algorithm 3 is $O(\varepsilon^{-1} \cdot \log n + \log m)$ whenever $\varepsilon \geqslant (mn)^{-1}$.

Proof. Each cell of C contains the total frequency of the tokens mapped by h to this cell. As this total frequency must be upper bounded by n, we get that each cell of C requires only $O(\log n)$ bits. Hence, the entire array C requires a space complexity of

$$k \cdot O(\log n) = O(k \cdot \log n) = O(\varepsilon^{-1} \cdot \log n).$$

It remains to upper bound the space complexity required for the hash function h. Let m' be the smallest power of two which is at least m. As we saw in Chapter 5, there exists a pairwise independent hash functions family H' of hash functions from $[m']$ to $[k]$ whose individual functions can be represented using $O(\log m' + \log k) = O(\log m + \log n)$ space (where the equality holds since $k < 4/\varepsilon \leqslant 4mn$ and $m' < 2m$). We now note that by restricting the domain of the functions of H' to $[m]$, we get a pairwise independent hash functions family H of hash functions from $[m]$ to $[k]$. Moreover, the space complexity required for representing individual functions of H is not larger than the space complexity required for representing individual functions of H'. Hence, for an appropriate choice of H, it is possible to represent h using $O(\log m + \log n)$ bits. $\qquad\square$

We summarize the properties of Algorithm 3 that we have proved in Theorem 1.

Theorem 1. *In the strict turnstile model, Algorithm 3 produces a sketch such that:*

- *for a fixed choice of the hash function h, sketches produced for different streams can be combined,*
- *the size of the sketch is $O(\varepsilon^{-1} \cdot \log n + \log m)$ whenever $\varepsilon \geqslant (mn)^{-1}$,*
- *given the sketch and an arbitrary token t, generating an estimate $\tilde{f}_t$ for the frequency f_t of t in the way given by Algorithm 3 guarantees that, with probability at least $1/2$, $f_t \leqslant \tilde{f}_t \leqslant f + \varepsilon \cdot \|f\|_1$. Moreover, the first inequality always holds.*

Algorithm 4: Count-Min (ε, δ)

1. Let k be the least power of two such that $k \geqslant 2/\varepsilon$, and let $r = \lceil \log_2 \delta^{-1} \rceil$.
2. Let C be an array of size $r \times k$ whose cells are all initially zero.
3. Independently choose r random hash functions $h_1, h_2, \ldots, h_t \colon [m] \to [k]$ from a pairwise independent hash functions family H.
4. **while** there are more update events **do**
5.   Let (t, c) be the next update event.
6.   **for** $i = 1$ to r **do**
7. $C[i, h_i(t)] \leftarrow C[i, h_i(t)] + c$.
8. **sketch:** the sketch consists of C and the hash functions $h_1, h_2, \ldots, h_r$.
9. **query:** given a token t, output $\min\limits_{1 \leqslant i \leqslant r} C[i, h_i(t)]$ as an estimate for f_t.

As mentioned above, our next objective is to improve the probability that the estimate $\tilde{f}_t$ for the frequency f_t is good. In the previous chapters we have usually used the median technique to improve such probabilities. However, here the error in the estimate $\tilde{f}_t$ is one sided, in the sense that $\tilde{f}_t$ can overestimate f_t, but can never underestimate it. This allows us to improve the probability of success by executing multiple independent parallel copies of Algorithm 3, and then simply outputting the minimum among the estimates produced by all the copies. The algorithm obtained this way is equivalent to the algorithm that produces the full Count-Min sketch. Due to the importance of this sketch, we give a standalone version of the algorithm generating it as Algorithm 4. However, the reader is encouraged to verify that it is indeed equivalent to executing multiple independent copies of Algorithm 3 and outputting their minimum estimate. We note that the Count-Min sketch has two accuracy parameters: $\varepsilon, \delta \in (0, 1]$.

The properties of the Count-Min sketch are summarized by Theorem 2.

Theorem 2. *In the strict turnstile model, the Count-Min sketch has the following properties*:

- *for a fixed choice of the hash functions $h_1, h_2, \ldots, h_r$, sketches produced for different streams can be combined,*
- *the size of the sketch is $O(\log \delta^{-1} \cdot (\varepsilon^{-1} \cdot \log n + \log m))$ whenever $\varepsilon \geqslant (mn)^{-1}$,*

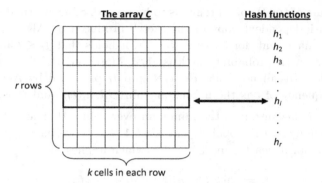

Figure 7.1. A graphical illustration of the Count-Min sketch. The sketch includes an array C which contains r rows, each of size k. Each row i is associated with an independently chosen hash function h_i.

- *given the sketch and an arbitrary token t, generating an estimate $\tilde{f}_t$ for the frequency f_t of t in the way given by Algorithm 4 guarantees that, with probability at least $1 - \delta$, $f_t \leqslant \tilde{f}_t \leqslant f + \varepsilon \cdot \|f\|_1$.*

Proof. The Count-Min sketch consists of two parts. The first part is an array C which has r rows, each of size k. The second part is a list of r hash functions, each of which is associated with one row of C (see Figure 7.1). The important observation to make is that if we restrict our attention to a single row of C and to its corresponding hash function, then Algorithm 4 updates them in the same way that Algorithm 3 updates its sketch. Thus, one can view each line of the array C, together with its corresponding hash function, as an independent sketch of the kind produced by Algorithm 3.

This already proves the first part of the theorem since we know, by Observation 2, that sketches of the kind produced by Algorithm 3 can be combined when they are based on the same hash function. Moreover, the second part of the theorem follows since each sketch of the kind produced by Algorithm 3 takes $O(\varepsilon^{-1} \cdot \log n + \log m)$ space by Observation 3 (when $\varepsilon \geqslant (mn)^{-1}$), and thus, the Count-Min sketch (which consists of r such sketches) has a space complexity of

$$r \cdot O(\varepsilon^{-1} \cdot \log n + \log m) = O(r \cdot (\varepsilon^{-1} \cdot \log n + \log m))$$
$$= O(\log \delta^{-1} \cdot (\varepsilon^{-1} \cdot \log n + \log m)).$$

The last part of the theorem remains to be proved. Since we treat each row of C as an independent copy of the sketch produced by Algorithm 3, we get by Lemma 1 that, for every $1 \leqslant i \leqslant r$, it holds that $f_t \leqslant C[i, h_i(t)] \leqslant f_t + \varepsilon \cdot \|f\|_1$ with probability at least $1/2$. Moreover, the first inequality always holds. Recall now that the estimate $\tilde{f}_t$ produced by Algorithm 4 for the frequency of t is the minimum $\min\limits_{1 \leqslant i \leqslant r} C[i, h_i(t)]$, and thus, it must be at least f_t because it is the minimum over values that are all at least f_t. Additionally, with probability at least $1 - 2^{-r}$, we have $C[i, h_i(t)] \leqslant f_t + \varepsilon \cdot \|f\|_1$ for at least some $1 \leqslant i \leqslant r$, which implies

$$\tilde{f}_t = \min_{1 \leqslant i \leqslant r} C[i, h_i(t)] \leqslant f_t + \varepsilon \cdot \|f\|_1.$$

The theorem now follows since $1 - 2^{-r} \geqslant 1 - 2^{-\log_2 \delta^{-1}} = 1 - \delta$. $\square$

The Min-Cost sketch applies only to the strict turnstile model. However, its main ideas can be generalized to the general turnstile model. This extension is studied in Exercises 4 and 5.

Exercise 4. Consider a modified version of Algorithm 3 in which k is increased to be the least power of two such that $k \geqslant 6/\varepsilon$, and let us denote by $\tilde{f}_t$ the output of this modified version when queried on t. Prove that, in the turnstile model, $\Pr[|f_t - \tilde{f}_t| > \varepsilon \cdot \|f\|_1] \leqslant \frac{1}{3}$.

The modified version of Algorithm 3 suggested by Exercise 4 succeeds with a constant probability to produce a good estimate for the frequency of a token t. Once again, we would like to improve this success probability by combining multiple independent copies of the algorithm. Unfortunately, the error here is two-sided (i.e., $\tilde{f}_t$ can be both larger and smaller than f_t), which means that we cannot simply run multiple independent copies of the algorithm and output the minimum estimate they produce (like we did in Algorithm 4). Instead, we have to employ the median technique. In other words, we need to execute multiple copies of the modified version of Algorithm 3, and then output the median of their estimates. Exercise 5 presents and analyzes an algorithm implementing this idea.

Exercise 5. Consider Algorithm 5. The sketch produced by this algorithm is known as the Count-Median sketch. Like the Count-Min sketch, this sketch also has two accuracy parameters, $\varepsilon, \delta \in (0, 1]$.

Algorithm 5: Count-Median (ε, δ)

1. Let k be the least power of two such that $k \geqslant 6/\varepsilon$, and let $r = \lceil 48 \log_2 \delta^{-1} \rceil$.
2. Let C be an array of size $r \times k$ whose cells are all initially zero.
3. Independently choose r random hash functions $h_1, h_2, \ldots, h_r : [m] \rightarrow [k]$ from a pairwise independent hash functions family H.
4. **while** there are more update events **do**
5.   Let (t, c) be the next update event.
6.   **for** $i = 1$ to r **do**
7. $C[i, h_i(t)] \leftarrow C[i, h_i(t)] + c$.
8. **sketch:** the sketch consists of C and the hash functions $h_1, h_2, \ldots, h_r$.
9. **query:** given a token t, output the median of $C[1, h_1(t)]$, $C[2, h_2(t)], \ldots, C[r, h_r(t)]$ as an estimate for f_t.

Prove that, in the turnstile model, the Count-Median sketch has the following properties:

- for a fixed choice of the hash functions $h_1, h_2, \ldots, h_r$, sketches produced for different streams can be combined,
- the size of the sketch is $O(\log \delta^{-1} \cdot (\varepsilon^{-1} \cdot \log n + \log m))$ whenever $\varepsilon \geqslant (mn)^{-1}$,
- given the sketch and an arbitrary token t, generating an estimate $\tilde{f}_t$ for the frequency f_t of t in the way specified by Algorithm 5 guarantees that $\Pr[|f_t - \tilde{f}_t| > \varepsilon \cdot \|f\|_1] \leqslant 1 - \delta$.

7.3 The Count Sketch

The Count-Min and Count-Median sketches that we have seen in Section 7.2 estimate frequencies up to an error term that depends on the ℓ^1 norm of the frequency vector f. For some applications that is not good enough since the ℓ^1 norm, which is the sum of the absolute values of all the frequencies, tends to be quite large. Intuitively, the reason that the ℓ^1 norm appears in the error term is that every cell of the above sketches contains the sum of the frequencies of many tokens, and when the frequencies are non-negative, this sum often builds up to be on the order of $\varepsilon \cdot \|f\|_1$. In this section, we will see a different sketch, called the Count sketch, in which the frequencies of the tokens mapped to a single cell of the sketch tend to cancel each other rather than build up, yielding a different error term which is often better.

The Count sketch is constructed by Algorithm 6. One can observe that its general structure is very similar to the structure of the Count-Min and Count-Median sketches. Specifically, the Count sketch contains a two-dimensional array C and associates two independent hash functions h_i and g_i with every row i of C.[3] The function h_i specifies which tokens are mapped to each cell of row i. In contrast, the function g_i (which does not appear in the previous sketches) specifies whether the frequency of the token is added or removed from the cell. Note that the randomness of g_i means that some frequencies are added, while others are removed, which gives the frequencies a fair chance to cancel each other out instead of building up. Finally, we would like to note that the Count sketch uses the same two accuracy parameters $\varepsilon, \delta \in (0, 1]$ used by the Count-Min and Count-Median sketches.

Algorithm 6: Count (ε, δ)

1. Let k be the least power of two such that $k \geqslant 3/\varepsilon^2$, and let $r = \lceil 48 \log_2 \delta^{-1} \rceil$.
2. Let C be an array of size $r \times k$ whose cells are all initially zero.
3. Independently choose r random hash functions $h_1, h_2, \ldots, h_r \colon [m] \to [k]$ from a pairwise independent hash functions family H_1.
4. Independently choose r random hash functions $g_1, g_2, \ldots, g_r \colon [m] \to \{-1, 1\}$ from a pairwise independent hash functions family H_2.
5. **while** there are more update events **do**
6.   Let (t, c) be the next update event.
7.   **for** $i = 1$ to r **do**
8. $C[i, h_i(t)] \leftarrow C[i, h_i(t)] + g_i(t) \cdot c$.
9. **sketch:** the sketch consists of C and the hash functions h_1, $g_1, h_2, g_2 \ldots, h_r, g_r$.
10. **query:** given a token t, output the median of $g_1(t) \cdot C[1, h_1(t)], g_2(t) \cdot C[2, h_2(t)], \ldots, g_r(t) \cdot C[r, h_r(t)]$ as an estimate for f_t.

---

[3]Like in the cases of Count-Min and Count-Median, one can treat each row of C and its two associated hash functions as an independent sketch, and then view the Count sketch as a collection of such sketches.

Exercise 6 studies some of the properties of the Count sketch.

Exercise 6. Prove that, in the turnstile model, the Count sketch has the following properties:

- for a fixed choice of the hash functions $h_1, h_2, \ldots, h_r$ and $g_1, g_2, \ldots, g_r$, sketches produced for different streams can be combined,
- the size of the sketch is $O(\log \delta^{-1} \cdot (\varepsilon^{-2} \cdot \log n + \log m))$ whenever $\varepsilon \geqslant (mn)^{-1}$.

To complete the study of the Count sketch, we still need to determine the quality of the frequency estimations that can be obtained from it. As a first step toward this goal we develop an expression for $g_i(t) \cdot C[i, h_i(t)]$. For every $1 \leqslant i \leqslant r$ and two tokens t and t', let $X^i_{t,t'}$ be an indicator for the event that t and t' are mapped to the same cell of row i, i.e., $h_i(t) = h_i(t')$. Using this notation, we get

$$C[i, h_i(t)] = g_i(t) \cdot f_t + \sum_{\substack{t' \in [m] \setminus \{t\} \\ h_i(t) = h_i(t')}} g_i(t') \cdot f_{t'}$$

$$= g_i(t) \cdot f_t + \sum_{t' \in [m] \setminus \{t\}} g_i(t') \cdot X^i_{t,t'} \cdot f_{t'},$$

which implies, since $g_i(t) \in \{-1, 1\}$,

$$g_i(t) \cdot C[i, h_i(t)] = f_t + \sum_{t' \in [m] \setminus \{t\}} g_i(t) \cdot g_i(t') \cdot X^i_{t,t'} \cdot f_{t'}.$$

Lemmata 2 and 3 use the last equality to prove properties of $g_i(t) \cdot C[i, h_i(t)]$.

Lemma 2. *For every $1 \leqslant i \leqslant r$, the expectation of $g_i(t) \cdot C[i, h_i(t)]$ is f_t.*

Proof. Intuitively, the lemma holds since each token $t' \neq t$ has an equal probability to contribute either $f_{t'}$ or $-f_{t'}$ to $g_i(t) \cdot C[i, h_i(t)]$, and thus, does not affect the expectation of this expression. A more formal argument is based on the linearity of the expectation. The pairwise independence of g_i implies that $g_i(t)$ and $g_i(t')$ are independent whenever $t \neq t'$. Moreover, both these values are independent from the variable $X^i_{t,t'}$ since the last variable depends only on the function h_i. Thus, by the linearity of expectation,

$$E[g_i(t) \cdot C[i, h_i(t)]] = E\left[f_t + \sum_{t' \in [m] \setminus \{t\}} g_i(t) \cdot g_i(t') \cdot X_{t,t'}^i \cdot f_{t'}\right]$$

$$= f_t + \sum_{t' \in [m] \setminus \{t\}} E[g_i(t)] \cdot E[g_i(t')] \cdot E[X_{t,t'}^i] \cdot f_{t'}.$$

We now observe that $E[g_i(t')] = 0$ for every token t'. Plugging this observation into the previous equality proves the lemma. □

Lemma 3. *For every $1 \leqslant i \leqslant r$, the variance of $g_i(t) \cdot C[i, h_i(t)]$ is at most $k^{-1} \cdot \sum_{t' \in [m]} f_{t'}^2$.*

Proof. Since adding a constant does not change the variance, we get

$$\mathrm{Var}[g_i \cdot C[i, h_i(t)]] = \mathrm{Var}\left[f_t + \sum_{t' \in [m] \setminus \{t\}} g_i(t) \cdot g_i(t') \cdot X_{t,t'}^i \cdot f_{t'}\right]$$

$$= \mathrm{Var}\left[\sum_{t' \in [m] \setminus \{t\}} g_i(t) \cdot g_i(t') \cdot X_{t,t'}^i \cdot f_{t'}\right].$$

Thus, we only need to upper bound the variance on the rightmost side of the last equality. We do that by calculating the expectation of the expression inside this variance and the expectation of the square of this expression. As a first step, we note that, by Lemma 2,

$$E\left[\sum_{t' \in [m] \setminus \{t\}} g_i(t) \cdot g_i(t') \cdot X_{t,t'}^i \cdot f_{t'}\right] = E[g_i \cdot C[i, h_i(t)]] - f_t = 0.$$

Next, we observe that, since $g_i(t) \in \{-1, 1\}$ and $X_{t,t'}^i \in \{0, 1\}$,

$$E\left[\left(\sum_{t' \in [m] \setminus \{t\}} g_i(t) \cdot g_i(t') \cdot X_{t,t'}^i \cdot f_{t'}\right)^2\right]$$

$$= E\left[\sum_{t' \in [m] \setminus \{t\}} X_{t,t'}^i \cdot f_{t'}^2 + \sum_{\substack{t', t'' \in [m] \setminus \{t\} \\ t' \neq t''}} g_i(t') \cdot g_i(t'') \cdot X_{t,t'}^i \cdot X_{t,t''}^i \cdot f_t \cdot f_{t''}\right]$$

$$= \sum_{t' \in [m] \setminus \{t\}} E[X^i_{t,t'}] \cdot f^2_{t'}$$

$$+ \sum_{\substack{t',t'' \in [m] \setminus \{t\} \\ t' \neq t''}} E[g_i(t')] \cdot E[g_i(t'')] \cdot E[X^i_{t,t'} \cdot X^i_{t,t''}] \cdot f_t \cdot f_{t''},$$

where the second equality holds for two reasons. First, like in the proof of Lemma 2, the pairwise independence of the hash functions family from which the function g_i is drawn implies that $g_i(t')$ and $g_i(t'')$ are independent whenever $t' \neq t''$, and second, both these values are independent from the variables $X^i_{t,t'}$ and $X^i_{t,t''}$ whose values are determined by the function h_i alone. We now recall that $E[g_i(t')] = 0$ for every token t' and observe that $E[X^i_{t,t'}] = k^{-1}$ due to the pairwise independence of h_i. Plugging these observations into the last equality gives

$$E\left[\left(\sum_{t' \in [m] \setminus \{t\}} g_i(t) \cdot g_i(t') \cdot X^i_{t,t'} \cdot f_{t'}\right)^2\right] = k^{-1} \cdot \sum_{t' \in [m] \setminus \{t\}} \cdot f^2_{t'}.$$

The lemma now follows by observing that

$$\mathrm{Var}[g_i \cdot C[i, h_i(t)]] = \mathrm{Var}\left[\sum_{t' \in [m] \setminus \{t\}} g_i(t) \cdot g_i(t') \cdot X^i_{t,t'} \cdot f_{t'}\right]$$

$$= E\left[\left(\sum_{t' \in [m] \setminus \{t\}} g_i(t) \cdot g_i(t') \cdot X^i_{t,t'} \cdot f_{t'}\right)^2\right]$$

$$- \left(E\left[\sum_{t' \in [m] \setminus \{t\}} g_i(t) \cdot g_i(t') \cdot X^i_{t,t'} \cdot f_{t'}\right]\right)^2$$

$$= k^{-1} \cdot \sum_{t' \in [m] \setminus \{t\}} \cdot f^2_{t'} \leqslant k^{-1} \cdot \sum_{t' \in [m]} \cdot f^2_{t'}.$$

$\square$

Corollary 1. *For every* $1 \leqslant i \leqslant r$, $\Pr\left[|g_i(t) \cdot C[i, h_i(t)] - f_t| \geqslant \varepsilon \cdot \sqrt{\sum_{t' \in [m]} f^2_{t'}}\right] \leqslant \frac{1}{3}$.

Proof. Since the expectation of $g_i(t) \cdot C[i, h_i(t)]$ is f_t by Lemma 2, Chebyshev's inequality yields

$$\Pr \left[|g_i(t) \cdot C[i, h_i(t)] - f_t| \geqslant \varepsilon \cdot \sqrt{\sum_{t' \in [m]} f_{t'}^2} \right]$$

$$\leqslant \frac{\text{Var}[g_i(t) \cdot C[i, h_i(t)]]}{\left(\varepsilon \cdot \sqrt{\sum_{t' \in [m]} f_{t'}^2} \right)^2} \leqslant \frac{k^{-1} \cdot \sum_{t' \in [m]} f_{t'}^2}{\varepsilon^2 \cdot \sum_{t' \in [m]} f_{t'}^2} \leqslant \frac{1}{3}.$$

$\square$

The expression $\sqrt{\sum_{t' \in [m]} f_{t'}^2}$ which appears in the last corollary is known as the ℓ^2 norm of the frequency vector f, and is usually denoted by $\|f\|_2$. We will discuss the ℓ^2 norm in more detail later in this section, but for now we just note that Corollary 1 can be rephrased using this norm as follows:

Corollary 1 (rephrased). *For every* $1 \leqslant i \leqslant r$, $\Pr[|g_i(t) \cdot C[i, h_i(t)] - f_t| \geqslant \varepsilon \cdot \|f\|_2] \leqslant \frac{1}{3}$.

Corollary 1 proves that, for every $1 \leqslant i \leqslant r$, with a constant probability the cell $g_i(t) \cdot C[i, h_i(t)]$ is a good estimation for f_t. The probability that the median of these cells is a good estimation for f_t remains to be determined.

Theorem 3. *Given a Count sketch and an arbitrary token t, generating an estimate $\tilde{f}_t$ for the frequency f_t of t in the way given by Algorithm 6 guarantees that* $\Pr[|f_t - \tilde{f}_t| < \varepsilon \cdot \|f\|_2] \leqslant 1 - \delta$.

Proof. For every $1 \leqslant i \leqslant r$, let X_i be an indicator for the event that $|g_i(t) \cdot C[i, h_i(t)] - f_t| < \varepsilon \cdot \|f\|_2$. Note that the indicators X_i are independent. Moreover, by Corollary 1, each one of these indicators takes the value 1 with a probability of at least $2/3$.

Recall now that the estimate $\tilde{f}_t$ produced by Algorithm 6 is the median of the expressions $g_1(t) \cdot C[1, h_1(t)], g_2(t) \cdot C[2, h_2(t)], \ldots, g_r(t) \cdot C[r, h_r(t)]$. Thus, the error in this estimate is less than $\varepsilon \cdot \|f\|_2$ whenever more than half of these expressions estimate f_t up to this amount of error. In other words, to prove the theorem it is enough to prove the inequality

$$\Pr \left[\sum_{i=1}^{r} X_i > \frac{r}{2} \right] \geqslant 1 - \delta,$$

which is equivalent to the inequality

$$\Pr\left[\sum_{i=1}^{r} X_i \leqslant \frac{r}{2}\right] \leqslant \delta. \tag{7.2}$$

Thus, in the rest of the proof we concentrate on proving this inequality. Note that the probability of $\sum_{i=1}^{r} X_i \leqslant r/2$ increases when the probabilities of the individual indicators $X_1, X_2, \ldots, X_r$ taking the value 1 decrease. Thus, for the purpose of proving (7.2), we can assume that each one of these indicators takes the value 1 with probability exactly $2/3$ (rather than at least $2/3$). By the Chernoff bound, we now get

$$\Pr\left[\sum_{i=1}^{r} X_i \leqslant \frac{r}{2}\right]$$

$$= \Pr\left[\sum_{i=1}^{r} X_i \leqslant \frac{3}{4}\mathrm{E}\left[\sum_{i=1}^{r} X_i\right]\right] \leqslant e^{-(1/4)^2 \cdot \mathrm{E}[\sum_{i=1}^{r} X_i]/2}$$

$$= e^{(2r/3)/32} = e^{-r/48} = e^{-\lceil 48\log_2 \delta^{-1}\rceil/48} \leqslant e^{-\log_2 \delta^{-1}} = \delta. \qquad \square$$

At this point we would like to compare the properties of the main sketches discussed in this chapter for estimating token frequencies. Table 7.1 summarizes the properties of these sketches. As is evident from the table, for fixed ε and δ the space complexity of the Count sketch is larger than the space complexity of the Count-Min and Count-Median sketches. However, the three sketches also differ in the guarantee on the quality of the estimations that can be produced from them. The Count-Min and Count-Median have a guarantee which depends on the ℓ^1 norm, while the

Table 7.1. A comparison of the main sketches presented in this chapter for estimating token frequencies. For every sketch, the table summarizes the model in which it works, its space complexity and its guarantee for the difference between the estimated frequency $\tilde{f}_t$ and the true frequency f_t.

Sketch Name	Model	Space Complexity	With Probability $1 - \delta$
Count-Min	Strict Turnstile	$O(\log \delta^{-1} \cdot (\varepsilon^{-1} \cdot \log n + \log m))$	$\tilde{f}_t - f_t \in [0, \varepsilon \cdot \|f\|_1]$
Count-Median	Turnstile	$O(\log \delta^{-1} \cdot (\varepsilon^{-1} \cdot \log n + \log m))$	$\tilde{f}_t - f_t \in [-\varepsilon \cdot \|f\|_1, \varepsilon \cdot \|f\|_1]$
Count	Turnstile	$O(\log \delta^{-1} \cdot (\varepsilon^{-2} \cdot \log n + \log m))$	$\tilde{f}_t - f_t \in [-\varepsilon \cdot \|f\|_2, \varepsilon \cdot \|f\|_2]$

Count sketch has a guarantee depending on the ℓ^2 norm. Hence, the use of the Count sketch is preferred, despite its larger space complexity, when the ℓ^2 norm is much smaller than the ℓ^1 norm.

It is known that for every vector $v \in \mathbb{R}^m$ the following inequalities hold (and moreover, there are vectors which make each one of these inequalities tight)

$$\frac{\|v\|_1}{\sqrt{m}} \leqslant \|v\|_2 \leqslant \|v\|_1.$$

Hence, the ℓ^2 norm is never larger than the ℓ^1 norm, and it can sometimes be much smaller than it. Exercise 7 gives some intuitive idea about the factors affecting the ratio between the two norms. Specifically, it shows that for "spread out" vectors the ℓ^2 norm is much smaller than the ℓ^1 norm, while for "concentrated" vectors the two norms take similar values.

Exercise 7. In this exercise, we consider two kinds of vectors and study the ratio between the ℓ^1 and ℓ^2 norms of both kinds of vectors.

(a) In vectors of the first kind we consider all the coordinates are equal. In other words, in a vector $v_a \in \mathbb{R}^m$ of this kind, all m coordinates are equal to some real value a. Prove that for such a vector $\|v_a\|_1 = \sqrt{m} \cdot \|v_a\|_2$.

(b) In vectors of the second kind we consider only one coordinate has a non-zero value. Specifically, in a vector $u_a \in \mathbb{R}^m$ of this kind, all the coordinates are zero except for one coordinate which takes the value a. Prove that for such a vector $\|u_a\|_1 = \|u_a\|_2$.

7.4 Linear Sketches

Linear sketches are an important class of sketches encompassing many of the sketches that are currently known, including all the sketches presented in this chapter. A formal definition of linear sketches is outside the scope of this book. However, in a nutshell, a linear sketch is defined by a matrix, and the sketch is obtained by multiplying this matrix with the frequency vector of the stream.

Consider now a stream σ in the turnstile model, and let f_σ be its frequency vector. Additionally, let $\text{comp}(\sigma)$ be a stream that is the complement of σ, in the sense that $f_\sigma + f_{\text{comp}(\sigma)} = \bar{0}$, where $f_{\text{comp}(\sigma)}$ is the frequency vector of $\text{comp}(\sigma)$ and $\bar{0}$ is the vector of all zeros (in other words, if f_σ contains in total r appearances of some token t, then $\text{comp}(\sigma)$

contains exactly $-r$ appearances of t in total). An important property of linear sketches is that, given the linear sketch $DS(\sigma)$ corresponding to the stream σ, one can calculate the sketch $DS(\text{comp}(\sigma))$ corresponding to the stream $\text{comp}(\sigma)$ by simply replacing each number in the sketch $DS(\sigma)$ with its complement.

‖ **Exercise 8.** Verify that you understand why that is the case for the sketches ‖ presented in this chapter.

Let us now present an application in which the above-mentioned property of linear sketches is very useful. Assume that we are given linear sketches $DS(\sigma_1)$, $DS(\sigma_2)$, ..., $DS(\sigma_k)$ for k streams. Based on these sketches, we can calculate for every two streams σ_i and σ_j the sketch

$$DS(\sigma_i \cdot \text{comp}(\sigma_j)) = \text{COMB}(DS(\sigma_i), DS(\text{comp}(\sigma_j))).[4]$$

The important observation to make now is that the stream $\sigma_i \cdot \text{comp}(\sigma_j)$ can be intuitively viewed as the difference between the streams σ_i and σ_j because the frequency of every token t in $\sigma_i \cdot \text{comp}(\sigma_j)$ is equal to the frequency of t in σ_i minus its frequency in σ_j. Thus, having the sketch corresponding to $\sigma_i \cdot \text{comp}(\sigma_j)$ allows us to answer questions about the difference between the streams σ_i and σ_j.

To make this more concrete, consider for example the Count-Median sketch — which is linear like all the other sketches in this chapter. Let us now assume that we have k computers and each one of these computers gets a different stream and calculates the Count-Median sketch corresponding to this stream (to make sure that their sketches can be combined, all the computers use a shared set of hash functions for their sketches). Given these sketches, we would like to get information about the differences between the original k streams. This can be done using the above ideas, however, to explain the details of how to do it we first need to define some notation. Let us denote by σ_1, σ_2, ..., σ_k the k streams, and let S denote the list of the k Count-Median sketches corresponding to these streams. Note that by the above arguments it is possible to calculate the Count-Median sketch of the stream $\sigma_i \cdot \text{comp}(\sigma_j)$ for every $1 \leqslant i, j \leqslant k$ based on the sketches in S alone, and this sketch gives us an estimate $\tilde{f}_t$ for the frequency of every

---

[4]Recall that $COMB$ is the algorithm that given sketches of two streams σ and σ' produces the sketch for the concatenated stream $\sigma \cdot \sigma'$. Such an algorithm must exist for every type of sketch by definition.

token t in $\sigma_i \cdot \text{comp}(\sigma_j)$. Since the frequency of t in $\sigma_i \cdot \text{comp}(\sigma_j)$ is equal to the difference between the frequencies of t in σ_i and σ_j, we can conclude that we have managed to get from the sketches of S an estimate for this difference.

Exercise 9. In the above discussion we have used the Count-Median sketch. Could we use either the Count-Min or Count sketches instead?

7.5 Bibliographic Notes

The first sketch is often attributed to the work of Alon *et al.* (1999), which studies a sketch known as "Tug-of-War". However, this work does not refer to the term "sketch" or to its definition since they were both introduced only at a later point. Hence, the attribution of the first sketch by Alon *et al.* (1999) is only in a retrospective view.

Charikar *et al.* (2002) introduced the Count sketch. They also came up with the technique explained in Section 7.4 which, given linear sketches for two streams, allows one to get information about the difference between the streams. Later, Cormode and Muthukrishnan (2005) introduced the Count-Min and Count-Median sketches that improve the space complexity of the Count sketch (at the cost of having an error guarantee depending on the ℓ^1 norm rather than on the ℓ^2 norm).

N. Alon, Y. Matias and M. Szegedy. The Space Complexity of Approximating the Frequency Moments. *Journal of Computer and System Sciences*, 58(1): 137–147, 1999.

M. Charikar, K. Chen and M. Farach-Colton. Finding Frequent Items in Data Streams. In *Proceedings of the 29th International Colloquium on Automata Languages and Programming (ICALP)*, 693–703, 2002.

G. Cormode and S. Muthukrishnan. An Improved Data Stream Summary: The Count-Min Sketch and its Applications. *Journal of Algorithms*, 55(1): 58–75, 2005.

Exercise Solutions

Solution 1

One can observe that Algorithm 1 calculates the sum

$$\sum_{t \in M} f_t,$$

where M is the set of possible tokens. This sum is equal to $\|f\|_1$ when the frequencies of the elements are all non-negative. Since this is the case in both the cash register and the strict turnstile models, we get that Algorithm 1 calculates $\|f\|_1$ in these models.[5]

It remains to be shown that Algorithm 1 might fail to calculate $\|f\|_1$ in the general turnstile model. According to the above observation, such a failure requires an element with a negative frequency. Consider a data stream consisting of two update events corresponding to the ordered pairs ("a", 1) and ("b", −1) (i.e., in the first update event, one copy of the token "a" arrives, and in the second update event, one copy of the token "b" leaves). The output of Algorithm 1 given this data stream is

$$\sum_{t \in M} f_t = f'_{a'} + f'_{b'} = 1 + (-1) = 0.$$

In contrast, the ℓ^1 norm corresponding to this data stream is

$$\sum_{t \in M} |f_t| = |f'_{a'}| + |f'_{b'}| = |1| + |-1| = 2.$$

Solution 2

The variant of Algorithm 2 we suggest for the cash register model is given as Algorithm 7. One can observe that Algorithm 7 updates its internal state following the arrival of an update event (t, c) in the same way that Algorithm 2 updates its internal state following the arrival of c copies of token t in a row. Hence, the analysis of Algorithm 2 from Chapter 1 carries over to Algorithm 7, and shows that the set produced by this algorithm contains exactly the tokens whose frequency is larger than n/k. Furthermore, in the cash register model, n is equal to the final value of $\|f\|_1$ because $\|f\|_1$ can only increase over time in this model. Thus, we get that the set produced by Algorithm 7 contains exactly the tokens whose frequency is larger than $k^{-1} \cdot \|f\|_1$, as required.

The space complexity of Algorithm 7 remains to be analyzed. Like in the case of Algorithm 2, we assume that the implementation of Algorithm 7 stores explicitly only counters with a non-zero value. Moreover, one can recall from the analysis of Algorithm 2 in Chapter 1 that the size of the set F maintained by Algorithms 2 and 7 never exceeds k. Hence, Algorithm 7

---

[5]We note that the cash register is in fact a special case of the strict turnstile model, and thus, it would have been enough to just prove that Algorithm 1 calculates $\|f\|_1$ in the strict turnstile model.

Algorithm 7: Frequent Elements Algorithm — Cash Register Model (k)

1. **while** there are more update events **do**
2.   Let (t, c) be the next update event.
3.   Increase the counter of t by c.
4.   **if** there are at least k non-zero counters **then**
5.   Let d be the smallest value of a non-zero counter.
6.   Decrease all the non-zero counters by d.
7. Let F be the set of tokens currently having a non-zero counter.
8. Reset all the counters to zero.
9. Start the second pass over the input stream.
10. $n \leftarrow 0$.
11. **while** there are more update events **do**
12.   Let (t, c) be the next event.
13. $n \leftarrow n + c$.
14.   **If** $t \in F$ **then** increase the counter of t by c.
15. **return** the list of tokens whose counters are larger than n/k.

---

maintains at most k non-zero counters at every given time. The value of each such counter is upper bounded by the frequency of the token corresponding to this counter, and thus, also by n. Therefore, we get that all the tokens used by Algorithm 7 can be represented together using $O(k \log n)$ bits. Moreover, the variable d, which takes the value of one of these counters, can also be represented using this amount of bits. Next, let us consider the variable t and the set F. The variable t represents one token, and the set F contains up to k tokens. As there are at most m possible tokens, each token can be represented using $O(\log m)$ bits, and thus, t and F can both be represented using at most $O(k \log m)$ bits. Finally, we consider the variables c and n. The variable n is increasing over time, and its final value is the value of the parameter n. Furthermore, the variable c contains the increase in the frequency of one token in one update event, and thus, its value cannot exceed n since n is the sum of the frequencies of all the tokens. Hence, we get that both variables c and n are always upper bounded by the parameter n, and thus, can be represented using $O(\log n)$ bits.

Combining all the above observations, we get that the space complexity of Algorithm 7 is $O(k(\log m + \log n))$, and thus, Algorithm 7 is a streaming algorithm when k is considered to be a constant.

Solution 3

We first observe that the ℓ^1 norm can be calculated using the data stream algorithm given by Algorithm 1 in the cash register and strict turnstile models. Thus, it remains to be seen that, in these models, given only the two ℓ^1 norms n^1 and n^2 of two data streams σ_1 and σ_2, it is possible to calculate the ℓ^1 norm of $\sigma_1 \cdot \sigma_2$. For that purpose, the frequency vectors corresponding to these two data streams are denoted by f^1 and f^2. Then, assuming that M is the set of all possible tokens, we get that the ℓ^1 norm of $\sigma_1 \cdot \sigma_2$ is given by

$$\sum_{t \in M} |f_t^1 + f_t^2| = \sum_{t \in M} |f_t^1| + \sum_{t \in M} |f_t^2| = n^1 + n^2,$$

where the first equality holds since frequencies are always non-negative in the cash register and strict turnstile models.

Solution 4

Recall that in the sketch generated by Algorithm 3 the cell $C[h(t)]$ contains the total frequency of all the tokens mapped to this cell by the hash function h, and thus,

$$\tilde{f}_t = C[h(t)] = \sum_{\substack{t' \in [m] \\ h(t)=h(t')}} f_{t'} = f_t + \sum_{\substack{t' \in [m]\setminus\{t\} \\ h(t)=h(t')}} f_{t'}. \tag{7.3}$$

Like in the proof of Lemma 1, we now define for every token $t' \in [m]\setminus\{t\}$ an indicator $X_{t'}$ for the event that $h(t) = h(t')$. Since h is selected from a pairwise independent hash functions family, the probability that $X_{t'}$ takes the value 1 must be k^{-1}. Using this notation, we can now rewrite Equality (7.3) as

$$\tilde{f}_t - f_t = \sum_{t' \in [m]\setminus\{t\}} X_{t'} \cdot f_{t'}.$$

The sum on the right-hand side of this equality contains both tokens with positive frequencies and tokens with non-positive frequencies. It is useful to break it into two sums, one for each of these kinds of tokens. Hence, let us define M^+ as the set of tokens from $[m]\setminus\{t\}$ having a positive frequency, and let M^- be the set of the other tokens from $[m]\setminus\{t\}$. Using these sets, we get

$$|\tilde{f}_t - f_t| = \left| \sum_{t' \in M^+} X_{t'} \cdot f_{t'} + \sum_{t' \in M^-} X_{t'} \cdot f_{t'} \right|$$

$$\leqslant \max \left\{ \sum_{t' \in M^+} X_{t'} \cdot f_{t'}, - \sum_{t' \in M^-} X_{t'} \cdot f_{t'} \right\},$$

where the inequality holds since the sum $\sum_{t' \in M^+} X_{t'} \cdot f_{t'}$ is always non-negative, and the sum $\sum_{t' \in M^-} X_{t'} \cdot f_{t'}$ is always non-positive. Our objective is to bound both sums using Markov's inequality, and toward this goal we need to bound their expectations as follows:

$$\mathrm{E}\left[\sum_{t' \in M^+} X_{t'} \cdot f_{t'} \right] = \sum_{t' \in M^+} \mathrm{E}[X_{t'}] \cdot f_{t'}$$

$$= k^{-1} \cdot \sum_{t' \in M^+} |f_{t'}| \leqslant k^{-1} \cdot \|f\|_1 \leqslant \frac{\varepsilon \cdot \|f\|_1}{6}$$

and

$$\mathrm{E}\left[- \sum_{t' \in M^-} X_{t'} \cdot f_{t'} \right] = - \sum_{t' \in M^-} \mathrm{E}[X_{t'}] \cdot f_{t'}$$

$$= k^{-1} \cdot \sum_{t' \in M^-} |f_{t'}| \leqslant k^{-1} \cdot \|f\|_1 \leqslant \frac{\varepsilon \cdot \|f\|_1}{6}.$$

By Markov's inequality, we now get

$$\Pr\left[\sum_{t' \in M^+} X_{t'} \cdot f_{t'} \geqslant \varepsilon \cdot \|f\|_1 \right] \leqslant \frac{1}{6} \quad \text{and}$$

$$\Pr\left[- \sum_{t' \in M^-} X_{t'} \cdot f_{t'} \geqslant \varepsilon \cdot \|f\|_1 \right] \leqslant \frac{1}{6}.$$

Thus, by the union bound, the probability that the value of either $\sum_{t' \in M^+} X_{t'} \cdot f_{t'}$ or $- \sum_{t' \in M^-} X_{t'} \cdot f_{t'}$ is at least $\varepsilon \cdot \|f\|_1$ is upper bounded by 1/3, which implies

$$\Pr[|\tilde{f}_t - f_t| \geqslant \varepsilon \cdot \|f\|_1]$$

$$\leqslant \Pr\left[\max\left\{\sum_{t' \in M^+} X_{t'} \cdot f_{t'}, - \sum_{t' \in M^-} X_{t'} \cdot f_{t'}\right\} \geqslant \varepsilon \cdot \|f\|_1\right] \leqslant \frac{1}{3}.$$

Solution 5

Our first objective is to prove that Count-Median sketches produced for different streams can be combined when the hash functions $h_1, h_2, \ldots, h_r$ are fixed. Consider two streams σ_1 and σ_2, and, given some fixed choice for the above hash functions, let C^1, C^2 and C^{12} denote the content of the array C in the Count-Median sketches corresponding to the streams σ_1, σ_2 and $\sigma_1 \cdot \sigma_2$, respectively. We need to show that C^{12} can be calculated based on C^1 and C^2 alone. For that purpose, we observe that each cell of C contains the total frequency of all the tokens mapped to this cell by the hash function h_i, where i is the row of the cell. Hence, each cell of C^{12} is equal to the sum of the corresponding cells of C^1 and C^2, and thus, can be calculated using the values of these cells alone.

Our next objective is to bound the size of the Count-Median sketch, assuming $\varepsilon \geqslant (mn)^{-1}$. The Count-Median sketch consists of the array C and r hash functions. By the same argument used in the proof of Observation 3, we get that each one of the hash functions from the sketch can be represented using $O(\log m + \log k)$ bits. Hence, the total space complexity required for all the hash functions of the sketch is

$$r \cdot O(\log m + \log k) = O\left(\log \delta^{-1} \cdot \left(\log m + \log \frac{12}{\varepsilon}\right)\right)$$

$$= O(\log \delta^{-1} \cdot (\log m + \log(12mn)))$$

$$= O(\log \delta^{-1} \cdot (\log m + \log n)).$$

Let us now consider the space complexity required for the array C, which contains rk cells. Each cell of C contains the sum of the frequencies of the tokens mapped to this cell by the hash function corresponding to its row, and thus, the absolute value of the cell's value is upper bounded by n. Consequently, the entire array C can be represented using a space complexity of

$$rk \cdot O(\log n) = O(\log \delta^{-1} \cdot \varepsilon^{-1} \cdot \log n).$$

Combining the two bounds we proved above on the space required for the hash functions and the array C, we get that the total space complexity necessary for the Count-Median sketch is

$$O(\log \delta^{-1} \cdot (\log m + \log n)) + O(\log \delta^{-1} \cdot \varepsilon^{-1} \cdot \log n)$$
$$= O(\log \delta^{-1} \cdot (\log m + \varepsilon^{-1} \cdot \log n)).$$

Our last objective is to show that given a Count-Median sketch and an arbitrary token t, generating an estimate $\tilde{f}_t$ for the frequency f_t of t in the way described by Algorithm 5 guarantees that $\Pr[|f_t - \tilde{f}_t| > \varepsilon \cdot \|f\|_1] \leq 1 - \delta$. Toward this goal, we observe that the Count-Median sketch can be viewed as a collection of r independent sketches of the type produced by the modified version of Algorithm 3 given by Exercise 4. More specifically, when considering a single row of the array C and the hash function corresponding to this row, this row and hash function are updated by Algorithm 5 in the same way that the modified version of Algorithm 3 updates its sketch. Taking this point of view, the result of Exercise 4 implies that, for every $1 \leq i \leq r$,

$$\Pr[|f_t - C[i, h_i(t)]| > \varepsilon \cdot \|f\|_1] \leq \frac{1}{3}. \tag{7.4}$$

Let us denote now by X_i an indicator for the event that $|f_t - C[i, h_i(t)]| \leq \varepsilon \cdot \|f\|_1$, and let $X = \sum_{i=1}^{r} X_i$. Intuitively, each X_i is an indicator for the event that the cell $C[i, h_i(t)]$ contains a good estimation for f_t, and X is the number of such cells containing a good estimation for f_t. Recall now that Algorithm 5 outputs the median of the cells $C[1, h_1(t)], C[2, h_2(t)], \ldots, C[r, h_r(t)]$, and thus, it produces a good estimation for f_t whenever more than a half of these cells contain a good estimation for f_t. Thus, to prove the inequality that we want to prove, it is enough to prove

$$\Pr\left[X > \frac{r}{2}\right] \geq 1 - \delta,$$

which is equivalent to

$$\Pr\left[X \leqslant \frac{r}{2}\right] \leqslant \delta. \tag{7.5}$$

We now note that X is the sum of the r indicators $X_1, X_2, \ldots, X_r$, which are independent and take the value 1 with probability at least $2/3$ each by Inequality (7.4). Clearly, the probability that X takes a value of at most $r/2$ is increased when the probability of each X_i taking the value 1 is decreased. Hence, for the purpose of proving (7.5), we may assume without loss of generality that each X_i takes the value 1 with probability exactly $2/3$. Thus, by the Chernoff bound,

$$\Pr\left[X \leqslant \frac{r}{2}\right] = \Pr\left[X \leqslant \frac{3}{4} \cdot \mathrm{E}[X]\right] \leqslant e^{-(1/4)^2 \cdot \mathrm{E}[X]/2} = e^{-\mathrm{E}[X]/32}$$

$$= e^{-(2r/3)/32} = e^{-r/48} = e^{-\lceil 48 \log_2 \delta^{-1}\rceil/48} \leqslant e^{-\log \delta^{-1}} = \delta.$$

Solution 6

Our first objective is to prove that sketches produced for different streams can be combined when the hash functions $h_1, h_2, \ldots, h_r$ and $g_1, g_2, \ldots, g_r$ are all fixed. Consider two streams σ_1 and σ_2, and, given some fixed choice for the above hash functions, let C^1, C^2 and C^{12} denote the content of the array C in the Count sketches corresponding to the streams σ_1, σ_2 and $\sigma_1 \cdot \sigma_2$, respectively. We need to show that C^{12} can be calculated based on C^1 and C^2 alone. For that purpose, we observe that the value of cell number j in row i of C is given by the expression

$$\sum_{\substack{t \in [m] \\ h_i(t)=j}} g_i(t) \cdot f_t. \tag{7.6}$$

Note that this is a linear expression of the frequencies, which implies that each cell of C^{12} is equal to the sum of the corresponding cells of C^1 and C^2, and thus, can be calculated using the values of these cells alone.

Our next objective is to bound the size of the Count sketch, assuming $\varepsilon \geqslant (mn)^{-1}$. The Count sketch consists of the array C, r hash functions from $[m]$ to $[k]$ and r hash functions from $[m]$ to $\{-1, 1\}$. By the same argument used in the proof of Observation 3, we get that each one of the hash functions from $[m]$ to $[k]$ can be represented using $O(\log m + \log k)$

bits. Hence, the space complexity required for all these hash functions is

$$r \cdot O(\log m + \log k) = O\left(\log \delta^{-1} \cdot \left(\log m + \log \frac{6}{\varepsilon^2}\right)\right)$$

$$= O(\log \delta^{-1} \cdot (\log m + \log(6m^2 n^2)))$$

$$= O(\log \delta^{-1} \cdot (\log m + \log n)).$$

Consider next the hash functions from $[m]$ to $\{-1, 1\}$. One can observe that any hash function from $[m]$ to $[2]$ can be converted into a hash function from $[m]$ to $\{-1, 1\}$ by simply renaming the elements of the function's image. Thus, each hash function from $[m]$ to $\{-1, 1\}$ requires the same space complexity as a hash function from $[m]$ to $[2]$, and by the argument from the proof of Observation 3, such a hash function requires $O(\log m + \log 2) = O(\log m)$ bits. Since there are r hash functions from $[m]$ to $\{-1, 1\}$ in the Count sketch, their total space requirement is

$$r \cdot O(\log m) = O(\log \delta^{-1} \cdot \log m).$$

Let us now consider the space complexity required for the array C, which contains rk cells. We observe that the absolute value of each cell of C is upper bounded by n. The reason for that is that the content of cell j in row i of the array C is given by the sum (7.6), whose absolute value is upper bounded by n since the frequency of each token appears in it only once (either as a positive or as a negative term). Consequently, the entire array C can be represented using a space complexity of

$$rk \cdot O(\log n) = O(\log \delta^{-1} \cdot \varepsilon^{-2} \cdot \log n).$$

Combining the above bounds we got on the space required for the hash functions and the array C, we get that the total space complexity necessary for the Count-Median sketch is

$$O(\log \delta^{-1} \cdot (\log m + \log n)) + O(\log \delta^{-1} \cdot \log m) + O(\log \delta^{-1} \cdot \varepsilon^{-2} \cdot \log n)$$

$$= O(\log \delta^{-1} \cdot (\log m + \varepsilon^{-2} \cdot \log n)).$$

Solution 7

(a) Since all m coordinates of v_a are equal to a, we get

$$\|v_a\|_1 = m \cdot |a| = \sqrt{m} \cdot \sqrt{m \cdot |a|^2} = \sqrt{m} \cdot \sqrt{m \cdot a^2} = \sqrt{m} \cdot \|v_a\|_2.$$

(b) Since u_a has $m - 1$ coordinates which take the value 0 and one coordinate taking the value a, we get

$$\|u_a\|_1 = (m - 1) \cdot |0| + 1 \cdot |a| = |a|$$

$$= \sqrt{a^2} = \sqrt{(m - 1) \cdot 0^2 + 1 \cdot a^2} = \|u_a\|_2.$$

Solution 8

We explain why the sketch produced by Algorithm 3 has the property that $DS(\text{comp}(\sigma))$ can be obtained from $DS(\sigma)$ by simply complementing all the numbers in the sketch. The explanation for the other sketches given in this chapter is similar. Recall that each cell of the array C in Algorithm 3 contains the sum of the frequencies of the tokens mapped to this cell by the hash function h. Hence, in the sketch $DS(\sigma)$ the value of the ith cell of C is given by

$$C[i] = \sum_{\substack{t \in [m] \\ h(t)=i}} (f_\sigma)_t.$$

Similarly, the value of this cell in $DS(\text{comp}(\sigma))$ is

$$C[i] = \sum_{\substack{t \in [m] \\ h(t)=i}} (f_{\text{comp}(\sigma)})_t = \sum_{\substack{t \in [m] \\ h(t)=i}} (-f_\sigma)_t = - \sum_{\substack{t \in [m] \\ h(t)=i}} (f_\sigma)_t,$$

where the second equality holds since $f_\sigma + f_{\text{comp}(\sigma)}$ is the vector of all zeros.

Solution 9

The discussion before the exercise shows that given Count-Median sketches for two streams σ_1 and σ_2, one can get information about the difference between the two streams using a two-step process. In the first step, a Count-Median sketch for $\sigma_1 \cdot \text{comp}(\sigma_2)$ is produced from the sketches for σ_1 and σ_2, and in the second step, the sketch for $\sigma_1 \cdot \text{comp}(\sigma_2)$ is used to derive an estimate for the frequency of a token t in $\sigma_1 \cdot \text{comp}(\sigma_2)$.

In this exercise, we are asked whether the same process can also be applied with the Count-Min and Count sketches. To answer this question, we first need to determine the properties of the Count-Median sketch that allow the above two steps to work. The first step relies on the fact that the Count-Median sketch is a linear sketch because this linearity is the thing that enables us to derive a sketch for the stream $\text{comp}(\sigma_2)$ from the sketch of the stream σ_2. Fortunately, both the Count-Min and Count sketches are linear, so this step can also be performed with these two sketches.

The second step relies on the fact that we can get an estimate for the frequency of tokens in the stream $\sigma_1 \cdot \text{comp}(\sigma_2)$ based on the Count-Median sketch of this stream. This is true for the Count-Median sketch because it applies to the turnstile model, and thus, can handle any stream. However, this is not generally true for a sketch that applies only to the strict turnstile model because $\sigma_1 \cdot \text{comp}(\sigma_2)$ may contain tokens with a negative frequency even when the original streams σ_1 and σ_2 do not contain such a token. Hence, the second step can be performed with the Count sketch that applies to the turnstile model, but cannot be performed with the Count-Min sketch, which applies only to the strict turnstile model.

Chapter 8

Graph Data Stream Algorithms

In the previous chapters, we have studied algorithms that considered the stream as a "collection" of abstract tokens and did not attribute any specific "meaning" to the values of the tokens. Accordingly, these algorithms estimated properties of the stream, such as the number of distinct token values, which make sense even when the token values have no meaning (the sole exception to this rule was that in some places we assumed the existence of a natural order between token values, which requires the token values to have some slight meaning).

In contrast, many known data stream algorithms have been designed for settings in which the tokens of the stream do have meaningful values. For example, the tokens can represent points in a geometric space or edges of a graph. In this chapter, we study an important class of algorithms of this kind. Specifically, we study data stream algorithms whose input is a graph given in the form of a stream of edges. Section 8.1 presents a formal description of the model in which such algorithms operate.

8.1 Graph Data Stream Algorithms

A *graph data stream algorithm* is a data stream algorithm whose input data stream consists of the edges of a graph. More formally, the tokens of the data stream are the edges of the graph, and each edge is represented in the stream as a pair of vertices (its two endpoints). To make this more concrete, consider the graph given in Figure 8.1. A data stream corresponding to this graph contains, in some arbitrary order, the tokens: $(u, v), (v, w), (u, s)$ and (v, s). One can note that the above description of

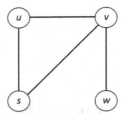

Figure 8.1.   An example of a graph.

graph data stream algorithms corresponds to the plain vanilla data stream model because we assume a single edge arrives at every time point, and additionally, edges are never removed. More general kinds of graph data stream algorithms corresponding to the other data stream models presented in Chapter 7 have also been studied, however, they are beyond the scope of this book.

As is customary with graphs, we use G, V and E to denote the graph corresponding to the input stream, its sets of vertices and its sets of edges, respectively. Additionally, we use n and m to denote the number of vertices and edges in the graph, respectively. Note that this notation is standard for graphs, but it is not consistent with the notation we have used so far in this book. For example, the length of the stream is equal to the number of edges, and is thus, given now by m; unlike in the previous chapters where we used n to denote this length (at least in the plain vanilla model). We adopt the convention that the meaning of n and m should be understood from the context. Specifically, in the context of data stream algorithms for graph problems, we assume that n and m represent the sizes of V and E, respectively, and in the context of non-graph-related data stream algorithms, we use n and m in the same way we did in the previous chapters.

We are now ready to present our first example of a graph data stream algorithm, which is an algorithm for determining whether a given graph is bipartite. This algorithm is given as Algorithm 1.

Algorithm 1 grows a forest F using the following process. Originally, F is empty. Then, every time that the algorithm gets an edge of the original graph, it adds this edge to F unless this would create a cycle in F. Observe that this construction process guarantees that F contains only edges of the original graph. While growing the forest F, the algorithm tests the original graph for bipartiteness by considering all the cycles that can be created by adding a single edge of the graph to F. If all these cycles are of even length, then the algorithm declares the graph to be bipartite. Otherwise,

---

Algorithm 1: Testing Bipartiteness

1. Let $F \leftarrow \varnothing$.
2. **while** there are more edges **do**
3.   Let (u, v) be the next edge.
4.   **if** $F \cup \{(u, v)\}$ contains an odd cycle (a cycle of an odd length) **then**
5.   **return** "The graph <u>is not</u> bipartite".
6.   **else if** $F \cup \{(u, v)\}$ does not contain a cycle **then**
7.   Update $F \leftarrow F \cup \{(u, v)\}$.
8. **return** "The graph <u>is</u> bipartite".

---

if the algorithm detects an odd cycle, then it declares the graph to be non-bipartite.

Lemma 1. *Algorithm 1 determined correctly whether its input graph G is bipartite or not.*

Proof. Recall that in a bipartite graph all the cycles are of an even length. Additionally, observe that Algorithm 1 does not declare a graph to be non-bipartite unless it finds in it an odd cycle. Combining both facts, we get that when Algorithm 1 is given a bipartite graph G, it declares G correctly to be bipartite. Thus, it remains to be proved that whenever Algorithm 1 declares that a graph G is bipartite, G is indeed bipartite.

Consider a graph G which Algorithm 1 declares to be bipartite. The forest F is clearly bipartite (all forests are bipartite), and thus, can be partitioned into two disjoint sets of vertices V_1 and V_2 such that no edge of F has its two endpoints in the same set V_1 or V_2. We will prove that this partition of the vertices is also good for showing that G is bipartite. In other words, we will show that no edge of G has its two endpoints in either V_1 or V_2. Consider an arbitrary edge $(u, v) \in E$, and let us prove that one of its endpoints belongs to V_1 and the other to V_2. If $(u, v) \in F$, then the claim follows from the definition of V_1 and V_2. Thus, we may assume that $(u, v) \notin F$. Since Algorithm 1 did not add (u, v) to F and did not declare G to be non-bipartite, $F \cup \{(u, v)\}$ must contain a (single) even cycle, which implies that F contains an odd path connecting u and v. Since every edge of F connects one vertex of V_1 and one vertex of V_2, the fact that there is an odd path from u to v implies that one of these nodes belong to V_1 and the other to V_2, which is what we needed to prove (see Figure 8.2 for a graphical illustration of this argument). $\square$

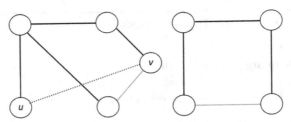

Figure 8.2. An illustration of the analysis of Algorithm 1. The black edges are the edges of F. The gray edges represent edges of G that have already arrived, but were not added to F. Finally, the dashed edge (u, v) is a new edge that has arrived now. Note that (u, v) closes an even cycle with F, and that in any presentation of F as a bipartite graph (i.e., a partitioning of its nodes into two sides with no edges within a side) u and v must appear in different sides of the graph since there is an odd length path between them.

Let us now analyze the space complexity of Algorithm 1.

Observation 1. Algorithm 1 has a space complexity of $O(n \log n)$.

Proof. Algorithm 1 keeps in its memory the edge that arrived last plus the edges of the forest F. Since a forest can contain at most $n - 1$ edges, this implies that Algorithm 1 needs only the space necessary for storing n edges. Each edge is represented using two vertices, and each one of these vertices can be represented using $O(\log n)$ space as there are only n vertices. Combining all these observations, we get that the space complexity necessary for Algorithm 1 is at most

$$n \cdot 2 \cdot O(\log n) = O(n \log n). \qquad \square$$

Note that Observation 1 does not imply that Algorithm 1 is a streaming algorithm because a data stream algorithm is a streaming algorithm only if its space complexity is polynomial in $\log n$ and $\log m$. Furthermore, one can observe that Algorithm 1 cannot be shown to be a streaming algorithm using a stronger space complexity analysis because there are many examples of graphs given which the space complexity of Algorithm 1 is indeed $\Theta(n \log n)$.

As it turns out, no algorithm can significantly improve over the space complexity of Algorithm 1 due to an impossibility result showing that any graph data stream algorithm for determining whether a graph is bipartite must use $\Omega(n)$ space. Interestingly, similar impossibility results exist for many other important graph problems. These impossibility results have led researchers to study graph data stream algorithms whose space complexity is somewhat larger than the space complexity allowed for streaming algorithms. Specifically, a lot of research has been devoted to algorithms whose space complexity is $O(n \cdot \log^c n \cdot \log^c m)$ for some constant $c \geqslant 0$. Such algorithms are known as *semi-streaming* algorithms, and they are interesting because they represent a sweet spot: on the one hand, they allow a high enough space complexity to avoid impossibility results such as the one mentioned above for the problem of determining whether a given graph is bipartite. On the other hand, they still require significantly less space than what is necessary for storing the entire input graph (assuming the graph is not too sparse, i.e., that m is not bounded by $O(n \log^c n)$ for any constant $c \geqslant 0$).[1] Since m is always upper bounded by n^2, a simpler and equivalent way to define a semi-streaming algorithm is as a graph data stream algorithm whose space complexity is $O(n \log^c n)$ for some constant $c \geqslant 0$.

The above definition of semi-streaming algorithms allows us to summarize our results for Algorithm 1 by theorem 1.

Theorem 1. *Algorithm 1 is a semi-streaming algorithm which determines correctly whether its input graph is bipartite.*

Exercise 1. Find a semi-streaming algorithm that determines whether its input graph is connected. The algorithm may assume to have prior knowledge of the vertices of the graph (note that the problem cannot be solved without this assumption because the algorithm cannot learn from the stream of edges about the vertices of the graph whose degree is 0).

8.2 Maximum Weight Matching

A particular graph problem which has been studied extensively in the context of the graph data stream model is the *maximum weight matching* problem. In this problem, the input consists of a graph with positive edge weights, and the objective is to find a matching in the graph

---

[1]The term "semi-streaming algorithm" tends to have different meanings in different contexts. For example, in some places it is used to denote any data stream algorithm whose space complexity is lower than the space complexity necessary to store the input of the algorithm, but not low enough to make it a streaming algorithm. In this book, we refer to semi-streaming algorithms only in the context of graph problems, and we stick either to the definition of semi-streaming algorithms given above or to a close variant of it described in Chapter 9.

whose weight (i.e., the total weight of the edges in it) is as large as possible.

One kind of data stream algorithms that have been developed for the maximum weight-matching problem estimates the size of the maximum weight matching, without explicitly producing any matching. Such algorithms are estimation algorithms because, like most of the algorithms we have seen so far in this book, they simply estimate some numerical value related to the stream; in this case, the weight of its maximum weight matching. We note that many estimation algorithms exist for the maximum weight matching problem, and in some cases they manage to achieve non-trivial results even using a space complexity which is low enough to make them streaming algorithms. Nevertheless, in this chapter we are interested in algorithms that do more than estimating the weight of the maximum weight matching. Specifically, we want algorithms that output a matching whose weight is close to the weight of the maximum weight matching. Such algorithms are called *approximation algorithms.* More generally, an approximation algorithm is an algorithm which given an optimization problem (such as maximum weight matching) finds a solution which approximately optimizes the objective function of the problem.

As a simple first example for an approximation algorithm, let us consider Algorithm 2. Algorithm 2 is an algorithm for the special case of maximum weight matching in which the weight of all the edges is equal to 1. In other words, in this special case the objective is to find the largest matching. We note that this special case of maximum weight matching is often called the maximum cardinality matching problem.

Algorithm 2 grows its solution matching M using the following process. Originally, M is empty. Then, whenever the algorithm gets a new edge, it adds the edge to M unless this will make M an illegal matching. Clearly, this

---

Algorithm 2: Greedy Algorithm for Maximum Cardinality Matching

1. Let $M \leftarrow \emptyset$.
2. **while** there are more edges **do**
3.   Let (u, v) be the next edge.
4.   **if** $M \cup \{(u, v)\}$ is a valid matching **then**
5.   Add (u, v) to M.
6. **return** M.

growth process guarantees that M is a legal matching when Algorithm 2 terminates. Exercise 2 analyzes the space complexity of Algorithm 2.

‖ **Exercise 2.** Prove that Algorithm 2 is a semi-streaming algorithm.

It is important to observe that one cannot expect an approximation algorithm for maximum cardinality matching to have a space complexity better than linear because at the very least such an algorithm must store its output matching. Thus, the fact that Algorithm 2 is a semi-streaming algorithm implies that it has an optimal space complexity up to a factor of $O(\log^c n)$ for some constant $c \geq 0$. The next step in the analysis of Algorithm 2 is to determine the quality of the approximation it produces, i.e., to show that the size of the matching it produces is not much smaller than the maximum size of any matching of the graph G.

Lemma 2. *Algorithm 2 produces a matching whose size is at least half the size of the largest matching of G.*

In what follows, we give the formal proof of Lemma 2. Intuitively, this formal proof is based on the observation that the matching produced by Algorithm 2 is maximal, in the sense that no edge of G can be added to it without violating feasibility. In general, it can be shown that the size of any maximal matching of a graph is at least half the size of the largest matching in the graph. However, for simplicity, we only prove this for the matching produced by Algorithm 2.

Proof. Let us now denote by M the matching produced by Algorithm 2 and by OPT an arbitrary maximum size matching of G. Consider now an arbitrary edge $e \in OPT \setminus M$. The fact that e was not added to M implies that M already contained at this point an edge e' which has a common vertex u with e. Since e' prevented the addition of e to M, we say that e' is blamed through u for the exclusion of e (see Figure 8.3 for a graphical illustration of the blame concept).

Note that the membership of e in OPT implies that no other edge of OPT can have a common vertex with e, and this has two important

Figure 8.3. An illustration of the analysis of Algorithm 2. The middle edge is an edge of M which is blamed for the exclusion of two edges of OPT (presented as dashed edges). Note that the middle edge cannot be blamed for the exclusion of any additional edges of OPT because this will require two edges of OPT to have a common vertex.

consequences: first, that e' must belong to $M \backslash OPT$, and second, that e' is not blamed through u for the exclusion of any other edge of OPT. Combining both consequences, we get that only edges of $M \backslash OPT$ can be blamed for the exclusion of edges of $OPT \backslash M$, and each such edge can be blamed for the exclusion of at most two edges of $OPT \backslash M$ (one through each one of its end points). Thus, the size of $OPT \backslash M$ is at most twice the size of $M \backslash OPT$, which implies

$$|OPT \backslash M| \leqslant 2 \cdot |M \backslash OPT| \Rightarrow |OPT| \leqslant 2 \cdot |M| . \qquad \square$$

Guarantees of a similar form to the one given by Lemma 2 appear often in the subsequent chapters of this book. Definition 1 will allow us to state them in a clearer way.

Definition 1. Given a maximization problem which has a set J of instances and a deterministic algorithm ALG for this problem, the *approximation ratio* of ALG is

$$\inf_{I \in J} \frac{ALG(I)}{OPT(I)},$$

where $ALG(I)$ is the value of the solution produced by the algorithm ALG given the instance I, and $OPT(I)$ is the value of the optimal solution for the instance I — i.e., the solution with the maximal value.

Informally, the approximation ratio of an algorithm is a number $x \in [0, 1]$ such that it is guaranteed that the value of the solution produced by the algorithm is never worse than the value of an optimal solution by more than a factor of x. Note that this implies that the closer the approximation ratio is to 1, the better it is. For example, an algorithm which always outputs an optimal solution has an approximation ratio of 1, while an algorithm whose approximation ratio is $1/2$ is only guaranteed to produce a solution whose value is at least half the value of an optimal solution. To simplify the writing, we often write that an algorithm is an x-approximation algorithm, for some $x \in [0, 1]$, instead of writing that its approximation ratio is at least x.

Recall that Lemma 2 shows that Algorithm 2 produces for every given graph (instance of the problem) a matching whose size (value) is at least half the size of the maximum size matching. By definition, this implies that the approximation ratio of Algorithm 2 is at least $1/2$; or equivalently, that Algorithm 2 is a $(1/2)$-approximation algorithm. Using this observation, we can now restate our results for Algorithm 2 by Theorem 2.

Theorem 2. *Algorithm 2 is a semi-streaming (1/2)-approximation algorithm for the maximum cardinality matching problem.*

Two remarks about the approximation ratio are now in order.

- The definition given above for the approximation ratio works only for maximization problems and deterministic algorithms. Variants of this definition for minimization problems and randomized algorithms exist as well, and we will present some of them later in this book when needed.
- Even for maximization problems and deterministic algorithms, there is an alternative (slightly different) definition of the approximation ratio which is occasionally used. Specifically, according to this alternative definition, the approximation ratio is defined as

$$\sup_{I \in J} \frac{OPT(I)}{ALG(I)}.$$

Note that this definition yields approximation ratios in the range $[1, \infty)$, which is more convenient in some cases. The two definitions, however, are very close and one can observe that the approximation ratio according to one definition is exactly the inverse of the approximation ratio according to the other definition. For example, Algorithm 2 is a 2-approximation algorithm according to the last definition. To avoid confusion, in this book we stick to the definition of the approximation ratio given by Definition 1.

Exercise 3. Above, we have shown that the approximation ratio of Algorithm 2 is at least 1/2. Prove that it is in fact equal to 1/2, i.e., find an example of an input for which Algorithm 2 produces a matching of size exactly one half of the size of the maximum size matching.

At this point, we conclude our discussion on the special case of maximum cardinality matching, and go back to the more general problem of maximum weight matching. The algorithm we study for this problem is given as Algorithm 3. Note that Algorithm 3 gets a parameter $\varepsilon \in (0, 1]$ which controls the quality of its output.

Algorithm 3 consists of two main parts. In its first part, the algorithm grows a stack of edges that are potential candidates to appear in the output, and in its second part, the algorithm creates a matching based on the edges

---

Algorithm 3: Algorithm for Maximum Weight Matching (ε)

1. Let S be an empty stack.
2. For every node $u \in V$, let $p_u \leftarrow 0$.
3. **while** there are more edges **do**
4.   Let (u, v) be the next edge, and let $w(u, v)$ be its weight.
5.   Let $w'(u, v) \leftarrow w(u, v) - p_u - p_v$.
6.   **If** $w'(u, v) \geqslant \varepsilon \cdot w(u, v)$ **then**
7.   Push (u, v) to the top of the stack S.
8.   Increase both p_u and p_v by $w'(u, v)$.
9. Let $M \leftarrow \varnothing$.
10. **while** the stack S is not empty **do**
11.   Pop an edge (u, v) from the top of the stack.
12.   **if** $M \cup \{(u, v)\}$ is a valid matching **then**
13.   Add (u, v) to M.
14. **return** M.

---

in the stack. Let us now explain each one of these parts in more detail. In the first part, the algorithm maintains for every vertex $u \in V$ a potential p_u. Originally, this potential is set to 0, and it grows as more and more edges hitting the vertex are added to the stack.[2] The algorithm then allows an edge to be added to the stack only if its weight is significantly larger than the sum of the potentials of its two endpoints. Intuitively, this makes sense because it prevents a new edge (u, v) from being added to the stack unless it is significantly heavier than edges that are already in the stack and hit either u or v. More formally, whenever Algorithm 3 gets an edge (u, v), it calculates for this edge a *residual weight* $w'(u, v)$ by subtracting the potentials of p_u and p_v from the weight of (u, v). If the residual weight is negligible compared to the original weight, then the algorithm simply discards the edge. Otherwise, the algorithm pushes the edge into the stack and increases the potentials of u and v by the edge's residual weight.

We now get to the second part of Algorithm 3, in which the algorithm creates a matching from the edges of the stack. This is done by simply popping the edges from the stack one by one, and adding any popped edge to the matching, unless this addition makes the matching illegal.

---

[2] We say that an edge *hits* a vertex if and only if it is incident to it.

Exercise 4. As given, the pseudocode of Algorithm 3 assumes prior knowledge of the set V of vertices. Can that assumption be dropped? In other words, can the algorithm be implemented without this knowledge?

Let us now begin the analysis of Algorithm 3. In this analysis, we assume that the weights of all the edges are integers in the range $[1, n^c]$ for some constant $c \geqslant 1$. Intuitively, this assumption says that no edge of the graph is extremely light compared to the maximum weight edge of the graph. One can note that this is not a very restrictive assumption since it is safe to simply ignore very light edges because they cannot contribute much to the value of the solution anyhow. Furthermore, it is in fact possible to develop this intuitive idea into a variant of Algorithm 3 which is not based on the above assumption, but we will not do that in this book.

Exercise 5. Use the above assumption to prove that the stack S maintained by Algorithm 3 contains at no time more than $O(\varepsilon^{-1} \cdot n \log n)$ edges. **Hint:** First, show that the potential p_u of a vertex u grows exponentially with the number of edges hitting u in the stack S.

Using the last exercise, we can easily upper bound the space complexity of Algorithm 3.

Corollary 1. *The space complexity of Algorithm 3 is $O(\varepsilon^{-1} \cdot n \log^2 n)$. Hence, for a constant ε it is a semi-streaming algorithm.*

Proof. Let us begin by upper bounding the space required by Algorithm 3 for storing edges. At every given time Algorithm 3 needs to keep in its memory the edges of the stack S, the edges of the matching M and potentially one more edge. According to Exercise 5, the stack S contains no more than $O(\varepsilon^{-1} \cdot n \log n)$ edges. Additionally, the matching M contains no more than $O(n)$ edges since it is a legal matching. Thus, we get that the number of edges that Algorithm 3 has to keep at every given time is upper bounded by

$$O\left(\varepsilon^{-1} \cdot n \log n\right) + O(n) + 1 = O(\varepsilon^{-1} \cdot n \log n),$$

and since each edge can be stored using $O(\log n)$ space, all these edges can be stored using a space complexity of only $O(\varepsilon^{-1} \cdot n \log^2 n)$.

In addition to the edges, Algorithm 3 also stores one more thing, which is the potentials of the vertices. One can observe that the potential of each vertex is an integer, and furthermore, it is upper bounded by the total weight of the edges hitting this vertex. Since there are at most n such edges, we get that the potential of every vertex is upper bounded by $n \cdot n^c = n^{c+1}$, and thus, can be represented using $O(\log n^{c+1}) = O(\log n)$ space. Hence, the potentials of all the vertices together require no more than $O(n \log n)$ space. □

Our next objective is to bound the approximation ratio of Algorithm 3. Observe that all the edges that end up in M come from S, and thus, it is natural to first prove that the edges of S have a large total weight. Lemma 3 proves that they even have, in fact, a large total residual weight. To state this lemma, we need some additional notation. Let $S_{m'}$ be the stack S immediately after the first m' edges have been processed by Algorithm 3, and let us denote by OPT an arbitrary maximum weight matching of G. To avoid confusion, we note that the notation $w'(u,v)$ stands for the residual weight of the edge (u,v) as calculated by Algorithm 3 when it processed this edge.

Lemma 3.

$$\sum_{(u,v) \in S_m} w'(u,v) \geqslant \frac{1-\varepsilon}{2} \cdot \sum_{(u,v) \in OPT} w(u,v).$$

Proof.   For every $0 \leqslant m' \leqslant m$, let us denote by $p_{u,m'}$ the potential of vertex u immediately after the first m' edges have been processed by (the first part of) Algorithm 3. Additionally, let $E_{m'}$ be the set of these first m' edges. We now want to prove that the following expression is a non-decreasing function of m'.

$$2 \cdot \sum_{(u,v) \in S_{m'}} w'(u,v) + \sum_{(u,v) \in OPT \setminus E_{m'}} [(1-\varepsilon) \cdot w(u,v) - (p_{u,m'} + p_{v,m'})].$$

$$(8.1)$$

Before we get to the proof of this claim, let us explain why it proves the lemma. Since the potentials all start as 0 and $S_0 = E_0 = \emptyset$, the value of (8.1) for $m' = 0$ is

$$\sum_{(u,v) \in OPT} (1-\varepsilon) \cdot w(u,v) = (1-\varepsilon) \cdot \sum_{(u,v) \in OPT} w(u,v).$$

Thus, by proving that (8.1) is a non-decreasing function of m', we will get that the value of (8.1) for $m' = m$ is lower bounded by the last expression. Since $E_m = E \supseteq OPT$, this implies

$$2 \cdot \sum_{(u,v) \in S_m} w'(u,v) \geqslant (1 - \varepsilon) \cdot \sum_{(u,v) \in OPT} w(u,v),$$

which (in its turn) implies the lemma. Thus, it remains to be proven that (8.1) is indeed a non-decreasing function of m'. Specifically, fix an arbitrary $1 \leqslant r \leqslant m$. Our objective is to prove that the value of (8.1) for $m' = r$ is at least as large as the value of (8.1) for $m' = r - 1$. Let (u_r, v_r) be the edge at place r in the stream, i.e., (u_r, v_r) is the single edge of $E_r \backslash E_{r-1}$. We now need to consider a few cases, as follows:

- **Case 1** — The first case we consider is that (u_r, v_r) does not belong to OPT, and additionally, it is not added to the stack S. In this case, $S_r = S_{r-1}$ and $OPT \backslash E_r = OPT \backslash E_{r-1}$, which together imply that the value of (8.1) is identical for both $m' = r$ and $m' = r - 1$.
- **Case 2** — The second case is that (u_r, v_r) belongs to OPT, but is not added to the stack S. In this case $S_r = S_{r-1}$ and $OPT \backslash E_r = (OPT \backslash E_{r-1}) \backslash \{(u_r, v_r)\}$, which together imply that the change in the value of (8.1) when m' is increased from $r - 1$ to r is

$$-[(1 - \varepsilon) \cdot w(u_r, v_r) - (p_{u_r, r-1} + p_{v_r, r-1})].$$

One can observe that this change is equal, by definition, to $\varepsilon \cdot w(u_r, v_r) - w'(u_r, v_r)$, and thus, it must be positive because the residual weight of an edge that is not added to the stack must be smaller than an ε fraction of its regular weight.

- **Case 3** — The third case is that (u_r, v_r) does not belong to OPT, but is added to the stack S. In this case, $S_r = S_{r-1} \cup \{(u_r, v_r)\}$, which implies that the change in the first term of (8.1) when m' is increased from $r - 1$ to r is $2 \cdot w'(u_r, v_r)$. Analyzing the change in the second term of (8.1) is more involved. Since $OPT \backslash E_r = OPT \backslash E_{r-1}$, we might be tempted to think that this term does not change. However, the fact that (u_r, v_r) is added to the stack implies that the potentials of u_r and v_r are both increased by $w'(u_r, v_r)$ when (u_r, v_r) is processed by Algorithm 3. As each one of these potentials can appear in the second term at most once (because OPT is a valid matching), we get that the decrease in the second term of (8.1) when m' is increased from $r - 1$ to

r is at most $2 \cdot w'(u_r, v_r)$. Adding all the above, we get that the total change in the value of (8.1) when m' is increased from $r - 1$ to r is non-negative in this case, too.

- **Case 4** — The final case is that (u_r, v_r) belongs to OPT, and additionally, it is added to the stack S. Like in the previous case, we again get that the change in the first term of (1) when m' is increased from $r - 1$ to r is $2 \cdot w'(u_r, v_r)$. Let us now analyze the change in the second term of (8.1). Since $OPT \backslash E_r = (OPT \backslash E_{r-1}) \backslash \{(u_r, v_r)\}$, the decrease in this term is given by $(1 - \varepsilon) \cdot w(u_r, v_r) - (p_{u_r, r-1} + p_{v_r, r-1})$. Note that this time there is no need to take into account the change in potentials following the addition of (u_r, v_r) to the stack because the value of (8.1) for $m' \geqslant r$ does not depend on the potentials of u_r and v_r (no other edge of OPT can involve these vertices). It now remains to be observed that, by definition,

$$(1 - \varepsilon) \cdot w(u_r, v_r) - (p_{u_r, r-1} + p_{v_r, r-1}) = w'(u_r, v_r) - \varepsilon \cdot w(u_r, v_r),$$

which implies that, in this case, the total change in the value of (8.1) when m' is increased from $r - 1$ to r is

$$2 \cdot w'(u_r, v_r)$$
$$-[w'(u_r, v_r) - \varepsilon \cdot w(u_r, v_r)] = w'(u_r, v_r) + \varepsilon \cdot w(u_r, v_r) \geqslant 0,$$

where the last inequality holds since the fact that (u_r, v_r) is added to the stack implies that $w'(u_r, v_r)$ is positive.   □

To prove an approximation ratio for Algorithm 3, it remains to show that the weight of its output matching M is related to the residual weights of the edges in S_m.

Lemma 4. *The weight of the output matching M is at least $\sum_{(u,v) \in S_m} w'(u, v)$.*

Proof. Consider an arbitrary edge $(u, v) \in S_m \backslash M$. The fact that (u, v) was not added to M implies that, when (u, v) was considered by Algorithm 3 for inclusion in M, there was already an edge in M which contained either u or v. Let us say that we blame (u, v) on u if there was already an edge in M which contained u. Similarly, we say that we blame (u, v) on v if there was already an edge in M which contained v (note that we might blame

(u, v) on both u and v if there were edges in M containing both of them when (u, v) was considered).

Consider now an edge $(u, v) \in M$, and let us denote by B_u and B_v the sets of edges of $S_m \setminus M$ that we blame on u and v, respectively. Clearly, both u and v did not appear in any edge of M before (u, v) was added to M. Thus, every edge of B_u and B_v (which is blamed on either u or v by definition) must appear lower in the stack S_m than the edge (u, v). As Algorithm 3 pushes edges into the stack in the order in which they arrive, this implies that the edges of $B_u \cup B_v$ arrived before (u, v). The crucial observation now is that every edge of B_u that arrived before (u, v) must have contributed to the potential of u at the moment that (u, v) arrived, and similarly, every edge of B_v that arrived before (u, v) must have contributed to the potential of v at the moment that (u, v) arrived. Thus, if we denote by p_u and p_v the potentials of u and v, respectively, at the moment that (u, v) arrived, then we get

$$p_u + p_v \geqslant \sum_{(u', v') \in B_u} w'(u', v') + \sum_{(u', v') \in B_v} w'(u', v')$$

$$\Rightarrow w(u, v) \geqslant w'(u, v) + \sum_{(u', v') \in B_u} w'(u', v') + \sum_{(u', v') \in B_v} w'(u', v'),$$

where the second line follows from the first line since $w'(u, v) = w(u, v) - p_u - p_v$. Summing up the last inequality over all the edges of M, we get

$$\sum_{(u, v) \in M} w(u, v)$$

$$\geqslant \sum_{(u, v) \in M} \left[w'(u, v) + \sum_{(u', v') \in B_u} w'(u', v') + \sum_{(u', v') \in B_v} w'(u', v') \right]$$

$$\geqslant \sum_{(u, v) \in S_m} w'(u, v).$$

where the last inequality holds due to two observations: first, that every edge of $S_m \setminus M$ must be blamed on some endpoint of an edge of M, and second, that the residual weights of edges in the stack are always positive (and so are the residual weights of the edges of M because $M \subseteq S_m$). $\square$

Combining Lemmata 3 and 4, we get that the weight of the matching produced by Algorithm 3 is at least a fraction of $(1 - \varepsilon)/2$ out of the weight of a maximum weight matching. Thus, Algorithm 3 is a $\frac{1-\varepsilon}{2}$-approximation algorithm. Theorem 3 summarizes the main properties that we have proved for Algorithm 3.

Theorem 3. *For a constant $\varepsilon \in (0,1)$, Algorithm 3 is a semi-streaming $\frac{1-\varepsilon}{2}$-approximation algorithm for the maximum weight matching problem.*

We conclude this section with two exercises extending Algorithms 2 and 3 to a generalization of graphs known as hypergraphs.

Exercise 6. A hypergraph is a generalization of a graph in which an edge may be incident to any number of vertices (rather than to exactly two, as in a graph). More formally, a hypergraph G consists of a set V of vertices and a set E of edges, where every edge $e \in E$ is a subset of V. Analogously to the case of graphs, a matching in a hypergraph is a set of edges such that the intersection of every two edges is empty (namely, the edges are pairwise disjoint as subsets of V). Additionally, for a value k, we say that a given hypergraph is k-*uniform* if all its edges are of size k (i.e., contain exactly k vertices).

In this exercise, we are interested in finding a maximum size matching in a k-uniform hypergraph. The algorithm we study for this problem is a generalization of Algorithm 2 given as Algorithm 4. Prove that this algorithm is a semi-streaming $(1/k)$-approximation algorithm for the above problem.

Algorithm 4: Greedy Algorithm for Maximum Cardinality Matching in Hypergraphs

1. Let $M \leftarrow \varnothing$.
2. **while** there are more edges **do**
3.   Let e be the next edge.
4.   **if** $M \cup \{e\}$ is a valid matching **then**
5.   Add e to M.
6. **return** M.

Algorithm 5: Algorithm for Maximum Weight Matching in Hypergraphs (ε, k)

1. Let S be an empty stack.
2. For every node $u \in V$, let $p_u \leftarrow 0$.
3. **while** there are more edges **do**
4.   Let e be the next edge, and let $w(e)$ be its weight.
5.   Let $w'(e) \leftarrow w(e) - \sum_{u \in e} p_u$.
6.   **If** $w'(e) \geqslant \varepsilon \cdot w(e)$ **then**
7.   Push e to the top of the stack S.
8.   Increase p_u by $w'(e)$ for every vertex $u \in e$.
9. Let $M \leftarrow \varnothing$.
10. **while** the stack S is not empty **do**
11.   Pop an edge e from the top of the stack.
12.   **if** $M \cup \{e\}$ is a valid matching **then**
13.   Add e to M.
14. **return** M.

Exercise 7. In this exercise, we again consider hypergraphs, however, this time we are interested in the maximum weight matching problem on k-uniform hypergraphs. The algorithm we study for this problem is a generalization of Algorithm 3 given as Algorithm 5. Prove that, for any constant integer $k \geqslant 2$ and constant $\varepsilon \in (0, 1)$, this algorithm is a semi-streaming $\frac{1-\varepsilon}{k}$-approximation algorithm for the above problem.

8.3 Triangle Counting

Another interesting graph problem is the problem of counting the number of triangles in a given graph. Algorithms for this problem are often used as tools in the study of social networks and other networks of interest. Unfortunately, it can be shown that even determining whether a given graph contains any triangles requires $\Omega(n^2)$ space in the graph data stream model. Thus, to get an interesting data stream algorithm for triangle counting, we must assume something about the input graph (more on that later in this section).

Algorithm 6: Basic Triangle Counting

1. Pick an edge (u, v) uniformly at random from the input stream.
2. Pick a vertex w uniformly at random from $V/\{u, v\}$.
3. **if** (u, w) and (w, v) both appear after (u, v) in the stream **then**
4.   Output $m(n - 2)$ as an estimate for the number of triangles in G.
5. **else**
6.   Output 0 as an estimate for the number of triangles in G.

We begin the study of the triangle counting problem with a basic algorithm which is given as Algorithm 6. In this algorithm, and in the rest of the section, we assume that the graph G contains at least 3 vertices (if it does not, then the triangle counting problem can be easily solved using constant space).

Exercise 8. As given, it is not clear that Algorithm 6 is a graph data stream algorithm. Explain how Algorithm 6 can be implemented in the graph data stream model using a space complexity of $O(\log n)$ assuming that the algorithm has prior knowledge of V (and that the space required for representing V is not counted toward the space complexity of Algorithm 6). **Hint:** Use the reservoir sampling method introduced in Chapter 4.

We begin the analysis of Algorithm 6 by showing that the expectation of its output is equal to the value that it tries to estimate, i.e., the number of triangles in the graph. Let X be the output of Algorithm 6, and let T_G be the number of triangles in the graph G.

Lemma 5. $E[X] = T_G$.

Proof. Let $T_{(u,v)}$ be the number of triangles in G whose first edge in the stream is (u, v). Since each triangle has a unique first edge in the stream,

$$T_G = \sum_{(u,v) \in E} T_{(u,v)}. \tag{8.2}$$

Let us explain now how the value of w affects the output of Algorithm 6. If there is a triangle consisting of the vertices u, v and w which is counted by $T_{(u,v)}$, then Algorithm 6 will find the edges (u, w) and (v, w) after (u, v) in the stream, and will output $m(n - 2)$. Otherwise, Algorithm 6 will not find both these edges after (u, v) in the stream, and thus, will output 0. Hence, for a fixed choice of the edge (u, v), Algorithm 6 will output $m(n - 2)$ with probability $T_{(u,v)}/|V \setminus \{u, v\}| = T_{(u,v)}/(n-2)$. More formally, for every edge $(u', v') \in E$,

$$E[X \,|\, (u, v) = (u', v')] = \frac{T_{(u',v')}}{n-2} \cdot [m(n-2)] + \left(1 - \frac{T_{(u',v')}}{n-2}\right) \cdot 0 = mT_{(u',v')}.$$

It remains to be observed that, by the law of total expectation,

$$E[X] = \sum_{(u',v') \in E} \Pr[(u, v) = (u', v')] \cdot E[X \,|\, (u, v) = (u', v')]$$

$$= \sum_{(u',v') \in E} \frac{1}{m} \cdot mT_{(u',v')} = \sum_{(u',v') \in E} T_{(u',v')} = T_G,$$

where the last equality holds by (8.2). $\qquad\square$

The next step in the analysis of Algorithm 6 is to bound the variance of its output.

Lemma 6. $\mathrm{Var}[X] \leqslant mn \cdot T_G$.

Proof. Algorithm 6 produces only two distinct outputs: 0 and $m(n-2)$. Thus, $X/[m(n-2)]$ is a Bernoulli variable. If we denote by p the probability of this variable taking the value 1, then the fact that $E[X] = T_G$ implies

$$T_G = E[X] = m(n-2) \cdot E\left[\frac{X}{m(n-2)}\right] = p[m(n-2)] \Rightarrow p = \frac{T_G}{m(n-2)}.$$

Thus,

$$\mathrm{Var}[X] = [m(n-2)]^2 \cdot \mathrm{Var}\left[\frac{X}{m(n-2)}\right] = [m(n-2)]^2 \cdot p(1-p)$$

$$\leqslant [m(n-2)]^2 \cdot p = \frac{[m(n-2)]^2 \cdot T_G}{m(n-2)} \leqslant mn \cdot T_G.$$

$\qquad\square$

One can observe that the above variance is too large to allow us to get a reasonable estimation of T_G using Algorithm 6. To solve this issue, we can use the averaging technique introduced in Chapter 3. Recall that this technique is based on executing multiple copies of Algorithm 6 and averaging their outputs. More formally, the averaging technique gives us Algorithm 7. Algorithm 7 gets two parameters: a number $\varepsilon \in (0, 1)$ and an integer $B \geqslant 0$. These parameters are used to determine the number of copies of Algorithm 6 that are used.

Algorithm 7: Averaging Multiple Copies of Algorithm 6 (ε, B)

1. Initialize $h = \lceil B/\varepsilon^2 \rceil$ copies of Algorithm 6, each using independent randomness.
2. Each time that an edge of the input stream arrives, forward it to all the copies of Algorithm 6.
3. For every $1 \leqslant i \leqslant h$, let X_i be the output of the i-th copy.
4. Return $\bar{X} = \frac{1}{h} \sum_{i=1}^{h} X_i$.

Lemma 7 uses Lemmata 5 and 6 to prove bounds on the expectation and variance of the output of Algorithm 7. Note that the expectation of the output of Algorithm 7 is identical to the expectation of the output of Algorithm 6. However, due to the use of the averaging technique, the output of Algorithm 7 enjoys a smaller variance compared to the output of Algorithm 6.

Lemma 7. $E[\bar{X}] = T_G$ and $\mathrm{Var}[\bar{X}] \leqslant \frac{\varepsilon^2 \cdot mn \cdot T_G}{B}$.

Proof. By the properties of the expectation and Lemma 5,

$$E\left[\bar{X}\right] = E\left[\frac{1}{h} \cdot \sum_{i=1}^{h} X_i\right] = \frac{1}{h} \cdot \sum_{i=1}^{h} E\left[X_i\right] = \frac{1}{h} \cdot \sum_{i=1}^{h} T_G = T_G.$$

Similarly, since the variables $X_1, X_2, \ldots, X_h$ are independent, we get by the properties of the variance and Lemma 6,

$$\mathrm{Var}\left[\bar{X}\right] = \mathrm{Var}\left[\frac{1}{h} \cdot \sum_{i=1}^{h} X_i\right] = \frac{1}{h^2} \cdot \sum_{i=1}^{h} \mathrm{Var}\left[X_i\right] \leqslant \frac{1}{h^2} \cdot \sum_{i=1}^{h} (mn \cdot T_G)$$

$$= \frac{mn \cdot T_G}{h} = \frac{mn \cdot T_G}{\lceil B/\varepsilon^2 \rceil} \leqslant \frac{\varepsilon^2 \cdot mn \cdot T_G}{B}. \qquad \square$$

Corollary 2. *Algorithm 7 estimates the number of triangles T_G up to a relative error of ε with probability at least $1 - mn/(B \cdot T_G)$.*

Proof. By Chebyshev's inequality,

$$\Pr\left[\,\left|\bar{X} - T_G\right| > \varepsilon \cdot T_G\right] = \Pr\left[\,\left|\bar{X} - E\left[\bar{X}\right]\right| > \varepsilon \cdot T_G\right]$$

$$\leqslant \frac{\mathrm{Var}\left[\bar{X}\right]}{(\varepsilon \cdot T_G)^2} \leqslant \frac{\varepsilon^2 \cdot mn \cdot T_G/B}{\varepsilon^2 \cdot T_G^2} = \frac{mn}{B \cdot T_G}. \qquad \square$$

Let us give the last corollary an intuitive meaning. This corollary states that when we are given a bound B such that we are guaranteed that the number of triangles in G is large enough to make mn/T_G at most $B/3$, then Algorithm 7 is guaranteed to estimate the number of triangles up to a relative error ε with probability at least $2/3$. In other words, if we think of all the graphs that have enough triangles to guarantee $mn/T_G \leqslant B/3$ as a class of graphs parametrized by B, then Corollary 2 states that Algorithm 7 produces a good estimate for the number of triangles with a constant probability when the graph belongs to this class of graphs. Note that this corresponds well with the beginning of this section, where we learned that obtaining an estimate for the number of triangles in a graph using a non-trivial space requires us to assume something on the graph (for example, that it belongs to some class of graphs).

Observe that increasing the value of the parameter B extends the class of graphs for which Corollary 2 guarantees a good estimate (with constant probability). However, there is a cost for this increase in the form of a larger space complexity.

Exercise 9. Prove that the space complexity of Algorithm 7 is $O((n + \varepsilon^{-2}B) \cdot \log n)$.

Theorem 4 summarizes the results that we have proved in this section.

Theorem 4. *For every integer value* $B \geqslant 1$, *Algorithm 7 is an* $O((n + \varepsilon^{-2}B) \cdot \log n)$ *space algorithm that estimates the number of triangles up to a relative error of* ε *with probability at least* $2/3$ *when the input graph is guaranteed to have enough triangles to obey*

$$B \geqslant \frac{3mn}{T_G}.$$

Two remarks about Algorithm 7 are now in place.

- When T_G is large enough, Algorithm 7 estimates it with a constant probability of $2/3$. This probability can be improved to $1 - \delta$, for every $\delta \in (0, 1)$, using the median technique, at the cost of increasing the space complexity of Algorithm 7 by a factor of $O(\log \delta^{-1})$. As the median technique has been demonstrated multiple times in previous chapters, we omit the details. However, if you are not sure how to apply the median technique here, we encourage you to reread about the median technique in Chapter 3.

- The trivial algorithm for triangle counting stores the entire graph, which requires a space complexity of $\Theta(m \log n)$. Hence, Algorithm 7 is only interesting when B is much smaller than m; which is equivalent to saying that Algorithm 7 is only interesting when we are guaranteed that the number of triangles in G is much larger than n.

8.4 Bibliographic Notes

The graph data stream model (and, in particular, the study of semi-streaming algorithms in this model) has been popularized by a work of Feigenbaum *et al.* (2005), although some work on this model has been done earlier. As explained above, one of the main motivations for the study of semi-streaming algorithms is the existence of impossibility results showing that many simple graph problems require $\Omega(n)$ space. For example, Feigenbaum *et al.* (2005) proved that this amount of space is necessary for a large class of graph problems, including the problems of determining whether a given graph is connected or bipartite. Semi-streaming algorithms for both these problems can be found in Feigenbaum *et al.* (2005).

The trivial greedy algorithm given above as Algorithm 2 is still the best-known single-pass semi-streaming approximation algorithm for the maximum cardinality matching problem. However, many single-pass semi-streaming approximation algorithms have been suggested for the maximum weight matching problem over the years. The first of these algorithms was a $(1/6)$-approximation algorithm given by the works of Feigenbaum *et al.* (2005). The approximation ratio obtained by this algorithm was improved by a long series of works due to (McGregar, 2014; Zelke, 2012; Epstein *et al.*, Croud and Stubbs, 2014; Grigorescu *et al.*, 2016) culminating with the work of Paz and Schwartzman (2017) which described a $(1/2 - \varepsilon)$-approximation algorithm for the problem (Algorithm 3 is a close variant of this algorithm). Further improving the approximation ratio for the maximum weight matching problem is considered a very difficult problem as it will induce a better approximation ratio also for maximum cardinality matching — a problem which still does not admit any non-trivial semi-streaming algorithm despite being the focus of much research. It should be pointed out that the above-mentioned references are only a little part of a large body of literature on various questions related to matching problems in the data stream models. Doing justice with all this body of literature is beyond the scope of these bibliographic notes, but a lot of information about it can be found in a (slightly outdated) survey by McGregor (2014).

The study of the triangle counting problem in the context of the data stream model started with the work of Bar-Yossef *et al.* (2002). In particular, this work proved that any algorithm that determines with a constant probability (larger than $1/2$) whether a given graph contains any triangles must use $\Omega(n^2)$ space. The algorithm given in this chapter for triangle counting (Algorithm 7) was first described in a later work by Buriol *et al.* (2006).

Z. Bar-Yossef, R. Kumar and D. Sivakumar. Reductions in Streaming Algorithms, with an Application to Counting Triangles in Graphs. In *Proceedings of the 30th Annual ACM-SIAM Symposium on Discrete Algorithms (SODA)*, 623–632, January 2002.

L. S. Buriol, G. Frahling, S. Leonardi, A. Marchetti-Spaccamela and C. Sohler. Counting Triangles in Data Streams. In *Proceedings of the 21st ACM SIGACT-SIGMOD-SIGART Symposium on Principles of Database Systems (PODS)*, 253–262, June 2006.

M. Crouch and D. S. Stubbs. Improved Streaming Algorithms for Weighted Matching, via Unweighted Matching. In *17th International Workshop on Approximation Algorithms for Combinatorial Optimization Problems (APPROX), and 18th International Workshop on Randomization and Computation (RANDOM)*, 96–104, September 2014.

L. Epstein, A. Levin, J. Mestre and D. Segev. Improved Approximation Guarantees for Weighted Matching in the Semi-streaming Model. *SIAM Journal on Discrete Mathematics*, 25(3): 1251–1264, 2011.

J. Feigenbaum, S. Kannan, A. McGregor, S. Suri and J. Zhang. Graph Distances in the Data-Stream Model. *SIAM Journal on Computing*, 38(5): 1709–1727, 2008.

J. Feigenbaum, S. Kannan, A. McGregor, S. Suri and J. Zhang. On Graph Problems in a Semi-streaming Model. *Theoretical Computer Science*, 348(2-3): 207–216, 2005.

E. Grigorescu, M. Monemizadeh and S. Zhou. Streaming Weighted Matchings: Optimal Meets Greedy. CoRR abs/1608.01487, 2016.

A. McGregor. Finding Graph Matchings in Data Streams. In *8th International Workshop on Approximation Algorithms for Combinatorial Optimization Problems (APPROX), and 9th International Workshop on Randomization and Computation (RANDOM)*, 170–181, 2005.

A. McGregor. Graph Stream Algorithms: A Survey. *SIGMOD Record*, 43(1): 9–20, 2014.

A. Paz and G. Schwartzman. A $(2 + \varepsilon)$-Approximation for Maximum Weight Matching in the Semi-Streaming Model. In *Proceedings of the 28th Annual ACM-SIAM Symposium on Discrete Algorithms (SODA)*, 2153–2161, 2017.

M. Zelke. Weighted Matching in the Semi-streaming Model. *Algorithmica*, 62(1-2): 1–20, 2012.

Exercise Solutions

Solution 1

The algorithm we suggest for determining whether a graph is connected is given as Algorithm 8. Note that this algorithm indeed assumes knowledge of the set V of vertices as suggested by the exercise.

The main data structure maintained by Algorithm 8 is the collection C. Observation 2 gives an important property of C. Formally, this observation can be proved using induction on m'.

Observation 2. Let m' be an integer between 0 and m, let $G_{m'}$ be the graph obtained from G by dropping all edges except for the first m' edges of the stream and let $C_{m'}$ be the collection C after Algorithm 8 processes m' edges. Then, the sets in the collection $C_{m'}$ correspond to the connected components of $G_{m'}$. More formally, there is a one-to-one mapping between sets of $C_{m'}$ and connected components of $G_{m'}$ such that each connected component of $G_{m'}$ is mapped to a set in $C_{m'}$ containing exactly the vertices of this connected component.

We now claim that Observation 2 implies that Algorithm 8 decides correctly whether G is a connected graph. To see why that is the case, note that by Observation 2 the size of the collection C_m is equal to the number of connected components in $G_m = G$. Thus, G is connected if and only if C_m contains only one set. Since C_m is the final value of the collection

---

Algorithm 8: Testing Connectedness

1. Let $C \leftarrow \{\{v\} | v \in V\}$.
2. **while** there are more edges **do**
3.   Let (u, v) be the next edge.
4.   Let C_u and C_v be sets in C containing u and v, respectively.
5.   **if** $C_u \neq C_v$ **then**
6.   Remove C_u and C_v from C and add $C_u \cup C_v$ to C instead.
7. Declare the graph to be connected if $|C| = 1$, and unconnected otherwise

C, one can determine the connectivity of G by checking whether the final collection C has only one set, which is exactly the test used by Algorithm 8 to determine its output.

To complete the answer for the exercise, it only remains to be shown that Algorithm 8 is a semi-streaming algorithm. Towards this goal, note that Algorithm 8 only needs enough space to maintain the current edge, the collection C of nodes and the two pointers C_u and C_v into this collection. The current edge is represented using two vertices, and Observation 2 implies that the total size of the sets in C is always exactly n. Thus, the collection and the edge together require only enough space to store $O(n)$ vertices. As there are n vertices, each vertex can be represented using $O(\log n)$ space, which implies that the space complexity of the collection and the edge together is only

$$O(n) \cdot O(\log n) = O(n \log n).$$

The space complexity necessary for the two pointers C_u and C_v remains to be analyzed. By Observation 2, the collection C contains at most n sets at every given time. Thus, each pointer to one of these sets requires only $O(\log n)$ bits. Combining all these space bounds, we get that the space complexity required for the entire Algorithm 8 is

$$O(n \log n) + 2 \cdot O(\log n) = O(n \log n),$$

which means that Algorithm 8 is indeed a semi-streaming algorithm, as required.

Solution 2

Algorithm 2 has to store only two things: the current edge and the matching M. Since M is a legal matching, it contains at most $n/2$ edges. Moreover, since any edge is represented using two vertices, we get that the space complexity of Algorithm 2 is upper bounded by the space necessary for storing $2(n/2 + 1) = n + 2 = O(n)$ vertices. Recall that each vertex can be represented using a space of $O(\log n)$ because there are only n vertices, which implies that the space complexity of Algorithm 2 is

$$O(n) \cdot O(\log n) = O(n \log n).$$

Thus, Algorithm 2 is indeed a semi-streaming algorithm.

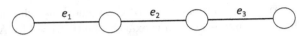

Figure 8.4. A graph showing that the approximation ratio of Algorithm 2 is not better than 1/2.

Solution 3

Consider the graph given in Figure 8.4. Clearly, the maximum size matching in this graph consists of the edges e_1 and e_3. However, if the edge e_2 appears first in the input stream, then Algorithm 2 will add it to its output matching M, which will prevent any other edge from being added to M later. Hence, we have found an input for which the ratio between the size of the matching produced by Algorithm 2 (which is 1) and the size of the largest possible matching (which is 2) is 1/2, as required.

Solution 4

The pseudocode of Algorithm 3 assumes prior knowledge of the set V of vertices only for the purpose of initializing the potentials of all the vertices to 0. However, in an implementation this can be done implicitly. In other words, an implementation of the algorithm can check every time before accessing the potential of a vertex if this potential was set before, and treat the potential as 0 if the answer is negative (i.e., the potential was never set before). Thus, Algorithm 3 can be implemented without assuming prior knowledge of V. Note that the algorithm learns, however, the non-isolated vertices of V since these vertices appear inside the edges that the algorithm gets during its execution.

Solution 5

Following the hint, we first prove Lemma 8.

Lemma 8. *Let S_u be the number of edges hitting u in the stack S. Then, $S_u \geqslant 1$ implies $p_u \geqslant (1 + \varepsilon)^{S_u - 1}$.*

Proof. We prove the lemma by induction on S_u. First, assume $S_u = 1$. In this case, the stack S contains a single edge (u, v) hitting u. When this edge was added to the stack, the potential p_u was increased by an amount equal to the residual weight $w'(u, v)$. Moreover, since the edge was added to the stack, this residual weight was at least a fraction of ε of the original weight of the edge. Finally, we can observe that residual weights and potentials are always integrals. Combining all these observations, we get

$$p_u \geqslant w'(u,v) \geqslant \lceil \varepsilon \cdot w\,(u,v) \rceil \geqslant \lceil \varepsilon \cdot 1 \rceil = 1 = (1+\varepsilon)^{S_u-1}.$$

Assume now that $S_u > 1$ and that the lemma holds for $S_u - 1$, and let us prove it for S_u. Let (u,v) be the last edge hitting u that was added to the stack S. Before (u,v) was added, the stack contained $S_u - 1$ edges hitting u, and thus, by the induction hypothesis, the potential of u at this point (which we denote by p'_u) was at least $(1+\varepsilon)^{S_u-2}$. Additionally, since (u,v) was added to the stack, we get

$$w'(u,v) \geqslant \varepsilon \cdot w(u,v) \Rightarrow w\,(u,v) - p'_u \geqslant \varepsilon \cdot w\,(u,v)$$
$$\Rightarrow p'_u \leqslant (1-\varepsilon) \cdot w\,(u,v) \leqslant w\,(u,v).$$

Recalling that the addition of (u,v) to the stack increases the potential of u by $w'(u,v)$, we conclude that the new potential of u after the addition of (u,v) to the stack is at least

$$p'_u + w'\,(u,v) \geqslant p'_u + \varepsilon \cdot w\,(u,v) \geqslant p'_u\,(1+\varepsilon)$$
$$\geqslant (1+\varepsilon)^{S_u-2} \cdot (1+\varepsilon) = (1+\varepsilon)^{S_u-1}.$$

$\square$

It remains to derive from Lemma 8 an upper bound on the number of edges that can appear in the stack S. Consider an arbitrary vertex $u \in V$, and assume towards a contradiction that S contains at some point more than $\log_{1+\varepsilon} n^c + 2$ edges hitting u (recall that n^c is an upper bound on the weight of any given edge). Lemma 8 guarantees that even before the last of these edges was added to S, the potential of u was at least

$$(1+\varepsilon)^{\log_{1+\varepsilon} n^c} = n^c.$$

As the weight of all edges, including (u,v), is at most n^c, this implies that the residual weight of (u,v) is non-positive, which contradicts the fact that (u,v) was add to the stack. As a consequence of this contradiction, we get that the number of edges in the stack hitting every given vertex is at most $\log_{1+\varepsilon} n^c + 2$. Moreover, since there are n vertices, and each edge must hit two of them, we also get the following upper bound on the number of edges in the stack.

$$\frac{n \cdot \left(\log_{1+\varepsilon} n^c + 2\right)}{2} = \frac{n \cdot \ln n^c}{2\ln\,(1+\varepsilon)} + n \leqslant \frac{n \cdot \ln n^c}{\varepsilon} + n = O\left(\varepsilon^{-1} \cdot n \log n\right).$$

Solution 6

Let us begin the solution for this exercise by proving that Algorithm 4 is a semi-streaming algorithm. Algorithm 4 has to store only two things: the current edge and the matching M. Since M is a legal matching, it contains at most n/k edges (each edge of M includes k vertices, and no vertex can belong to more than one edge in a legal matching). Moreover, since any edge is represented using k vertices, we get that the space complexity of Algorithm 2 is upper bounded by the space necessary for storing $k(n/k + 1) = n + k = O(n)$ vertices. Recall that each vertex can be represented using a space of $O(\log n)$ because there are only n vertices, which implies that the space complexity of Algorithm 2 is

$$O(n) \cdot O(\log n) = O(n \log n).$$

Thus, Algorithm 2 is indeed a semi-streaming algorithm.

To complete the solution for the exercise, we still need to show that the size of M is at least $1/k$ of the size of the largest matching in the hypergraph. Let us denote by OPT the last matching, and consider now an arbitrary edge $e \in OPT \backslash M$. The fact that e was not added to M implies that M already contained at this point an edge e' which has a common vertex u with e. Since e' prevented the addition of e to M, we say that e' is blamed through u for the exclusion of e.

Note that the membership of e in OPT implies that no other edge of OPT can have a common vertex with e, and this has two important consequences: first, that e' must belong to $M \backslash OPT$, and second, that e' is not blamed through u for the exclusion of any other edge of OPT. Combining both consequences, we get that only edges of $M \backslash OPT$ can be blamed for the exclusion of edges of $OPT \backslash M$, and each such edge can be blamed for the exclusion of at most k edges of $OPT \backslash M$ (one through each one of its end points). Thus, the size of $OPT \backslash M$ is at most k times the size of $M \backslash OPT$, which implies

$$|OPT \backslash M| \leqslant k \cdot |M \backslash OPT| \Rightarrow |OPT| \leqslant k \cdot |M|.$$

Solution 7

The analysis of Algorithm 5 is very similar to the analysis of Algorithm 3, and therefore, we concentrate here only on the places in the analyses where they differ.

We begin with the analysis of the space complexity of Algorithm 5. One can verify that the result given by Exercise 5 — i.e., that the number of edges in the stack S is never larger than $O(\varepsilon^{-1} \cdot n \log n)$ — holds for Algorithm 5 as well. Moreover, the same applies also to the part of the proof of Corollary 1 using this result to show that Algorithm 5 has to maintain at every given time at most $O(\varepsilon^{-1} \cdot n \log n)$ edges. We now note that every edge consists of k vertices and a weight. Moreover, each vertex can be represented using $O(\log n)$ space since there are only n vertices, and each weight can also be represented using $O(\log n^c) = O(\log n)$ space since we assume that the weights are integers between 1 and n^c (for a constant c). Thus, each edge can be represented using a space of $(k + 1) \cdot O(\log n) = O(\log n)$, which implies that the total space required by Algorithm 5 for storing edges is only $O(\varepsilon^{-1} \cdot n \log^2 n)$.

In addition to the edges, Algorithm 5 also stores one more thing, which is the potentials of the vertices. One can observe that the potential of each vertex is an integer, and furthermore, it is upper bounded by the total weight of the edges hitting this vertex. Since there are at most n^{k-1} such edges, we get that the potential of every vertex is upper bounded by $n^{k-1} \cdot n^c = n^{c+k-1}$, and thus, can be represented using $O(\log n^{c+k-1}) = O(\log n)$ space. Hence, the potentials of all the vertices together require no more than $O(n \log n)$ space. This completes the proof that Algorithm 5 is a semi-streaming algorithm (for constant ε and k).

The next step in the analysis of Algorithm 5 is to prove an analog for Lemma 3. Specifically, we prove Lemma 9.

Lemma 9. $\sum_{e \in S_m} w'(e) \geqslant \frac{1-\varepsilon}{k} \cdot \sum_{e \in OPT} w(e)$.

Proof. Recall that the proof of Lemma 3 is done by arguing that (1) is a non-decreasing function of m'. The proof of this lemma follows in the same way from the claim that the next expression is non-decreasing (recall that $p_{u,m'}$ is the potential of vertex u after the algorithm has processed the first m' edges and $E_{m'}$ is the set of these first m' edges).

$$k \cdot \sum_{e \in S_{m'}} w'(u,v) + \sum_{e \in OPT \setminus E_{m'}} \left[(1 - \varepsilon) \cdot w(u,v) - \sum_{u \in e} p_{u,m'} \right].$$

To prove this claim, we need to use the same partition into four cases used in the proof of Lemma 3. As the proofs of the individual cases here are identical (up to some technical changes) to the proofs of the corresponding cases in the proof of Lemma 3, we omit them. □

We also need the following analog for Lemma 4. The proof of this analog differs from the proof of Lemma 4 only in some technical details.

Lemma 10. *The weight of the output matching M is at least* $\sum_{e \in S_m} w'(e)$.

Combining Lemmata 9 and 10, we get that the weight of the matching produced by Algorithm 5 is at least a fraction of $(1 - \varepsilon)/k$ out of the weight of a maximum weight matching. Thus, Algorithm 5 is a $\frac{1-\varepsilon}{k}$-approximation algorithm, which completes the solution for the exercise.

Solution 8

Assume first that we are given a magical helper that selects a uniformly random edge from the stream and signals when this edge arrives. It is not difficult to see that given such a helper Algorithm 6 can be implemented as a graph data stream algorithm. Specifically, we use the edge selected by the helper to implement Line 1 of the algorithm, i.e., to sample a uniformly random edge (u, v). Since the helper signals its choice as soon as (u, v) arrives, we can also select at this point a vertex $w \in V \setminus \{u, v\}$, and then scan the rest of the stream for the edges (u, w) and (v, w) whose presence or absence from the part of the stream appearing after (u, v) determines Algorithm 6's output.

Unfortunately, we do not have such a magical helper. Instead, we can use a reservoir sampling algorithm to implement Line 1 of Algorithm 6. The difference between a reservoir sampling algorithm and the above magical helper is that the reservoir sampling algorithm maintains a sample that changes occasionally over time. More specifically, every time that the reservoir sampling algorithm receives an edge, it decides with some probability to make this edge the new sample, and the final output of the algorithm is the last edge that was made into a sample this way. This means that we can never be sure (before the stream terminates) whether the current sample of the reservoir sampling algorithm will be replaced with a new edge later on or will end up as the output sample.

To solve this issue, every time after the reservoir sampling algorithm selects a new edge as its sample, Algorithm 6 should assume that this edge is the final sample and continue executing based on this assumption. If this assumption turns out to be false (i.e., the reservoir sampling algorithm picks a new edge as its sample at a later stage), then Algorithm 6 can simply discard everything that it did based on the previous sample, and again start assuming that the new sample is the final edge (u, v).

Recall that the reservoir sampling algorithm stores only the length of the stream and a constant number of tokens (i.e., edges) at every given time.

The length of the stream is m, and thus, can be stored using $O(\log m) = O(\log n^2) = O(\log n)$ space. Moreover, storing each edge can be done by storing its two endpoints, which again requires $O(\log n)$ space. Hence, the space complexity necessary for the reservoir sampling algorithm is only $O(\log n)$. In addition to the space required for this algorithm, Algorithm 6 requires only $O(\log n)$ additional space for storing the three vertices u, v and w and the values of the parameters m and n. Thus, we can conclude that Algorithm 6 can be implemented as a graph data stream algorithm using $O(\log n)$ space.

Solution 9

Algorithm 7 uses h copies of Algorithm 6. Each one of these copies can be implemented using a space complexity of $O(\log n)$ by Exercise 8 assuming prior knowledge of V, but without taking into account the space necessary for representing V. The total space complexity required for all these copies is

$$h \cdot O(\log n) = O(B/\varepsilon^2) \cdot O(\log n) = O(\varepsilon^{-2} B \cdot \log n).$$

Adding the space necessary for representing V, which is $O(n \log n)$, we get that the total space complexity necessary for Algorithm 7 is $O((n + \varepsilon^{-2} B) \cdot \log n)$.

Chapter 9

The Sliding Window Model

While presenting the data stream model in Chapter 1, we explained it using two examples. In one example, the input for the algorithm appeared on a magnetic tape which can be efficiently accessed only in a sequential manner. In this example, the reason that we got the input in the form of a data stream is technical (it is the only way to efficiently read the input), and has nothing to do with the nature of the problem that the algorithm tried to solve. The other motivating example in Chapter 1 was a network monitoring element which views the packets going through the network, and has to perform certain calculations based on these packets. For example, the monitoring element might have to raise the alarm if it detects malicious network activity. Note that in this example the fact that the monitoring element receives the packets in the form of a data stream is a natural consequence of the nature of the problem itself. In other words, the input for this problem consists of a set of "events" (each event is the pass of a single packet through the network), and the stream contains these events in the order in which they occurred.

In problems of the last kind, events that happened long ago are usually not important for the decisions that the algorithm has to make at the current point. For example, it is unlikely that we need access to packets that passed through the network a year ago to make a decision regarding the current existence of malicious activity in the network. This means that for problems of this kind, we can assume that we receive an infinite stream and must make a decision at every given time based only on the recent tokens (or events) that appeared in the stream. In Section 9.1, we describe the *sliding window model*, which is a formal model capturing the above point of view.

9.1 The Sliding Window Model

An algorithm for the sliding window model (also known as a *sliding window algorithm*) receives a data stream and a *window length* parameter which we denote by W. At every given time point, the *active window* of the algorithm contains the last W tokens that arrived in the stream (if less than W tokens arrived so far, all of them are considered to be part of the active window). The algorithm should treat the content of its active window as its input instance, and must be ready to produce a solution corresponding to this instance when asked. A toy example of a sliding window algorithm is given as Algorithm 1. This algorithm determines whether the sequence consisting of the token "a" followed by the token "b" appears inside its active window.

Algorithm 1: Sliding Window Algorithm for Detecting "ab"

Initialization

1. *LastAppearance* ← "*Never*"
2. *LastTokenWasA* ← "*False*"

Token Processing

3. Every time that a token t arrives do:
4.   **if** $t =$ 'b' and *LastTokenWasA* = "*True*" **then** *LastAppearance* ← 0.
5.   **else if** *LastAppearance* $= W - 2$ **then** *LastAppearance* ← *Never*.
6.   **else if** *LastAppearance* $\neq$ "*Never*" **then** Increase *LastAppearance* by 1.
7.   Set *LastTokenWasA* to "*True*" if $t =$ 'a', and to "*False*" otherwise.

Query

8.   **If** *LastAppearance* = "*Never*" **then**
9.   **return** "ab" does not appear in the active window.
10. **else**
11.   **return** "ab" appears in the active window.

It is natural to present a sliding window algorithm as consisting of three parts. The first part is an initialization part that sets up the data structure used by the algorithm. In the case of Algorithm 1, this data structure consists of two variables. The first variable is called *LastAppearance*, and it stores the number of tokens that have arrived since the last appearance of the sequence "*ab*" in the active window (or the value "*Never*" if this sequence does not appear in the current active window). The second variable kept by Algorithm 1 is called *LastTokenWasA*, and it indicates whether the last token viewed by the algorithm was "*a*".

The second part of a sliding window algorithm is a token processing part in which the algorithm reads the tokens of the stream and updates its data structure accordingly. In the case of Algorithm 1, this part of the algorithm updates the two variables maintained by the algorithm as follows: first, it updates the *LastAppearance* variable in one of the following two ways:

- If the new token is "*b*" and the last token was "*a*", then the algorithm has detected a new appearance of "*ab*" in the active window, which implies that zero tokens have arrived since the last appearance of this sequence.
- Otherwise, the algorithm either increases the *LastAppearance* by 1 to indicate that one more token has arrived after the last appearance of the sequence "*ab*", or set it to "*Never*" if so many tokens have arrived since this last appearance that the sequence "*ab*" is not part of the active window anymore.

Finally, the token processing part of Algorithm 1 updates *LastTokenWasA* to indicate whether the newly read token was "*a*" or not.

The third and final part of a sliding window algorithm is a query part that should produce the appropriate answer for the instance represented by the active window. For example, Algorithm 1 answers whether the sequence "*ab*" appears in the input stream by checking the value of the variable *LastAppearance*.

Exercise 1. Execute Algorithm 1 on the input stream "*aababaab*" with the window length $W = 3$. Note that this means first executing the initialization part of the algorithm, and then executing the token processing part for each one of the tokens of the stream in order. Verify that at every given point, the query part of the algorithm can be used to determine correctly whether the sequence "*ab*" appears in the current active window.

Before concluding this section, we note that since Algorithm 1 is a toy algorithm, we did not discuss its space complexity, and more generally, we did not discuss the space complexity that we expect from a good sliding window algorithm. We defer the last discussion to Section 9.2, in which we will see our first non-toy example of a sliding window algorithm.

9.2 Graph Connectivity in the Sliding Window Model

We are now ready to present our first non-toy example of an algorithm for the sliding window model. Algorithm 2 is a sliding window algorithm that gets a stream of edges, and its objective is to determine whether the graph induced by the edges in its active window is connected. We assume that Algorithm 2 has prior knowledge of the set V of vertices. Recall that without such prior knowledge one cannot determine whether a graph is connected or not because it is not possible to learn from the stream of edges about vertices of degree zero.

Algorithm 2 maintains a forest F of edges from the active window. Every time that a new edge arrives, it is added to F. This addition might

---

Algorithm 2: Testing Connectedness in the Sliding Window Model

<u>Initialization</u>

1. Let F be a forest over the vertices of V having no edges.

<u>Token Processing</u>

2. Every time that an edge (u, v) arrives do:
3.   Add (u, v) to the forest F.
4.   **if** F contains now a cycle $C_{(u,v)}$ **then**
5.   Remove from F the oldest edge of $C_{(u,v)}$ to make it a forest again.
6.   Remove from F edges that are no longer inside the active window.

<u>Query</u>

7.   **If** F is connected **then**
8.   **return** "the active window induces a connected graph".
9.   **else**
10.   **return** "the active window <u>does not</u> induce a connected graph".

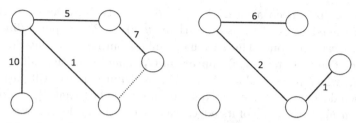

Figure 9.1. An update performed by Algorithm 2 following the arrival of a single edge. On the left side we see the forest F before the processing of the new edge (the new edge appears in it as a dashed line). Beside each edge of F we have number indicating its age (the last edge that arrived has an age of 1, the edge that arrived before it has an age of 2, and so on). We assume in this example that $W = 10$, hence, the edge marked with the age 10 is about to leave the active window. On the right side we see the forest F after the processing of the new edge. The addition of the new edge to F created a cycle, which forced Algorithm 2 to remove the oldest edge of this cycle. Additionally, the age of all the edges increased by 1, which means that the edge whose age used to be 10 is no longer part of the active window, and has been, thus, removed.

create a cycle in the forest F, which is fixed by the removal of a single edge from this cycle. The removed edge is chosen as the oldest edge of the cycle. Additionally, edges of F that are no longer part of the active window (i.e., are too old) also get removed from the forest. See Figure 9.1 for a graphical illustration of the changes made in F during the processing of a new edge.

Lemma 1. *At every given point, Algorithm 2 answers correctly (if queried) whether the graph induced by the edges in its active window is connected.*

Proof. Let G_m be the graph induced by the edges of the active window after Algorithm 2 has processed m edges (for some positive integer m), and let F_m be the forest F at this point. Observe that the forest F_m solely consists of edges of G_m. Thus, when F_m is connected, so must be G_m. To complete the proof of the lemma, we have to also prove the other direction, i.e., that F_m is connected whenever G_m is connected. To show that, we prove by induction on m the stronger claim that for every edge (u, v) in G_m there must be a path $P_{(u,v)}$ in F_m between u and v such that none of the edges of $P_{(u,v)}$ is older than (i.e., arrived before) the edge (u, v).

For $m = 0$ this claim is trivial since G_m contains no edges. Assume now that the claim holds for G_{m-1}, and let us prove it for G_m. Consider an arbitrary edge (u, v) of G_m. If (u, v) is a new edge that did not appear in G_{m-1}, then we can choose the path $P_{(u,v)}$ as the edge (u, v) itself because a new edge is always added to F. Otherwise, by the induction hypothesis, there must have been a path $P'_{(u,v)}$ in F_{m-1} between u and v such that none of the edges of $P'_{(u,v)}$ is older than (u,v). If $P'_{(u,v)}$ appears in F_m as well, then we are done. Thus, let us assume from now on that this is not the case. The fact that (u,v) appears in G_m guarantees that all the edges of $P'_{(u,v)}$, which are not older than (u,v) by definition, are still part of the active window. Thus, the only explanation for the fact that $P'_{(u,v)}$ does not appear in F_m is that one of its edges was part of the cycle that was created when edge number m of the stream arrived.

Let us denote this edge (i.e., edge number m of the stream) by (u',v'). Additionally, let $C_{(u',v')}$ denote the cycle that was created when (u',v') was added to F, and let (u_R, v_R) denote the edge of $P'_{(u,v)}$ that belongs also to $C_{(u',v')}$ and was removed following the arrival of (u',v'). Since Algorithm 2 removes the oldest edge of the cycle, (u_R, v_R) must be the oldest edge of $C_{(u',v')}$. Thus, $C_{(u',v')} \setminus \{(u_R, v_R)\}$ is a path between u_R and v_R in G_m such that all the edges in this path are younger than (u_R, v_R), and thus, also younger than (u,v). Adding this path to $P'_{(u,v)}$ instead of the edge (u_R, v_R) creates a new path between u and v which appears in F_m and contains only edges that are not older than (u,v), which completes the proof of the lemma (see Figure 9.2 for a graphical illustration). $\square$

After proving that Algorithm 2 works correctly, let us now discuss its time and space efficiency. We begin with the study of the token processing time of Algorithm 2 (the time used by Algorithm 2 to process a single edge). This time strongly depends on the data structures we use to handle two main tasks. The first task is updating the forest F, which includes: adding the new edge to the forest, detecting the cycle that is created (if it exists), finding the oldest edge of the cycle, removing the oldest edge of the cycle

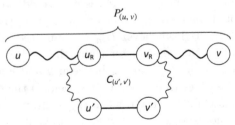

Figure 9.2.   Illustration of the construction of the path $P_{(u,v)}$ based on the path $P'_{(u,v)}$ and the cycle $C_{(u',v')}$. The path $P_{(u,v)}$ is identical to the path $P'_{(u,v)}$, except that the edge (u_R, v_R) of $P'_{(u,v)}$ is replaced with the other edges of $C_{(u',v')}$.

and removing edges that are no longer in the active window. The second task is updating the ages of the edges and detecting edges that are too old to be in the active window. Using a naïve representation of F, updating F can take as long as $\Theta(n)$ time.[1] However, using more involved data structures, it is possible to significantly decrease the time required for updating F. As the data structures required for that are quite complex and have little to do with sliding window algorithms in general, we do not present them in this book. Instead, we concentrate on the second task mentioned above (i.e., updating edge ages and detecting edges that are no longer within the active window).

A naïve way to handle this task is to associate an age counter with every edge, and let this counter count the number of edges that have arrived after the edge in question. Unfortunately, having such age counters means that the algorithm will have to spend $\Theta(n)$ time following the arrival of every new edge on updating these counters because every one of the counters has to be increased by 1 following the arrival. A more efficient way to maintain the ages of the edges is to have a single counter C tracking time. This counter starts with the value 0, and is increased by 1 following the arrival of every edge. The existence of C allows us to track the ages of edges in a much easier way. Every time that an edge arrives, we store its arrival time (i.e., the value of C at that time) in the edge. Then, when we want to determine the age of a given edge, it is enough to consider the difference between the current time (value of C) and the time in which the edge arrived. Moreover, as Algorithm 2 discards edges whose age is more than W, we can safely make C a counter modulo with some value $p = \Theta(W)$, i.e., it does not need to be an unbounded counter. This observation is important because it means that the space complexity of C does not need to grow with the length of the stream (we discuss this point in more detail later).

Exercise 2. The second task presented above consists of two parts: tracking the ages of the edges and detecting edges whose age is large enough to place them outside the active window. The last paragraph explains how to efficiently track the ages of the edges, which is the first part of the task. Explain how to efficiently implement the second part of the task, i.e., describe an efficient way to detect edges of F whose age puts them outside the active window.

---

[1] Recall that we use n to denote the number of vertices in graph-related problems.

As we did not describe the exact data structure used to store F, it is difficult to calculate the space complexity of Algorithm 2. However, if we assume for simplicity that F is represented using the natural data structure, then we get Observation 1.

Observation 1. The space complexity of Algorithm 2 is $O(n \cdot (\log n + \log W))$.

Proof. Algorithm 2 has to maintain the edges of F plus a constant number of other edges. Since F is a forest, it cannot contain more than $n - 1$ edges, and thus, Algorithm 2 has to maintain only $O(n)$ edges. Each edge consists of three fields: its two endpoints and its arrival time (i.e., the value of the counter C at the time of the edge's arrival). Each endpoint requires $O(\log n)$ space since there are n vertices, and the value of the counter C is an integer between 0 and some value $p = \Theta(W)$, and thus, can be stored using $O(\log p) = O(\log W)$ space. Adding all these observations, we get that Algorithm 2 requires a space of $O(n \cdot (\log n + \log W))$ for storing edges.

In addition to storing edges, Algorithm 2 requires space for two additional things. First, it requires $O(\log W)$ space for storing the counter C itself. Additionally, it requires $O(n \log n)$ space for a data structure used to detect edges of F whose age puts them outside the active window (this data structure is described in the solution for Exercise 2). The observation now follows by adding all the above space requirements. $\qquad\square$

As we can see, the space complexity of Algorithm 2 depends on the length W of the window, but not on the total length of the stream. This is a desirable property because in the context of the sliding window algorithms, we often think of the stream as infinite, or at least, much larger than the window length. Accordingly, the definitions of streaming and semi-streaming algorithms are modified in this context to refer to the window length W instead of the stream length. For example, a sliding window algorithm for a graph problem is a semi-streaming algorithm if its space complexity is $O(n \cdot \log^c n \cdot \log^c W)$ for some constant $c \geqslant 0$. Using this definition, we can now summarize most of our discussion of Algorithm 2 using Theorem 1.

Theorem 1. *Algorithm 2 is a semi-streaming sliding window algorithm which detects correctly whether the graph induced by the edges in its active window is connected.*

Exercise 3. A graph is called 2-edge-connected if there are at least two edges crossing every non-trivial cut in it (i.e., for every set $S \subseteq V$ of vertices which is not empty and does not contain all the vertices, there are at least two edges between the vertices of S and the vertices of $V \setminus S$). 2-edge-connected graphs are interesting because they are robust to single edge removal, i.e., they remain connected even after the removal of any single edge. This is useful, for example, when the graph represents a communication network; in which case 2-connectivity implies that the communication network remains connected even if one communication link (edge) fails. Prove that Algorithm 3 is a semi-streaming sliding window algorithm that answers correctly (when queried) whether the edges in its active window induce a 2-connected graph. **Hint:** Consider an arbitrary non-trivial cut. Prove that if there are at least two edges within the active window that cross this cut, then the two youngest edges among them must belong to either F_1 or F_2.

Before concluding this section, we would like to draw attention to the relationship between the sliding window and strict turnstile models. The two models are similar in the sense that in both of them tokens can both arrive and leave ("exit the active window" in the terminology of the sliding window model). However, there is also a crucial difference between these two models. In the turnstile model, the departure of a token is done by an explicit event that the algorithm reads from its input stream. In contrast, in the sliding window model, the departure of a token happens implicitly when the token drops out of the active window. Interestingly, it is not possible to say that one of these models is more difficult than the other because each model lets algorithms for it enjoy a different advantage. An algorithm for the turnstile model gets an explicit notification when a token leaves, and this notification includes the leaving token itself. In contrast, an algorithm for the sliding window model does not know the identity of the leaving token (unless space was used to save this token when it arrived), but enjoys a very simple rule regarding the leave times of tokens. Specifically, every token leaves exactly when the token that appears W places after it in the stream arrives.

Algorithm 3: Testing 2-Edge-Connectedness in the Sliding Window Model

Initialization

1. Let F_1 and F_2 be two forests over the vertices of V having no edges.

Token Processing

2. Every time that an edge (u, v) arrives do:
3.   Add (u, v) to the forest F_1.
4.   **if** F_1 contains now a cycle $C_{(u,v)}$ **then**
5.   Remove from F_1 the oldest edge of $C_{(u,v)}$ to make it a forest again.
6.   Denote the removed edge by (u', v'), and add it to the forest F_2.
7.   **if** F_2 contains now a cycle $C_{(u',v')}$ **then**
8.   Remove from F_2 the oldest edge of $C_{(u',v')}$ to make it a forest again.
9.   Remove from F_1 and F_2 edges that are no longer inside the active window.

Query

10. **If** the union of the edges of F_1 and F_2 induces a 2-connected graph **then**
11.   **return** "the active window induces a 2-connected graph".
12. **else**
13.   **return** "the active window <u>does not</u> induce a 2-connected graph".

9.3 Smooth Histograms

Assume that we are given a data stream algorithm ALG for the plain vanilla data stream model. This algorithm can be transformed into an algorithm for the sliding window model using a very simple trick. Specifically, every time a new token arrives, we create a new instance of ALG and feed the new token to all the instances of ALG that we have. This guarantees that at every point in time we have an instance of ALG which has received exactly the tokens of the currently active window, and thus, we can use the value produced by this instance as the output of our sliding window algorithm. Moreover, it is possible to slightly improve this trick by deleting instances of ALG that are too old, i.e., instances of ALG that received in the past tokens

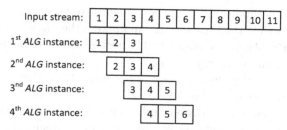

Figure 9.3. An illustration of the trick used to convert a plain vanilla data stream algorithm ALG into a sliding window algorithm. A new instance of ALG is created every time that a token of the stream arrives. The first instance gets the W first tokens of the stream (here we assume that $W = 3$). The second instance gets the W tokens starting at place 2 of the stream, and so on. There are two important observations to make here. The first observation is that at every given point, one instance of ALG received exactly the tokens of the active window, and thus, the sliding window algorithm can use the output of this instance of ALG to answer queries. The second observation is that we never need to keep more than W instances of ALG. For example, by the time we receive token number 4 and create the fourth instance of ALG, the first instance can be discarded because it received in the past a token (token number 1) that has already left the active window.

which have already left the active window (see Figure 9.3 for a graphical illustration). However, even after this improvement, the space complexity of the sliding window algorithm obtained using this trick is larger by a factor of W compared to the space complexity of ALG because the sliding window algorithm has to keep W instances of ALG, which is usually unacceptable.

Let us denote by J the set of instances of ALG maintained by the sliding window algorithm produced by the above trick. In many cases, it is possible to save space by keeping only a subset J' of the instances of J, and still produce roughly the same answers when queried. Intuitively, this is possible because two instances from J that were created at close time points receive similar streams, and thus, often produce very similar answers. To use this intuition, we should strive to choose the subset J' in a way which guarantees that every instance of $J \backslash J'$ started at a close enough time to one of the instances of J' to guarantee that both instances share a similar answer. Clearly, if we succeed in doing that, then we can use the instances of J' to produce a query answer which is similar to the answer that would have been produced by keeping all the instances of J.

Many existing sliding window algorithms are based on the idea described by the last paragraph. Often these algorithms use additional insights that are necessary for the implementation of this idea in the context of the specific problems solved by these algorithms. Nevertheless, there exists a method, known as the *smooth histograms* method, which is applicable to a wide range of settings and allows the implementation of the above idea in a black box manner. The rest of this section is devoted to presenting and analyzing this method.

Assume that the data stream algorithm ALG that we are given calculates some numerical function f of its input stream σ.[2] For example, $f(\sigma)$ can be the number of distinct tokens in σ, or the size of the maximum matching in the graph induced by the edges of σ (assuming σ is a graph stream). We would like to use the above intuitive idea to construct a sliding window algorithm that efficiently estimates the value of f over the content of the active window. The smooth histograms method shows that Algorithm 4 achieves this goal when f is "nice" in the sense captured by Definition 1.

Definition 1. A function f is (α, β)-*smooth* for $0 < \beta \leqslant \alpha < 1$, if it has the following properties:

1. $f(\sigma)$ is positive for every non-empty stream σ,
2. adding tokens to the beginning of a stream can never decrease the value of f for this stream. More formally, for a stream σ and a suffix σ' of this stream, $f(\sigma) \geqslant f(\sigma')$,
3. consider a stream σ and a suffix σ' of it. If $f(\sigma') \geqslant (1 - \beta) \cdot f(\sigma)$, then $f(\sigma' \cdot \sigma'') \geqslant (1 - \alpha) \cdot f(\sigma \cdot \sigma'')$, for any other stream σ'',
4. for every non-empty stream σ, the ratio between $f(\sigma)$ and the value of f for the suffix of σ containing only the last token of σ is upper bounded by a polynomial in m and $|\sigma|$.[3]

Do not worry if you do not understand at this point the intuitive meaning of some of the properties described by Definition 1. Their meaning will become clearer when we use them later to analyze Algorithm 4. The pseudocode of this algorithm uses some new notation. First, given an instance a of ALG, $f(a)$ is used to denote the value that a would have produced if we passed no more tokens to it (equivalently, $f(a)$ is the value of f over the part of the stream that the instance a has received so far). Second, an instance of ALG is called "active" if all the tokens it has received so far belong to the active window; otherwise, it is called "inactive".

---

[2]A numerical function is a function whose range includes only numbers.

[3]Here, m represents the number of possible tokens. As usual, for graph problems it should be replaced with n — the number of vertices. Additionally, we would like to remind you that $|\sigma|$ is the length of the stream σ, i.e., the number of tokens in it.

Algorithm 4: Smooth Histograms Algorithm

Initialization

1. Let A be an empty list of instances of ALG, and let a_i denote instance number i in this list.

Token Processing

2. Every time that a new token t arrives do:
3.   Append a new instance of ALG to the end of A.
4.   Forward t to all instances of ALG in A.
5.   **if** A contains inactive instances **then**
6.   Remove all of them, except for the last one.
7.   **while** there are instances a_i, a_{i+2} in A with $(1-\beta) \cdot f(a_i) < f(a_{i+2})$ **do**
8.   Remove instance a_{i+1} from A.

Query

9.   Let a be the first active instance in A.
10. **return** the value $f(a)$.

Following the intuition given at the beginning of this section, Algorithm 4 maintains a list A of all instances of ALG. This list is sorted according to the time in which each instance of ALG was created. Consequently, if we denote by a_i the instance at location i of the list and by σ_i the stream of tokens it has received, then σ_i is a suffix of σ_j whenever $i > j$. This, together with Property 2 of Definition 1, implies that $f(\sigma_1), f(\sigma_2), \ldots, f(\sigma_{|A|})$ (or, equivalently, $f(a_1), f(a_2), \ldots, f(a_{|A|})$) is a non-increasing list of values. Lemma 2 bounds the rate at which the values in this list decrease.

Lemma 2. *For every $1 \leqslant i \leqslant |A| - 2, (1-\beta) \cdot f(\sigma_i) \geqslant f(\sigma_{i+2})$. In contrast, for every $1 \leqslant i < |A|, (1 - \alpha) \cdot f(\sigma_i) \leqslant f(\sigma_{i+1})$, unless σ_i contains exactly one more token compared to σ_{i+1}.*

Before proving Lemma 2, let us first explain its importance. Lemma 2 consists of two parts. The first part proves that advancing two places in the above list decreases the value by at least a factor of $1 - \beta$. As the ratio between the values at the two ends of the list is polynomial by Property 4 of Definition 1, this will allow us later to bound the length of the list, and thus, analyze the space complexity of Algorithm 4. The second part of Lemma 2 shows that advancing a single place in the list decreases the value by no more than a factor of $1 - \alpha$ (with some exception). This allows us to estimate $f(\sigma')$ for every suffix σ' of σ_1 using the following trick. If $\sigma' = \sigma_i$ for some i, then we already have $f(\sigma')$. Otherwise, we locate the i for which σ' is a suffix of σ_{i-1}, but not of σ_i. Clearly, $f(\sigma_{i-1}) \geqslant f(\sigma') \geqslant f(\sigma_i)$, which means that $f(\sigma_i)$ can be used as an estimate for $f(\sigma')$ because we know that the ratio between $f(\sigma_{i-1})$ and $f(\sigma_i)$ is relatively small. In particular, we will show that this observation allows Algorithm 4 to estimate the value of the suffix of σ_1 corresponding to the currently active window.

Proof of Lemma 2. The first part of the lemma follows immediately from the fact that Algorithm 4 explicitly looks for instances a_i, a_{i+2} violating the inequality $(1 - \beta) \cdot f(\sigma_i) \geqslant f(\sigma_{i+2})$, and continues to delete instances from the list A as long as such a violating pair of instances exists. Proving the second part of the lemma is a bit more involved. Consider the iteration in which the instance a_{i+1} of ALG was created, and let a'_{i+1} be the instance of ALG created by the iteration before that. One can observe that Algorithm 4 never removes from A the last instance of ALG. Thus, a'_{i+1} was still part of A when the instance a_{i+1} was created. There are now two cases to consider. The first case is that $a_i = a'_{i+1}$. This case implies that a_i and a_{i+1} were created in consecutive iterations of Algorithm 4, and thus, σ_i contains exactly one more token compared to σ_{i+1}, which completes the proof of the lemma for this case.

The second case that we need to consider is the case $a_i \neq a'_{i+1}$. This case implies that a_i and a_{i+1} were not adjacent in A when a_{i+1} was first added to A. Thus, they must have become adjacent when some instance a' that appeared between them was removed. The removal of a' could not have been due to inactivity of a' because that would have caused the removal of a_i as well. Thus, the removal of a' must have been done because at the time of the removal it was true that $(1 - \beta) \cdot f(a_i) < f(a_{i+1})$. At this point, we need to invoke Property 3 of Definition 1. This property guarantees that if $f(\sigma_{i+1})$ was smaller than $f(\sigma_i)$ by at most a factor of $1 - \beta$ at some point, then adding the new tokens that arrived after this point to both σ_i and σ_{i+1} cannot make the ratio $f(\sigma_{i+1})/f(\sigma_i) = f(a_{i+1})/f(a_i)$ smaller than $1 - \alpha$. In other words, $f(a_i)$ and $f(a_{i+1})$ must obey now the inequality $(1 - \alpha) \cdot f(a_i) \leqslant f(a_{i+1})$ because they obeyed the inequality $(1 - \beta) \cdot f(a_i) < f(a_{i+1})$ at some point in the past. $\square$

Corollary 1. *The space complexity of Algorithm 4 is $O(\beta^{-1} \cdot (\log W + \log m))$ times the space complexity of ALG.*

Proof. Note that Algorithm 4 stores nothing besides the instances of *ALG* that appear in the list A. Thus, to prove the lemma it is enough to show that A contains no more than $O(\beta^{-1} \cdot (\log W + \log m))$ *ALG* instances. Clearly, A can contain at most one inactive instance. Let us now also upper bound the number of active instances in A. Toward this goal, let us denote by a_i and a_j the first and last active instances in A, respectively. Properties 2 and 4 of Definition 1 together imply that the ratio between $f(a_i)$ and $f(a_j)$ is bounded by a polynomial in m and $|\sigma_i| \leqslant W$. Thus,

$$\ln(f(a_i)/f(a_j)) = O(\log W + \log m).$$

Recall now that, by Lemma 2, every value in the list $f(a_1), f(a_2), \ldots, f(a_{|A|})$ must be smaller by at least a factor of $1 - \beta$ compared to the value that appears in the list two places earlier. As the first value in the list corresponding to an active instance is $f(a_i)$, and the last value in the list corresponding to an active instance is $f(a_j)$, this implies that the number of values in the list corresponding to active instances is upper bounded by

$$
\begin{aligned}
2 + 2 \cdot \log_{1-\beta}\left(\frac{f(a_j)}{f(a_i)}\right) &= 2 + 2 \cdot \frac{\ln\left(f(a_j)/f(a_i)\right)}{\ln(1-\beta)} \\
&\leqslant 2 + 2 \cdot \frac{\ln\left(f(a_i)/f(a_j)\right)}{\beta} \\
&= O\left(\beta^{-1} \cdot (\log W + \log m)\right),
\end{aligned}
$$

where the inequality follows from the inequality $\ln(1 - \beta) \leqslant -\beta$, which holds for every real value β. □

The quality of the estimation produced by Algorithm 4 remains to be analyzed. We begin with Observation 2.

Observation 2. The list A contains at most one inactive instance. Moreover, if there is such an instance, then it is the first instance of A. In contrast, if there are only active instances in A, then the first instance of A has received exactly the tokens of the active window.

Proof. While Algorithm 4 receives the first W tokens, it never drops the first instance of A, which implies that this instance receives exactly the tokens of the active window. When Algorithm 4 eventually gets token number $W + 1$, the first instance of A becomes inactive. Starting at this point, Algorithm 4 always has an inactive instance as the first instance of A. The reason for that is that Algorithm 4 removes the first instance of A only when there are multiple inactive instances in A, and when that happens, one inactive instance is saved from deletion and becomes the new first instance of A (inactive instances always appear in A before active ones).   □

Corollary 2. *Let σ_W be the part of the stream corresponding to the active window (which makes $f(\sigma_W)$ the value that we want to estimate). Then, the output of Algorithm 4 (when queried) belongs to the range $[(1 - \alpha) \cdot f(\sigma_W), f(\sigma_W)]$.*

Proof. Assume first that the list A contains no inactive instances. In this case, Observation 2 guarantees that the first instance of ALG in A has received all the tokens of the active window, and thus, its output (which is also the output of Algorithm 4 when queried) is exactly $f(\sigma_W)$, which completes the proof for this case. Thus, we can assume from now on that A contains an inactive instance — which must be a_1 due to Observation 2.

The next instance in A (which is a_2) is the first active instance in A. Note that the output of a_2 is the output of Algorithm 4 in this case, and thus, it remains to be proved that $f(\sigma_2) \in [(1 - \alpha) \cdot f(\sigma_W), f(\sigma_W)]$. If a_2 happened to receive exactly the tokens of the active window, then $f(\sigma_2) = f(\sigma_W)$, and we are done. Otherwise, σ_2 must be shorter than σ_1 by more than one token, which implies (by Lemma 2) that $f(\sigma_2) \geq (1-\alpha) \cdot f(\sigma_1)$. We now observe that the facts that a_1 is inactive and a_2 is active imply that σ_W is a suffix of σ_1 and that σ_2 is a suffix of σ_W. Thus, $f(\sigma_1) \geq f(\sigma_W) \geq f(\sigma_2)$. Combining the inequalities we have got yields, as required,

$$f(\sigma_W) \geq f(\sigma_2) \geq (1 - \alpha) \cdot f(\sigma_1)$$
$$\geq (1 - \alpha) \cdot f(\sigma_W) \Rightarrow f(\sigma_2) \in [(1 - \alpha) \cdot f(\sigma_W), f(\sigma_W)].$$ □

We can now summarize the properties of the smooth histograms method we have proved using Theorem 2.

Theorem 2. *Given a plain vanilla data stream algorithm ALG calculating an (α, β)-smooth function f, Algorithm 4 estimates the value of f on the content of the active window up to a relative error of α using a space complexity of $O(\beta^{-1} \cdot (\log W + \log m))$ times the space complexity of ALG.*

Algorithm 5: Integers Summing

1. Let $s \leftarrow 0$.
2. Every time that a new integer t arrives do:
3.   Updates $s \leftarrow s + t$.
4. **return** s.

To exemplify the use of the smooth histograms method, consider Algorithm 5. This algorithm is a data stream algorithm that receives a stream of integer numbers between 1 and c, for some integer constant $c \geqslant 1$, and calculates the sum of the integers it has received.

Exercise 4. Algorithm 5 calculates a function f defined as follows. For every stream σ of integers between 1 and c, $f(\sigma)$ is the sum of the integers in σ.

(a) Prove that this function f is $(\varepsilon, \varepsilon)$-smooth for every $\varepsilon \in (0, 1/2)$.
(b) Show that the space complexity of Algorithm 5 is $O(\log n)$ — recall that n is the length of the stream.

Combining Exercise 4 and the smooth histograms method (Theorem 2), we get that for every constant $\varepsilon \in (0, 1/2)$ there exists a sliding window algorithm (which we call *SlidingSum*) which approximates the sum of the integers in the active window up to a relative error of ε using a space complexity of $O(\varepsilon^{-1} \cdot (\log W + \log m) \cdot \log n)$. This is already a non-trivial result; however, it is not quite satisfactory because the space complexity of *SlidingSum* depends on the length n of the stream, which we assume to be very large. In particular, this result fails to prove that *SlidingSum* is a streaming sliding window algorithm because the space complexity of a streaming sliding window algorithm should be a polynomial function of only $\log W$ and $\log m$.

To solve the above issue, we need to improve the space complexity analysis of *SlidingSum* beyond the space complexity guarantee given by Theorem 2. Recall that the algorithm we call *SlidingSum* is in fact Algorithm 4, with the algorithm ALG chosen as Algorithm 5. Thus, according to the proof of Corollary 1, *SlidingSum* maintains at most $O(\varepsilon^{-1} \cdot (\log W + \log m))$ instances of Algorithm 5, and its space complexity is equal to the sum of the space complexities of these instances. Simply plugging in the upper bound of $O(\log n)$, given by Exercise 4, on the space complexity of every instance of Algorithm 5 yields the above-mentioned unsatisfactory upper bound of $O(\varepsilon^{-1} \cdot (\log W + \log m) \cdot \log n)$ on the space complexity of *SlidingSum*. Thus, to get a better upper bound on the space complexity of *SlidingSum*, we need to find a better bound on the space complexity of the instances of Algorithm 5 used by *SlidingSum*.

‖ **Exercise 5.** Prove that every instance of Algorithm 5 used by *SlidingSum* ‖ has a space complexity of $O(\log W)$.

Combining Exercise 5 with the discussion in the last paragraph, we immediately get that the space complexity of *SlidingSum* is $O(\varepsilon^{-1} \cdot (\log W + \log m) \cdot \log W) = O(\log^2 W)$, where the equality holds since ε is a constant and m is equal to the constant c. Thus, *SlidingSum* is a streaming sliding window algorithm.

The work we had to do above in order to prove that *SlidingSum* is a streaming sliding window algorithm represents an important weakness of Theorem 2. Specifically, Theorem 2 does not guarantee that Algorithm 4 is a streaming sliding window algorithm whenever ALG is a streaming data stream algorithm. Recall that the reason for this weakness is that the space complexity of ALG might depend on $\log n$, while the space complexity of a streaming sliding window algorithm should be a polynomial function of only $\log W$ and $\log m$. One way to solve this problem is to observe that the space complexity of an instance of ALG depends only on the length of the stream it views, not on the length of the original stream. Thus, as long as an instance of ALG receives only $O(W)$ tokens, the fact that it is a streaming data stream algorithm implies that its space complexity is polynomial in $\log W$ and $\log m$, which is what we want. In other words, if we could prove that every instance of ALG in Algorithm 4 views only $O(W)$ tokens, then we could prove the following stronger version of Theorem 2. Note that this stronger version yields, by the above discussion, a streaming sliding window algorithm whenever ALG is a streaming data stream algorithm.

Theorem 3. *Given a plain vanilla data stream algorithm ALG calculating an (α, β)-smooth function f, there exists a sliding window algorithm which estimates the value of f on the content of the active window up to a relative error of α. Moreover, the space complexity of this algorithm is $O(\beta^{-1} \cdot (\log W + \log m))$ times the space complexity of ALG on streams of length $O(W)$.*

Unfortunately, in some extreme cases (for example, when f has the same value for every input) Algorithm 4 may feed its entire input stream to a single instance of ALG. Hence, as is, Algorithm 4 cannot be used to prove Theorem 3. Exercise 6 studies a variant of Algorithm 4 which does not suffer from this problem, and thus, induces Theorem 3.

Exercise 6. Consider Algorithm 6, which is a variant of Algorithm 4. The difference between the two algorithms is that Algorithm 6 marks one out of every W instances of ALG that it creates. The marked instances are then partially protected from deletion. Specifically, a marked instance gets deleted only when the following two conditions hold: the marked instance is inactive, and there are other inactive instances that appear after it in the list A.

(a) Prove that Algorithm 6 has the same estimation guarantee as Algorithm 4. In other words, prove that given a plain vanilla data stream algorithm ALG calculating an (α, β)-smooth function f, Algorithm 4 estimates the value of f on the content of the active window up to a relative error of α.

(b) Prove that the list A of ALG instances maintained by Algorithm 6 contains $O(\beta^{-1} \cdot (\log W + \log m))$ instances.

(c) Prove that every instance of ALG appearing in the list A of Algorithm 6 receives an input stream of length $O(W)$.

Algorithm 6: Smooth Histogram Algorithm

Initialization

1. Let A be an empty list of instances of ALG, and let a_i denote instance number i in this list.

Token Processing

2. Every time that a new token t arrives do:
3. Append a new instance of ALG to the end of A. If the location of t in the stream is $k \cdot W$ for some integer k, mark this new instance.
4. Forward t to all instances of ALG in A.
5. **if** A contains inactive instances **then**
6.   Remove all of them, except for the last one.
7. **while** there are instances a_i, a_{i+1}, a_{i+2} in A such that a_{i+1} is not marked and $(1 - \beta) \cdot f(a_i) < (fa_{i+2})$ **do**
8. Remove instance a_{i+1} from A.

Query

9. Let a be the first active instance in A.
10. **return** the value $f(a)$.

9.4 Bibliographic Notes

The sliding window model was first studied by Datar *et al.* (2002). Among other things, Datar *et al.* presented a general method, called the *exponential histograms method*, for converting a data stream algorithm which evaluates a numerical function f into a sliding window algorithm which estimates the value of the same function over the active window. The exponential histograms method works whenever the function f belongs to a class of functions that exhibit (in some sense) a weakly additive behavior.

The smooth histograms method was suggested by Braverman and Ostrovsky (2007). For many problems, this method provides improved results compared to the older exponential histograms method, although the set of functions to which the two methods can be applied is somewhat different. It should also be noted that both methods have generalized versions that work even when the given data stream algorithm only provides an estimate of the value of the function f.

Since its introduction by Datar *et al.* (2002), the sliding window model has been studied with problems from various domains. The work of Crouch *et al.* (2013) has been the first work to study graph problems in this model, and all the algorithms presented in this chapter for graph problems are based on this work.

V. Braverman and R. Ostrovsky. Smooth Histograms for Sliding Windows. In *Proceedings of the 48ᵗʰ Annual IEEE Symposium on Foundations of Computer Science (FOCS)*, 283–293, 2007.

M. S. Crouch, A. McGregor and D. Stubbs. Dynamic Graphs in the Sliding-Window Model. In *Proceedings of the 21ˢᵗ European Symposium on Algorithms (ESA)*, 337–348, 2013.

M. Datar, A. Gionis, P. Indyk and R. Motwani. Maintaining stream statistics over sliding windows. *SIAM Journal on Computing*, 31(6): 1794–1813, 2002.

Exercise Solutions

Solution 1

The following table summarizes the changes in the state of Algorithm 1 during its execution. The first row of the table corresponds to the state of the algorithm immediately after the execution of its initialization part, while the rows after that correspond to the states of the algorithm after the processing of each token of the stream (in order). Each row contains a few pieces of information, including the value of the two variables of the algorithm at the time corresponding to the row, the content of the active window at that time (i.e., the last 3 tokens that have arrived) and the answer of the query part of the algorithm if executed at this time. Note that the query part indicates correctly whether the sequence "*ab*" appears in the active window.

Arriving Token	LastAppearance	Last Token WasA	Active Window	Query Answer
Initialization	"Never"	"False"	""	Does not appear
"a"	"Never"	"True"	"a"	Does not appear
"a"	"Never"	"True"	"aa"	Does not appear
"b"	0	"False"	"aab"	Appears
"a"	1	"True"	"aba"	Appears
"b"	0	"False"	"bab"	Appears
"a"	1	"True"	"aba"	Appears
"a"	"Never"	"True"	"baa"	Does not appear
"b"	0	"False"	"aab"	Appears

Solution 2

We need to explain how to detect edges of F whose age is large enough to put them outside the active window. A naïve solution is to maintain a queue which contains all the edges of the active window. Every time that a new edge arrives, it should be added to the queue. If the size of the queue exceeds W following this addition, then we know that the first edge of the queue is now outside the active window, and we can remove it from both the queue and F. This naïve solution is very time-efficient, but unfortunately, it uses a lot of space because it requires the algorithm to store W edges.

To improve the space efficiency of the solution, we need to remove from the queue edges that are no longer in F. Note that this reduces the size of the queue to $O(n)$ because a forest over n nodes contains at most $n-1$ edges. Moreover, such a removal can be done efficiently if the queue is represented as a doubly linked list. One should note, however, that, as a consequence of the removal of these edges, we can no longer determine whether the first edge of the queue belongs to the active window by simply checking the size of the queue. However, as explained in the paragraph before this exercise, we can calculate the age of the first edge of the queue by comparing its arrival time with the current time as captured by the counter C. Hence, we can still determine in $O(1)$ time whether the first edge of the queue is outside the active window (and thus, needs to be removed from the queue and from F).

Solution 3

We begin this solution by analyzing the space complexity of Algorithm 3. Note that the main difference between the things that Algorithms 2 and 3 have to store is that Algorithm 3 stores two forests F_1 and F_2, as opposed to Algorithm 2 which stores only one forest F. The analysis of the space complexity of Algorithm 2, as given by the proof of Observation 1, bounds the space complexity used for storing the forest F by showing two things. First, that each edge requires $O(\log n + \log W)$ space, and second, that F contains $O(n)$ edges because it is a forest with n vertices. These two things together imply that F can be represented using $O(n(\log n + \log W))$ space. Clearly, this analysis of the space complexity of F is based on no properties of F, other than the mere fact that it is a forest. Thus, there is no reason preventing the same analysis from being applied to F_1 and F_2 as well. In other words, the two forests F_1 and F_2 require $O(n(\log n + \log W))$ space — just like F. Recalling that the replacement of F with F_1 and F_2 is the main difference between the data structures used by Algorithms 2 and 3, we get that the space complexity bound proved by Observation 1 for Algorithm 2 applies also to Algorithm 3. Hence, we have proved that Algorithm 3 is a semi-streaming algorithm.

Let us now shift our attention to proving that Algorithm 3 answers correctly (when queried) whether the graph induced by the edges in its active window is a 2-edge-connected graph. In other words, we need to show that the graph induced by the union of the edges of F_1 and F_2 (which we denote by H from now on) is 2-edge-connected if and only if the graph induced by all the edges in the active window (which we denote by G from now on) is 2-edge-connected. Observe that both F_1 and F_2 include only edges from the active window, which implies that H is a subgraph of G. Thus, the number of edges of G crossing every given cut is at least as large as the number of such edges of H. In particular, a cut that is crossed by at least two edges in H is also crossed by at least two edges in G, which guarantees that G is 2-edge-connected whenever H is 2-edge-connected. The other direction, namely, that H is 2-edge-connected whenever G is remains to be proved. For that purpose, let us assume from now on that G is 2-edge-connected. We will show that the 2-edge-connectivity of H follows from this assumption.

Consider an arbitrary non-trivial cut between the vertices of a set $\varnothing \neq S \subset V$ and the vertices of $V \backslash S$. Since G is 2-edge-connected, there must be at least two edges in it crossing this cut. Let us denote the youngest edge among these by e_1 and the second youngest among them by e_2. To prove that H is 2-edge-connected, it is enough to show that it contains both edges e_1 and e_2 because $(S, V \backslash S)$ was chosen as an arbitrary non-trivial cut. When e_1 arrived, Algorithm 3 added it to F_1 because it adds every new edge to F_1. Assume, by way of contradiction, that e_1 was removed from F_1 at a later point. Since e_1 belongs to G, it is part of the active window, which implies that its removal from F_1 was due to its membership in a cycle C_1 which contained only younger edges than e_1 itself. However, such a cycle C_1 must include a second edge e_1' (other than e_1) that crosses the cut $(S, V \backslash S)$, which contradicts the definition of e_1 because we got that e_1' crosses the cut $(S, V \backslash S)$ and is younger than e_1 due to its membership in C_1 (see Figure 9.4 for a graphical illustration). This contradiction implies that e_1 must be part of F_1, and thus, also part of H.

Consider now the edge e_2. When e_2 arrived, it was added to F_1 by Algorithm 3. If e_2 was never removed from F_1, then it is also part of H, and we are done. Thus, we can safely assume in the rest of the proof that e_2 was removed from F_1. When that happened, it was added to F_2 by Algorithm 3. Using an analogous argument to the one used in the last paragraph, we can show that if e_2 was removed from F_2 later, then there must exist an edge e_2' which was at F_2 at some point, crosses the cut $(S, V \backslash S)$ and is younger than e_2. However, the existence of such an edge e_2' leads to a contradiction

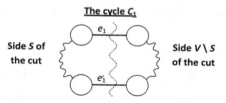

Figure 9.4. A graphical illustration of the proof that e_1 has not been removed from F_1. The cycle C_1 is a hypothetical cycle which caused e_1's removal. As such, this cycle must contain beside e_1 only edges younger than it. Additionally, this cycle must cross at least twice the cut $(S, V \backslash S)$ because e_1 crosses this cut and each cycle crosses each cut an even number of times. Thus, C_1 must contain an edge e_1' which is both younger than e_1 and crosses the cut $(S, V \backslash S)$, which contradicts e_1's definition.

since the fact that e_1 remains in F_1 implies that e_2 is the youngest edge crossing the cut $(S, V \backslash S)$ that was ever added to F_2. Thus, we have proved that e_2 remains in F_2, and hence, it belongs to H, which completes the proof that H is 2-edge-connected.

Solution 4

(a) Fix a value $\varepsilon \in (0, 1/2)$, and let f be the function that given a stream σ of integers between 1 and c returns the sum of the integers in the stream. We need to show that f is $(\varepsilon, \varepsilon)$-smooth. To do that, we need to prove that it obeys the four properties given in Definition 1.

- Property 1 requires f to be positive on every non-empty string σ, which is true because $f(\sigma)$ is the sum of a positive number of positive integers.
- To prove Property 2, we need to show that for every stream σ and a suffix σ' of it, the inequality $f(\sigma) \geqslant f(\sigma')$ holds. To see why that is true, we first observe that f is linear, in the sense that given two streams σ_1 and σ_2, we always have $f(\sigma_1 \cdot \sigma_2) = f(\sigma_1) + f(\sigma_2)$. Thus, if we denote by σ'' the part of σ appearing before the suffix σ', then we get

$$f(\sigma) = f(\sigma'' \cdot \sigma') = f(\sigma'') + f(\sigma') \geqslant f(\sigma'),$$

  where the inequality follows from the non-negativity of f.
- To prove Property 3, we need to show that if a stream σ and a suffix σ' of it obey $f(\sigma') \geqslant (1 - \varepsilon) \cdot f(\sigma)$, then the inequality $f(\sigma' \cdot \sigma'') \geqslant (1 - \varepsilon) \cdot f(\sigma \cdot \sigma'')$ holds for any other stream σ''. To prove the last inequality, we use again the linearity of f as follows:

$$f(\sigma' \cdot \sigma'') = f(\sigma') + f(\sigma'') \geqslant (1 - \varepsilon) \cdot f(\sigma) + f(\sigma'')$$
$$\geqslant (1 - \varepsilon) \cdot [f(\sigma) + f(\sigma'')] = (1 - \varepsilon) \cdot f(\sigma \cdot \sigma''),$$

  where the second inequality follows from the non-negativity of f.
- To prove Property 4, we need to show that, for every non-empty stream σ and its suffix σ' which contains only the last token of σ, the ratio between $f(\sigma)$ and $f(\sigma')$ is upper bounded by a polynomial in m and $|\sigma|$. To do that, we observe that $f(\sigma)$ is upper bounded by

$|\sigma| \cdot c$ because every token in σ is upper bounded by c. In contrast, $f(\sigma')$ is lower bounded by 1 because σ' contains one token. Thus,

$$\frac{f(\sigma)}{f(\sigma')} \leqslant \frac{c \cdot |\sigma|}{1} = c \cdot |\sigma|.$$

Since c is a constant, the rightmost side of the last inequality is a polynomial in $|\sigma|$.

(b) Algorithm 5 stores in memory only the variables t and s. The variable t contains a single token, which is an integer between 1 and the constant c, and thus, requires only $O(1)$ space. In contrast, the variable s is the sum of up to n such integers, and thus, it is an integer between 1 and cn. Storing such an integer requires a space complexity of $O(\log cn) = O(\log n)$. Combining the space complexities required for the two variables, we get that the total space complexity required for Algorithm 5 is

$$O(1) + O(\log n) = O(\log n).$$

Solution 5

Consider an arbitrary instance a of Algorithm 5 used by *SlidingSum*. If at some point a is an active instance, then (by definition) a received at most W tokens so far. Hence, from the point of view of a, the length of its input stream is at most W. Combining that with Exercise 4, we get that the space complexity used by a at this point is $O(\log W)$. Thus, in the rest of this solution we may assume that a is an inactive instance of Algorithm 5.

According to Observation 2, the inactive instance a is the only inactive instance in the list A, and it appears as the first instance in this list. Let us denote the second instance in this list by a_2. Since a_2 is an active instance, it received at most W tokens so far, and thus, its variable s has a value of at most $c \cdot W$. Observe now that when an instance of Algorithm 5 reaches the end of its stream, it returns the value of its variable s. Thus, Lemma 2 implies in this context that one of two things must happen:

- The first case is that the value of the variable s of the instance a is larger than the value of the variable s of the instance a_2 by at most a factor of $(1 - \varepsilon)^{-1} \leqslant 2$. Combining this with the upper bound we have on the value of the variable s of a_2, we get that in this case the value of the variable s of the instance a is at most $2c \cdot W$.

- The other case is that a has received exactly one token more than a_2, which means that it has received at most $W + 1$ tokens in total. Thus, in this case we also get that the value of the variable s of a is upper bounded by $c \cdot (W + 1) \leqslant 2c \cdot W$.

The above case analysis proves that the variable s of a is an integer upper bounded by $2c \cdot W$, and thus, the space necessary for storing it is $O(\log(2c \cdot W)) = O(\log W)$. In addition to the space used for storing s, the instance a needs space only for storing the variable t. As this variable takes only integer values between 1 and the constant c, it can be stored using $O(1)$ space. Hence, the total space complexity required for the instance a of Algorithm 5 is

$$O(1) + O(\log W) = O(\log W).$$

Solution 6

(a) It is enough to prove that Corollary 2 applies to Algorithm 6 as well. This corollary is based on Observation 2 and on the second part of Lemma 2, and it can be observed that the proofs of both of these work for Algorithm 6 without any modification. Thus, the same is also true for Corollary 2.

(b) Let us begin this solution with a few observations, as follows:

- The first part of Lemma 2 does not apply to Algorithm 6. However, it is still true that, for every $1 \leqslant i \leqslant |A| - 2$, either $(1 - \beta) \cdot f(\sigma_i) \geqslant f(\sigma_{i+2})$ or σ_{i+1} is marked. The reason for that is that Algorithm 6 explicitly looks for triplets a_i, a_{i+1}, a_{i+2} which do not have either of the above properties, and deletes the instance a_{i+1} whenever it finds such a triplet.

- A can contain at most one inactive instance because Algorithm 6 deletes all the inactive instances except for the last one.

- At most one of the active instances in A can be marked. The reason for that is that the active instances are all instances that were created by Algorithm 6 following the arrival of a token that currently belongs to the active window, and at most one token out of an active window of length W can have a location in the stream of the form $k \cdot W$ for some integer k.

Let us explain now how these observations can be used to bound the total number of instances in A. Let a_i and a_j be the first and last active instances in A, respectively. Properties 2 and 4 of Definition 1 together imply that the ratio between $f(a_i)$ and $f(a_j)$ is bounded by a polynomial in m and $|\sigma_i| \leqslant W$. Thus,

$$\ln(f(a_i)/f(a_j)) = O(\log W + \log m).$$

If there are no marked instances in A, then the first observation implies that every value in the list $f(a_1), f(a_2), \ldots, f(a_{|A|})$ must be smaller by at least a factor of $1 - \beta$ compared to the value that appears in the list two places earlier. If there are marked instances in A, then this might not be true for some values in the list. Specifically, for every marked instance there is one value in the list (the one corresponding to the instance that appears in the list immediately after the marked instance) which might not be smaller by a factor of $1 - \beta$ compared to the value that appears in the list two places earlier. However, Property 2 of Definition 1 still guarantees that a value in the above list can never be larger than the value that appears in the list two places earlier.

As there can be only two marked instances in A (an active one and an inactive one), we get that the number of instances in A between a_i and a_j, including a_i and a_j themselves, is upper bounded by

$$6 + 2 \cdot \log_{1-\beta}\left(\frac{f(a_j)}{f(a_i)}\right) = 6 + 2 \cdot \frac{\ln(f(a_j)/f(a_i))}{\ln(1 - \beta)}$$

$$\leqslant 6 + 2 \cdot \frac{\ln(f(a_i)/f(a_j))}{\beta}$$

$$= O(\beta^{-1} \cdot (\log W + \log m)),$$

where the inequality follows from the inequality $\ln(1 - \beta) \leqslant -\beta$, which holds for every real value β. Recalling that a_i and a_j are the first and last active instances in A, respectively, the last bound implies that there are at most $O(\beta^{-1} \cdot (\log W + \log m))$ active instances in A, and thus, at most $1 + O(\beta^{-1} \cdot (\log W + \log m)) = O(\beta^{-1} \cdot (\log W + \log m))$ instances in A in total.

(c) Assume, by way of a contradiction, that there exists an instance a of ALG in the list A which has already received more than $2W + 1$ tokens, and let a_m be the first marked instance that was created after a. Let us denote by t and t_m the tokens whose arrival caused Algorithm 6 to create the instances a and a_m, respectively. Observe that the location of t_m in the stream can be at most W places after the location of t because one out of every W instances of ALG created by Algorithm 6 is marked,

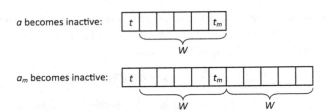

Figure 9.5. A graphical illustration of some properties of the instances of ALG used in part (c) of Solution 6. The upper part of the figure represents the situation at the time point in which the instance a became inactive. Since t is the token whose arrival triggered the creation of a, this is also the time point in which t dropped out of the active window. As the active window is of size W, at this time point there must exist a token t_m in the active window whose arrival triggered the creation of the marked instance a_m. The lower part of the figure represents the situation that exists at the moment a_m becomes inactive. One can observe that a receives at most $2W + 1$ tokens up to this moment.

and the first marked instance created after the arrival of t becomes a_m. Additionally, one can recall that a_m, as a marked instance, cannot be deleted before it becomes inactive. Thus, it is guaranteed that a_m becomes inactive, and it does so at the latest when a receives its $2W+1$ token (see Figure 9.5 for a graphical explanation). Immediately when this happens, a is removed from A because a and a_m are both inactive instances and a_m appears later in A than a. However, this contradicts our assumption that a has received more than $2W + 1$ tokens.

Part II: Sublinear Time Algorithms

Part II: Sublinear-Time Algorithms

Chapter 10

Introduction to Sublinear Time Algorithms

Traditionally, an algorithm is considered efficient if it has a polynomial time complexity. However, as modern applications require algorithms to process more and more data, it is often necessary for a truly practical algorithm to have a much better time complexity guarantee than merely being polynomial. Accordingly, faster and faster algorithms have been developed over the last decades for many computation problems. Usually, the fastest algorithm that people hope for is a linear time algorithm since this time complexity is necessary even for just reading the entire input. Nevertheless, in this part of this book we will consider *sublinear time algorithms*, i.e., algorithms that break the above barrier and use (significantly) less than linear time. As a sublinear time algorithm cannot even read all of its input, its output is always only an approximate solution in some sense. However, despite this clear weakness, sublinear time algorithms have gained importance because they often provide a practical way to solve problems on very large datasets.

10.1 A Naïve Example

To make the existence of sublinear time algorithms less mysterious, let us begin with a very simple such algorithm. Consider the following problem. Given a string w, we would like to determine the number of "a" characters in it.

Exercise 1. Prove that any deterministic algorithm that **exactly** determines the number of "a" characters in the string w must use $\Omega\left(|w|\right)$ time.

Algorithm 1: (Count '*a*' characters)

1. Let $s \leftarrow 0$ and $h \leftarrow \lceil 3\log(2/\delta)/\varepsilon^2 \rceil$.
2. **do** h times:
3.   Pick a uniformly random character t from w.
4.   **if** $t = $ '*a*' **then** increase s by 1.
5. **return** $(n/h) \cdot s$.

Remark. The result of this exercise applies in fact also to randomized algorithms, and the interested reader can find a proof for this claim in the solutions section.

Exercise 1 shows that getting a sublinear time algorithm for the above problem will require us to give up hope of getting an exact answer. Fortunately, as it turns out, once we give up this hope, there are very fast algorithms for the problem. One such algorithm is given as Algorithm 1. This algorithm gets as input a string w of length n and quality control parameters $\varepsilon, \delta \in (0, 1)$.

Recall that we assume in this book that standard operations on numbers use constant time. In particular, we will assume that sampling a number from a range can be done in constant time. Given this assumption, we get the following observation.

Observation 1. Algorithm 1 has a time complexity of $\Theta(\varepsilon^{-2} \cdot \log \delta^{-1})$. Hence, it is a sublinear time (and even constant time) algorithm when ε and δ are considered constants.

The quality of the estimation produced by Algorithm 1 remains to be analyzed.

Lemma 1. *With probability at least $1 - \delta$, Algorithm 1 estimates the number of "a" characters in its input string up to an error of $\varepsilon \cdot n$.*

Proof. Let us denote by $\#_a$ the true number of "a" characters in the input string of Algorithm 1. Note that when $\#_a = 0$ (i.e., the input string includes no "a" characters) Algorithm 1 is guaranteed to output a correct estimate. Hence, in the rest of the proof we assume $\#_a \geqslant 1$.

Let X_i be an indicator for the event that the ith character picked by Algorithm 1 is "a". One can observe that the expected value of X_i is $\#_a/n$. Thus, the sum $\sum_{i=1}^{h} X_i$ is distributed according to the binomial distribution

$B(h, \#_a/n)$, and by the Chernoff bound,

$$\Pr\left[\sum_{i=1}^{h} X_i \geqslant \frac{h \cdot (\#_a + \varepsilon \cdot n)}{n}\right]$$

$$= \Pr\left[\sum_{i=1}^{h} X_i \geqslant E\left[\sum_{i=1}^{h} X_i\right] \cdot \left(1 + \frac{\varepsilon \cdot n}{\#_a}\right)\right]$$

$$\leqslant e^{-\frac{\min\left\{\varepsilon \cdot n/\#_a, \varepsilon^2 \cdot n^2/\#_a^2\right\} \cdot E\left[\sum_{i=1}^{h} X_i\right]}{3}}$$

$$= e^{-\frac{\min\left\{h\varepsilon, h\varepsilon^2 \cdot n/\#_a\right\}}{3}} \leqslant e^{-h\varepsilon^2/3} \leqslant e^{\log(\delta/2)} = \frac{\delta}{2},$$

where the penultimate inequality holds since $\#_a \leqslant n$ by definition and $\varepsilon \in (0, 1)$. Let us upper bound now the probability that the sum $\sum_{i=1}^{h} X_i$ is much smaller than its expectation. Since this sum is non-negative, when $\#_a < \varepsilon \cdot n$ we get

$$\Pr\left[\sum_{i=1}^{h} X_i \leqslant \frac{h \cdot (\#_a - \varepsilon \cdot n)}{n}\right] \leqslant \Pr\left[\sum_{i=1}^{h} X_i < 0\right] = 0.$$

Otherwise, when $\#_a \geqslant \varepsilon \cdot n$, we get

$$\Pr\left[\sum_{i=1}^{h} X_i \leqslant \frac{h \cdot (\#_a - \varepsilon \cdot n)}{n}\right]$$

$$= \Pr\left[\sum_{i=1}^{h} X_i \leqslant E\left[\sum_{i=1}^{h} X_i\right] \cdot \left(1 - \frac{\varepsilon \cdot n}{\#_a}\right)\right]$$

$$\leqslant e^{-\frac{(\varepsilon \cdot n/\#_a)^2 \cdot E\left[\sum_{i=1}^{h} X_i\right]}{2}}$$

$$= e^{-\left(h\varepsilon^2/2\right) \cdot (n/\#_a)} \leqslant e^{-h\varepsilon^2/2} \leqslant e^{\log(\delta/2)} = \frac{\delta}{2}.$$

Combining all the above, and using the union bound, we get that with probability at least $1 - \delta$, the sum $\sum_{i=1}^{h} X_i$ is equal to its expectation $h\#_a/n$ up to an error of $h\varepsilon$. Observe now that the output of Algorithm 1 is equal to this sum times n/h. Thus, the expectation of this output is $\#_a$, and with probability at least $1 - \delta$, it is equal to this expectation up to an error of $\varepsilon \cdot n$. $\qquad\square$

Combining the results we have proven for Algorithm 1, we obtain Theorem 1.

Theorem 1. *For $\varepsilon, \delta \in (0,1)$, there exists a $\Theta(\varepsilon^{-2} \cdot \log \delta^{-1})$ time algorithm that with probability at least $1 - \delta$ estimates up to an error of $\varepsilon \cdot n$ the number of "a" characters in a string of length n.*

10.2 Estimating the Diameter

We would like to now present a more surprising example of a sublinear time algorithm. Consider a set P of n points, and assume that the distances between the points of P are specified by a matrix M. In other words, the matrix M has a column and a row for every point of P, and the distance from a point u to a point v is given by the cell that appears on the column of u and the row of v (see Figure 10.1 for a graphic explanation). Given such a matrix M, our objective is to find the largest distance between any two points of P. This distance is also known as the diameter of P.

The kind of algorithms that can be used for this problem depends on what we assume about the distances between the points. For example, if the distances are Euclidean, then we can use techniques from the field of computational geometry. In contrast, if we assume nothing about the distances, then Exercise 2 shows that any deterministic algorithm must read the entire matrix M even to get an estimate of the diameter up to a finite relative error. Moreover, we will not prove it here, but the result of this exercise can be extended to show that a randomized algorithm must also read a linear fraction of M to get an estimate of the distance up to

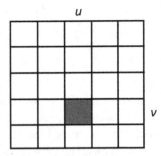

Figure 10.1. A graphical representation of the matrix M. The distance from u to v appears in the gray cell.

a finite relative error, and thus, such an estimate cannot be obtained by a sublinear time algorithm.

Exercise 2. Prove that given no assumption about the distances in M, every deterministic algorithm that distinguishes between the case that the diameter is 0 and the case that the diameter is 1 must read all of M (at least given some inputs).

Given the above discussion, it is clear that we must state explicitly the assumptions that we make. Thus, we will assume from now on that the distances in M have the following four properties. In the statement of these properties, we denote by $M(u, v)$ the distance from point u to point v.

- All the distances are non-negative.
- The distance between every point and itself is 0.
- Symmetry: $M(u, v) = M(v, u)$ for points $u, v \in P$.
- Triangle inequality: $M(u, v) \leqslant M(u, w) + M(w, v)$ for points $u, v, w \in P$.

One can observe that standard Euclidean distances always obey these properties. However, many other distances also obey them. For example, if the points of P are the vertices of a connected graph, then the distances between these vertices according to the graph obey all the above properties (recall that the distance between vertices of a graph is the length of the shortest path between them). In general, distances that obey the four above properties are often called *pseudometric*.

Before presenting our algorithm for estimating the diameter, let us state once more the problem that we want to solve. Given a set P of points and a matrix M of distances between them which form a pseudometric, we are interested in estimating the diameter of P. The algorithm we suggest for this problem is given as Algorithm 2.

Algorithm 2: Diameter Estimation

1. Let u be an arbitrary point in P.
2. Let $d \leftarrow 0$.
3. **for** every other point v **do**
4.   **if** $M(u, v) > d$ **then** $d \leftarrow M(u, v)$.
5. **return** d.

Exercise 3. Consider the pseudometric[1] defined by a star over $n \geqslant 3$ vertices (in other words, each point of the pseudometric is a vertex of the star, and the distance between two points is the number of edges on the path between them). Consider two executions of Algorithm 2 on this pseudometric: one in which the center vertex is selected as u on Line 1 of the algorithm, and one in which another vertex is selected as u. How close does the output of Algorithm 2 estimate the diameter in each case?

Theorem 2 analyzes Algorithm 2. Note that the relationship it guarantees between the output of Algorithm 2 and the diameter of P is tight due to the answer for Exercise 3. Moreover, the time complexity proved by Theorem 2 is sublinear since the size of the input for the problem we consider is the size of the matrix M, which contains $|P|^2$ cells.

Theorem 2. *Let d be the output of Algorithm 2, and let D be the diameter of P, then $d \in [D/2, D]$. Moreover, the time complexity of Algorithm 2 is $O(|P|)$.*

Proof. The bound of $O(|P|)$ on the time complexity of Algorithm 2 follows immediately from the observation that the algorithm contains a single loop, and this loop iterates exactly $|P| - 1$ times. Therefore, in the rest of the proof we concentrate on proving that $d \in [D/2, D]$.

Let v and w be points in P such that $M(v, w) = D$ (i.e., the distance between v and w is the diameter of P). Additionally, let u be the point selected by Line 1 of Algorithm 2. The symmetry and triangle inequality properties of pseudometrics guarantee that

$$M(u, v) + M(u, w) = M(v, u) + M(u, w) \geqslant M(v, w) = D.$$

Observe now that the output d of Algorithm 2 is equal to the maximum distance of u from any other point of P. Thus, on the one hand,

$$d = \max_{p \in P \setminus \{u\}} M(u, p) \geqslant \frac{M(u, v) + M(u, w)}{2} \geqslant \frac{D}{2},$$

and on the other hand, by definition, D is at least as large as the distance between any two points of P, which implies

$$d = \max_{p \in P \setminus \{u\}} M(u, p) \leqslant \max_{v \in P} \max_{p \in P \setminus \{v\}} M(v, p) = D. \qquad \square$$

---

[1]Readers who are familiar with the definition of metrics might observe that this pseudometric is in fact a metric. However, this is irrelevant for our purpose.

We conclude this section by noting that Algorithm 2 is a deterministic algorithm, which is a rare property for a sublinear time algorithm. Most of the other sublinear time algorithms we will see in this book are randomized.

10.3 Query Complexity

We have observed from the above analysis that a sublinear time algorithm can read only a sublinear part of its input. In some situations reading the input is very costly, which makes the property of reading only a sublinear part of the input important on its own right, regardless of the time complexity. For example, consider an algorithm diagnosing a disease, and assume that the input for such an algorithm consists of the outputs of various medical tests. One way to use such an algorithm is to do all the possible medical tests, and then execute the algorithm on their outputs. Obviously, the usage of the algorithm in this way is problematic since it means that some medical tests will be performed even when they are not necessary for making a decision regarding the diagnosis. This observation motivates a different way to use the algorithm. Namely, we start executing the algorithm, and every time that the algorithm asks for the result of some test, we perform the test and feed its output to the algorithm. If the algorithm reads only a small part of its input, then this improved usage method will allow us to save many unnecessary (and costly) medical tests.

The importance of algorithms that read only a sublinear part of their input has led to the definition of a concept known as *query complexity*. The query complexity of an algorithm is the number of units of information it reads from its input, where the definition of a "unit of information" depends on the exact problem being considered. For example, in the problem of estimating the number of "*a*" characters in a string, a unit of information is a character; while, in the problem of estimating the diameter, a unit of information is the distance between a single pair of points. Given this definition, one can observe that the query complexities of Algorithms 1 and 2 are equal to their respective time complexity. This is roughly true for many sublinear time algorithms, but there are cases in which the time complexity is significantly larger than the query complexity.

Exercise 4. Are there algorithms whose query complexity is larger than their time complexity? Give an example of such an algorithm, or explain why such an algorithm cannot exist.

The importance of the query complexity has made its optimization an important factor, along with the time complexity, in the design of new sublinear time algorithms. Moreover, due to the usual similarity between the values of the two complexity measures, many works on sublinear time algorithms discuss only the query complexity and neglect to mention the time complexity at all.

10.4 Bibliographic Notes

Initially, sublinear time algorithms have been studied mainly in the context of property testing problems, such as program testing (Blum *et al.*, 1993; Rubinfeld and Sudan, 1996) and probabilistically checkable proofs (Arora *et al.*, 1998; Arora and Safra, 1998) (see Chapter 11 for more information on property testing). However, later works often study sublinear time algorithms also in the context of other problems.

The algorithm for estimating the diameter of a set of points given as Algorithm 2 is considered a folklore result, and a version of it can be found, for example, in the works of Aingworth *et al.* (1999).

D. Aingworth, C. Chekuri, P. Indyk and R. Motwani. Fast Estimation of Diameter and Shortest Paths (Without Matrix Multiplication). *SIAM Journal on Computing*, 28(4): 1167–1181, 1999.

S. Arora, C. Lund, R. Motwani, M. Sudan and M. Szegedy. Proof Verification and the Hardness of Approximation Problems. *Journal of the ACM*, 45(3): 501–555, 1998.

S. Arora and S. Safra. Probabilistic Checking of Proofs: A New Characterization of NP. *Journal of the ACM*, 45(1): 70–122, 1998.

M. Blum, M. Luby and R. Rubinfeld. Self-Testing/Correcting with Applications to Numerical Problems. *Journal of Computer and System Sciences*, 47(3): 549–595, 1993.

R. Rubinfeld and M. Sudan. Robust Characterizations of Polynomials with Applications to Program Testing. *SIAM Journal on Computing*, 25(2): 252–271, 1996.

Exercise Solutions

Solution 1

Assume by way of contradiction that there exists a deterministic Algorithm A that given a string w can exactly determine the number of "a" characters in w using $o(|w|)$ time. In particular, this means that there exists a large enough n such that algorithm A determines the number of "a" characters in strings of size n using less than n time. Note that this implies that, given such an input string, Algorithm A does not read all of it.

Consider now an arbitrary string w of length n. By the above discussion, there exists a character in w which is not read by A when w is its input string. Let us denote the location of this character by i, and let w' be a string of length n which is equal to w in every location other than i and contains the character "a" in location i if and only if w does not contain it in this location. Clearly, w and w' have a different number of "a" characters. However, as A does not read location i of w when given w as input, it will execute in exactly the same manner given either w or w'. Thus, A will produce the same output given both inputs; which leads to a contradiction.

The result of this exercise can be extended to randomized algorithms by fixing the random choices of the algorithm. In other words, consider a randomized algorithm A which uses $o(|w|)$ time and always determines correctly the number of "a" characters in its input string. One can fix the random choices of this algorithm as follows. Whenever A asks for a random bit, we forward it a bit from a predetermined sequence of bits (which could even be all zeros for the sake of this proof). This fixing of the random choices converts A into a deterministic algorithm. The important observation now is that the resulting deterministic version of A represents one possible execution path of the original algorithm A, and thus, is also guaranteed to use $o(|w|)$ time and determine correctly the number of "a" characters in its input string; which contradicts our previous result regarding deterministic algorithms.

Solution 2

Consider an arbitrary deterministic algorithm A, and assume that it does not read all of the matrix M when M contains only zeros. Let C be one of the cells that A does not read when M contains only zeros, and consider the execution of A on a matrix M' which contains zeros in all cells other than C and 1 in the cell C. We now need to make two observations, as follows.

First, since A does not read the cell C given the matrix M, it will follow the same execution path given M and M', and thus, will produce the same answer given both of them. The second observation is that M corresponds to a diameter of 0, while M' corresponds to a diameter of 1 (note that the diameter is simply the maximum of the matrix entries), and thus, A fails to distinguish between a diameter of 0 and a diameter of 1.

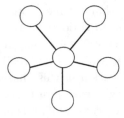

Figure 10.2.   A star over six vertices.

Solution 3

Figure 10.2 depicts a star over six vertices. We encourage you to use it as a visual aid while reading this solution.

We begin the solution by observing that the diameter of a star is 2 since this is the distance between any two non-center vertices of the star. Consider now the output of Algorithm 2 given that it selects the center vertex of the star as u. Since the distance of the center vertex from any other vertex of the star is 1, Algorithm 2 outputs in this case the value 1, which underestimates the true diameter by a factor of 2.

Consider now an execution of Algorithm 2 in which it selects a non-center vertex as u. Since the distance between any pair of non-center vertices is 2, the algorithm outputs 2 in this case — i.e., its estimate for the distance is completely accurate.

Solution 4

Reading a unit of information from the input requires a unit of time. Thus, the query complexity of an algorithm is always a lower bound on its time complexity, which implies that the query complexity can never be larger than the time complexity.

Chapter 11

Property Testing

Many computational problems ask an algorithm to check whether a given object has a certain property. For example, given a graph we might be interested in determining whether it is connected or not. Unfortunately, very often such problems cannot be solved by sublinear time algorithms because the difference between an object that obeys the property and an object that does not obey it can be very subtle, which effectively forces any algorithm for testing whether an object has the property to read most of the object. *Property testing algorithms* are algorithms that avoid the above issue by relaxing their guarantee a bit. More specifically, a property testing algorithm should detect correctly that the object has the property when it has it, and it should also detect correctly that the object does not have the property when it is far from having it (in some sense). However, the property testing algorithm is allowed to answer in either way when the object almost has the property. For example, a property testing algorithm for connectivity of graphs should indicate correctly that a connected graph is connected, and should also indicate correctly that a graph with many connected components is not connected. However, such an algorithm is allowed to answer in either way given an unconnected graph with only a few connected components.

One of the most immediate uses of property testing algorithms is to filter objects that are far from having the property. This can be useful as a pre-processing step before running a slower exact algorithm for determining which of the objects have the property. The pre-processing eliminates some of the objects, and thus, reduces the number of objects on which we need to execute the slower exact algorithm. In other cases, the answer of the property testing algorithm might be useful enough to make the application of an exact algorithm redundant altogether. Following are two such cases:

- Some inputs, such as the graph representing the World Wide Web, change constantly. For such inputs, it does not make much sense to distinguish between objects that have the property and objects that roughly have the property, since the input can easily alternate between these two states. However, the distinction between having the property and being far from having it is often still meaningful, as it is less likely for the input to switch between these very distinct states.
- In real-world scenarios' inputs often either have the property or are far from having it. When this happens, the output of a property testing algorithm is as good as the output of an exact algorithm.

Later in this chapter we will see a few examples of property testing algorithms. However, before we can do that, we need to have a more formal definition of a property testing algorithm.

11.1 Formal View on Property Testing Algorithms

A property testing problem is formally defined using three components. The first component is the set N of possible input objects, the second component is the subset P of these objects that obey the property and the last component is a distance function d that assigns a distance $d(x, y) \in [0, 1]$ for every pair of objects $x, y \in N$ and also obeys $d(x, x) = 0$ for every object $x \in N$. To make this definition clearer, let us consider a specific property testing problem and see how it fits this definition.

The property testing problem we consider is the problem of testing whether a given list of n numbers is free of duplicates. The set N of possible input objects for this problem is simply the set of all possible lists of n numbers, and among these lists, the set $P \subseteq N$ contains all the lists that are free of duplicates (and thus, have the property we are looking for). There are numerous natural ways in which one can define the distance function d for this problem. One natural function that is used in many problems defines the distance between a pair of objects as the fraction of units of information that need to be changed to get from one object to the second one. Applying this general idea to our problem of testing whether a given list of n numbers contains duplicates, we get that the distance between any two lists of n numbers is the fraction of the positions in which the two lists differ. For example, given the lists "1, 5, 7, 8" and "6, 5, 1, 8", one can observe that these lists differ in positions 1 and 3, which are half of the positions, and thus, the distance between them is $1/2$. Note that this distance function always outputs a distance between 0 and 1 because the fraction of the positions in which two lists differ is always a number between 0 and 1. Moreover, since a list does not differ from itself in any position, the distance between a list and itself is always 0, as required.

Exercise 1. Describe one natural way in which the problem of testing whether a graph over n vertices is connected can be formalized.

A deterministic algorithm for a property testing problem gets an object $o \in N$ and a value $\varepsilon \in (0,1)$ as its input, and should output "Yes" when o belongs to P, i.e., has the property. If o does not belong to P, then the requirement from the output of the algorithm depends on the distance of the object o from the set P, which is defined as the minimal distance of o from an object of P. More formally, the distance of o from P is defined as

$$d(o, P) = \min_{p \in P} d(o, p).$$

Intuitively, this distance measures how far o is from having the property P, and it becomes 0 when o belongs to P. If the distance $d(o, P)$ of an element o from P is at least ε, then we say that o is ε-*far* from having the property and the algorithm for the property testing problem should output "No". In contrast, if the distance of o from P is smaller than ε, but o does not belong to P (i.e., the object o is close to having the property, but does not really have it), then the algorithm is allowed to output either "Yes" or "No".

A randomized algorithm for a property testing problem is very similar to a deterministic one, except that it is only required to output the appropriate answer with probability at least $2/3$. In other words, given an object $o \in P$, the algorithm must output "Yes" with probability at least $2/3$, and given an object o which is ε-far from having the property, the algorithm must output "No" with probability at least $2/3$.

One should note that the number $2/3$ in the above definition of randomized algorithms for property testing problems is arbitrary. Exercise 2 shows that increasing it to any number smaller than 1 will not make much of a difference.

Exercise 2. Show that given a property testing algorithm ALG and any value $\delta \in (0, 1/3]$, one can create a new property testing algorithm ALG_δ for the same problem such that

(a) ALG_δ outputs the appropriate answer with probability at least $1 - \delta$.
(b) The query complexity of ALG_δ is larger than the query complexity of ALG by only an $O(\log \delta^{-1})$ factor.

Hint: ALG_δ should make use of $\Theta (\log \delta^{-1})$ independent executions of ALG.

11.2 Testing a List of n Numbers for Being Free of Duplicates

Let us now give our first property testing algorithm, which is an algorithm for determining whether a given list of n numbers is free of duplicates. Note that when $\varepsilon^{-1} = \Omega(\sqrt{n})$, one can easily determine whether the list contains duplicates by simply reading the entire list, which results in a query complexity of only $O(\sqrt{n}/\varepsilon)$. Thus, we only need to describe a property testing algorithm for the case that $\varepsilon\sqrt{n} \geqslant c$ for some large enough constant c. This algorithm is given as Algorithm 1. Intuitively, the algorithm takes a random sub-list of $O(\sqrt{n}/\varepsilon)$ numbers from the list and declares the original list free of duplicates if and only if the sampled sub-list is free of duplicates.

Observation 1 shows that Algorithm 1 has a sublinear query complexity. It is not difficult to verify that it is also possible to implement Algorithm 1 using a sublinear time complexity.

Observation 1. The query complexity of Algorithm 1 is $h = O(\sqrt{n}/\varepsilon)$.

Algorithm 1: (Testing Duplicate Freeness)

1. Let $h \leftarrow \lceil \sqrt{n} \rceil + \lceil 22\sqrt{n}/\varepsilon \rceil$, and let L be the input list.
2. Let D be a list of h independent uniformly random positions in L.
3. Let S be a sub-list of L obtained by keeping only the positions of L appearing in D.
4. **if** S is free of duplicates **then**
5.   **return** "Yes"
6. **else**
7.   **return** "No".

Proof.   There are at most h distinct positions in D, and thus, Algorithm 1 reads at most h numbers (data items) from its input list.   □

It remains to prove that Algorithm 1 outputs the appropriate answer with probability at least 2/3. Observation 2 shows that this is the case when the input list is free of duplicates.

Observation 2.   Given a list which is free of duplicates, Algorithm 1 always outputs "Yes".

Proof.   Since the list is free of duplicates, any sub-list of it must also be free of duplicates. In particular, the sub-list S produced by Algorithm 1 is free of duplicates, which makes the algorithm output "Yes".   □

The other (and more complicated) case that we need to consider is the case in which Algorithm 1 gets a list L which is ε-far from being free of duplicates. We need to show that in this case Algorithm 1 outputs "No" with probability at least 2/3. The first step toward proving this is to show that the fact that L is ε-far from being free of duplicates implies that it must have some structural property.

Lemma 1.   *There must be a set Q of at least $\varepsilon n/3$ disjoint pairs of position (between 1 and n) such that the two positions corresponding to any given pair in Q contain the same number in L.*

Proof.   Since L is ε-far from being free of duplicates, one must change at least εn positions in L to get a duplicates free list. Thus, there must be at least εn positions in L which contain numbers that also appear in another position in L. Let us denote the set of these positions by R. Consider now an arbitrary number m which appears multiple times in L, and let R_m be the subset of R containing the positions in which m appears in L. Since $|R_m| \geqslant 2$ by the definition of m, we can create at least $\lfloor |R_m|/2 \rfloor \geqslant |R_m|/3$ disjoint pairs from the positions in R_m. Repeating this for every number m which appears multiple times in L, we are guaranteed to get at least $|R|/3 \geqslant \varepsilon n/3$ disjoint pairs such that the two positions corresponding to every pair contain the same number in L.   □

We would like to show that with a probability of at least 2/3, the two positions of some pair of Q both appear in the list D. Let D_1 be the prefix of D of length $\lceil \sqrt{n} \rceil$, and let D_2 be the rest of the list D. Additionally, let Q_1 be the subset of Q containing only pairs whose first positions appear in D_1.

Lemma 2. *With probability at least* $5/6$, $|Q_1| \geqslant \varepsilon \cdot \sqrt{n}/12$.

Proof. Let Y_i be an indicator for the event that position i in D_1 appears as the first position of some pair in Q. Clearly, Y_i takes the value 1 with probability $|Q|/n$ since the pairs in Q are disjoint. Thus,

$$E\left[\sum_{i=1}^{|D_1|} Y_i\right] = \sum_{i=1}^{|D_1|} E[Y_i] = \frac{|D_1| \cdot |Q|}{n} \geqslant \frac{\sqrt{n} \cdot (\varepsilon n/3)}{n} = \frac{\varepsilon \cdot \sqrt{n}}{3}.$$

Moreover, since the Y_i variables are independent, using the Chernoff bound, we get

$$\Pr\left[\sum_{i=1}^{|D_1|} Y_i < \frac{\varepsilon \cdot \sqrt{n}}{6}\right] \leq \Pr\left[\sum_{i=1}^{|D_1|} Y_i < \frac{E\left[\sum_{i=1}^{|D_1|} Y_i\right]}{2}\right] \leqslant e^{-\frac{(1/2)^2 \cdot (\varepsilon \cdot \sqrt{n}/3)}{2}}$$

$$\leq e^{-\frac{\varepsilon \cdot \sqrt{n}}{24}} \leqslant \frac{1}{12},$$

where the last inequality holds when $\varepsilon\sqrt{n}$ is large enough (recall that we only need to consider the case that $\varepsilon\sqrt{n}$ is larger than some large enough constant c).

We have proved that with probability at least $11/12$, the sum $\sum_{i=1}^{|D_1|} Y_i$ is at least $\varepsilon \cdot \sqrt{n}/6$. Unfortunately, that is not good enough to prove the lemma because D_1 might contain repetitions, which implies that the first position of some pairs in Q might appear multiple times in D_1. To solve this, we need to show that D_1 is not likely to contain many repetitions. Let Z_{ij} be an indicator for the event that locations i and j in D_1 contain the same value. One can observe that the size of $|Q_1|$ is lower bounded by the expression

$$\sum_{i=1}^{|D_1|} Y_i - \sum_{i=1}^{|D_1|} \sum_{j=i+1}^{|D_1|} Z_{ij}.$$

We have already seen that the first term is usually large. Let us now show that the second term is usually small. Clearly, Z_{ij} takes the value 1 with probability $1/n$ when $i \neq j$. Thus, by Markov's inequality, we obtain

$$\Pr\left[\sum_{i=1}^{|D_1|} \sum_{j=i+1}^{|D_1|} Z_{ij} > 12\right] \leq \Pr\left[\sum_{i=1}^{|D_1|} \sum_{j=i+1}^{|D_1|} Z_{ij} > \frac{6|D_1|\,(|D_1|-1)}{n}\right]$$

$$= \Pr\left[\sum_{i=1}^{|D_1|} \sum_{j=i+1}^{|D_1|} Z_{ij} > 12 \cdot E\left[\sum_{i=1}^{|D_1|} \sum_{j=i+1}^{|D_1|} Z_{ij}\right]\right]$$

$$\leq \frac{1}{12}.$$

By the union bound, we get that with probability at least $5/6$ the sum $\sum_{i=1}^{|D_1|} Y_i$ is at least $\varepsilon \cdot \sqrt{n}/6$ and the sum $\sum_{i=1}^{|D_1|} \sum_{j=i+1}^{|D_1|} Z_{ij}$ is at most 12. When that happens, the size of $|Q_1|$ can be lower bounded by

$$\sum_{i=1}^{|D_1|} Y_i - \sum_{i=1}^{|D_1|} \sum_{j=i+1}^{|D_1|} Z_{ij} \geqslant \frac{\varepsilon \cdot \sqrt{n}}{6} - 12 \geqslant \frac{\varepsilon \cdot \sqrt{n}}{12},$$

where the last inequality holds when $\varepsilon \cdot \sqrt{n}$ is large enough. $\qquad\square$

Next, let us show that when $|Q_1|$ is large, Algorithm 1 is likely to detect a duplicate. Note that Algorithm 1 returns "No" whenever D_2 contains the second position of some pair in Q_1 because this means that both positions of this pair appear in D.

Lemma 3. *When $|Q_1| \geqslant \varepsilon \cdot \sqrt{n}/12$, D_2 contains the second position of some pair in Q_1 with probability at least $5/6$.*

Proof. First, we observe that Q_1 depends only on D_1, and thus, is completely independent of D_2. Hence, the probability that a given location in D_2 does not contain the second position of any pair in Q_1 is at most $1 - |Q_1|/n$. As the positions of D_2 are independent, this implies that the probability that none of them contains the second position of a pair in Q_1 is at most

$$\left(1 - \frac{|Q_1|}{n}\right)^{|D_2|} \leqslant \left(1 - \frac{\varepsilon}{12\sqrt{n}}\right)^{\frac{22\sqrt{n}}{\varepsilon}} \leqslant e^{-\frac{\varepsilon}{12\sqrt{n}} \cdot \frac{22\sqrt{n}}{\varepsilon}} = e^{-\frac{22}{12}} \leqslant \frac{1}{6}.$$

$\qquad\square$

Combining Lemmata 2 and 3, we get that when L is ε-far from being free of duplicates, Algorithm 1 outputs "No" with probability at least $(5/6)^2 \geqslant 2/3$. We summarize this in Theorem 1.

Theorem 1.   *Algorithm 1 is a property testing algorithm for testing whether a list of length n is free of duplicates whose query complexity is $O(\sqrt{n}/\varepsilon)$.*

By definition, a property testing algorithm is guaranteed to output with probability at least 2/3 "Yes" given an object obeying the property and "No" given an object which is ε-far from having the property. However, this definition still allows the algorithm to make a mistake (i.e., produce the wrong output) for every such input with probability at most 1/3. We consider the mistake of outputting "No" given an object obeying the property as one kind of mistake, and the mistake of outputting "Yes" given an object which is ε-far from having the property as a second kind of mistake. If the algorithm has a non-zero probability to make both kinds of mistakes, then we say that it is a *two-sided error algorithm*. However, some algorithms can only make one of the above two kinds of mistakes. Such algorithms are called *one-sided error algorithms*.

‖ **Exercise 3.** Determine whether Algorithm 1 is a one-sided error or two-sided ‖ error algorithm.

11.3 The List Model and Testing Lists for Being Sorted

Recall that a property testing problem consists of three components: a set N of possible input objects, a subset P of the objects that obey the property and a distance function d. Intuitively, the set N and the distance function d describe the world in which the problem resides, i.e., what kinds of objects exist, and how is the distance between them defined. In contrast, the subset P describes the property that we are looking for in objects of this world (by including exactly the objects having this property). Due to this intuitive point of view, the pair of N and d is often called the *model* to which the problem belongs, and the subset P is often simply referred to as the *property* of the problem.

Often there are many interesting properties that one might want to test within the context of a single model (or world). For example, the problem of testing a list of n numbers for being free of duplicates lives in a model in which the set of objects is the set of all lists of n numbers and the distance between two lists is the fraction of the n positions in which the two lists differ. This model is often called the *list model*. Beside the property of being free of duplicates, there are other properties that one might want to test in this model. For example, one might be interested in testing in this model the property of being a sorted list.

‖ **Exercise 4.** Give an additional example of a natural property one might want
‖ to test in the list model.

In the rest of this section, we study algorithms for testing the property of being a sorted list in the list model. In other words, we are interested in a property testing algorithm for testing whether a list of n numbers is sorted (in a non-decreasing order). Exercise 5 demonstrates that this problem is not trivial by showing that two very natural algorithms for the problem can fail with a high probability to detect that a list is not sorted even when it is very far from being sorted.

‖ **Exercise 5.** For every one of the following two algorithms, describe a list
‖ which is 1/2-far from being sorted, but the algorithm declares it to be sorted
‖ with a probability of at least $1 - O(1/n)$.

‖ (a) The algorithm that picks a uniformly random location i between 1 and
‖ $n - 1$, and declares the list to be sorted if and only if the number at
‖ location i is not larger than the number at location $i + 1$.
‖ (b) The algorithm that picks a uniformly random pair of locations $1 \leqslant i <$
‖ $j \leqslant n$, and declares the list to be sorted if and only if the number at
‖ location i is not larger than the number at location j.

Remark: The algorithms considered by Exercise 5 are natural but simplistic, in the sense that they only make one random test. One can argue that a more realistic algorithm should repeat this random test multiple times, and declare the list to be sorted only if it passes the test every time. Such a repetition will of course increase the probability of the algorithm to detect that the list is not sorted. However, it is not difficult to prove that getting this probability to be constant even for lists which are 1/2-far from being sorted will require at least a linear number of repetitions.

Given the failure of the two natural algorithms described in Exercise 5, we need to consider somewhat less natural algorithms. In particular, we will show that the algorithm given as Algorithm 2 has a significant probability to detect that a list is not sorted when it is ε-far from being sorted (conditioned on an assumption that we will present soon).

Algorithm 2: (Testing Being Sorted)

1. Pick a uniformly random position i between 1 and n.
2. Let v_i be the value at position i in the list.
3. Use binary search to look for the value v_i in the list.
4. **if** the binary search reported i as the position of v_i **then**
5.   **return** "Yes" (the list is sorted).
6. **else**
7.   **return** "No" (the list is not sorted).

Intuitively, Algorithm 2 picks a uniformly random value from the list, and then checks whether a binary search for this value will recover the right location in the list of the value. One can observe that even sorted lists might fail this test if they contain duplicates, because given duplicates, there are multiple answers that the binary search might return. To avoid this issue, we assume in the rest of this section that the input list is free of duplicates. One possible way to remove this assumption will be discussed in Exercise 6.

Observation 3. Given a (duplicate-free) sorted list, Algorithm 2 always returns "Yes".

Proof. Binary search works correctly given a sorted list. Thus, regardless of what value v_i is picked by Algorithm 2, the binary search will return the position of v_i in the list given v_i as the input. □

The more involved part in the analysis of Algorithm 2 is to upper bound the probability that it will declare as sorted a list which is ε-far from being sorted. Toward this goal, let us say that a number v_i is *good* if Algorithm 2 returns "Yes" when it selects v_i. Additionally, let V_G be the set of good values in the list.

Lemma 4. *The values of V_G appear in a sorted order in the list.*

Proof. Recall that binary search maintains at all times a potential range in which its target value might appear. At every iteration, it picks a pivot value from the middle of this potential range, and compares it with the value it is looking for. If the last value is larger than the pivot value, then the part of the potential range before the pivot value is dropped, and otherwise, the other part of the potential range is dropped (see Figure 11.1 for a graphical illustration of a single iteration of binary search).

Consider now two distinct good values v_i and v_j that appear in locations i and j in the list, and consider the behavior of binary search when it is

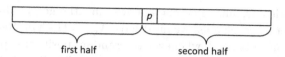

first half   second half

Figure 11.1. A graphical illustration of a single iteration of binary search. The rectangle in the above figure represents the range in which the value searched for may reside. Binary search compares the value it is looking for with a pivot value from the middle of this range (the pivot is denoted by p in this figure). If the target value is smaller than the pivot, then only the first half of the range is kept for the next iteration, otherwise only the second half of the range is kept.

given either v_i or v_j as its input. In both cases, the algorithm selects pivot values, compares them to its input and acts according to the results of the comparisons. As long as the comparison of the pivot to v_i and v_j gives the same result, the algorithm continues with the same execution path given either v_i or v_j. However, this cannot go on forever. To see why that is the case, note that the fact that v_i and v_j are good values implies that binary search manages to find them when it looks for them. Thus, v_i is the sole value remaining in the potential range of binary search until the search terminates when v_i is given as the input, and similarly v_j is the sole value that remains in the potential range until the search terminates when v_j is the input. Thus, at some point binary search must get a different answer when comparing the pivot to v_i or v_j.

Let us denote the pivot for which the comparison resulted in a different answer by p. Thus, either $v_i < p \leqslant v_j$ or $v_j < p \leqslant v_i$, and let us assume without loss of generality that the first option is true. When comparing v_i with p, binary search learns that v_i is smaller than p, and thus, it removes the second half of the potential range. However, we already know that v_i remains in the potential range until the end when v_i is the input for the binary search. Thus, v_i must appear before p in the list. A similar argument shows that either $p = v_j$ or v_j appears after p in the list. Hence, we have proved that the relative order in the list of v_i and v_j is consistent with their order as numbers. Since this is true for every two good values, it proves the lemma. $\qquad\square$

Corollary 1. *Given a list which is ε-far from being sorted, Algorithm 2 returns "No" with probability at least ε.*

Proof. Observe that a list of length n in which there is a subset of m values that appear in the right order can be sorted by changing only the other $n - m$ values. Thus, a list which is ε-far from being sorted cannot contain a subset of more than $(1 - \varepsilon)n$ values that appear in the right order. In particular, since Lemma 4 shows that the good values appear in the right order, for such a list we must have $|V_G| \leqslant (1-\varepsilon)n$. Recall now that Algorithm 2 outputs "No" whenever the random position it picks contains a value that does not belong to V_G. Thus, the probability of this algorithm to output "No" given a list which is ε-far from being sorted is at least

$$\frac{n - |V_G|}{n} \geqslant \frac{n - (1 - \varepsilon)n}{n} = \varepsilon. \qquad \square$$

Observation 3 and Corollary 1 together show that Algorithm 2 correctly answers when its input list is sorted, and has a significant probability to correctly answer when its input list is ε-far from being sorted. However, to get a property testing algorithm, we need the last probability to be at least $2/3$. This can be achieved by executing Algorithm 2 multiple times, and outputting that the list is sorted if and only if all the executions of Algorithm 2 report this answer. A formal presentation of the algorithm we get in this way is given as Algorithm 3.

Theorem 2. *Algorithm 3 is a one-sided error property testing algorithm for testing whether a list of length n is sorted whose query complexity is $O(\varepsilon^{-1} \log n)$.*

Proof. Let us begin by proving that Algorithm 3 is a one-sided error property testing algorithm for testing whether a list of length n is sorted. Consider first the case that the input list is sorted. Algorithm 3 executes h copies of Algorithm 2 on this list. According to Observation 3, all the h copies of Algorithm 2 return "Yes" in this case, and thus, Algorithm 3 also returns "Yes" (i.e., it detects correctly that the list is sorted).

Consider now the case that the input list is ε-far from being sorted. In this case Corollary 1 guarantees that each one of the h copies of Algorithm 2 has a probability of at least ε to return "No". Since the h copies are

---

Algorithm 3: (Final Testing Being Sorted)

1. Let $h \leftarrow \lceil 2/\varepsilon \rceil$.
2. Execute h independent copies of Algorithm 2 on the input list.
3. **if** all the copies answer "Yes" **then**
4.   **return** "Yes" (the list is sorted).
5. **else**
6.   **return** "No" (the list is not sorted).

independent, the probability that at least one of the copies returns "No" is at least

$$1 - (1 - \varepsilon)^h \geqslant 1 - e^{-\varepsilon h} = 1 - e^{-\varepsilon \lceil 2/\varepsilon \rceil} \geqslant 1 - e^{-2} \geqslant \frac{2}{3},$$

where the first inequality follows from the inequality $1 - x \leqslant e^{-x}$, which holds for every real value x. Hence, given a list which is ε-far from being sorted, Algorithm 3 detects that it is not sorted with probability at least $2/3$; which completes the proof that it is a one-sided error property testing algorithm.

It remains to bound the query complexity of Algorithm 3. Consider first the query complexity of Algorithm 2. This algorithm uses one query to read v_i, and then makes some additional queries through the use of binary search. However, binary search has a time complexity of $O(\log n)$, and thus, its query complexity cannot be larger than that. Hence, we got that the query complexity of Algorithm 2 is upper bounded by $1 + O(\log n) = O(\log n)$. Let us consider now Algorithm 3. One can observe that it accesses its input list only through the h copies of Algorithm 2 that it uses. Thus, the query complexity of Algorithm 3 is upper bounded by h times the query complexity of Algorithm 2, i.e., by

$$h \cdot O(\log n) = \lceil 2/\varepsilon \rceil \cdot O(\log n) = O(\varepsilon^{-1} \cdot \log n). \qquad \square$$

Exercise 6. The analysis of Algorithm 3 is based on the assumption that no value appears in the list more than once. Describe one way in which this assumption can be removed. **Hint:** The input list for Algorithm 3 contains real numbers. However, one can observe that the only property of real numbers that the algorithm and its analysis depend on is the ability to compare real numbers, i.e., the existence of an order over the real number. Thus, Algorithm 3 and its analysis work when the input list contains elements of any set, as long as it is possible to compare elements of this set.

11.4 The Pixel Model and Testing for Half-Planes

In the previous sections of this chapter, we have studied two property testing problems, both of which belonged to the list model. In this section, we will consider a different model, known as the *pixel model*. The set of the objects in this model is the set of all black and white images of size n on n. In

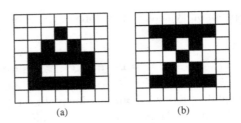

(a)   (b)

Figure 11.2.   Two objects (images) in the pixel model.

other words, an object in this model (or an image) is a square array of n^2 pixels, where each pixel can be either black or white (see Figure 11.2 for two examples of images belonging to this model). Formally, if we treat the black pixels as zeros and the white pixels as ones (or vice versa), then an image is simply a square binary matrix of size n. However, in this section it will be more useful to view it as a graphical object than as a matrix.

Since the basic unit of information in the pixel model is the color of a pixel, it is natural to define the distance between a pair of images as the fraction of the n^2 pixels in which they differ. For example, the distance between the images (a) and (b) of Figure 11.2 is 12/49 because they differ in 12 out of their 49 pixels. Note that by now we have described the set of objects in the pixel model and the distance function between them, and thus, we have completed the definition of this model.

Let us now define the property testing problem we will consider in this model. Intuitively, an image is a half-plane if there exists a line such that all the pixels on one side of the line are black and all the pixels on the other side of the line are white (see Figure 11.3 for a few examples of half-plane images). This intuitive definition will be good enough for us in this section. However, a more formal definition is that an image is a half-plane if and only if there exist two linear functions f_{row} and f_{column} such that a pixel on row i and column j is black if and only if $f_{row}(i) \leqslant f_{column}(j)$. Convince yourself that this formal definition indeed corresponds to the above intuitive definition.

In the rest of this section, we describe a property testing algorithm for determining whether an image is a half-plane (or ε-far from being a half-plane). This algorithm starts by determining the number of edges of the image that have end points with different colors (see Figure 11.4 for a graphical illustration of these terms). Figure 11.3 includes examples of images in which the number of edges with non-identical end point colors is 0 (the leftmost image), 4 (the rightmost image) or 2 (the two middle

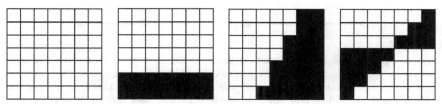

Figure 11.3. A few additional examples of images in the pixel model. The three images on the left are half-planes, while the rightmost image is not a half-plane since no straight line can separate the white and black pixels in it.

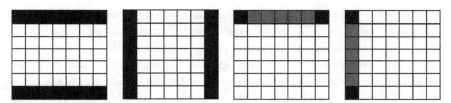

Figure 11.4. A graphical illustration of the terms "edge" and "end points". In the leftmost image, the top and bottom edges of the image are marked in black. Note that these are simply the top and bottom rows of the image, respectively. In the second image from the left, the left and right edges of the image are marked in black. Note that these are the leftmost and rightmost columns of the image, respectively. Finally, in the third and fourth images we mark in black the end points of the top and left edges, respectively (the edges themselves are marked in gray). Note that the end points of an edge are its two pixels that fall on the corners of the image.

images), but no example in which this number is 1 or 3. It is not difficult to prove that this is no coincidence, i.e., that no image can have exactly 1 or 3 edges with non-identical end point colors. Thus, our algorithm needs to handle only three possible values for the number of edges with non-identical end point colors. Exercises 7 and 8 deal with two of these values.

Exercise 7. Show that an image having four edges with non-identical end point colors is never a half-plane.

Exercise 8. Describe a property testing algorithm with a query complexity of $O(\varepsilon^{-1})$ for determining whether an image having zero edges with non-identical end point colors is a half-plane. **Hint:** Observe that there are only two half-plane images having zero edges with non-identical end point colors.

Figure 11.5. Consider three pixels w, b and m on an edge that have the following properties: w is white, b is black and m is in the middle between w and b. There are two possibilities for the color of m, however, this figure demonstrates that regardless of the color of m, there exists a pair of pixels on the edge that have non-identical colors and the distance between them is half the distance between w and b. (a) shows that the pair of m and b has these properties when m is white, and (b) shows that the pair of m and w has these properties when m is black.

The case that the image has exactly two edges with non-identical end point colors remains to be considered. Consider one of these edges. We already know that one of its end points is black, while the other one is white. In other words, we have two pixels of the edge which have different colors and the distance between them is n. Let us denote the black pixel by b and the white pixel by w. If we now pick the middle pixel m between b and w (or roughly the middle pixel if there is no pixel exactly in the middle), then it must be either black or white. If it is white, then b and m are two pixels on the edge which have different colors and the distance between them is roughly half the distance between b and w. Similarly, if m is black, then w and m are two pixels on the edge having the above properties. Thus, regardless of the color of m, given two pixels b and w on the edge which have different colors and a distance of n, we managed to get a pair of pixels on the edge which have different colors and a distance of about half of n (see Figure 11.5 for a graphical illustration). Repeating this process $O(\log \varepsilon^{-1})$ times, we end up with a pair of pixels on the edge which have different colors and a distance of at most $\max\{\varepsilon n/2, 1\}$.

Recall now that we assume that the image has two edges whose end points have non-identical colors. Applying the above process to both these edges, we get a pair (b_1, w_1) of pixels on one edge and a pair (b_2, w_2) of pixels on the other edge, such that: the distance between the pixels in each pair is at most $\max\{\varepsilon n/2, 1\}$, the pixels b_1 and b_2 are both black and the pixels w_1 and w_2 are both white. We now connect b_1 and b_2 by a section S_b, and also w_1 and w_2 by a section S_w. If the two sections intersect, then clearly the image is not a half-plane. Thus, we may assume that the two sections partition the image into three areas as follows:

- an area B consisting of the part of the image separated from w_1 and w_2 by the section S_b (including S_b itself),

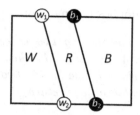

Figure 11.6. The partitioning of an image into the three areas W, R and B based on the locations of the pixels w_1, w_2, b_1 and b_2.

- an area W consisting of the part of the image separated from b_1 and b_2 by S_w (including S_w itself),
- and an area R consisting of the part of the image between the two sections.

See Figure 11.6 for a graphical illustration of the above three areas.

One can observe that since B is separated from the white pixels w_1 and w_2 by a section ending with two black pixels, it cannot include any white pixels unless the image is not a half-plane. Similarly, the image is not a half-plane if W contains any black pixels. Thus, one can try to determine whether the image is a half-plane by looking for pixels in B that are white and pixels in W that are black. If such pixels can be found, then the image is certainly not a half-plane. This idea is the basis of the algorithm we suggest, which is given as Algorithm 4, for determining whether an image having two edges with non-identical end point colors is a half-plane.

Algorithm 4: Test for Half-Plane (2 Edges with Non-Identical End Point Colors)

1. Construct S_b, S_w, B and W as described above.
2. **if** S_b and S_w intersect **then**
3. **return** "No" (the image is not a half-plane).
4. Let $h \leftarrow \lceil 4/\varepsilon \rceil$.
5. **do** h times:
6. Select a uniformly random pixel from the image.
7. **if** the selected pixel is white and belongs to B or is black and belongs to W **then**
8.   **return** "No" (the image is not a half-plane).
9. **return** "Yes" (the image is a half-plane).

The above discussion implies Lemma 5 immediately.

Lemma 5. *Given an image having two edges with non-identical end points colors, if Algorithm 4 returns "No", then the image is not a half-plane. Thus, given a half-plane image having two edges with non-identical end point colors, the algorithm always return "Yes".*

Lemma 6 proves the other direction, i.e., that Algorithm 4 is likely to return "No" given an image which is far from being a half-plane (assuming ε is not too small).

Lemma 6. *Assuming $\varepsilon \geqslant 2/n$, given an image having two edges with non-identical end point colors which is ε-far from being a half-plane, Algorithm 4 returns "No" with probability at least $2/3$.*

Proof. Let us assume that the sections S_b and S_w do not intersect (otherwise we are done), and let us begin the proof by upper bounding the number of pixels in the area R (the area between the sections S_b and S_w, excluding the sections themselves). By construction, the distance between the end points b_1 and p_1 of these sections is at most $\varepsilon n/2$, and so is the distance between their other end points. One can verify that this implies that there are at most $\varepsilon n^2/2$ pixels between the sections, i.e., in the area R.

Consider now one way in which the input image can be made a half-plane. First, we make all the pixels of B and R black, and then we make all the pixels of W white. Since the image is known to be ε-far from a half-plane, this way of making it a half-plane must require the change of at least εn^2 pixels. In particular, since R contains at most $\varepsilon n^2/2$ pixels, at least $\varepsilon n^2/2$ of the changed pixels must belong to the areas W and B. In other words, there must be at least $\varepsilon n^2/2$ pixels that are black and reside in W or are white and reside in B.

Using the above observation we get that whenever Algorithm 4 picks up a random pixel, it has a probability of at least $\varepsilon/2$ to pick a white pixel in B or a black pixel in W. Thus, the probability that the algorithm returns "No" is at least

$$1 - \left(1 - \frac{\varepsilon}{2}\right)^h \geqslant 1 - e^{-\varepsilon h/2} \geqslant 1 - e^{-2} \geqslant 2/3. \qquad \square$$

To complete the analysis of Algorithm 4, it remains to upper bound its query complexity.

Observation 4. Algorithm 4 has a query complexity of $O(\varepsilon^{-1})$.

Proof. Constructing S_b and S_w in the way explained above requires $O(\log \varepsilon^{-1})$ queries. After this construction, Algorithm 4 requires only $O(h) = O(\varepsilon^{-1})$ additional queries. $\qquad \square$

Combining all the claims proved earlier, we get Theorem 3.

Theorem 3. *For $\varepsilon \geqslant 2/n$, Algorithm 4 is a property testing algorithm with a query complexity of $O(\varepsilon^{-1})$ for determining whether an image of size n on n having two edges with non-identical end point colors is a half-plane.*

Observe that by combining Theorem 3 with the claims proved by Exercises 7 and 8, one can get for $\varepsilon \geqslant 2/n$ a property testing algorithm with a query complexity of $O(\varepsilon^{-1})$ for determining whether a general image of size n on n is a half-plane.

Exercise 9. Theorem 3 only works when ε is not too small. Explain why the above analysis of Algorithm 4 fails when $\varepsilon < 2/n$, and suggest a modification for the algorithm that will make it work also in this case.

11.5 Concluding Remark

In this chapter, we have seen property testing algorithms for three problems. All three algorithms had a sublinear query (and time) complexity, but it is still interesting to compare their query complexities. The worst query complexity was presented by our algorithm for determining whether a list is free of duplications, whose query complexity was $O(\sqrt{n}/\varepsilon)$, i.e., polynomial in the natural size n of the instance. Our algorithm for determining whether a list is sorted had a better query complexity of $O(\varepsilon^{-1} \log n)$, which depends only logarithmically on the natural size of the instance. A logarithmic dependence on the size of the instance is much more desirable than a polynomial dependence because it allows the algorithm to deal with much larger instances. However, the most desirable algorithms are algorithms whose query complexity is completely independent of the size of the input instance. Intuitively, it is quite surprising that such algorithms can exist at all. However, we have already seen one such algorithm. Specifically, our algorithm for determining whether an image is a half-plane has a query complexity of $O(\varepsilon^{-1})$, which is independent of the size n^2 of the input.

11.6 Bibliographic Notes

Property testing first appeared in an implicit form in the work of Blum *et al.* (1993), and was later made explicit by Rubinfeld and Sudan (1996). Both these works focused on testing algebraic properties of functions. The extension of property testing beyond this specific field was first made by Goldreich *et al.* (1998), who studied property testing in graphs.

The algorithm presented above for testing whether a list is duplicates free (Algorithm 1) is closely related to the well-known birthday paradox. One analysis of this algorithm can be found in the works of Ergün *et al.* (2000), however, the specific analysis given in this chapter is based on an analysis appearing in the lecture notes of a course given by Ronitt Rubinfeld in 2014 at Tel Aviv University. It should also be noted that the analysis we give is not optimal, and can be slightly improved.

The algorithm we have presented for testing whether a list is sorted (Algorithm 3) was first suggested by Ergün *et al.* (2000), and the algorithm for testing whether an image is a half-plane was first given by Raskhodnikova (2003).

M. Blum, M. Luby and R. Rubinfeld. Self-testing/correcting with Applications into Numerical Problems. *Journal of the ACM*, 47(3): 549–595, 1993.

F. Ergün, S. Kannan, R. Kumar, R. Rubinfeld and M. Viswanathan. Spot-Checkers. *Journal of Computer and System Sciences*, 60(3): 717–751, 2000.

O. Goldreich, S. Goldwasser and D. Ron. Property Testing and its Connection to Learning and Approximation. *Journal of the ACM*, 45(4): 653–750, 1998.

S. Raskhodnikova. Approximate Testing of Visual Properties. In *Proceedings of the 6th International Workshop on Approximation Algorithms for Combinatorial Optimization Problems (APPROX)*, 370–381, August 2003.

R. Rubinfeld and M. Sudan. Robust Characterization of Polynomials with Applications to Program Testing. *SIAM Journal on Computing*, 25(2): 252–271, 1996.

Exercise Solutions

Solution 1

In the problem of testing whether a graph over n vertices is connected, the set N of possible inputs is the set of all graphs over n vertices, and the set P is the subset of the connected graphs in N. If we think of the graph as represented by its adjacency matrix, then it is natural to define the distance between two graphs as the fraction of the entries in this matrix in which the two graphs differ (see Figure 11.7 for an example).

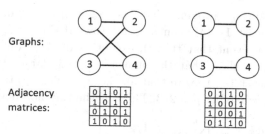

Graphs:

Adjacency matrices:

Figure 11.7. Two graphs on 4 vertices and their corresponding adjacency matrices. The two matrices differ in 8 cells, which are half of the cells of each matrix. Thus, the distance between the two graphs is 1/2.

We note that one might be tempted to define the distance between two graphs in the context of this problem as the difference between the number of connected components in these graphs (up to some normalization to keep the distance within the range $[0, 1]$). While such a definition is formally correct, it fails to capture the intuition that we usually look for in a distance function. In other words, such a distance function will be more about the distance of a graph from the property that we have in mind, and less about the distance between the pairs of graphs. As a rule of thumb, we are interested in distance functions that are natural for the representation of the objects and are independent of the property that we have in mind.

Solution 2

Consider the algorithm ALG_δ given as Algorithm 5. As this algorithm accesses the input object only by executing ALG on it h times, it is clear that the query complexity of ALG_δ is larger than the query complexity of ALG by a factor of $h = \Theta(\log \delta^{-1})$. Thus, it remains to show that ALG_δ outputs the appropriate answer with probability at least $1 - \delta$.

Algorithm 5: $ALG_\delta(o, \varepsilon)$

1. Let $h \leftarrow 48\lceil \log \delta^{-1} \rceil$.
2. Independently execute h times the algorithm ALG on the object o.
3. **if** most of the executions outputted "Yes" **then**
4.   return "Yes"
5. **else**
6.   return "No".

Let us begin by proving that the algorithm outputs "Yes" with probability at least $1 - \delta$ when $o \in P$. Toward this goal, let X_i be an indicator for the event that the ith execution of ALG outputted "Yes". Then, we need to show that the sum $\sum_{i=1}^{h} X_i$ is larger than $h/2$ with probability at least $1 - \delta$. Note that all the X_i indicators take the value 1 with the same probability $p \geqslant 2/3$. Thus, by the Chernoff bound, we obtain

$$\Pr\left[\sum_{i=1}^{h} X_i \leqslant \frac{h}{2}\right] = \Pr\left[\sum_{i=1}^{h} X_i \leqslant \frac{1/2}{p} \cdot ph\right]$$

$$= \Pr\left[\sum_{i=1}^{h} X_i \leqslant \frac{1/2}{p} \cdot E\left[\sum_{i=1}^{h} X_i\right]\right]$$

$$\leqslant e^{-\frac{\left(1-\frac{1/2}{p}\right)^2 \cdot ph}{2}} \leqslant e^{-\frac{\left(1-\frac{1/2}{2/3}\right)^2 \cdot (2/3)h}{2}} = e^{-\frac{h}{48}} \leqslant e^{\log \delta} = \delta.$$

Consider now the case that o is ε-far from having the property. In this case, we need to show that ALG_δ outputs "No" with probability at least $1 - \delta$, which is equivalent to showing that the sum $\sum_{i=1}^{h} X_i$ is at most $h/2$ with that probability. Since ALG is a property testing algorithm, we get that in this case each indicator X_i takes the value 1 with some probability $p \leqslant 1/3$. Using the Chernoff bound again, we get

$$\Pr\left[\sum_{i=1}^{h} X_i > \frac{h}{2}\right] = \Pr\left[\sum_{i=1}^{h} X_i > \frac{1/2}{p} \cdot ph\right]$$

$$= \Pr\left[\sum_{i=1}^{h} X_i > \frac{1/2}{p} \cdot E\left[\sum_{i=1}^{h} X_i\right]\right]$$

$$\leqslant e^{-\frac{\min\left\{\frac{1/2}{p}-1,\left(\frac{1/2}{p}-1\right)^2\right\} \cdot ph}{3}}$$

$$= e^{-\frac{\min\left\{1,\frac{1/2}{p}-1\right\} \cdot (1/2-p)h}{3}} \leqslant e^{-\frac{\min\left\{1,\frac{1/2}{1/3}-1\right\} \cdot (1/2-1/3)h}{3}}$$

$$= e^{-\frac{h}{36}} \leqslant e^{\log \delta} = \delta.$$

Solution 3

As proved by Observation 2, given a list L which is free of duplicates, Algorithm 1 always outputs "Yes". In other words, it never makes the mistake of outputting "No" given a list obeying the property, and thus, it is a one-sided error algorithm.

Solution 4

Recall that the objects in the list model consist of all the lists of n numbers. There are many natural properties of such lists that one might be interested in testing. A very partial list of them includes the following:

- the list contains only positive numbers,
- the sum of the numbers in the list is positive,
- there is an increasing sequence of at least three consecutive numbers in the list,
- no number in the list is divisible by another number appearing in the list.

Solution 5

(a) Assume for simplicity that n is even, and consider the list whose first half consists of the integer numbers $n/2 + 1$ to n and its second half consists of the integer numbers 1 to $n/2$ (for example, if $n = 8$, then we get the list "5, 6, 7, 8, 1, 2, 3, 4"). To make this list sorted, one must either change all the numbers in its first half, or all the numbers in its second half, thus, this list is $\frac{1}{2}$-far from being sorted.

Consider now the algorithm described by part (a) of the exercise. This algorithm picks a value i between 1 and $n-1$, and then compares the values of the list in locations i and $i+1$. Given the above list, the numbers in these locations will always be compatible with a sorted list, unless $i = n/2$. Thus, the algorithm will declare the list to be sorted with probability

$$\Pr[i \neq n/2] = \frac{\#\text{ possible values for } i \text{ other than } n/2}{\#\text{ possible values for } i}$$

$$= \frac{n-2}{n-1} = 1 - O(1/n).$$

(b) Assume for simplicity that n is even, and consider the list which contains in its odd locations the even numbers 2 to n, and in its even locations the odd numbers 1 to $n-1$ (for example, if $n = 8$, then we get the list "2, 1, 4, 3, 6, 5, 8, 7"). For every $1 \leqslant k \leqslant n/2$, consider the numbers at positions $2k-1$ and $2k$ in the list. As the first of these numbers is larger than the second one, at least one of them has to be changed to make the list sorted. Moreover, since this is true for every one of the $n/2$ possible values for k, we get that making the above list sorted requires changing at least $n/2$ values in it. Thus, the list is $\frac{1}{2}$-far from being sorted.

Consider now the algorithm described by part (b) of the exercise. This algorithm picks two random locations $i < j$, and then compares the values of the list in these locations. Given the above list, the numbers in locations i and j will be consistent with a sorted list, unless $i = 2k - 1$ and $j = 2k$ for some integer $1 \leqslant k \leqslant n/2$. Thus, the algorithm will declare the list to be sorted with probability

$$\Pr \begin{bmatrix} \text{There is no integer } k \text{ such} \\ \text{that } i = 2k - 1 \text{ and } j = 2k \end{bmatrix}$$

$$= 1 - \frac{n/2}{\#\text{possible } i, j \text{ values such that } 1 \leqslant i < j \leqslant n}$$

$$= 1 - \frac{n/2}{n(n-1)/2} = 1 - O(1/n).$$

Solution 6

Consider a pre-processing algorithm that takes the input list for Algorithm 3 and replaces every number v in it with an ordered pair (v, i), where i is the location of v in the original list. Let us define for such ordered pairs a comparison according to the following lexicographic rule. A pair (v_1, i_1) is larger than a pair (v_2, i_2) if $v_1 > v_2$ or $v_1 = v_2$ and $i_1 > i_2$. Let us now make a few observations as follows:

1. The pre-processing algorithm will convert a sorted list of numbers into a sorted list of pairs and a non-sorted list of numbers into a non-sorted list of pairs.
2. The pre-processing algorithm never produces a list of pairs with duplicates (because the second component of every pair is equal to the location of the pair).
3. According to the hint following the exercise, Algorithm 3 can be used to detect whether the list of pairs is sorted or not because we have defined a way to compare pairs.

It is easy to see that these observations together imply that the combination of the pre-processing algorithm and Algorithm 3 yields a property testing algorithm for testing whether a list of numbers is sorted, and moreover, this property testing algorithm does not need the assumption of no duplications. The only problem is that, as given, the pre-processing algorithm needs to read the entire input list, and thus, has a linear query complexity. However, this can be solved by performing the pre-processing in a lazy manner. In other words, we execute Algorithm 3 without performing the pre-processing. Then, whenever Algorithm 3 tries to read a pair from the list, we make a single query to the original list of numbers, and generate the pair that Algorithm 3 tries to read. This way, the query complexity of the algorithm we get is identical to the query complexity of the original Algorithm 3.

Solution 7

Consider an image whose four edges all have non-identical end-point colors. In such an image, no two adjacent corners can have the same color, and thus, it must have two black corners on one diagonal, and two white corners on the other diagonal. Assume now, by way of contradiction, that this image is a half-plane. Then, there must be a straight line separating the white and black pixels in it. Let us study the relationship of this separating line with the diagonals of the image. There are a few cases to consider as follows:

- The first case is that the separating line does not intersect the diagonals. This case implies that all the corners of the image appear on one side of the image, and thus, should have the same color; which leads to a contradiction.
- The second case is that the separating line intersects one of the diagonals at a point which is not a corner. In this case, the two corners of this diagonal appear on different sides of the separating lines, and should have different colors; which again leads to a contradiction.
- The third case is that the separating line intersects the diagonals (and therefore, also the image) only in the corners. In this case, the two or three corners of the images that are not intersected by the separating line appear on the same side of the separating line, and thus, should have identical colors. This leads to a contradiction once more, because each diagonal has at least one corner which is not intersected by the separating line.

Solution 8

Consider a half-plane image having zero edges with non-identical end point colors. All the corners of this image must have the same colors, which means that they are all on the same side of the straight line separating the white and black pixels of the image. Note that this implies that the entire image is on one side of the separating line, and thus, the entire image must have one color. In other words, as claimed by the hint, there are only two half-plane images having zero edges with non-identical end point colors: the image which is all white, and the image which is all black.

This last observation suggests the following simple algorithm for determining whether an image having zero edges with non-identical end point colors is a half-plane. The algorithm first selects a random subset of pixels, and compares their colors with the color of the corners. If the algorithm detects any pixel whose color differs from the color of the corners, then it declares that the image is not a half-plane. However, if all the pixels selected by the algorithm have the same color as the corners, then the algorithm declares the image to be a half-plane. A more formal description of this algorithm is given as Algorithm 6.

Let us prove that Algorithm 6 is a property testing algorithm with a query complexity of $O(\varepsilon^{-1})$. This follows from the next three claims.

Observation 5. Algorithm 6 has a query complexity of $O(\varepsilon^{-1})$.

Proof. Algorithm 6 queries exactly h pixels from the image, and thus, its query complexity is $O(h) = O(\varepsilon^{-1})$. $\qquad\square$

Observation 6. Algorithm 6 always return "Yes" given a half-plane having zero edges with non-identical end point colors.

Proof. According to the above discussion, a half-plane image having zero edges with non-identical end point colors must be colored entirely with a single color. Thus, given such an image, whenever Algorithm 6 picks a pixel

---

Algorithm 6: Test for Half-Plane (0 Edges with Non-Identical End Point Colors)

1. Let $h \leftarrow \lceil 2/\varepsilon \rceil$.
2. **do** h times:
3.   Select a uniformly random pixel from the image.
4.   **if** the selected pixel has a different color than the image corners **then**
5.   **return** "No" (the image is not a half-plane).
6. **return** "Yes" (the image is a half-plane).

from the image, the color of this pixel will match the colors of the corners of the image (and the color of every other pixel in the image). Hence, given an image of the above type, the condition of the "if" statement on Line 4 of Algorithm 6 will never evaluate to "true", which will make the algorithm return "Yes". □

Lemma 7. *Algorithm 6 returns "No" with probability at least 2/3 given an image having zero edges with non-identical end point colors which is ε-far from being a half-plane.*

Proof. Consider an image having zero edges with non-identical end point colors which is ε-far from being a half-plane and assume without loss of generality that the corners of the image are white. We need to show that Algorithm 6 returns "No" given this image with probability at least 2/3. Toward this goal, we claim that there must be at least $\varepsilon \cdot n^2$ black pixels in the image. To see why that must be the case, note that if there were less than $\varepsilon \cdot n^2$ black pixels in the image, then it could not be ε-far from being a half-plane, since it could be transformed into the all-white half-plane image by changing the color of only these less than $\varepsilon \cdot n^2$ black pixels.

Consider now a single random pixel picked by Algorithm 6. The probability that this pixel is black is at least ε by the above discussion. Since the random pixels picked by Algorithm 6 are independent, this means that the probability that at least one of them is black is at least

$$1 - (1 - \varepsilon)^h \geqslant 1 - e^{-\varepsilon h} = 1 - e^{-\varepsilon \lceil 2/\varepsilon \rceil} \geqslant 1 - e^{-2} \geqslant \frac{2}{3}.$$

The proof now completes by observing that Algorithm 6 outputs "No" whenever one of the random pixels it picks is black since we assumed the corners of the image are white. □

Solution 9

One of the first steps of Algorithm 4 is finding two pairs of pixels (one pair consists of b_1 and w_1, and the other of b_2 and w_2) such that the pixels in each pair have non-identical colors and the distance between them is upper bounded by $n\varepsilon/2$. Naturally, this cannot be done when $\varepsilon < 2/n$, since this will require finding two disjoint pixels whose distance from each other is less than 1. The best alternative is to find pairs of the above kind such that the distance between the pixels in each pair is exactly 1. Unfortunately, this might result in an area R containing $\Theta(n)$ pixel. To see why that is problematic, one can note that, when $\varepsilon < 2/n$, a property testing algorithm must detect that an image is not a half-plane even when it can be made a half-plane by changing as few as $\varepsilon n^2 \leqslant 2n$ pixels. Thus, in the regime of $\varepsilon < 2/n$, one cannot ignore a part of the image of size $\Theta(n)$. In particular, to make Algorithm 4 apply to this regime as well, we must take into consideration the pixels of R in some way.

Assume from now on that we are in the regime $\varepsilon < 2/n$, and consider the modified version of Algorithm 4 given as Algorithm 7. Algorithm 7 differs from Algorithm 4 in two things. First, it uses pairs (b_1, w_1) and (b_2, w_2) whose distance is 1 rather than $\varepsilon n/2$. As discussed above, this leads to an area R containing $O(n)$ pixels. The second modification is that the algorithm constructs an image I which is black in the area B (of the original image), white in the area W and agrees with the original image on the area R. Constructing I requires the algorithm to read all the pixels of R from the original image, however, in the regime $\varepsilon < 2/n$ this can be done without making the query complexity of the algorithm exceed $O(\varepsilon^{-1})$.

Algorithm 7: Modified Test for Half-Plane (2 Edges with Non-Identical End Point Colors)

1. On each one of the edges with non-identical end point color, find a pair of adjacent pixels with different colors. Denote these pairs by (b_1, w_1) and (b_2, w_2).
2. Construct S_b, S_w, B and W based on the pairs (b_1, w_1) and (b_2, w_2).
3. **if** S_b and S_w intersect **then**
4.   **return** "No" (the image is not a half-plane).
5. Let $h \leftarrow \lceil 4/\varepsilon \rceil$.
6. **do** h times:
7.   Select a uniformly random pixel from the image.
8.   **if** the selected pixel is white and belongs to B or is black and belongs to W **then**
9.   **return** "No" (the image is not a half-plane).
10. Consider an image I in which the area B is completely black, the area W is completely white and the area R is identical to the area R of the original image.
11. **if** I is not a half-plane **then**
12.   **return** "No" (the image is not a half-plane).
13. **else**
14.   **return** "Yes" (the image is a half-plane).

It remains to be explained why Algorithm 7 is a property testing algorithm for testing whether its input image is a half-plane. First, consider the case that it gets an image which is a half-plane. For such an image, the area B will contain only black pixels, while the area W will contain only white pixels, and this has two consequences. The first consequence is that whenever the algorithm picks a random pixel from one of these two areas, the pixel will be in the right color, and will not make the algorithm return "No". The second consequence is that the image I constructed by the algorithm is identical to the input image, and thus, will be a half-image. Thus, the algorithm will output "Yes", as required.

Consider now the case that Algorithm 7 gets an input image which is ε-far from being a half-plane. If given this input image, Algorithm 7 constructs an image I which is not a half-plane, then it will return "No", and we are done. Otherwise, the fact that the input image is ε-far from being a half-plane implies that it differs from I in at least εn^2 places. As the two images are identical in the area R, we get that there are at least εn^2 pixels in the original image that are either white and belong to B or black and belong to W. Observe that if any one of these pixels is ever selected by the algorithm, then the algorithm returns "No". Moreover, since the algorithm selects each pixel independently, the probability that this happens is at least

$$1 - \left(1 - \frac{\varepsilon n^2}{n^2}\right)^h = 1 - (1 - \varepsilon)^h \geqslant 1 - e^{-\varepsilon h} \geqslant 1 - e^{-4} \geqslant \frac{2}{3}.$$

Chapter 12

Algorithms for Bounded Degree Graphs

There are multiple natural representations for graphs. For example, a graph can be represented by its adjacency matrix, or by storing the adjacency list of each vertex. Traditionally, the designer of a graph algorithm is free to assume that the algorithm's input graph is given in any one of the standard representations. This assumption often makes sense because the graph can be easily converted from one representation to another in polynomial (or often even linear) time. However, in the context of sublinear time algorithms, the algorithm does not have enough time to convert the input graph from one representation to another, and thus, the representation in which the input graph is given can have a major impact on the things that can be performed in sublinear time. For example, it might be possible to determine in sublinear time whether a graph is connected when it is given in one representation, but not when it is given in another representation.

The above issue implies that we should study sublinear time algorithms for graph problems separately for every one of the standard graph representations. In this chapter and in Chapter 13, we do this for two such representations. In particular, in this chapter we study sublinear algorithms that assume a representation of graphs which is appropriate for graphs with a bounded degree, and in Chapter 13 we study a sublinear time algorithm that assumes the adjacency matrix representation.

12.1 Counting Connected Components

In this chapter, we are interested in graphs whose degree is bounded by some parameter d (in other words, no vertex in the graph has more than

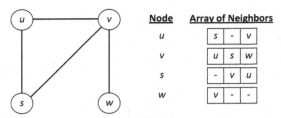

Figure 12.1. A graph, and its bounded degree representation for $d = 3$. Cells in the arrays of neighbors which are empty are designated with the character "-".

d neighbors). The representation we assume for such graphs is as follows. For every vertex u of the graph, the representation includes an array of size d which stores the list of neighbors of u. We assume that the array includes no repetitions, i.e., every neighbor of u appears exactly once in the array of u. In particular, this implies that if u has less than d neighbors, then some of the cells in its array are left empty. In the rest of the chapter, we refer to this graph representation as the *bounded degree graph representation*. A graphical example of such a representation can be found in Figure 12.1.

The first computational problem we would like to solve for bounded degree graphs is estimating the number of connected components in a graph $G = (V, E)$. Toward this goal, we observe that if the number of nodes in the connected component of a node $u \in V$ is denoted by n_u, then the number of connected components in G can be expressed using the following formula.

$$\sum_{u \in V} \frac{1}{n_u}. \tag{12.1}$$

Exercise 1. Prove that (12.1) is indeed equal to the number of connected components in G.

One natural approach for trying to estimate the sum (12.1) is to pick a few random terms of this sum, and then calculate the value of the sum under the assumption that the terms we evaluated are average terms. A more formal statement of this approach is given as Algorithm 1. The algorithm gets parameters $\varepsilon, \delta \in (0, 1]$ which control the quality of its output. Additionally, it uses n to denote the number of nodes in the graph G.

Algorithm 1: Connected Components Estimation — First Attempt (ε, δ)

1. Let $h \leftarrow \lceil 12\epsilon^{-2} \cdot \log(2/\delta) \rceil$ and $S \leftarrow 0$.
2. For every $1 \leqslant i \leqslant h$, let $u(i)$ be an independent uniformly random node of G.
3. **return** $\frac{n}{h} \cdot \sum_{i=1}^{h} \frac{1}{n_{u(i)}}$.

‖ **Exercise 2.** Prove that the expected output of Algorithm 1 is exactly the ‖ number of connected components in G.

Implementing Algorithm 1 requires us to evaluate $n_{u(i)}$. One standard way to do this is to run a BFS algorithm from the vertex $u(i)$, and let it discover all the nodes of the connected components of $u(i)$. This works very well when the connected component of $u(i)$ is small, but might take too much time to allow for a sublinear time complexity when the connected component of $u(i)$ is large. The workaround we will use to solve this problem is to stop the BFS after it has discovered $\lceil 2/\varepsilon \rceil$ nodes. This will guarantee that the BFS terminates after $O(d/\varepsilon)$ time (because the BFS scans at most d edges for every node it discovers). Moreover, if we denote by $\hat{n}_u$ the number of nodes discovered by the BFS when it starts from u, then $\hat{n}_u$ obeys by definition the formula

$$\hat{n}_u = \min\{n_u, 2/\varepsilon\}.$$

If we now replace $n_{u(i)}$ with $\hat{n}_{u(i)}$ in Algorithm 1, then we get the algorithm given as Algorithm 2.

The big advantage of Algorithm 2 over Algorithm 1 is that we can implement it in sublinear time (which is even independent of the number of nodes in G — see Observation 1). However, unlike Algorithm 1 whose

---

Algorithm 2: Connected Components Estimation (ε, δ)

1. Let $h \leftarrow \lceil 12\epsilon^{-2} \cdot \log(2/\delta) \rceil$ and $S \leftarrow 0$.
2. For every $1 \leqslant i \leqslant h$, let $u(i)$ be an independent uniformly random node of G.
3. **return** $\frac{n}{h} \cdot \sum_{i=1}^{h} \frac{1}{\hat{n}_{u(i)}}$.

---

expected output is equal to (12.1), the expected output of Algorithm 2 is equal to the slightly different sum

$$\sum_{u \in V} \frac{1}{\hat{n}_u} \tag{12.2}$$

(the proof for this fact is identical to the proof of Exercise 2). Hence, the expected output of Algorithm 2 is not necessarily equal to the number of connected components in G. Exercise 3 solves this issue by proving that the values of (12.1) and (12.2) do not differ by much, which implies that the expected output of Algorithm 2 is always close to the number of connected components in G (which we proved to be equal to (12.1)).

‖ **Exercise 3.** Prove that $0 \leqslant \sum_{u \in V} 1/\hat{n}_u - \sum_{u \in V} 1/n_u \leqslant \varepsilon n/2$.

To complete the analysis of Algorithm 2, we still need to do two things. First, we need to formally analyze its time complexity, and second, we need to show that its output is usually close to its expected value. This is done by the following two claims.

Observation 1. The time complexity of Algorithm 2 is $O(d \cdot \log \delta^{-1}/\varepsilon^3)$.

Proof. Excluding the calculation of the terms $\hat{n}_{u(i)}$, one can observe that the time complexity of Algorithm 2 is $O(h)$ given our standard assumption that arithmetic operations take $\Theta(1)$ time. According to the above discussion, evaluating each one of the terms $\hat{n}_{u(i)}$ requires $O(d/\varepsilon)$ time. Thus, the total time complexity of Algorithm 2 is given by

$$O(h) + h \cdot O\left(\frac{d}{\varepsilon}\right) = O\left(\frac{hd}{\varepsilon}\right) = O\left(\frac{d \cdot \log \delta^{-1}}{\varepsilon^3}\right). \qquad \square$$

Lemma 1. *Algorithm 2 estimates the value of (12.2) up to an error of $\varepsilon n/2$ with probability at least $1 - \delta$.*

Proof. For every $1 \leqslant i \leqslant h$, let $Y_i = 1/\hat{n}_{u(i)}$. Observe that the variables $Y_1, Y_2, \ldots, Y_h$ take values only from the range $[\varepsilon/2, 1]$. Thus, we can bound the expectation of their sum by

$$\frac{h\varepsilon}{2} \leqslant E\left[\sum_{i=1}^{h} Y_i\right] \leqslant h.$$

We now observe that the variables $Y_1, Y_2, \ldots, Y_h$ are also independent, and thus, by the Chernoff bound, we get

$$\Pr\left[\sum_{i=1}^{h} Y_i \geqslant E\left[\sum_{i=1}^{h} Y_i\right] + \frac{h\varepsilon}{2}\right]$$

$$= \Pr\left[\sum_{i=1}^{h} Y_i \geqslant \left(1 + \frac{h\varepsilon}{2E[\sum_{i=1}^{h} Y_i]}\right) \cdot E\left[\sum_{i=1}^{h} Y_i\right]\right]$$

$$\leqslant e^{-\left(\frac{h\varepsilon}{2E\left[\sum_{i=1}^{h} Y_i\right]}\right)^2 E\left[\sum_{i=1}^{h} Y_i\right]/3}$$

$$= e^{-\frac{h^2\varepsilon^2}{12E[\sum_{i=1}^{h} Y_i]}} \leqslant e^{-h\varepsilon^2/12} = e^{-\lceil 12\varepsilon^{-2} \cdot \log(2/\delta)\rceil \cdot \varepsilon^2/12}$$

$$\leqslant e^{\log(\delta/2)} = \frac{\delta}{2}.$$

Similarly,

$$\Pr\left[\sum_{i=1}^{h} Y_i \leqslant E\left[\sum_{i=1}^{h} Y_i\right] - \frac{h\varepsilon}{2}\right]$$

$$= \Pr\left[\sum_{i=1}^{h} Y_i \leqslant \left(1 - \frac{h\varepsilon}{2E[\sum_{i=1}^{h} Y_i]}\right) \cdot E\left[\sum_{i=1}^{h} Y_i\right]\right]$$

$$\leqslant e^{-\left(\frac{h\varepsilon}{2E\left[\sum_{i=1}^{h} Y_i\right]}\right)^2 E\left[\sum_{i=1}^{h} Y_i\right]/2}$$

$$= e^{-\frac{h^2\varepsilon^2}{8E[\sum_{i=1}^{h} Y_i]}} \leqslant e^{-h\varepsilon^2/8} = e^{-\lceil 12\varepsilon^{-2} \cdot \log(2/\delta)\rceil \cdot \varepsilon^2/8}$$

$$\leqslant e^{\log(\delta/2)} = \frac{\delta}{2}.$$

Combining the last two inequalities using the union bound, we see that with probability at least $1 - \delta$ the sum $\sum_{i=1}^{h} Y_i$ does not deviate from its expectation by more than $h\varepsilon/2$, which implies

$$\Pr\left[\left|\frac{n}{h} \cdot \sum_{i=1}^{h} Y_i - E\left[\frac{n}{h} \cdot \sum_{i=1}^{h} Y_i\right]\right| \leqslant \frac{n\varepsilon}{2}\right] \geqslant 1 - \delta.$$

It now remains to recall that the expression $\frac{n}{h} \cdot \sum_{i=1}^{h} Y_i$ is equal to the output of Algorithm 2, and thus, its expectation is equal to (12.2). The lemma now follows by combining this observation with the last inequality. $\qquad\Box$

Corollary 1. *Algorithm 2 estimates the value of* (12.2) *up to an error of* εn *with probability at least* $1 - \delta$.

Proof. Observe that Exercise 3 implies that (12.2) always estimates (12.1) up to an error of $\varepsilon n/2$. The corollary now follows by combining this observation with Lemma 1, i.e., with the fact that Algorithm 2 estimates the value of (12.2) up to an error of $\varepsilon n/2$ with probability at least $1 - \delta$. $\qquad\Box$

Theorem 1 summarizes the properties that we have proved for Algorithm 2.

Theorem 1. *Algorithm 2 has a time complexity of* $O(d\varepsilon^{-3} \cdot \log \delta^{-1})$, *and with probability at least* $1 - \delta$, *it estimates the number of connected components in* G *up to an error of* εn.

Theorem 1 shows that with a large probability, the error in the estimation produced by Algorithm 2 is bounded by εn. Note that this error can be very large compared to the estimated value when G contains few connected components. One might hope to improve that by finding an algorithm that estimates the number of connected components up to a relative error of ε, but unfortunately, Exercise 4 shows that this cannot be done.

Exercise 4. Prove that no sublinear time algorithm can estimate the number of connected components in a bounded degree graph up to a relative error of $1/4$ with a probability $1/2 + \varepsilon$ for any constant $\varepsilon > 0$. **Hint:** Consider the graph G_1 which is a path of length n and the random graph G_2 which is obtained from G_1 by removing a uniformly random edge from it. Show that with a high probability, every sublinear time algorithm must output the same value given either G_1 or G_2.

12.2 Minimum Weight Spanning Trees

The next computational problem for which we would like to develop a sublinear time algorithm is the problem of estimating the weight of the minimum weight spanning tree of a graph. Naturally, this problem only makes sense for connected weighted graphs, and thus, we assume

---

Algorithm 3: Kruskal's Algorithm

1. Let $T \leftarrow \emptyset$.
2. Order the edges of G in a non-decreasing weight order.
3. **for** every edge e in that order **do**
4.   **if** $T \cup \{e\}$ is a tree **then**
5.   Add e to T.
6. **return** T.

---

throughout this section that the input graph is connected and that its edges have integer weights between 1 and some positive integer w.

One of the standard algorithms for finding a minimum weight spanning tree is the well-known algorithm of Kruskal. Pseudocode of this algorithm is given as Algorithm 3.

Exercise 5 proves an important property of the tree constructed by Kruskal's algorithm. Let T be the tree produced by Kruskal's algorithm for the graph G, and let us denote by $T_{\leqslant i}$ the set of the edges of T whose weight is at most i. Similarly, let us denote by $G_{\leqslant i}$ the subgraph obtained from G by removing all edges whose weight exceed i. Finally, given a graph G, we denote by $CC(G)$ the set of connected components of G.

‖ **Exercise 5.** Prove that $|T_{\leqslant i}| = n - |CC(G_{\leqslant i})|$ for every $1 \leqslant i \leqslant w$.

Remark: It can be shown that the claim made by Exercise 5 is true for every minimum weight spanning tree of G. However, this is not necessary for our purposes.

Using Exercise 5, it is now possible for us to assign a formula for the weight of T in terms of the number of connected components in various subgraphs of G.

Observation 2. The weight of the minimum weight spanning tree T is $n - w + \sum_{i=1}^{w-1} |CC(G_{\leqslant i})|$.

Proof. Exercise 5 implies that the number of edges of T of weight 1 is

$$|T_{\leqslant 1}| = n - |CC(G_{\leqslant 1})|,$$

and for every $2 \leqslant i \leqslant n$, the number of edges of T of weight i is

$$|T_{\leqslant i}| - |T_{\leqslant i-1}| = [n - |CC(G_{\leqslant i})|] - [n - |CC(G_{\leqslant i})|]$$

$$= |CC(G_{\leqslant i-1})| - |CC(G_{\leqslant i})|.$$

Thus, the total weight of T is

$$n - |CC(G_{\leqslant 1})| + \sum_{i=2}^{w} i \cdot (|CC(G_{\leqslant i-1})| - |CC(G_{\leqslant i})|)$$

$$= n - w \cdot |CC(G_{\leqslant w})| + \sum_{i=1}^{w-1} |CC(G_{\leqslant i})|$$

$$= n - w + \sum_{i=1}^{w-1} |CC(G_{\leqslant i})|,$$

where the last equality holds since $G_{\leqslant w}$ is equivalent to the original graph G, and we assume that G is connected (i.e., has a single connected component). $\qquad\square$

An immediate consequence of the last observation is that estimating the weight of T boils down to estimating the number of connected components in the graphs $G_{\leqslant 1}, G_{\leqslant 2}, \ldots, G_{\leqslant w-1}$, which is a task for which we have already developed an algorithm in Section 12.1. The algorithm obtained this way for estimating the weight of the minimum weight spanning tree is given as Algorithm 4. As usual, the algorithm gets parameters $\varepsilon', \delta' \in (0, 1]$ which control the quality of its output. Additionally, it uses n to denote the number of nodes in graph G.

Lemma 2. *With probability at least $1 - \delta'$, Algorithm 4 estimates the weight of the minimum weight spanning tree of G up to an error of $\varepsilon' n$.*

Proof. Theorem 1 guarantees that with probability at least $1 - \delta$, Algorithm 2 estimates the number of connected components in its input graph

---

Algorithm 4: Estimating the Weight of the Minimum Weight Spanning Tree (ε', δ')

1. **for** $i = 1$ to $w - 1$ **do**
2.   Execute Algorithm 2 on the graph $G_{\leqslant i}$ with parameters $\varepsilon = \varepsilon'/(w - 1)$ and $\delta = \delta'/(w - 1)$. Let C_i be the estimate produced by the algorithm for $|CC(G_{\leqslant i})|$.
3. **return** $n - w + \sum_{i=1}^{w-1} C_i$.

up to an error of εn. Thus, by the union bound, with probability at least $1 - (w - 1)\delta = 1 - \delta'$ we have

$$|C_i - |CC(G_{\leqslant i})|| \leqslant \varepsilon n \quad \forall_{1 \leqslant i \leqslant w - 1}.$$

One can now observe that whenever these inequalities hold, we also have

$$\left| \left(n - w + \sum_{i=1}^{w-1} C_i \right) - \left(n - w + \sum_{i=1}^{w-1} |CC(G_{\leqslant i})| \right) \right|$$

$$= \left| \sum_{i=1}^{w-1} C_i - \sum_{i=1}^{w-1} |CC(G_{\leqslant i})| \right| \leqslant \sum_{i=1}^{w-1} |C_i - |CC(G_{\leqslant i})||$$

$$\leqslant (w - 1) \cdot \varepsilon n = \varepsilon' n,$$

which is equivalent to claiming that the error in the estimate produced by Algorithm 4 is at most $\varepsilon' n$. □

Exercise 6. Prove that the time complexity of Algorithm 4 is $O(dw^4/(\varepsilon')^3 \cdot \log(w/\delta'))$.

Theorem 2 summarizes the claims we have proved about Algorithm 4.

Theorem 2. *Algorithm 4 has a time complexity of $O(dw^4/(\varepsilon')^3 \cdot \log(w/\delta'))$, and with probability at least $1 - \delta'$, it estimates the weight of the minimum weight spanning tree of G up to an error of $\varepsilon' n$.*

The time complexity proved by Theorem 2 for Algorithm 4 is quite poor, especially when w is large. Better results are known, but unfortunately, one cannot do better than a time complexity of $\Omega(dw/\varepsilon^2)$. Still, the time complexity of Algorithm 4 is independent of n, which can make it useful when d and w are both small.

Exercise 7. Suggest an algorithm for estimating the weight of the minimum weight spanning tree of G when the weights of the edges of G belong to the continuous range $[1, w]$. What is the time complexity of your algorithm? **Hint:** Pick a discrete set of weights between 1 and w, and round every weight to the closest value in this set. If the set is chosen to be dense enough, then this rounding should not change the weight of any tree by much.

12.3 Minimum Vertex Cover

A *vertex cover* of a graph is a set of vertices from the graph such that every edge of the graph is adjacent to at least one vertex of the vertex cover (see Figure 12.2 for an example). Finding a minimum size vertex cover for a given graph is an NP-complete problem, but there are simple approximation algorithms which find a vertex cover whose size is at most twice the size of a minimum vertex cover. In this section, our objective is to develop a sublinear time algorithm for estimating the size of the minimum vertex cover. However, we will do this in a few steps, and will get to know two new types of algorithms along the way.

We begin by introducing the first of these types of algorithms. Usually, when we design an algorithm for a graph problem, we assume that our algorithm has a global view of the input graph, i.e., that it has access to every part of it. *Local distributed algorithms* assume a very different setting in which there are multiple processors, each having only a local view on some part of the graph, and these processors must communicate with each other in order to make some calculation about the entire graph. More formally, the input for a *local distributed algorithm* is a graph $G = (V, E)$, and we assume that every vertex of this graph is a processor which executes the algorithm. Initially, each processor has very little information about the input graph. Specifically, the information it has includes only a unique ID identifying the processor, the set of edges hitting the vertex of the processor and possibly some problem-specific parameters of the graph (such as the maximum degree in it or the total number of vertices). However, over time the processors can learn additional information about the graph G by communicating with each other. This communication is done in rounds. In each communication round, every processor can send an arbitrary message to each one of its neighbors, and can process the messages it receives from its neighbors. A toy example of a *local distributed algorithm* is given by

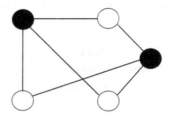

Figure 12.2.   An example of a graph and a vertex cover of it. The black vertices form a vertex cover of this graph because each edge hits at least one black vertex.

Algorithm 5: Simple Local Distributed Algorithm

1. In the first communication round, send my ID to every one of my neighbors. Let I be the set of IDs received from my neighbors in this round.
2. In the second communication round, send the set I to each one of my neighbors. Let us denote by $I_1, I_2, \ldots, I_a$ the sets obtained from my neighbors in this round.
3. **return** the union of $I_1, I_2, \ldots, I_a$ and I.

Algorithm 5 (while reading Algorithm 5, keep in mind that it is executed by every processor/vertex in the graph).

Algorithm 5 uses two rounds of communication. In the first communication round, every vertex sends its ID to its neighbors, which means that by the end of this round every vertex knows the set I of the IDs of its neighbors. In the second communication round, every vertex sends this set I to each one of its neighbors. At the end of this round a vertex u of degree a has $a+1$ sets: a set I containing the ID of each one of its neighbors, and sets $I_1, I_2, \ldots, I_a$, each containing the IDs of the neighbors of a different neighbor of u. One can observe that the union of these sets, which is the output of Algorithm 5, is a set of IDs which includes the IDs of all the nodes that can be reached from u using a path of length at most 2.

At this point, we would like to consider a locally distributed algorithm for a real computational problem, namely for the problem of calculating an approximate minimum vertex cover for the input graph. This algorithm is given as Algorithm 6, and it assumes knowledge about a parameter d which upper bounds the maximum degree of a vertex in the graph.

Algorithm 6 works in $\lceil \log_2 d \rceil$ rounds. In each round, the algorithm checks the condition on Line 3, and based on the answer, makes one of two possible decisions. The first option is that it declares itself (or more correctly, the vertex in which it runs) to be part of the vertex cover. If this happens, then the algorithm sends this decision to all the neighbors of the vertex, and stops executing. The second option is that the algorithm does not declare itself to be part of the vertex cover. In this case, the algorithm simply updates the variable h, which counts the number of neighbors of the current vertex which have not declared themselves to be part of the vertex cover so far.

Algorithm 6: Local Distributed Algorithm for Minimum Vertex Cover

1. Let h be the degree of the vertex of this processor.
2. **for** $i = 1$ to $\lceil \log_2 d \rceil$ **do**
3.   **if** $h \geqslant d/2^i$ **then**
4.   In round i, let my neighbors know that I am part of the vertex cover.
5.   **return** "I am part of the vertex cover"
6.   **else**
7.   Get all the messages in round i, and let h_i denote the number of my neighbors that declared themselves to be in the vertex cover in this round.
8. $h \leftarrow h - h_i$.
9. **return** "I am not part of the vertex cover".

Note that by the time Algorithm 6 terminates, each vertex knows whether it is part of the vertex cover or not, but there is no place that stores the entire solution (i.e., the set of all the vertices in the vertex cover). This is a standard property of local distributed algorithms. In other words, when such an algorithm terminates, we only require the processor of each vertex to know the part of the solution corresponding to that particular vertex. Nevertheless, there exists a global solution that can be obtained by combining the parts of the solution calculated by the different processors, and we refer to this global solution as the output of the algorithm. In particular, the output of Algorithm 6 is the set of vertices which declare themselves to be part of the vertex cover when all the vertices execute this algorithm.

Observation 3. The output of Algorithm 6 is a vertex cover of the input graph G.

Proof. Assume, by way of contradiction, that the observation is false. Then, there must exist an edge uv in G such that neither u nor v are declared part of the vertex cover by Algorithm 6. Let us consider the events during iteration $\lceil \log_2 d \rceil$ of Algorithm 6 in vertex u. During this iteration, the variable h still has a value of at least 1 since the edge uv connects it to a node v, which by our assumption did not declare itself to be part of the vertex cover so far. Thus, the condition

$$h \geqslant 1 \geqslant \frac{d}{2^{\lceil \log_2 d \rceil}} = \frac{d}{2^i}$$

on Line 3 of the algorithm holds in this iteration, which contradicts our assumption that u never declares itself to be part of the vertex cover. $\square$

Our next objective is to show that the vertex cover outputted by Algorithm 6 is not much larger than the minimum vertex cover.

Lemma 3. *Let C^* be the minimum vertex cover of the input graph G, and let C_A be the vertex cover produced by Algorithm 6, then $|C_A| \leqslant (1 + 2 \cdot \lceil \log_2 d \rceil) \cdot |C^*|$.*

Proof. To prove the lemma, we need to show that no more than $2|C^*|$ vertices that are not part of C^* declare themselves to be part of the vertex cover in every given iteration of Algorithm 6. We will do that by charging one unit to nodes of C^* for every vertex outside C^* that declares itself to be part of the vertex cover, and then showing that in each iteration no more than two units of charge are assigned to each vertex of C^*. One can note that this will indeed imply that no more than $2|C^*|$ units of charge are assigned in every given iteration, and thus, this is also an upper bound on the number of vertices outside C^* which declare themselves to be a part of the vertex cover in this iteration.

Consider some iteration i of Algorithm 6, and let G_i be the graph obtained from G by removing all the vertices which have already declared themselves to be part of the vertex cover in previous iterations (and the edges hitting these vertices). Consider now an arbitrary vertex $u \notin C^*$ that declares itself to be a part of the vertex cover in iteration i. One can observe that the fact that u declares itself to be a part of the vertex cover implies that u has at least $d/2^i$ neighbors in G_i. Moreover, each one of these $d/2^i$ neighbors must be a vertex of C^* because the edges between them and u must be covered by C^*. Thus, we can charge a unit to the vertices of C^* by charging at most $2^i/d$ units to each neighbor of u.

Consider now an arbitrary vertex $v \in C^*$. As discussed above, we need to show that v is not assigned more than a charge of 2 in iteration i. If v does not appear in G_i, then it is not assigned any charge in iteration i, and we are done. Otherwise, the fact that v appears in G_i implies that it did not declare itself to be a part of the vertex cover in any of the previous iterations, and thus, its degree in G_i is at most $d/2^{i-1}$. Each neighbor of v in G_i can cause a charge of at most $2^i/d$ to be assigned to v if this neighbor declares itself a part of the vertex cover in iteration i. However, as v has at most $d/2^{i-1}$ neighbors in G_i, even if all of them declare themselves to be part of the vertex cover, the total charge that will be assigned to v in iteration i will be at most

$$\frac{d}{2^{i-1}} \cdot \frac{2^i}{d} = 2. \qquad \square$$

Recall now that an approximation algorithm for an optimization problem is an algorithm that finds a feasible solution for the problem which approximately optimizes the objective function of the problem. According to this definition, Algorithm 6 is an approximation algorithm because it produces a feasible vertex cover whose size approximates the size of the minimum vertex cover. The quality of the approximation obtained by an approximation algorithm is usually measured using their approximation ratios. In Chapter 8, we defined the approximation ratio for deterministic algorithms for maximization problems. The following slightly different definition defines the approximation ratio for deterministic algorithms for minimization problems.

Definition 1. Given a minimization problem which has a set J of instances and a deterministic algorithm ALG for this problem, the *approximation ratio* of ALG is

$$\sup_{I \in J} \frac{ALG(I)}{OPT(I)},$$

where $ALG(I)$ is the value of the solution produced by the algorithm ALG given the instance I, and $OPT(I)$ is the value of the optimal solution for the instance I — i.e., the solution with the minimal value.

Informally, the approximation ratio of an algorithm for a minimization problem is a number $x \in [1, \infty)$ such that it is guaranteed that the value of the solution produced by the algorithm is never larger than the value of an optimal solution by more than a factor of x. For example, an algorithm with an approximation ratio of 1 always outputs an optimal solution, while an algorithm with an approximation ratio of 2 outputs solutions whose value is no more than twice the value of an optimal solution. To simplify the writing, we often state that an algorithm is an x-approximation algorithm, for some $x \geqslant 1$, instead of writing that its approximation ratio is at most x. Using this notation, we can now restate Lemma 3 as follows:

Lemma 3 (rephrased). *Algorithm 6 is a* $(1 + 2 \cdot \lceil \log_2 d \rceil)$*-approximation algorithm.*

We complete the analysis of Algorithm 6 by observing that it can be implemented using $\lceil \log_2 d \rceil$ communication rounds. Thus, Theorem 3 summarizes our results for this algorithm.

Theorem 3. *Algorithm 6 is a local distributed* $(1 + 2 \cdot \lceil \log_2 d \rceil)$*-approximation algorithm for the minimum vertex cover problem which uses* $\lceil \log_2 d \rceil$ *communication rounds.*

One can observe that we did not analyze the time complexity of Algorithm 6. This omission is not accidental. While analyzing local distributed algorithms, it is customary to assume that local computation is very cheap compared to the cost of communication. Thus, it is usually considered much more important to bound the number of communication rounds than to bound the time complexity of the local computations done within the processors. In fact, the tendency to ignore the cost of the local computation is so strong that people occasionally assume that the local computation is done in zero time, which makes the time complexity of the algorithm simply a synonym for the number of communication rounds it uses.

Exercise 8. Consider the problem of finding a legal coloring for graph vertices, i.e., finding a color for every vertex of the graph such that no edge connects two vertices that have the same color. Algorithm 7 is a local distributed algorithm for this problem, which colors the graph with up to $2d$ colors (where d is the maximum degree of a vertex in the graph). For simplicity, the algorithm refers to the $2d$ colors as numbers between 1 and $2d$.

(a) Prove that if Algorithm 7 terminates for all vertices, then its output is a legal coloring.

(b) Let n be the number of vertices in the input graph, and assume that $d \geqslant 1$. Prove that given this assumption, Algorithm 7 terminates after $4 \cdot \lceil \log_2 n \rceil$ communication rounds with probability at least $1 - 1/n$.

We now would like to present an additional type of algorithms, known as *local computation algorithms*, but before doing so, let us describe a situation motivating the use of such algorithms. Assume that one would like to find the social community of a given social network user. One way to do this would be to partition the entire social network into communities. For example, by applying an appropriate clustering algorithm to the graph

---

Algorithm 7: Local Distributed Algorithm for Coloring

1. Let C be a list of colors, originally containing all the colors of the range $1, 2, \ldots, 2d$.
2. **while** no final color was chosen for me yet **do**
3.   Pick a uniformly random color c from C.
4.   Let my neighbors know about the color c that I have picked, and get the colors they have picked.
5.   **if** none of my neighbors picked the color c **then**
6.   Let my neighbors know that my final color is c.
7.   **return** "my final color is c"
8.   **else**
9.   Remove from C any color that was chosen by one of my neighbors as its final color.

---

underlying the social network, and then looking up the community in which the user we are interested in happens to be. While this approach is natural, it suffers from a very significant disadvantage, namely, that getting the social community of just a single user requires us to construct a partition for all the users of the social network. If the social network is small, this disadvantage is not too problematic, but if the social network is large, the overhead of partitioning the entire network into social communities can easily make this approach impractical. An alternative way to describe this situation in somewhat more abstract terms is as follows. Our algorithm creates a "global solution" by partitioning the entire social network into social communities. Then, we drop most of this global solution and keep only the part of it which we are interested in, which is the social community which includes the user we are interested in. A much more efficient approach would be to somehow generate only the part of the global solution in which we are interested, without going through the time-consuming task of generating the entire global solution. This is exactly the objective that local computation algorithms try to achieve.

Let us now consider a more specific example. Consider the problem of finding a minimum weight spanning tree. A local computation algorithm for this problem gets a graph G and a single edge e in it, and should output whether e belongs to the minimum weight spanning tree of G (hopefully in less time than what is necessary for calculating the entire minimum weight spanning tree). One can observe that as long as G has a single minimum weight spanning tree, the task faced by the local computation algorithm is well defined. However, it is unclear what answer the algorithm should produce when there are several minimum weight spanning trees in G. For example, suppose G is a cycle and all its edges have equal weights of 1, then for every edge e of G, there exists some minimum weight spanning tree of G which includes it, and a different minimum weight spanning tree which does not include it. The way we solve this issue is by requiring the local computation algorithm to have a fixed minimum weight spanning tree in mind. In other words, if we denote by $A(G, e)$ the answer produced by the algorithm when it is given the graph G and the edge e, then the set $\{e|A(G, e) = \text{true}\}$ should be some minimum weight spanning tree of G.

More formally, a local computation algorithm gets an instance I of some computational problem and a specification of the part of the solution for this problem in which we are interested. The algorithm should then behave as if it has calculated a fixed solution S for the instance I without looking at the part of the solution we asked for, and then output the requested part of S (we refer to S as the *global solution* of the algorithm).[1] A trivial way to get a local computation algorithm will be to really calculate such a global solution S, but this usually results in a slow algorithm. Thus, what we are interested in is local computation algorithms that can produce the above behavior without really calculating a full solution for their input instance. We will exemplify this by describing a local computation algorithm for the minimum vertex cover problem, which is given as Algorithm 8.

For every vertex $u \in V$, let $C_A(G, u)$ be a boolean variable which is true if and only if Algorithm 8 indicates that u belongs to the vertex cover when given the graph G. Additionally, let $C_A(G) = \{u \in V|C_A(G, u) = \text{true}\}$.

Algorithm 8: Local Computation Algorithm for Minimum Vertex Cover (G, u)

1. Let $G'(u)$ be the subgraph of G containing only vertices that are at distance at most $\lceil \log_2 d \rceil + 1$ from u.
2. Execute Algorithm 6 on every vertex of $G'(u)$ in parallel.
3. Return the answer of Algorithm 6 for vertex u.

---

[1] This definition works for deterministic local computation algorithms, but a slightly more involved definition can be used to also define randomized local computation algorithms.

Observation 4. $C_A(G)$ is identical to the output of Algorithm 6 on the graph G, and thus, it is a vertex cover of G.

Proof. Let us assume, by way of contradiction, that there exists a vertex u such that u belongs to $C_A(G)$ but not to the output of Algorithm 6 on the graph G, or vice versa. This means that by examining the output of Algorithm 6 for the vertex u, one can determine whether the algorithm was executed on G or $G'(u)$. If we now define by V' the set of nodes that appear in G but not in G', then the last claim can be restated as claiming that the output of Algorithm 6 for the vertex u depends on the existence or inexistence of the nodes of V'. Thus, the copy of Algorithm 6 executed by u must receive information about this existence or inexistence during the execution of Algorithm 6.

According to Theorem 3, Algorithm 6 uses only $\lceil \log_2 d \rceil$ rounds of communication, and thus, any piece of information can travel a distance of at most $\lceil \log_2 d \rceil$ while this algorithm executes. In particular, the information about the existence or inexistence of V' can only travel a distance of at most $\lceil \log_2 d \rceil$. Hence, u (which is aware of this information when the algorithm terminates by the above discussion) must be located at a distance of at most $\lceil \log_2 d \rceil$ from a node that is aware of this information when the algorithm starts. However, the existence or inexistence of the nodes of V' is originally known only to the neighbors in G of the nodes of V'. Thus, there must be a neighbor of a node of V' whose distance from u is at most $\lceil \log_2 d \rceil$, which implies the existence a node of V' whose distance from u is at most $\lceil \log_2 d \rceil + 1$, and therefore, contradicts the definition of $G'(u)$. □

The last observation proves that Algorithm 8 acts as if it calculates the vertex cover $C_A(G)$ and then answers whether u is part of this vertex cover. Since $C_A(G)$ is independent of u, this implies that Algorithm 8 is a true local computation algorithm having $C_A(G)$ as its global solution.

Let us now consider the approximation ratio of Algorithm 8. Recall that the approximation ratio is a measure for the quality of the solution produced by an algorithm. Thus, it is not immediately clear how to define it for a local computation algorithm since such an algorithm only outputs a part of a solution (for example, Algorithm 8 only answers whether one particular vertex is part of the vertex cover). However, there is a natural way to bypass this difficulty by treating the global solution of the local computation algorithm as its output solution, and defining the approximation ratio of the algorithm using this global solution.

Corollary 2. *Algorithm 8 is a* $(1 + 2 \cdot \lceil \log_2 d \rceil)$*-approximation algorithm.*

Proof. Theorem 3 guarantees that the approximation ratio of Algorithm 6 is at most $(1 + 2 \cdot \lceil \log_2 d \rceil)$, which is equivalent to saying that the size of its output solution is larger than the size of the minimum vertex cover by at most a factor of $1 + 2 \cdot \lceil \log_2 d \rceil$. Observation 4 tells us that $C_A(G)$ is identical to the output solution of Algorithm 6, and thus, the size of $C_A(G)$ is also upper bounded by $1 + 2 \cdot \lceil \log_2 d \rceil$ times the size of the minimum vertex cover. The proof of the corollary now completes by recalling that $C_A(G)$ is the global solution of Algorithm 8. □

Exercise 9 concludes the analysis of Algorithm 8 by bounding its time complexity.

‖ **Exercise 9.** Prove that the time complexity of Algorithm 8 is $O(d)^{O(\log d)}$.

For convenience, we summarize in Theorem 4 all the properties of Algorithm 8 that we have proved.

Theorem 4. *Algorithm 8 is a* $(1 + 2 \cdot \lceil \log_2 d \rceil)$*-approximation local computation algorithm for the minimum vertex cover problem whose time complexity is* $O(d)^{O(\log d)}$.

We are now ready to present the promised sublinear time algorithm for the minimum vertex cover problem. This algorithm is given as Algorithm 9, and it gets a parameter $\varepsilon > 0$ which controls the quality of its output. Intuitively, this algorithm tries to estimate the size of the global solution $C_A(G)$ of Algorithm 8 by sampling random vertices of G and checking how many of these sampled vertices belong to the global solution. Since we

---

Algorithm 9: Sublinear Time Algorithm for Minimum Vertex Cover (G, ε)

1. Let $s = \lceil 12/\varepsilon \rceil$.
2. Sample uniformly and independently s vertices $u_1, u_2, \ldots, u_s$ from the graph G.
3. For each sampled vertex u_i, check whether it belongs to the vertex cover according to Algorithm 8.
4. Let r be the number of sampled vertices for which Algorithm 8 returns a positive answer (i.e., they belong to the vertex cover).
5. **return** nr/s.

already know that $C_A(G)$ is a vertex cover which is not much larger than the minimum vertex cover, an estimate of its size is also an estimate for the size of the minimum vertex cover. Lemma 4 quantifies the quality of the estimate that Algorithm 9 gets for the size of $C_A(G)$. In this lemma, we denote by $|C_A(G)|$ the number of nodes in the vertex cover $C_A(G)$.

Lemma 4. *For every $\varepsilon > 0$, with probability at least 2/3, the output of Algorithm 9 belongs to the range $[0.5|C_A(G)| - \varepsilon n, 2|C_A(G)| + \varepsilon n]$.*

Proof. Let X_i be an indicator for the event that u_i belongs to $C_A(G)$. One may observe that the output of Algorithm 9 is equal to

$$\frac{n}{s} \cdot \sum_{i=1}^{s} X_i, \tag{12.3}$$

and moreover, the expectation of this expression is

$$\mathrm{E}\left[\frac{n}{s} \cdot \sum_{i=1}^{s} X_i\right] = \frac{n}{s} \cdot \sum_{i=1}^{s} \mathrm{E}[X_i] = \frac{n}{s} \cdot \sum_{i=1}^{s} \frac{|C_A(G)|}{n} = |C_A(G)|.$$

Thus, to prove the lemma we need to show that (12.3) does not deviate from its expectation by too much. Let us first prove that (12.3) is smaller than $0.5|C_A| - \varepsilon n$ with probability at most 1/6. If $|C_A(G)| \leqslant 2\varepsilon n$, then this is trivial since (12.3) is always non-negative. Hence, it remains to consider the case that $|C_A(G)| > 2\varepsilon n$. Since the value of each indicator X_i is determined by the sample u_i, and the samples $u_1, u_2, \ldots, u_s$ are independent, we can use the Chernoff bound in this case to get

$$\Pr\left[\frac{n}{s} \cdot \sum_{i=1}^{s} X_i \leqslant 0.5 C_A(G) - \varepsilon n\right]$$

$$\leqslant \Pr\left[\sum_{i=1}^{s} X_i \leqslant \frac{s}{2n} \cdot C_A(G)\right] = \Pr\left[\sum_{i=1}^{s} X_i \leqslant \frac{1}{2} \cdot \mathrm{E}\left[\sum_{i=1}^{s} X_i\right]\right]$$

$$\leqslant e^{-\mathrm{E}[\sum_{i=1}^{s} X_i]/8} = e^{-s \cdot |C_A(G)|/(8n)} \leqslant e^{-s \cdot (2\varepsilon n)/(8n)} = e^{-s\varepsilon/4} \leqslant e^{-3} < \frac{1}{6}.$$

Next, we would like to prove that (12.3) is larger than $2|C_A| + \varepsilon n$ with probability at most 1/6. Let Y_i be an indicator that takes the value 1 with probability $\max\{\varepsilon/2, |C_A(G)|/n\}$. Since this probability is an upper bound on the probability that X_i takes the value 1, we get

$$\Pr\left[\frac{n}{s} \cdot \sum_{i=1}^{s} X_i \geqslant 2C_A(G) + \varepsilon n\right]$$

$$= \Pr\left[\sum_{i=1}^{s} X_i \geqslant \frac{2s}{n} \cdot C_A(G) + s\varepsilon\right] \leqslant \Pr\left[\sum_{i=1}^{s} Y_i \geqslant \frac{2s}{n} \cdot C_A(G) + s\varepsilon\right]$$

$$\leqslant \Pr\left[\sum_{i=1}^{s} Y_i \geqslant 2\mathrm{E}\left[\sum_{i=1}^{s} Y_i\right]\right] \leqslant e^{-\mathrm{E}\left[\sum_{i=1}^{s} Y_i\right]/3} \leqslant e^{-s\varepsilon/6} \leqslant e^{-2} < \frac{1}{6}.$$

The lemma now follows by applying the union bound to the two above results. □

Corollary 3. *With probability at least 2/3, the output of Algorithm 9 is at least $OPT/2 - \varepsilon n$, where OPT is the size of the minimum vertex cover, and at most $(2 + 4 \cdot \lceil \log_2 d \rceil) \cdot OPT + \varepsilon n$.*

Proof. The corollary follows immediately by combining Lemma 4 with the fact that Algorithm 8 is a $(1 + 2 \cdot \lceil \log_2 d \rceil)$-approximation algorithm by Theorem 4, and thus, its global solution $C_A(G)$ obeys

$$OPT \leqslant |C_A(G)| \leqslant (1 + 2 \cdot \lceil \log_2 d \rceil) \cdot OPT$$

(the first inequality holds since $C_A(G)$ is a legal vertex cover). □

Exercise 10. Lemma 4 shows that Algorithm 9 estimates $|C_A(G)|$ up to a multiplicative factor of 2 and an additive error of εn. Prove that the choice of the multiplicative factor in this lemma is arbitrary, in the sense that it can be replaced with an arbitrary constant factor $c \in (1, 2]$ if we increase s to $\lceil 6c/[(c-1)^2\varepsilon] \rceil$.

Let us now analyze the time complexity of Algorithm 9.

Observation 5. The time complexity of Algorithm 9 is $O(d)^{O(\log d)}/\varepsilon$.

Proof. Algorithm 9 samples s vertices of the graph G, and then executes Algorithm 8 on each one of these samples. Thus, its time complexity is s times the time complexity of Algorithm 8. Recalling that the time complexity of Algorithm 8 is $O(d)^{O(\log d)}$ according to Theorem 4, we get that the time complexity of Algorithm 9 is

$$s \cdot O(d)^{O(\log d)} = \lceil 12/\varepsilon \rceil \cdot O(d)^{O(\log d)} = O(d)^{O(\log d)}/\varepsilon. \qquad \square$$

Theorem 5 summarizes all the properties of Algorithm 9 that we have proved.

Theorem 5. *For every $\varepsilon > 0$, with probability at least $2/3$, Algorithm 9 outputs a value which is at least $OPT/2 - \varepsilon n$, where OPT is the size of the minimum vertex cover, and at most $(2 + 4 \cdot \lceil \log_2 d \rceil) \cdot OPT + \varepsilon n$. Moreover, the time complexity of Algorithm 9 is $O(d)^{O(\log d)}/\varepsilon$.*

The time complexity of Algorithm 9 has a quite bad dependence on d, but it is completely independent of n, and thus, Algorithm 9 is a sublinear time algorithm when d is considered to be a constant. It should be noted that there are better sublinear time algorithms for the minimum vertex cover problem which achieve both a better dependence of the time complexity on d and a better approximation, but we will not cover these algorithms in this book. We also note that, as usual, the median technique can be used to increase the probability of success of Algorithm 9 from $2/3$ to $1 - \delta$ (for every constant $\delta > 0$) at the cost of increasing the time complexity of the algorithm by a factor of $O(\log \delta^{-1})$.

12.4 Testing Whether a Graph is Connected

The last computational problem we would like to consider in this chapter is the problem of determining whether a bounded degree graph is connected, and we will later describe a property testing algorithm for it. However, before we can do that, we first need to present the model that we will assume in this problem, which is known as the *bounded degree graph model*.

The bounded degree graph model has two parameters: the number n of vertices and a bound d on the maximum degree of any single vertex. Given these parameters, the set N of the possible objects in this model is the set of all bounded degree representations (with this value of d) of graphs over n vertices. Additionally, as usual, we define the distance between two objects of N (i.e., two bounded degree representations) as the fraction of the entries in which the two representations differ, where we think of every cell in the lists of neighbors of the representation as a different entry. Unfortunately, the above definition suffers from a minor technical issue which stems from the fact that a graph can have multiple bounded degree representations (see Figure 12.3 for an example). This fact implies that a bounded degree graph might correspond to multiple objects in N, and moreover, these objects can be quite far from each other according to the distance function. To alleviate this technical issue, we will use the term

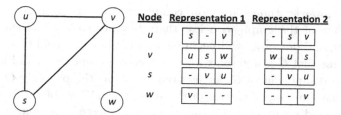

Node	Representation 1			Representation 2		
u	s	-	v	-	s	v
v	u	s	w	w	u	s
s	-	v	u	-	v	u
w	v	-	-	-	-	v

Figure 12.3. Two bounded degree representations of the single graph (for the same $d = 3$). Cells in the representations which are empty are designated with the character "-". Note that, despite the fact that both representations correspond to the same graph, the distance between them is $7/12$ because the two representations are different in 7 out of the 12 cells each of them has.

graph as a synonym for a bounded degree representation in the context of the bounded degree graph model. Thus, for example, we will interpret the problem of determining whether a graph is connected or is far from being connected as equivalent to the problem of determining whether a given bounded degree representation corresponds to a connected graph or is far from every bounded degree representation of a connected graph. For completeness of the formal presentation of this problem, we note that the property set P corresponding to this problem is the set of all bounded degree representations of connected graphs.

Let us begin the study of the above problem by presenting a useful lemma that characterizes graphs that are far from being connected. We assume in this lemma, and in the rest of the discussion about this problem, that $d \geqslant 2$. It is quite easy to lift this assumption if necessary because a graph with a maximum degree of $d < 2$ is clearly not connected (unless it has 2 vertices or less).

Lemma 5. *A graph G which is ε-far from being connected must have at least $\varepsilon dn/2$ connected components.*

Proof. We will prove the lemma by showing that a graph G with less than $\varepsilon dn/2$ connected components cannot be ε-far from being connected. Recall that a graph containing h connected components can be made connected by adding to it $h - 1$ edges. Thus, one might assume that any such graph can be made connected by modifying at most $2(h-1)$ entries in its bounded degree representation. As we will see later in this proof, this intuition works when there are at least two empty entries in the lists of neighbors of the vertices of every single connected component of the graph (because the above-mentioned $h - 1$ edges can be added by modifying these empty entries). However, things are more complicated when there are connected components of the graph with less than 2 empty entries in their lists of neighbors, and our proof will begin by showing how to avoid this case.

Assume that G is a graph with h connected components, and for every connected component of G, let us say that it has the property Q if there are at least two empty entries in the lists of neighbors of the vertices of this connected component. Consider now a connected component C of G that does not have the property Q, and let T be a spanning tree of C. The fact that C does not have the property Q implies that it contains at least two vertices, and thus, T must have at least two leaves: t_1 and t_2. Let us denote now by e_1 an edge that hit t_1 and does not belong to T (if such an edge exists), and similarly, let us denote by e_2 an edge that hits t_2 and does not belong to T (again, if such an edge exists) — see Figure 12.4(a) for a graphical illustration of these edges. If neither e_1 nor e_2 exists, then each of t_1 and t_2 has an empty entry in its list of neighbors, which contradicts our choice of C as a connected component of G which does not have the property Q. Thus, either e_1 or e_2 must exist, and let us assume without loss of generality that e_1 exists. We now observe that by removing e_1 we can make C have the property Q, and moreover, this removal will not affect the connectivity of C because T is connected. Thus, we have found a way to make C have the property Q by removing a single edge, which requires us to change at most 2 entries. Repeating this process now for all the connected components of G which does not have the property Q will result in a graph G' in which all the connected components C have the property Q, and will require at most $2h$ entry modifications.

Our next objective is to explain how G' can be made connected by changing at most $2h$ entries in it. Let us denote the connected components

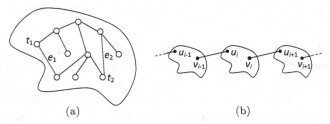

(a)   (b)

Figure 12.4. Illustrations for the proof of Lemma 5. (a) describes a single connected component of G, the tree T within it, the leaves t_1 and t_2 of this tree and the edges e_1 and e_2 that hit these leaves and are not part of T. (b) describes three consecutive connected components, C_{i-1}, C_i and C_{i+1} of G' and the edges that are added to connect them in G''.

of G' by $C_1, C_2, \ldots, C_h$. For every connected component C_i we choose two empty entries $e_{i,1}$ and $e_{i,2}$ from the lists of neighbors of the vertices of C_i, which is possible since each connected component of G' has the property Q. Let us now denote by u_i and v_i the vertices corresponding to the empty entries $e_{i,1}$ and $e_{i,2}$, respectively (we note that u_i and v_i might be the same vertex if $e_{i,1}$ and $e_{i,2}$ both belong to the list of neighbors of this vertex). We create a new graph G'' by adding to G' the edges $v_1 u_2, v_2 u_3, \ldots, v_{h-1} u_h$. Observe that because each one of the vertices of these edges has a different associated empty entry from the set $\{e_{i,1}, e_{i,2}\}_{i=1}^h$ in its list of neighbors, one can get G'' from G' by changing $2(h-1)$ entries from this list. Moreover, the above $h-1$ new edges connect all the connected components of G' (see Figure 12.4(b)), and thus, G'' is a connected graph.

Summarizing all the above in a naïve way, we get that a graph G with h connected components can be transformed into a connected graph G'' by changing at most $2h + 2(h-1) < 4h$ entries. However, it is possible to reduce the number of entries that need to be changed using a slightly more careful analysis. Specifically, one can recall that the transformation of G' into G'' changes only entries from the set $\{e_{i,1}, e_{i,2}\}_{i=1}^h$. This set contains two empty entries arbitrarily chosen from every connected component C_i of G'. In particular, we can choose these two empty entries so that they include any entry of C_i that was changed during the transformation of G into G' since every such entry is empty in G' by definition. Using this particular choice, we get that both the transformation of G to G' and the transformation of G' to G'' change only entries of the set $\{e_{i,1}, e_{i,2}\}_{i=1}^h$, whose size is $2h$, and thus, G can be transformed into a connected graph by changing at most $2h$ entries.

The lemma now follows because the last observation implies that a graph with $h < \varepsilon dn/2$ connected components can be made connected by changing at most $2h < \varepsilon dn$ of the dn entries in its representation; thus, its distance from being connected is less than ε. $\qquad\square$

Exercise 11. Lemma 5 proves that a bounded degree graph which is far from being connected has many more connected components than a connected graph (which has a single connected component). Thus, an algorithm for estimating the number of connected components in a graph, such as Algorithm 2, can be used to distinguish between such graphs. Show that this idea leads to a property testing algorithm for determining whether a bounded degree graph is connected whose time complexity is $O(d^{-2}\varepsilon^{-3})$.

To improve over the algorithm suggested in Exercise 11, we need to use Lemma 5 in a slightly more sophisticated way. Lemma 5 guarantees that a graph which is far from being connected has many connected components. Since every vertex of the graph appears in only one of these connected components, most connected components must be quite small. Corollary 4 proves this formally.

Corollary 4. *A graph G which is ε-far from being connected must have at least $\varepsilon dn/4$ connected components of size at most $4/(\varepsilon d)$.*

Proof. Assume, by way of contradiction, that the lemma is not true, i.e., there are less than $\varepsilon dn/4$ connected components in G whose size is at most $4/(\varepsilon d)$. Since G contains at least $\varepsilon dn/2$ connected components by Lemma 5, we get that it contains more than $\varepsilon dn/4$ large connected components of size larger than $4/(\varepsilon d)$. As these large connected components are vertex disjoint, the total number of vertices in them is more than

(bound on the number of large components)

$$\cdot \text{(minimum size of the large component)} > \frac{\varepsilon dn}{4} \cdot \frac{4}{\varepsilon d} = n,$$

which contradicts the fact that G has only n vertices. $\qquad\square$

Corollary 4 implies that, to determine whether a graph is connected or far from being connected, it is suffices to look for small connected components in the graph. If the graph is connected, then it has only a single (large) connected component, and if the graph is far from being connected, then it has many small connected components. This idea is the basis of the algorithm given as Algorithm 10. One should note that the above assumption that the single connected component of a graph is large is true only when the number of vertices in G is not very small (compared to $1/(\varepsilon d)$). When this does not happen, the above intuitive idea fails, and thus, an alternative method for determining whether G is connected must be employed. The first line of Algorithm 10 deals with this technical issue.

Lemma 6. *Algorithm 10 is a property testing algorithm for determining whether a bounded degree graph G is connected.*

Proof. If G contains at most $4/(\varepsilon d)$ vertices, then Algorithm 10 uses a BFS to explore the entire graph, and thus, always answers correctly whether the graph is connected or not. Thus, let us assume from now on that G contains more than $4/(\varepsilon d)$ vertices.

Algorithm 10: Determining Whether a Graph is Connected
(G, ε)

1. **if** $n \leqslant 4/(\varepsilon d)$ **then** use a BFS to determine whether G is connected, and terminate.
2. Let $s = \lceil 8/(\varepsilon d) \rceil$.
3. Sample uniformly and independently s vertices $u_1, u_2, \ldots, u_s$ from the graph G.
4. **for** each sampled vertex u_i **do**
5.   explore the connected component of u_i using BFS.
6.   **if** the BFS finds more than $4/(\varepsilon d)$ vertices in $u_i's$ connected component **then**
7.   Stop the BFS as soon as this happens.
8.   **else**
9.   **return** "G is not connected".
10. **if** the algorithm reaches this point **return** "G is connected".

If G is connected, then a BFS starting from every vertex of G will eventually discover all the vertices of G, which is more than $4/(\varepsilon d)$. Thus, Algorithm 10 is guaranteed to correctly detect if a connected graph is connected. That Algorithm 10 also detects with probability at least 2/3 that G is not connected when it is ε-far from being connected remains to be proved.

Assume that G is ε-far from being connected. Then, according to Corollary 4, it contains at least $\varepsilon dn/4$ connected components of size $4/(\varepsilon d)$ or less. Since each connected component of G must contain at least one vertex, this implies that every one of the vertices $u_1, u_2, \ldots, u_s$ has a probability of at least $(\varepsilon dn/4)/n = \varepsilon d/4$ to belong to a small connected component (i.e., a connected component with at most $4/(\varepsilon d)$ vertices. Observe now that if this happens, i.e., there is a vertex u_i that belongs to a small connected component, then the BFS starting from u_i will find at most $4/(\varepsilon d)$ vertices; which will make the algorithm output that the graph is not connected. Hence, to prove that Algorithm 10 detects that G is not connected with probability at least 2/3, it is enough to prove that one of the vertices $u_1, u_2, \ldots, u_s$ belongs to a small connected component with at least this probability.

Recall that the vertices $u_1, u_2, \ldots, u_s$ are chosen independently and each one of them belongs to a small connected component with probability at least $\varepsilon d/4$. Hence, the probability that at least one of them belongs to such a component is at least

$$1 - \left(1 - \frac{\varepsilon d}{4}\right)^s \geqslant 1 - e^{-\varepsilon d s/4} \geqslant 1 - e^{-\varepsilon d [8/(\varepsilon d)]/4} = 1 - e^{-2} > \frac{2}{3},$$

where the first inequality holds since $1 + x \leqslant e^x$ for every real number x. □

To complete the analysis of Algorithm 10 it remains to bound its time complexity.

Observation 6. The time complexity of Algorithm 10 is $O(d^{-1}\varepsilon^{-2})$.

Proof. If $n \leqslant 4/(\varepsilon d)$, then Algorithm 10 employs a single BFS execution, which requires $O(n + nd)$ time since G contains at most $nd/2$ edges. Since $n \geqslant 1$, we have in this case $d^{-1}\varepsilon^{-1} = \Omega(1)$, which means (together with the inequality $n \leqslant 4/(\varepsilon d)$) that the above time complexity is upper bounded by

$$O(n + nd) = O(nd) = O(\varepsilon^{-1}) = O(d^{-1}\varepsilon^{-2}).$$

The case that $n > 4/(\varepsilon d)$ remains to be considered. In this case, the time complexity of Algorithm 10 is dominated by the time required for the s executions of BFS that it uses. As seen above, in general, a single BFS execution can take time that depends on n, but fortunately, Algorithm 10 stops the BFS as soon as it finds $4/(\varepsilon d)$ vertices. Since BFS scans only the edges of vertices that it has already found, stopping the BFS in this fashion guarantees that its time complexity is only $O(4/(\varepsilon d) \cdot d) = O(\varepsilon^{-1})$. Thus, the total time complexity of Algorithm 10 is

$$s \cdot O(\varepsilon^{-1}) = \lceil 8/(\varepsilon d) \rceil \cdot O(\varepsilon^{-1}) = O(d^{-1}\varepsilon^{-2}). \qquad \Box$$

Theorem 6 summarizes all the claims that we have proved regarding Algorithm 10.

Theorem 6. *Algorithm 10 is a property testing algorithm for determining whether a bounded degree graph is connected, whose time complexity is* $O(d^{-1}\varepsilon^{-2})$.

Exercise 12. Both Algorithms 2 and 10 are based on executing BFS from random vertices of the graph. However, the algorithm suggested by Exercise 11, which is based on Algorithm 2, is significantly slower than Algorithm 10 (assuming ε^{-1} is significantly larger than d). Give an intuitive explanation for this difference.

12.5 Bibliographic Notes

The algorithms we presented for estimating the number of connected components in a graph (Algorithm 2) and estimating the weight of the minimum weight spanning tree (Algorithm 4) are simplified versions of algorithms suggested by Chazelle *et al.* (2005) for these tasks. The original algorithms have better time complexities of $O(d\varepsilon^{-2} \cdot \log(d/\varepsilon))$ and $O(dw\varepsilon^{-2} \cdot \log(dw/\varepsilon))$, respectively. Note that the last time complexity almost matches the lower bound mentioned in Section 2.3.2 on the time complexity required for any algorithm for estimating the weight of the minimum weight spanning tree (the lower bound is also due to (Chazelle *et al.*, 2005)). The simplified algorithms we presented are based on lecture notes of a course given by Grigory Yaroslavtsev in 2015 at the University of Pennsylvania.

The idea of obtaining a sublinear time algorithm by simulating a local distributed algorithm was suggested by Parnas and Ron (2007). They used their idea to suggest an algorithm for estimating the size of the minimum vertex cover of a bounded degree graph, which is very similar to the algorithm developed in this chapter for this task (Algorithm 9). It should be noted that, by combining this idea with more advanced local distributed algorithms, Parnas and Ron (2007) were able to also obtain additional results. In particular, they showed an algorithm which estimates the size of the minimum vertex cover up to a multiplicative error of 2 and an additive error of εn using only $d^{O(\log(d/\varepsilon))}$ queries.

Despite the way in which Algorithm 9 was presented, the original work of Parnas and Ron (2007) did not use a local computation algorithm as an intermediate step between the local distributed algorithm and the sublinear time algorithm. Local computation algorithms were suggested for the first time a few years later by Rubinfeld *et al.* (2010), who also spotted the relation between local computation algorithms and local distributed ones.

Finally, let us say a few words about the bounded degree graph model (for property testing). This model was originally defined by Goldreich and Ron (2002), who studied various problems in this model. In particular, they came up with the algorithm described above for determining whether a bounded degree graph is connected (Algorithm 10), and with a second property testing algorithm for the same problem whose time complexity is $O(\varepsilon^{-1} \cdot \log^2(\varepsilon d)^{-1})$; which is better when ε^{-1} is significantly larger than d.

B. Chazelle, R. Rubinfeld and L. Trevisan. Approximating the Minimum Spanning Tree Weight in Sublinear Time. *SIAM Journal on Computing*, 34(6): 1370–1379, 2005.

O. Goldreich and D. Ron. Property Testing in Bounded Degree Graphs. *Algorithmica*, 32(2): 302–343, 2002.

M. Parnas and D. Ron. Approximating the Minimum Vertex Cover in Sublinear Time and a Connection to Distributed Algorithms. *Theoretical Computer Science*, 381(1–3): 183–196, 2007.

R. Rubinfeld, G. Tamir, S. Vardi and N. Xie. Fast Local Computation Algorithms. In *Proceedings of the 1st Innovations in Computer Science (ICS)*, 223–238, 2010.

Exercise Solutions

Solution 1

Consider an arbitrarily connected component C of G. We will show that the nodes of C contribute exactly 1 to the expression (12.1), which proves that (12.1) is equal to the number of connected components in G since C is a generic connected component of G. The contribution of the nodes of C to (12.1) is

$$\sum_{u \in C} \frac{1}{n_u} = \sum_{u \in C} \frac{1}{|C|} = |C| \cdot \frac{1}{|C|} = 1.$$

Solution 2

For every $1 \leqslant i \leqslant h$, let Y_i be a random variable equal to $1/n_{u(i)}$. Since $u(i)$ is a uniformly random vertex of G, we get

$$E[Y_i] = \frac{\sum_{u \in V} 1/n_u}{n}.$$

Observe now that the output of Algorithm 1 can be written as $(n/h) \cdot \sum_{i=1}^{h} Y_i$. Thus, by the linearity of expectation, the expected output of the algorithm is equal to

$$\frac{n}{h} \cdot \sum_{i=1}^{h} E[Y_i] = \frac{n}{h} \cdot \sum_{i=1}^{h} \frac{\sum_{u \in V} 1/n_u}{n} = \sum_{u \in V} \frac{1}{n_u}.$$

This completes the proof since the rightmost side of the last equality is equal to (12.1), which was already proved to be equal to the number of connected components in G in Exercise 1.

Solution 3

Recall that $\hat{n}_u = \min\{n_u, 2/\varepsilon\}$. This equality implies that $\hat{n}_u$ is never larger than n_u. Thus,

$$\sum_{u \in V} \frac{1}{\hat{n}_u} \geqslant \sum_{u \in V} \frac{1}{n_u} \Rightarrow \sum_{u \in V} \frac{1}{\hat{n}_u} - \sum_{u \in V} \frac{1}{n_u} \geqslant 0.$$

To prove the other inequality of the exercise, we note that whenever $\hat{n}_u$ and n_u are not identical, $\hat{n}_u$ is equal to $2/\varepsilon$. Thus, $1/\hat{n}_u$ can be upper bounded by $1/n_u + \varepsilon/2$. Summing up this observation over all the nodes of G, we get

$$\sum_{u \in V} \frac{1}{\hat{n}_u} - \sum_{u \in V} \frac{1}{n_u} \leqslant \left(\sum_{u \in V} \frac{1}{n_u} + \frac{n\varepsilon}{2} \right) - \sum_{u \in V} \frac{1}{n_u} = \frac{n\varepsilon}{2}.$$

Solution 4

Following the hint, let us denote by G_1 the path over n vertices, and let G_2 be a random graph obtained from G_1 by removing a uniformly random edge from it. Consider now an arbitrary sublinear time algorithm ALG for estimating the number of connected components in a graph. We will prove that with probability $1 - o(1)$, ALG produces the same output given either G_1 or G_2.

Assume first that ALG is a deterministic algorithm, and let E_{ALG} be the edges of G_1 that ALG reads when it gets G_1 as its input. Consider the execution path that ALG follows when it gets G_1 as its input, and observe that removing any edge of G_1 outside of E_{ALG} cannot change this execution path because such an edge is never read by ALG. Thus, ALG will follow the same execution path given G_1 or G_2 (and will produce the same output) whenever E_{ALG} does not include the single edge that is removed from G_1 to get G_2. Since this edge is selected as a uniformly random edge of G_1, we get that ALG produces the same output given G_1 or G_2 with probability at least $|E_{ALG}|/(n-1)$. More formally, if we denote by $ALG(G)$ the output of ALG given a graph G, then

$$\Pr[ALG(G_1) = ALG(G_2)] \geqslant 1 - \frac{|E_{ALG}|}{n - 1}.$$

Recall that the above holds when ALG is deterministic, and let us now consider the case where ALG is randomized. An equivalent way to view

ALG is to assume that it gets a list of random bits, and that whenever it needs to make a random decision, it reads the next bit from this list. Given this point of view, executing ALG consists of two stages. In the first stage, we create the list of random bits, and in the second stage, we run the deterministic algorithm that ALG becomes given this list. In other words, executing ALG (like any other randomized algorithm) is equivalent to choosing a deterministic algorithm according to an appropriate distribution, and then executing it. To make things more formal, let us denote by A a random deterministic algorithm chosen according to the distribution defining ALG, and observe that $ALG(G)$ has the same distribution as $A(G)$.

Let B be the set of algorithms that A has a positive probability to be. Since every algorithm $A' \in B$ is deterministic, our above result for deterministic algorithms applies to it. Thus, by the law of total probability, we obtain

$$\Pr[A(G_1) = A(G_2)] = \sum_{A' \in B} \Pr[A'(G_1) = A'(G_2)|A = A'] \cdot \Pr[A = A']$$

$$\geqslant \sum_{A' \in B} \mathrm{E}\left[1 - \frac{|E_A|}{n-1}\Big|A = A'\right] \cdot \Pr[A = A']$$

$$= 1 - \frac{\mathrm{E}[|E_{ALG}|]}{n-1} = 1 - o(1),$$

where E_A is the set of edges read by algorithm A when it gets G_1. Note that the last equality holds since ALG reads all the edges of E_{ALG}, and thus, its sublinear time complexity upper bounds the size of E_{ALG}. Let us now denote by H_2 the set of graphs that G_2 has a positive probability to be. Then, by using again the law of total probability, we get

$$\sum_{G \in H_2} \Pr[G = G_2] \cdot \Pr[A(G_1) = A(G)] = \Pr[A(G_1) = A(G_2)] \geqslant 1 - o(1).$$

Since the sum $\sum_{G \in H_2} \Pr[G = G_2]$ is equal to 1, the last inequality implies that there must be a graph $G' \in H_2$ such that $\Pr[A(G_1) = A(G'))] \geqslant 1 - o(1)$.

Assume now, by way of contradiction, that ALG estimates the number of connected components in its input graph up to a relative error of $1/4$ with probability at least $1/2 + \varepsilon$ for some constant $\varepsilon > 0$. This means that given G_1, ALG must output a value of no more than $5/4$ with probability at least $1/2 + \varepsilon$ because G_1 has a single connected component. Similarly, given G', ALG must output a value of no less than $3/2$ with probability at least $1/2 + \varepsilon$. Since $3/2 > 5/4$, the two claims can be combined as follows:

$$\Pr[A(G_1) = A(G')]$$

$$\leqslant \Pr[A(G_1) = A(G') \geqslant 3/2] + \Pr[A(G_1) = A(G') \leqslant 5/4]$$

$$\leqslant \Pr[A(G_1) \geqslant 3/2] + \Pr[A(G') \leqslant 5/4]$$

$$\leqslant \Pr[A(G_1) > 5/4] + \Pr[A(G') < 3/2]$$

$$= \Pr[ALG(G_1) > 5/4] + \Pr[ALG(G') < 3/2] \leqslant 2 \cdot (1/2 - \varepsilon) = 1 - 2\varepsilon,$$

which contradicts the definition of G'.

Solution 5

By definition, $T_{\leqslant i}$ only contains edges of G whose weight is at most i, and thus, all its edges appear in $G_{\leqslant i}$. This implies that all the edges of $T_{\leqslant i}$ appear within connected components of $G_{\leqslant i}$. Thus, it is possible to count the number of edges in $T_{\leqslant i}$ by simply counting the number of edges from this set within every given connected component of $G_{\leqslant i}$. Thus, let us fix such a connected component C of $G_{\leqslant i}$.

Since all the edges of $T_{\leqslant i}$ belong to the tree T, they cannot contain a cycle. Thus, the number of such edges within C can be upper bounded by $|C| - 1$, where $|C|$ is the number of nodes in the connected component C. Let us now assume by way of contradiction that this upper bound is not tight, i.e., that $T_{\leqslant i}$ contains less than $|C| - 1$ edges inside the connected component C. This implies that C can be partitioned into two subsets C_1 and C_2 of nodes such that there is no edge of $T_{\leqslant i}$ between these subsets. However, since C is a connected component of $G_{\leqslant i}$, there must be an edge of weight at most i between C_1 and C_2. Let us denote this edge by e (see Figure 12.5 for a graphical illustration of the notation we use).

Let T_e be the set T maintained by Kruskal's algorithm immediately before it considers the edge e. Since e has a weight of at most i, but does not belong to $T_{\leqslant i}$, we get that it does not belong to T either. By definition, the fact that Kruskal's algorithm did not add e to T implies that the addition of e to T_e creates a cycle. In other words, T_e must already include a path between the two endpoints of e. Recalling that e connects nodes of C_1 and C_2, this implies the existence of a path in T_e between C_1 and C_2. Observe now that the edges of T_e must all have a weight of at most i because e has a weight of at most i (and Kruskal's algorithm considers the edges in a

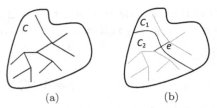

(a)   (b)

Figure 12.5. The connected component C of $G_{\leqslant i}$. Figure (a) presents the case that this connected component contains $|C| - 1$ edges of $T_{\leqslant i}$, which implies that these edges form a spanning tree of the component. Figure (b) presents the case that the component contains less edges of $T_{\leqslant i}$, and thus, it can be partitioned into two parts C_1 and C_2 such that no edge of $T_{\leqslant i}$ connects them. However, since C is connected in $G_{\leqslant i}$, there must be an edge e of this graph between the two parts.

non-decreasing weight order). One consequence of this observation is that the path in T_e between C_1 and C_2 must exist in $T_{\leqslant i}$ as well. As we have already proved that no edge of $T_{\leqslant i}$ connects the connected component C to the rest of the graph $G_{\leqslant i}$, the above path in $T_{\leqslant i}$ must be within C, and thus, must include an edge between C_1 and C_2; which contradicts the definition of C_1 and C_2.

The contradiction implies that the upper bound of $|C| - 1$ that we have on the number of $T_{\leqslant i}$ edges within the connected component of C is in fact tight. Summing this observation up over all the connected components of $G_{\leqslant i}$, we get

$$|T_{\leqslant i}| = \sum_{C \in CC(G_{\leqslant i})} (|C| - 1) = n - CC(G_{\leqslant i}).$$

Solution 6

Algorithm 4 uses $w - 1$ executions of Algorithm 2. By Theorem 1, each one of these executions uses $O(d/\varepsilon^3 \cdot \log \delta^{-1})$ time when its input graph $G_{\leqslant i}$ is pre-calculated. Unfortunately, pre-calculating $G_{\leqslant i}$ before executing Algorithm 2 on it requires too much time. However, one can observe that every time Algorithm 2 attempts to read some cell from the neighbors list of a vertex u of $G_{\leqslant i}$, we can calculate the content of this cell in constant time as follows. If the corresponding cell in the representation of G is empty, then the original cell of $G_{\leqslant i}$ should be empty as well. Otherwise, let us assume that the corresponding cell in the representation of G contains the neighbor v, and that the edge (u, v) has a weight of j in G. If $j > i$, then the edge (u, v) is not a part of $G_{\leqslant i}$, and thus, the original cell of $G_{\leqslant i}$ should be empty. Otherwise, the edge (u, v) is part of $G_{\leqslant i}$, and the original cell of $G_{\leqslant i}$ should contain the same vertex v as the cell of G.

Summing up the above, we get that since every cell in the representation of $G_{\leqslant i}$ can be calculated in constant time, executing Algorithm 2 should take the same amount of time (up to constants) as executing this algorithm on a pre-calculated input graph. Thus, each one of the executions of Algorithm 2 used by Algorithm 4 take $O(d/\varepsilon^3 \cdot \log \delta^{-1})$ time. Since there are $w - 1$ such executions, and Algorithm 4 uses only $O(w)$ time for the calculations it makes outside of these executions, we get that the total time complexity of Algorithm 4 is

$$O(w) + (w-1) \cdot O\left(\frac{d}{\varepsilon^3} \cdot \log \delta^{-1}\right) = O\left(\frac{dw}{\varepsilon^3} \cdot \log \delta^{-1}\right) = O\left(\frac{dw^4}{\varepsilon'} \cdot \log \frac{w}{\delta'}\right).$$

Solution 7

Let ε and δ be two values from $(0, 1]$, and let us assume without loss of generality that ε^{-1} is an integer (otherwise, we can replace ε with a value that obeys this property and belongs to the range $[\varepsilon/2, \varepsilon]$). Following the hint, we would like to round down the weight of every edge to an integer multiple of $\varepsilon/2$. Then, we can make all the weights integral by multiplying them with $2/\varepsilon$. Combining the two steps, we transform a weight i of an edge into a weight $\lfloor 2i/\varepsilon \rfloor$. Let us denote by G' the weighted graph obtained from G by this weights transformation.

We now execute Algorithm 4 on G' with $\varepsilon' = 1$ and $\delta' = \delta$. Since the weights of the edges in G' are integers between $2/\varepsilon \geqslant 1$ and $2w/\varepsilon$, Theorem 2 guarantees that Algorithm 4 executes in time $O(dw^4/\varepsilon^4 \cdot \log(w/(\varepsilon\delta)))$ when G' is pre-calculated, and moreover, with probability at least $1 - \delta$ it estimates the weight of the minimum weight spanning tree of G' up to an error of $\varepsilon'n = n$. Lemma 7 allows us to translate estimates on the weight of the minimum weight spanning tree of G' to estimates on the weight of the minimum weight spanning tree of G.

Lemma 7. *If W is an estimate for the weight of the minimum weight spanning tree of G' up to an error of n, then $\varepsilon W/2$ is an estimate for the weight of the minimum weight spanning tree of G up to an error of εn.*

Proof. Let T and T' be the minimum weight spanning trees of G and G', respectively, and let $v(T)$ and $v(T')$ denote their weights in G and G', respectively. Observe now that T is also a spanning tree in G', and its weight there is at most $2v(T)/\varepsilon$. Thus,

$$v(T') \leqslant 2v(T)/\varepsilon,$$

which implies

$$\frac{\varepsilon W}{2} - v(T) \leqslant \frac{\varepsilon W}{2} - \frac{\varepsilon}{2} \cdot v(T') = \frac{\varepsilon}{2} \cdot [W - v(T')] \leqslant \frac{\varepsilon}{2} \cdot n = \frac{\varepsilon n}{2} \leqslant \varepsilon n.$$

Similarly, T' is a spanning tree of G, and its weight there is at most $\varepsilon v(T')/2 + \varepsilon n/2$ (where the term $\varepsilon n/2$ is due to the rounding in the definition of the weights of G' and the observation that T' has at most n edges). Hence,

$$v(T) \leqslant \varepsilon v(T')/2 + \varepsilon n/2,$$

which implies

$$\frac{\varepsilon W}{2} - v(T) \geqslant \frac{\varepsilon W}{2} - \frac{\varepsilon}{2} \cdot v(T') - \frac{\varepsilon n}{2}$$
$$= \frac{\varepsilon}{2} \cdot [W - v(T')] - \frac{\varepsilon n}{2} \geqslant \frac{\varepsilon}{2} \cdot (-n) - \frac{\varepsilon n}{2} = -\varepsilon n. \qquad \square$$

The above discussion and the last lemma show that the algorithm given as Algorithm 11 estimates the weight of the minimum weight spanning tree of G up to an error of εn with probability at most $1 - \delta$. To determine the time complexity of Algorithm 11, we observe that it requires only $O(1)$ time in addition to the time required for executing Algorithm 4 on G'. Thus, it is enough to bound the last time complexity. When G' is pre-calculated, we saw above that the execution of Algorithm 4 takes only $O(dw^4/\varepsilon^4 \cdot \log(w/(\varepsilon\delta)))$ time. Unfortunately, calculating G' takes too much time, but we can generate in constant time every weight or neighbors list entry of G' that Algorithm 4 tries to read, which is as good as having a pre-calculated copy of G'. Hence, it is possible to implement Algorithm 11 using a time complexity of $O(dw^4/\varepsilon^4 \cdot \log(w/(\varepsilon\delta)))$.

Algorithm 11: Estimating the Weight of the Minimum Weight Spanning Tree — with Continuous Weights (ε, δ)

1. Execute Algorithm 4 on the graph G' obtained from G by replacing every edge weight i in G with $\lfloor 2i/\varepsilon \rfloor$. Let W be its output.
2. **return** $\varepsilon W/2$.

Solution 8

(a) Assume by way of contradiction that Algorithm 7 produced an illegal coloring, namely, there is an edge e whose end points u and v have the same final color c. Then, one of two things must have happened. Either u and v got the same final color c at the same time, or the end point u obtained its final color c before v (the reverse can also happen, but we can ignore it due to symmetry). Let us show that neither of these cases can happen.

Consider first the case that u and v got the same final color c at the same time. In the iteration of Algorithm 7 in which this has happened, both u and v must have picked this color c and then each one of them has reported to the other one about choosing c. Thus, both of them were informed that one of their neighbors has also chosen the color c, and this should have prevented them from finalizing c. Thus, we get a contradiction.

Consider now the second case in which the end point u of e has chosen a final color c, and then the other end point v decided to choose the same final color c at a later time. Consider the iteration of Algorithm 7 in which u has finalized its color. At the end of this iteration, u informs all its neighbors (including v) that it has finalized its color c, and consequently, these neighbors deleted c from their corresponding color lists C. Since a vertex picks colors only from its list C of colors, this means that v could not pick the color c at any time after u has finalized its choice of color, which leads us to a contradiction again.

(b) Every iteration of Algorithm 7 involves two rounds of communication. In the first round, every vertex informs its neighbors about the color it has picked from its list of colors C, and in the second round every vertex informs its neighbors whether it has finalized the color it has picked. Thus, we need to show that with probability at least $1 - 1/n$ Algorithm 7 terminates after $2 \cdot \lceil \log_2 n \rceil$ iterations. Fix an arbitrary vertex u of the input graph, and consider an arbitrary iteration of Algorithm 7 which starts before u has finalized its color. In this iteration, u picks an arbitrary color c_u, and this color is finalized if it is different from the colors picked by the neighbors of u that did not have their colors finalized as yet. If we denote by N_u the set of these neighbors of u (i.e., the neighbors of u with a final color), by c_v the color of a neighbor $v \in N_u$ and by C_u the list of colors that u has at the current iteration, then the probability that u finalizes its color at the end of this iteration is

$$\Pr[c_u \neq c_v \ \forall v \in N_u] = \Pr[c_u \notin \{c_v | v \in N_u\}] = 1 - \frac{|N_u|}{|C_u|}.$$

The important observation now is that every time that a neighbor of u finalizes its color, N_u loses a single vertex and C_u loses at most a single color. Since the original size of N_u is the degree of u, which is at most d, and the original size of C_u is $2d$, this implies that

$$1 - \frac{|N_u|}{|C_u|} \leqslant 1 - \frac{d - \begin{pmatrix} \text{number of neighbors of } u \\ \text{which have finalized their colors} \end{pmatrix}}{2d - \begin{pmatrix} \text{number of neighbors of } u \\ \text{which have finalized their colors} \end{pmatrix}} \leqslant 1 - \frac{d}{2d} = \frac{1}{2}.$$

Thus, we have proved that in every iteration of Algorithm 7, every vertex of the input graph finalizes its color with a probability at least $1/2$. Hence, after $2 \cdot \lceil \log_2 n \rceil$ iterations every one of these vertices finalizes its color with a probability at least

$$1 - \left(\frac{1}{2}\right)^{2 \cdot \lceil \log_2 n \rceil} \geqslant 1 - 2^{-2 \cdot \log_2 n} = 1 - n^{-2}.$$

Using the union bound, we get that the probability that all n vertices of the input graph finalized their color after $2 \cdot \lceil \log_2 n \rceil$ iterations of Algorithm 7 is at least $1 - n^{-1}$, which is what we wanted to prove (since the algorithm terminates after all the vertices choose their final colors).

Solution 9

The subgraph $G'(u)$ constructed by Algorithm 8 contains all the nodes of G whose distance from u is at most $\lceil \log_2 d \rceil + 1$. Thus, recalling that the degree of every node in G is upper bounded by d, we can upper bound the number of nodes in $G'(u)$ by

$$\sum_{i=0}^{\lceil \log_2 d \rceil + 1} d^i \leqslant (\lceil \log_2 d \rceil + 2) \cdot d^{\lceil \log_2 d \rceil + 1} = O(d)^{\lceil \log_2 d \rceil + 2}.$$

The construction of $G'(u)$ only requires us to read the list of neighbors of the nodes of $G'(u)$. Since each such list of neighbors is of length d, Algorithm 8 requires only a time complexity of $O(d) \cdot O(d)^{\lceil \log_2 d \rceil + 2} = O(d)^{O(\log d)}$ for this construction.

Aside from the construction of $G'(u)$, the only part of Algorithm 8 which requires a non-constant time is the execution of Algorithm 6 for every one of the nodes of $G'(u)$ in parallel. Thus, we need to calculate the time complexity of Algorithm 6. The loop of Algorithm 6 iterates $\lceil \log_2 d \rceil$ times, and each one of these iterations requires $O(d)$ time. Thus, each individual execution of Algorithm 6 requires $O(d \log d)$ time, and the total time complexity of all the executions of Algorithm 6 used by Algorithm 8 is

$$O(d)^{\lceil \log_2 d \rceil + 2} \cdot O(d \log d) = O(d)^{O(\log d)}.$$

Since both the construction of $G'(u)$ and the execution of Algorithm 6 for every one of its nodes in parallel require $O(d)^{O(\log d)}$ time, this is also the time complexity of Algorithm 8.

Solution 10

We need to show that, for every $\varepsilon > 0$ and $c \in (1, 2]$, when s is set to $\lceil 6c/[(c-1)^2 \varepsilon] \rceil$, then with probability at least $2/3$ the output of Algorithm 9 belongs to the range $[|C_A(G)|/c - \varepsilon n, c \cdot |C_A(G)| + \varepsilon n]$. The proof of this fact is very similar to the proof of Lemma 4, but we write it fully here for completeness.

Let X_i be an indicator for the event that u_i belongs to $C_A(G)$. Recall that the output of Algorithm 9 is equal to

$$\frac{n}{s} \cdot \sum_{i=1}^{s} X_i, \tag{12.4}$$

and moreover, the expectation of this expression is

$$\mathrm{E}\left[\frac{n}{s} \cdot \sum_{i=1}^{s} X_i \right] = \frac{n}{s} \cdot \sum_{i=1}^{s} \mathrm{E}[X_i] = \frac{n}{s} \cdot \sum_{i=1}^{s} \frac{|C_A(G)|}{n} = |C_A(G)|.$$

We now need to show that (12.4) does not deviate from its expectation by too much. Let us first prove that (12.4) is smaller than $|C_A|/c - \varepsilon n$ with probability at most $1/6$. If $|C_A(G)| \leqslant c \cdot \varepsilon n$, then this is trivial since (12.4) is always non-negative. Hence, the case that $|C_A(G)| > c \cdot \varepsilon n$ remains to be considered. Since the value of each indicator X_i is determined by the sample u_i, and the samples $u_1, u_2, \ldots, u_s$ are independent, we can use the

Chernoff bound in this case to get

$$\Pr\left[\frac{n}{s} \cdot \sum_{i=1}^{s} X_i \leqslant C_A(G)/c - \varepsilon n\right]$$

$$\leqslant \Pr\left[\sum_{i=1}^{s} X_i \leqslant \frac{s}{cn} \cdot C_A(G)\right] = \Pr\left[\sum_{i=1}^{s} X_i \leqslant \frac{1}{c} \cdot \mathrm{E}\left[\sum_{i=1}^{s} X_i\right]\right]$$

$$\leqslant e^{-(1-1/c)^2 \cdot \mathrm{E}[\sum_{i=1}^{s} X_i]/2} = e^{-(1-1/c)^2 s \cdot |C_A(G)|/(2n)}$$

$$\leqslant e^{-s(1-1/c)^2 \cdot (c\varepsilon n)/(2n)} = e^{-s(1-1/c)^2 \cdot (c\varepsilon)/2} \leqslant e^{-3} < \frac{1}{6}.$$

Next, we would like to prove that (12.4) is larger than $c|C_A| + \varepsilon n$ with probability at most $1/6$. Let Y_i be an indicator that takes the value 1 with probability $\max\{\varepsilon/c, |C_A(G)|/n\}$. Since this probability is an upper bound on the probability that X_i takes the value 1, we get

$$\Pr\left[\frac{n}{s} \cdot \sum_{i=1}^{s} X_i \geqslant c \cdot C_A(G) + \varepsilon n\right]$$

$$= \Pr\left[\sum_{i=1}^{s} X_i \geqslant \frac{cs}{n} \cdot C_A(G) + s\varepsilon\right] \leqslant \Pr\left[\sum_{i=1}^{s} Y_i \geqslant \frac{cs}{n} \cdot C_A(G) + s\varepsilon\right]$$

$$\leqslant \Pr\left[\sum_{i=1}^{s} Y_i \geqslant c\mathrm{E}\left[\sum_{i=1}^{s} Y_i\right]\right] \leqslant e^{-(c-1)^2 \mathrm{E}[\sum_{i=1}^{s} Y_i]/3}$$

$$\leqslant e^{-(c-1)^2 s\varepsilon/(3c)} \leqslant e^{-2} < \frac{1}{6}.$$

The claim that we need to prove now follows by applying the union bound to the two above results.

Solution 11

First, we note that when $\varepsilon \leqslant 8/(dn)$, the exercise asks for an algorithm that can determine whether a bounded degree graph is connected whose time complexity is at most $O(dn^3)$. It is easy to see that this time complexity is larger than the time complexity of BFS, and thus, the problem is trivial. Hence, in the rest of the solution we assume $\varepsilon > 8/(dn)$.

**Algorithm 12: Determining Whether a Graph is Connected —
Simple (G, ε)**

1. Use Algorithm 2 to find an estimate c for the number of connected components of G whose error is at most $\varepsilon dn/8$ with probability at least $2/3$.
2. **if** $c < \varepsilon dn/4$ **then return** "G is connected".
3. **else return** "G is not connected."

Consider now the algorithm given as Algorithm 12. Following the discussion in the exercise, this algorithm estimates the number of connected components in its input bounded degree graph, and based on this estimate determines whether the graph is connected or not.

Let us begin the analysis of Algorithm 12 by showing that it is indeed a property testing algorithm. This is done by Observations 7 and 8.

Observation 7. If G is a connected bounded degree graph, then Algorithm 12 indicates that it is connected with probability at least $2/3$.

Proof. Since G is connected, with probability at least $2/3$ the estimate c computed by Algorithm 12 for the number of connected components of G will be at most $1 + \varepsilon dn/8 < \varepsilon dn/8 + \varepsilon dn/8 = \varepsilon dn/4$, where the first inequality holds since we assume that $\varepsilon > 8/(dn)$. Thus, Algorithm 12 will declare G to be connected with probability at least $2/3$. □

Observation 8. If G is a bounded degree graph which is ε-far from being connected, then Algorithm 12 indicates that it is not connected with probability at least $2/3$.

Proof. Since G is ε-far from being connected, it must have at least $\varepsilon dn/2$ connected components by Lemma 5. Thus, with probability at least $2/3$ the estimate c computed by Algorithm 12 for the number of connected components of G will be at least $\varepsilon dn/2 - \varepsilon dn/8 = 3\varepsilon dn/8 > \varepsilon dn/4$. Thus, Algorithm 12 will declare G to be unconnected with probability at least $2/3$. □

It remains to bound the time complexity of Algorithm 12. According to Theorem 1, Algorithm 2 produces an estimate c with the required guarantee using $O(d(\varepsilon d)^{-3} \cdot \log(1/3)^{-1}) = O(d^{-2}\varepsilon^{-3})$ time. Since Algorithm 12 uses only a constant number of operations in addition to calculating c, this is also its time complexity.

Solution 12

The objective of Algorithm 2 is to estimate the number of connected components in the graph. To achieve this goal, the algorithm executes BFS from random vertices of the graph and then averages (in some sophisticated way) the number of vertices found by these BFS executions. To make the result of the algorithm trustworthy, the algorithm must use enough executions to guarantee that the average it calculates is close to its expectation, which requires many executions.

In contrast, for Algorithm 10 to detect that a graph is not connected, it is enough for it to have one BFS execution which finds a small number of vertices. In particular, it is not necessary for the algorithm to have enough BFS executions so that the fraction of the BFS executions which find a small number of vertices is close to its expectation. Thus, the algorithm can work with a significantly smaller number of BFS executions.

Chapter 13

An Algorithm for Dense Graphs

As discussed in Chapter 12, sublinear time algorithms for graph problems have to be studied separately for every one of the standard graph representations. Chapter 12 presented a few algorithms for a specific graph representation that is appropriate for bounded degree graphs, which are a family of sparse graphs. In this chapter, we present a property testing algorithm for graphs represented by their *adjacency matrix*, which is a representation that is more appropriate for dense graphs.

13.1 Model

We begin this chapter by defining the adjacency matrix and the property testing model we assume. Recall that the adjacency matrix of an (undirected) graph is a matrix which has a single column and a single row for every vertex of the graph. Each cell of this matrix is an indicator for the existence of an edge between the vertices corresponding to its column and row. In other words, the cell in the row corresponding to vertex u and the column corresponding to vertex v contains the value 1 if and only if there is an edge between u and v (see Figure 13.1 for an example). We would like to draw your attention to two properties of the adjacency matrix, as follows:

- The main diagonal of the matrix corresponds to edges between a vertex and itself, i.e., self-loops. When the graph is simple, which we assume throughout this chapter, then this diagonal contains only zeros.
- For every pair of vertices u and v, there are two cells of the matrix which indicate the existence of an edge between u and v: the cell at the row corresponding to u and the column corresponding to v, and the

Algorithms for Big Data

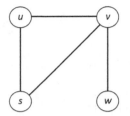 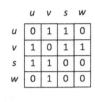

Figure 13.1. A graph and its adjacency matrix representation. Note that the matrix is symmetric (because the graph is not directed) and its main diagonal contains only zero entries (because there are no self-loops in the graph).

cell at the row corresponding to v and the column corresponding to u. Naturally, these two cells always contain the same value, which makes the adjacency matrix symmetric with respect to its main diagonal. We note that in directed graphs, one of these cells indicates the existence of an arc from u to v and the other indicates the existence of the reverse arc; thus, in directed graphs the adjacency matrix need not be symmetric. However, we consider only undirected graphs in this chapter.

At this point, we are ready to define the property testing model that we assume in this chapter, which is known as the *dense graph model*. In this model, the set N of possible objects is the set of all adjacency matrices of graphs over n vertices (n is a parameter of the model), and as usual, the distance d in this model between two adjacency matrices is the fraction of their n^2 cells in which the two matrices differ.

As a warmup exercise for the study of the dense graph model, let us consider the problem of determining whether a graph is connected. Recall that in Chapter 12 we studied this problem in the context of the bounded degree graph model and showed a non-trivial property testing algorithm for it. However, the following exercise shows that this problem is trivial in the dense graph model unless ε is very small.

Exercise 1. Show that no graph is ε-far from being connected in the dense graph model unless $\varepsilon < 2n^{-1}$.

13.2 Algorithm for Testing Bipartiteness

Our main objective in this chapter is to find a property testing algorithm in the dense graph model for determining whether a graph G is bipartite.

Algorithm 1: Testing Bipartiteness (G, s)

1. Pick uniformly at random a subset V' of s vertices of G.
2. **if** $G[V']$ is a bipartite graph **then**
3.   **return** "G is bipartite".
4. **else**
5.   **return** "G is not bipartite".

A very natural algorithm for this task is given as Algorithm 1. Algorithm 1 simply selects a random subset of s vertices of the input graph G (where s is a parameter of the algorithm), and then checks whether the subgraph *induced* by these vertices is bipartite. We remind the reader that given a graph G and a set V' of vertices of G, the subgraph induced by V' (which is denoted by $G[V']$) is a graph over the vertices of V' in which there is an edge between a pair of two vertices of V' if and only if there is such an edge in G.

To prove that Algorithm 1 is a property testing algorithm, we need to show that it detects correctly that bipartite graphs are bipartite and also detects correctly (with a significant probability) that graphs that are far from being bipartite are not bipartite. Exercise 2 asks you to prove the first of these claims.

Exercise 2. Prove that, when the value of the parameter s of Algorithm 1 is at least 2, given a bipartite graph, this algorithm detects correctly that it is bipartite.

To show that Algorithm 1 is a property testing algorithm, it remains to be proved that it also detects correctly that a graph which is far from being bipartite is indeed not bipartite. Observation 1 characterizes the graphs that are far from being bipartite, which is a first step toward proving this claim.

Let us denote by V the set of vertices of G. Given a disjoint partition of the vertices of G into two sets V_1 and V_2, we say that an edge e *violates* this partition if it connects two vertices of V_1 or two vertices of V_2. Clearly, G is bipartite if and only if there exists a disjoint partition of its vertices into sets V_1 and V_2 which is not violated by any edge of G.

Observation 1. If a graph G is ε-far from being bipartite, then every disjoint partition of V into two sets V_1 and V_2 is violated by at least $\varepsilon n^2 / 2$ edges of G.

Proof.   Assume that a graph G has a disjoint partition of V into two sets V_1 and V_2 such that the set E' of edges of G violating this partition is of size less than $\varepsilon n^2/2$. To prove the observation, we need to show that G is not ε-far from being bipartite, i.e., that one can make it bipartite by modifying less than εn^2 entries in its adjacency matrix. Clearly, we can make G bipartite by removing the edges of E' from it. Moreover, since removing any single edge requires us to make two changes in the adjacency of G, the number of entries in the adjacency matrix of G that need to be modified to remove all the edges of E' (and make G bipartite) is only

$$2 \cdot |E'| < 2 \cdot \frac{\varepsilon n^2}{2} = \varepsilon n^2. \qquad \square$$

Intuitively, the last observation shows that when G is ε-far from being bipartite, every partition of it is violated by many edges. This means that for every given partition there should be a high probability that the subgraph $G[V']$ selected by Algorithm 1 contains at least a single edge violating this partition. More formally, given a partition of V into two disjoint sets V_1 and V_2, let us denote by $A(V_1, V_2)$ the event that one of the edges violating this partition appears in $G[V']$. Then, the above intuitive argument claims that $A(V_1, V_2)$ should be a high probability event for every given partition of V.

Exercise 3. Prove that, when the value of the parameter s of Algorithm 1 is at least 2, $G[V']$ is not bipartite if and only if the event $A(V_1, V_2)$ occurs for all possible partitions of V into two disjoint sets V_1 and V_2.

The last exercise implies that our objective to prove that $G[V']$ is unlikely to be bipartite when G is far from being bipartite is equivalent to proving that, with a significant probability, the event $A(V_1, V_2)$ occurs for all possible partitions of V for such graphs G. Since we already argued that intuitively $A(V_1, V_2)$ is a high probability event, it is natural to lower bound the probability of the event that $A(V_1, V_2)$ occurs for all possible partitions of V using the union bound. As a first step, let us find a lower bound on the probability that the event $A(V_1, V_2)$ occurs for a given partition.

Lemma 1. *If G is ε-far from being bipartite and $s \geqslant 2$ (recall that s is a parameter of Algorithm 1), then for every given partition of V into two disjoint sets V_1 and V_2, $\Pr[A(V_1, V_2)] \geqslant 1 - e^{-\varepsilon s/3}$.*

Proof. Consider the set V' of vertices picked by Algorithm 1. We can pretend that the algorithm selects this set by repeatedly picking a uniform vertex G and adding it to V', until the set V' contains s vertices (which can require more than s iterations if the same vertex is added to V' multiple times). Let us denote the first s vertices added to V' according to this process by $u_1, u_2, \ldots, u_s$, and observe that these vertices are independent of each other.

Let us denote now by E' the set of edges violating the partition (V_1, V_2). Observation 1 shows that E' is of size at least $\varepsilon n^2/2$. Recall that the event $A(V_1, V_2)$ happens whenever at least one edge of E' belongs to $G[V']$, and note that an edge $e \in E'$ is guaranteed to belong to $G[V']$ if it is equal to the pair $u_i u_j$ for some $1 \leqslant i$, $j \leqslant s$. Thus,

$$1 - \Pr[A(V_1, V_2)] \leqslant \Pr[\forall_{1 \leqslant i,j \leqslant s} u_i u_j \notin E'] \leqslant \Pr[\forall_{1 \leqslant i \leqslant \lfloor s/2 \rfloor} u_{2i-1} u_{2i} \notin E']$$

$$= \prod_{i=1}^{\lfloor s/2 \rfloor} \Pr[u_{2i-1} u_{2i} \notin E'] = \prod_{i=1}^{\lfloor s/2 \rfloor} \left(1 - \frac{2|E'|}{n^2}\right)$$

$$\leqslant \prod_{i=1}^{\lfloor s/2 \rfloor} (1 - \varepsilon) \leqslant e^{-\varepsilon \lfloor s/2 \rfloor} \leqslant e^{-\varepsilon s/3},$$

where the first equality holds since the vertices u_1, $u_2, \ldots, u_s$ are independent of each other and the last inequality is true for any $s \geqslant 2$. □

As planned, we can now use the union bound to lower bound the probability that the event $A(V_1, V_2)$ happens for all possible partitions. Since there are $2^n - 2 \leqslant 2^n$ possible partitions, and for every given partition the event $A(V_1, V_2)$ happens with probability at least $1 - e^{-\varepsilon s/3}$ by Lemma 1, we get that the probability that the event $A(V_1, V_2)$ happens for all possible partitions is at least

$$1 - 2^n e^{-\varepsilon s/3} = 1 - e^{n \ln 2 - \varepsilon s/3}. \tag{13.1}$$

Unfortunately, to make this expression larger than 0, we must choose $s = \Omega(n/\varepsilon)$, which makes Algorithm 1 a linear time algorithm.[1] Thus, the natural approach of applying the lower bound proved by Lemma 1

---

[1] Technically speaking, to make expression (13.1) positive, we need to select a value s which is strictly larger than n, which cannot be done because it requires Algorithm 1 to select into V' more than all the vertices of G.

to all possible partitions of V fails because there are just too many such partitions.

13.3 Reducing the Number of Partitions to Check

To fix the issue presented at the end of the last section (namely that we consider all the partitions of V, and there are just too many of these partitions), we must reduce the number of partitions that we need to consider. We do this by logically breaking up the set V' into two disjoint sets: a set U that intuitively determines the partitions that we need to consider and a set W that has a significant probability to introduce a violating edge for every one of these partitions when G is ε-far. More formally, from this point on we think of V' as the union of two sets, as follows:

- a set U containing s_U uniformly random vertices of G (where s_U is some number between 1 and s to be chosen later),
- a set W containing $s - s_U$ uniformly random vertices of G that do not belong to U.

One can observe that $U \cup W$ is a uniformly random subset of s vertices of G, and thus, it indeed has the same distribution as V'.

Given a partition (U_1, U_2) of U, we are interested in the question whether there exists a partition (W_1, W_2) of W such that no edge of $G[V']$ violates the partition $(U_1 \cup W_1, U_2 \cup W_2)$ of V'. Let us first study this question under the simplifying assumption that every vertex $w \in V \setminus U$ has an edge connecting it in G to some vertex $u \in U$. Note that this assumption implies that if the vertex $w \in V \setminus U$ ends up in W, then it must be assigned to the side of the partition $(U_1 \cup W_1, U_2 \cup W_2)$ which does not include u because otherwise there is no hope that the last partition will not be violated by any edge of $G[V']$.

The last observation means that in order to determine whether there is a partition (W_1, W_2) of W such that no edge of $G[V']$ violates the partition $(U_1 \cup W_1, U_2 \cup W_2)$ there is essentially only a single partition of V that we need to consider. One side of this partition contains the vertices of U_1 and the vertices of $V \setminus U$ that must go to W_1 if they end up in W, while the other side of this partition contains the remaining vertices of V. Lemma 2 formally proves this intuitive claim. Given a set $S \subseteq U$ of vertices, we denote by $N(S)$ the set of vertices of $V \setminus U$ that have an edge connecting them to S.

Lemma 2. *Given our assumption that there exists an edge from every vertex of $V \setminus U$ to a vertex of U, there exists a partition (W_1, W_2) of W such that no edge of $G[V']$ violates $(U_1 \cup W_1, U_2 \cup W_2)$ if and only if the event $A(U_1 \cup N(U_2), V \setminus (U_1 \cup N(U_2)))$ does not occur.*

Proof. We begin by proving the simpler direction of the lemma, i.e., we assume that $(U_1 \cup W_1, U_2 \cup W_2)$ is violated by an edge of $G[V']$ regardless of the partition (W_1, W_2) of W chosen, and we show that this implies that event $A(U_1 \cup N(U_2), V \setminus (U_1 \cup N(U_2)))$ occurred. Let us choose $W_1 = W \cap N(U_2)$, then our assumption that $(U_1 \cup W_1, U_2 \cup W_2)$ is always violated by an edge of $G[V']$ implies that there exists an edge e of $G[V']$ violating the partition $(U_1 \cup (W \cap N(U_2)), U_2 \cup (W \setminus N(U_2)))$ of V'. Recall that this means that the edge e goes between two vertices belonging to the same side of this partition, and thus, it must also violate the partition $(U_1 \cup N(U_2), V \setminus (U_1 \cup N(U_2)))$ of V because every side of this partition includes one side of the previous partition. However, the last observation implies that the event $A(U_1 \cup N(U_2), V \setminus (U_1 \cup N(U_2)))$ occurred by definition.

We now need to prove the other direction of the lemma, i.e., we assume that the event $A(U_1 \cup N(U_2), V \setminus (U_1 \cup N(U_2)))$ occurred and prove that this implies that $(U_1 \cup W_1, U_2 \cup W_2)$ is violated by an edge of $G[V']$ regardless of the partition (W_1, W_2) of W chosen. The event $A(U_1 \cup N(U_2), V \setminus (U_1 \cup N(U_2)))$ implies that there is an edge e in $G[V']$ violating its partition. The edge e must be within one of the two sides of this partition, which gives us a few cases to consider.

- The first case is that e connects two vertices of U_1. In this case, e clearly violates $(U_1 \cup W_1, U_2 \cup W_2)$.
- The second case we consider is that e connects a vertex $u_1 \in U_1$ with a vertex $v \in N(U_2)$. By the definition of $N(U_2)$ there must be an edge between v and some vertex $u_2 \in U_2$. Thus, $G[V']$ contains a path of length two between a vertex u_1 on one side of the partition $(U_1 \cup W_1, U_2 \cup W_2)$ and a vertex u_2 on the other side of this partition (see Figure 13.2(a)). Regardless of the side of the partition in which we place the middle vertex v of this path, we are guaranteed that one of the edges of the path will be within a single side of the partition, i.e., will violate the partition.
- The third case we need to consider is that e connects two vertices v_1 and v_2 of $N(U_2)$. By the definition of $N(U_2)$, there must be an edge connecting v_1 to a vertex $u_1 \in U_2$ and an edge connecting v_2 to a vertex $u_2 \in U_2$ (possibly $u_1 = u_2$). Thus, $G[V']$ contains a path of length 3 that

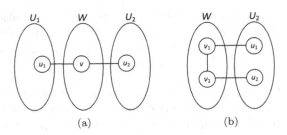

Figure 13.2. Illustration of two cases from the proof of Lemma 2.

starts and ends on the same side of the partition $(U_1 \cup W_1, U_2 \cup W_2)$ — see Figure 13.2(b). If the middle two vertices v_1 and v_2 of this path are on the same side of this partition, then the edge e between them violates it. Otherwise, at least one of these vertices must be on the same side of the partition as the end vertices u_1 and u_2, and thus, at least one of the non-middle edges $v_1 u_1$ or $v_2 u_2$ must violate the partition $(U_1 \cup W_1, U_2 \cup W_2)$.

- The case where e connects two vertices of $V \backslash (U_1 \cup N(U_2))$ remains to be considered. Since we assume that every vertex of $V \backslash U$ is connected by an edge to at least one vertex of U, we have $V \backslash (U_1 \cup N(U_2)) \subseteq U_2 \cup N(U_1)$. Thus, in this case e connects two vertices of $U_2 \cup N(U_1)$, which gives us three subcases: a subcase in which e connects two vertices of U_2, a subcase in which e connects a vertex of U_2 and a vertex of $N(U_1)$, and a subcase in which e connects two vertices of $N(U_1)$. One can observe that these three subcases are analogous to the three previous cases we considered, and hence, it can be shown in a similar way that in all these subcases there must be an edge of $G[V']$ violating the partition $(U_1 \cup W_1, U_2 \cup W_2)$. $\qquad\square$

Corollary 1. *Given our assumption that there exists an edge from every vertex of $V \backslash U$ to a vertex of U, $G[V']$ is bipartite if and only if there is a partition (U_1, U_2) of U such that the event $A(U_1 \cup N(U_2), V \backslash (U_1 \cup N(U_2)))$ does not occur.*

Proof. Clearly, $G[V']$ is bipartite if and only if there exists a partition (U_1, U_2) of U and a partition (W_1, W_2) of W such that no edge of $G[V']$ violates the partition $(U_1 \cup W_1, U_2 \cup W_2)$. Lemma 2 proves that the existence of such partitions of U and W is equivalent to the existence of a partition (U_1, U_2) of U such that the event $A(U_1 \cup N(U_2), V\backslash(U_1 \cup N(U_2)))$ does not occur, which completes the proof of the corollary. $\square$

Recall that in Section 13.2 we tried to prove that $G[V']$ is unlikely to be bipartite when G is ε-far from being bipartite by showing that for such a graph G there is a significant probability that the event $A(V_1, V_2)$ holds for every partition of V. Despite the fact that the event $A(V_1, V_2)$ holds for every given partition of V with high probability, we failed to prove that it holds for all the partitions at the same time with a significant probability because we had to consider all the possible partitions of V, and there were too many of these. Corollary 1 shows that (under our assumption) it is in fact sufficient to consider only a single partition of V for every partition of U. Since the number of such partitions is much smaller than the number of all possible partitions of V, we can use Corollary 1 to prove that $G[V']$ is unlikely to be bipartite when G is ε-far from being bipartite. However, before we can do that, we first need to deal with the technical issue that the partitions we now consider are defined by U, and thus, we need to show that the events corresponding to them happen with high probability even given a fixed choice of U. This is done by Exercise 4.

Exercise 4. Assuming $s - s_U \geqslant 2$, prove that, for every given set U of s_U vertices of G and a partition (U_1, U_2) of this set, the event $A(U_1 \cup N(U_2), V\backslash(U_1 \cup N(U_2)))$ happens with probability at least $1 - e^{-\varepsilon(s-s_U)/12}$ when G is ε-far from being bipartite.

We can now complete the proof that Algorithm 1 is a property testing algorithm given the assumption that we have made and a large enough value for the parameter s.

Corollary 2. *Let $c = 12 \cdot \ln 2$, and fix an $\varepsilon \in (0, 1]$. Given our assumption that every vertex of $V\backslash U$ is connected by an edge to a vertex of U, Algorithm 1 detects with probability at least $2/3$ that a graph G which is ε-far from being bipartite is not bipartite as long as $s \geqslant (c/\varepsilon + 1)s_U + 24/\varepsilon$.*

Proof. Assume that the input graph G for Algorithm 1 is ε-far from being bipartite and that $s \geqslant (c/\varepsilon + 1)s_U + 24/\varepsilon$. Note that the last inequality implies $s - s_U \geqslant cs_U/\varepsilon + 24/\varepsilon \geqslant 2$, and thus, Exercise 4 proves that the event $A(U_1 \cup N(U_2), V\backslash(U_1 \cup N(U_2)))$ happens with probability at least $1 - e^{-\varepsilon(s-s_U)/12}$ for every given partition (U_1, U_2) of the set U. Applying now the union bound over all the 2^{s_U} possible partitions of U, we get that the probability that the above event happens for all the possible partitions of U at the same time is at least

$$1 - 2^{s_U} \cdot e^{-\varepsilon(s-s_U)/12} = 1 - e^{s_U \ln 2 - \varepsilon(s-s_U)/12}$$

$$\geqslant 1 - e^{s_U \ln 2 - \varepsilon(cs_U/\varepsilon+24/\varepsilon)/12}$$

$$= 1 - e^{-2} > \frac{2}{3},$$

where the second equality holds due to the choice of c. To complete the proof of the corollary, it remains to observe that the last expression is also a lower bound on the probability that Algorithm 1 detects that G is not bipartite because Corollary 1 shows that $G[V']$ is not bipartite whenever the event $A(U_1 \cup N(U_2), V \setminus (U_1 \cup N(U_2)))$ happens for all the possible partitions of U. □

13.4 Removing the Assumption

In Section 13.3, we have proved that Algorithm 1 is a property testing algorithm given the assumption that every vertex of $V \setminus U$ is connected by an edge to a vertex of U. In this section, we would like to show that this assumption can be dropped. The most natural way to do that will be to show that the assumption holds with a significant probability when U is chosen as a uniformly random subset of s_U vertices. Intuitively, we might expect that this will indeed be the case when s_U is large enough because the larger U is, the more likely it is that a given vertex either ends up in U or ends up with a neighbor in U. Unfortunately, despite this intuition, U has to be of size $\Theta(n)$ to guarantee that the assumptions hold with a constant probability. To see that, consider an isolated vertex u. Such a vertex satisfies the assumption only when it is part of U, which happens with probability s_U/n.

Since we cannot prove that the assumption we used so far happens with a significant probability, we need to find a weaker property that, on the one hand, does happen with a significant probability, and on the other hand, provides enough structure for the proof that Algorithm 1 is a property testing algorithm to go through. Given a set U of vertices, let us denote by $R(U)$ the vertices of V/U that do not have an edge connecting them to U. We say that U has *good coverage* if there are at most $\varepsilon n^2/4$ edges in G hitting vertices of $R(U)$.

Lemma 3. *When $s_U \geqslant 8 \cdot \ln(48/\varepsilon)/\varepsilon$, the set U has a good coverage with probability at least $5/6$.*

Proof. In this proof, we pretend that the algorithm selects the set U by repeatedly picking a uniformly random vertex of G and adding it to U, until the set U contains s_U vertices (which can require more than s_U iterations if the same vertex is added to U multiple times). We denote by $u_1, u_2, \ldots, u_{s_U}$ the first s_U vertices selected by this process, and observe that they are independent random vertices of G.

Consider now an arbitrary vertex v of G of degree at least $\varepsilon n/8$. The probability that u_i is a neighbor of v, for any given $1 \leqslant i \leqslant s_U$, is at least $(\varepsilon n/8)/n = \varepsilon/8$, and thus, the probability that v belongs to $R(U)$ can be upper bounded by

$$\prod_{i=1}^{s_U} \left(1 - \frac{\varepsilon}{8}\right) \leqslant e^{-\varepsilon s_U/8} \leqslant e^{-\ln(48/\varepsilon)} = \frac{\varepsilon}{48}.$$

Let us now denote by X a random variable indicating the number of vertices of G that have a degree of at least $\varepsilon n/8$ and belong to $R(U)$. Since every vertex of G with such a degree has a probability at most $\varepsilon/48$ to be counted by X, the expected value of X is at most $\varepsilon n/48$. Thus, by Markov's inequality

$$\Pr\left[X \geqslant \frac{\varepsilon n}{8}\right] \leqslant \frac{\mathrm{E}[X]}{\varepsilon n/8} \leqslant \frac{\varepsilon n/48}{\varepsilon n/8} = \frac{1}{6}.$$

We are now ready to prove the lemma. By definition, $R(U)$ contains only X vertices of degree larger than $\varepsilon n/8$. Thus, we can upper bound the number of edges hitting the vertices of $R(U)$ using the expression

$$X \cdot n + (n - X) \cdot \frac{\varepsilon n}{8} \leqslant X \cdot n + \frac{\varepsilon n^2}{8}.$$

Recall that with probability at least $5/6$ we have $X < \varepsilon n/8$, which means that the last expression evaluates to less than $\varepsilon n^2/4$. □

Recall that the original assumption we used (i.e., that every vertex outside U is connected by an edge to a vertex of U) was useful because it allowed us to extend every partition of U into a partition of V in a natural way. Without this assumption, it is not obvious how to assign the vertices of $V \setminus U$ that are not connected by an edge to U (note that these are exactly the vertices of $R(U)$). We circumvent this issue by not assigning these vertices to any side of the partition, which should not make too much of a difference when only few edges hit these vertices — i.e., when U has a good coverage. More formally, a *partial partition* of V is a pair of disjoint subsets V_1 and V_2 of V whose union might not include the entire set V. Given a partition (U_1, U_2) of U, we construct a partial partition of V consisting of two sets: $U_1 \cup N(U_2)$ and $V/(U_1 \cup N(U_2) \cup R(U))$.

One can naturally extend the notation of violating edges to partial partitions as follows. Given a partial partition (V_1, V_2) of V, an edge e violates this partial partition if it connects two vertices of V_1 or two vertices of V_2. As usual, we define the event $A(V_1, V_2)$ as the event that some edge of $G[V']$ violates the partial partition (V_1, V_2). Using these definitions, we can state a weaker version of Lemma 2 that Exercise 5 asks you to prove.

Exercise 5. Prove that given a partition (U_1, U_2) of U, if the event $A(U_1 \cup N(U_2), V\backslash(U_1 \cup N(U_2)\backslash R(U)))$ occurs, then there does not exist a partition (W_1, W_2) of W such that no edge of $G[V']$ violates $(U_1 \cup W_1, U_2 \cup W_2)$.

Corollary 3. *If the event $A(U_1 \cup N(U_2), V\backslash(U_1 \cup N(U_2)\cup R(U)))$ occurs for every partition (U_1, U_2) of U, then $G[V']$ is not bipartite.*

Proof. Assume by way of contradiction that the event $A(U_1 \cup N(U_2), V\backslash(U_1 \cup N(U_2) \cup R(U)))$ occurs for every partition (U_1, U_2) of U, but $G[V']$ is bipartite. The fact that $G[V']$ is bipartite implies that there exists a partition (U_1, U_2) of U and a partition (W_1, W_2) of W such that no edge of $G[V']$ violates the partition $(U_1 \cup W_1, U_2 \cup W_2)$ of V'. However, this leads to a contradiction because Exercise 5 shows that the existence of such a partition is excluded by our assumption that the event $A(U_1 \cup N(U_2), V\backslash(U_1 \cup N(U_2) \cup R(U)))$ has happened. $\qquad\square$

We now need to prove that the event stated by the Exercise 5 is a high probability event. In general, this might not be true because many of the edges violating the partition $(U_1 \cup N(U_2), V\backslash(U_1 \cup N(U_2)))$ might not violate the partition $(U_1 \cup N(U_2), V\backslash(U_1 \cup N(U_2)\cup R(U)))$; however, there are only a few such edges when U has a good coverage.

Lemma 4. *If $s - s_U \geqslant 2$, then, for every given set U of s_U vertices that has a good coverage and a partition (U_1, U_2) of this set, the event $A(U_1\cup N(U_2), V\backslash(U_1 \cup N(U_2) \cup R(U)))$ happens with probability at least $1 - e^{-\varepsilon(s-s_U)/24}$ when G is ε-far from being bipartite.*

Before proving the lemma, we would like to point out that its proof is a slight generalization of the solution for Exercise 4, and thus, readers who read that solution will find most of the details in the following proof very familiar.

Proof. Let E' be the set of edges violating the partition $(U_1 \cup N(U_2), V \backslash (U_1 \cup N(U_2)))$. If there is an edge of E' that connects two vertices of U, then this edge is guaranteed to be in $G[V']$ and also violate the partial partition $(U_1 \cup N(U_2), V \backslash (U_1 \cup N(U_2) \cup R(U)))$, which implies that the event $A(U_1 \cup N(U_2), V \backslash (U_1 \cup N(U_2) \cup R(U)))$ happens with probability 1. Thus, we can safely assume from now on that this does not happen, which allows us to partition E' into three sets of edges: the set E'_1 contains the edges of E' that hit a single vertex of U and a single vertex of $V \backslash (U \cup R(U))$, the set E'_2 contains the edges of E' that hit two vertices of $V \backslash (U \cup R(U))$ and the set E'_3 contains the edges of E' that hit any vertices of $R(U)$. Note that, by Observation 1, the fact that G is ε-far from being bipartite guarantees that

$$|E'_1| + |E'_2| + |E'_3| = |E'| \geqslant \frac{\varepsilon n^2}{2} \Rightarrow |E'_1| + |E'_2| \geqslant \frac{\varepsilon n^2}{2} - |E'_3| \geqslant \frac{\varepsilon n^2}{4},$$

where the last inequality holds since the set E'_3 contains only edges hitting vertices of $R(U)$, and thus, its size is upper bounded by $\varepsilon n^2/4$ because U has a good coverage.

We now pretend that the set W is selected by repeatedly picking a uniform vertex of $V \backslash U$ and adding it to W, until the set W contains $s - s_U$ vertices. Let us denote the first $s - s_U$ vertices added to W according to this process by $u_1, u_2, \ldots, u_{s-s_U}$, and observe that these vertices are independent of each other. We also observe that the event $A(U_1 \cup N(U_2), V \backslash (U_1 \cup N(U_2) \cup R(U)))$ is guaranteed to happen when the vertices $u_1, u_2, \ldots, u_{s-s_U}$ include the two endpoints of an edge of E'_2 or the single vertex of an edge of E'_1 that does not belong to U (because in these two cases the edge in question is both a part of $G[V']$ and violates the partial partition of the event). Thus, if we denote by $U(e)$ the set of end points of an edge e that do not belong to U, then

$$1 - \Pr[A(U_1 \cup N(U_2), V \backslash (U_1 \cup N(U_2) \cup R(U)))]$$

$$\leqslant \Pr\left[\forall_{1 \leqslant i,j \leqslant s-s_u} u_i u_j \notin E'_2 \wedge \forall_{1 \leqslant i \leqslant s-s_u} u_i \notin \bigcup_{e \in E'_1} U(e) \right]$$

$$\leqslant \Pr\left[\forall_{1\leqslant i\leqslant \lfloor (s-s_u)/2 \rfloor} u_{2i-1} u_{2i} \notin E_2' \wedge \forall_{1\leqslant i\leqslant \lfloor (s-s_u)/2 \rfloor} u_{2i} \notin \bigcup_{e\in E_1'} U(e)\right]$$

$$= \prod_{i=1}^{\lfloor (s-s_u)/2 \rfloor} \Pr\left[u_{2i-1} u_{2i} \notin E_2' \wedge u_{2i} \notin \bigcup_{e\in E_1'} U(e)\right]$$

$$\leqslant \prod_{i=1}^{\lfloor (s-s_u)/2 \rfloor} \min\left\{\Pr[u_{2i-1} u_{2i} \notin E_2'], \Pr\left[u_{2i} \notin \bigcup_{e\in E_1'} U(e)\right]\right\},$$

where the equality holds since the vertices $u_1, u_2, \ldots, u_{s-s_U}$ are independent. We can now upper bound the two probabilities on the rightmost side as follows:

$$\Pr[u_{2i-1} u_{2i} \notin E_2'] = 1 - \frac{2|E_2'|}{|V\backslash U|^2} \leqslant 1 - \frac{2|E_2'|}{n^2}$$

and

$$\Pr\left[u_{2i} \notin \bigcup_{e\in E_1'} U(e)\right] = 1 - \frac{|\bigcup_{e\in E_1'} U(e)|}{|V\backslash U|} \leqslant 1 - \frac{|\bigcup_{e\in E_1'} U(e)|}{n} \leqslant 1 - \frac{|E_1'|}{n^2},$$

where the last inequality holds since a vertex can belong to at most $n-1$ edges. Combining all the inequalities we have proved so far, we get

$$1 - \Pr[A(U_1 \cup N(U_2), V\backslash(U_1 \cup N(U_2) \cup R(U)))]$$

$$\leqslant \prod_{i=1}^{\lfloor (s-s_u)/2 \rfloor} \min\left\{\Pr[u_{2i-1} u_{2i} \notin E_2'], \Pr\left[u_{2i} \notin \bigcup_{e\in E_1'} U(e)\right]\right\}$$

$$\leqslant \prod_{i=1}^{\lfloor (s-s_u)/2 \rfloor} \min\left\{1 - \frac{2|E_2'|}{n^2}, 1 - \frac{|E_1'|}{n^2}\right\} \leqslant \prod_{i=1}^{\lfloor (s-s_u)/2 \rfloor} \left(1 - \frac{|E_1'| + |E_2'|}{2n^2}\right)$$

$$\leqslant \prod_{i=1}^{\lfloor (s-s_u)/2 \rfloor} \left(1 - \frac{\varepsilon}{8}\right) \leqslant e^{-\varepsilon \lfloor (s-s_u)/2 \rfloor /8} \leqslant e^{-\varepsilon (s-s_u)/24},$$

where the second inequality holds since the minimum of two values is always upper bounded by their average and the last inequality follows from our assumption that $s - s_U \geqslant 2$. $\qquad\square$

Corollary 4 now follows from Lemma 3, Corollary 3 and Lemma 4.

Corollary 4. *Let $c = 24 \cdot \ln 2$, and fix an $\varepsilon \in (0,1]$. Algorithm 1 detects with probability at least $2/3$ that a graph G which is ε-far from being bipartite is not bipartite as long as $s_U \geqslant 8 \cdot \ln(48/\varepsilon)/\varepsilon$ and $s \geqslant (c/\varepsilon + 1)s_U + 48/\varepsilon$.*

Proof. Fix a graph G which is ε-far from being bipartite, let I_1 be the event that the set U has a good coverage and let I_2 be the event that Algorithm 1 detects that G is not bipartite. Lemma 3 shows that the event I_1 happens with probability at least $5/6$ given the constraint stated by the corollary on the size of s_U. Let us now lower bound the probability of the event I_2 given the event I_1.

Observe that the constraint on s given in the corollary guarantees $s - s_U \geqslant cs_U/\varepsilon + 48/\varepsilon \geqslant 2$, and thus, Lemma 4 proves that, conditioned on I_1, the event $A(U_1 \cup N(U_2), V \backslash (U_1 \cup N(U_2) \cup R(U)))$ happens with probability at least $1 - e^{-\varepsilon(s-s_U)/24}$ for every given partition (U_1, U_2) of the set U. Applying now the union bound over all the 2^{s_U} possible partitions of U, we get that conditioned on I_1 the probability that the above event happens for all the possible partitions of U at the same time is at least

$$1 - 2^{s_U} \cdot e^{-\varepsilon(s-s_U)/24} = 1 - e^{s_U \ln 2 - \varepsilon(s-s_U)/24}$$

$$\geqslant 1 - e^{s_U \ln 2 - \varepsilon(cs_U/\varepsilon + 48/\varepsilon)/24} = 1 - e^{-2} > \frac{5}{6},$$

where the second equality holds due to the choice of c. Observe now that the last expression is also a lower bound on the probability $\Pr[I_2|I_1]$ because Corollary 3 shows that $G[V']$ is not bipartite whenever the event $A(U_1 \cup N(U_2), V \backslash (U_1 \cup N(U_2) \cup R(U)))$ happens for all the possible partitions of U.

To complete the proof of the corollary, it remains to be observed that

$$\Pr[I_2] \geqslant \Pr[I_1] \cdot \Pr[I_2|I_1] \geqslant \left(\frac{5}{6}\right)^2 \geqslant \frac{2}{3}. \qquad \square$$

Let us now choose

$$s_U = \left\lceil \frac{8 \cdot \ln(48/\varepsilon)}{\varepsilon} \right\rceil = \Theta(\varepsilon^{-1} \cdot \ln \varepsilon^{-1}).$$

and

$$s = \min\left\{ \left\lceil \left(\frac{24 \cdot \ln 2}{\varepsilon} + 1\right) s_U + \frac{48}{\varepsilon} \right\rceil, n \right\}$$

$$= O[\varepsilon^{-1} \cdot (\varepsilon^{-1} \cdot \ln \varepsilon^{-1}) + \varepsilon^{-1}] = O(\varepsilon^{-2} \cdot \ln \varepsilon^{-1}).$$

Corollary 4 implies that given this choice for s, Algorithm 1 detects correctly with probability at least $2/3$ that its input graph is not bipartite when it is ε-far from being bipartite as long as $s \neq n$. Additionally, one can observe that the same thing is true also when $s = n$ because $s = n$ implies that the graph $G[V']$ is identical to the input graph of Algorithm 1. Together with Exercise 2, which showed that Algorithm 1 always detects correctly that a bipartite graph is bipartite, we get that Algorithm 1 is a property testing algorithm for determining whether its input graph is bipartite. Theorem 1 follows from this observation and from the observation that Algorithm 1 reads only the part of the representation of G corresponding to edges between the s vertices of V'.

Theorem 1. *For an appropriately chosen value* $s = O(\varepsilon^{-2} \cdot \ln \varepsilon^{-1})$, *Algorithm 1 is a one-side error property testing algorithm for determining whether its input graph is bipartite whose query complexity is* $O(s^2) = O(\varepsilon^{-4} \cdot \ln^2 \varepsilon^{-1})$.

> **Exercise 6.** In Chapter 11, we have seen a general result showing that the probability of error of a property testing algorithm can be reduced to $\delta \in (0, 1/3)$ by independently repeating the algorithm $O(\log \delta^{-1})$ times, which increases the query complexity of the algorithm by that factor. Show that it is also possible to reduce the error probability of a single execution of Algorithm 1 to δ by increasing the value of s to $O(\varepsilon^{-2} \cdot (\ln \varepsilon^{-1} + \log \delta^{-1}))$, which is slightly better than the previous option for some choices of the parameters.

13.5 Bibliographic Notes

The dense graph model and Algorithm 1 were both presented in a work by Goldreich *et al.* (1998). In this work, Goldreich *et al.* showed that Algorithm 1 is a property testing algorithm when $s = \Theta(\varepsilon^{-2} \cdot \log \varepsilon^{-1})$, which yields a query complexity of $O(\varepsilon^{-4} \cdot \log^2 \varepsilon^{-1})$. Moreover, they also showed that a slightly modified version of Algorithm 1, that queries only a subset of the entries of the adjacency matrix queried by the original algorithm, is a property testing algorithm with an improved query complexity of $O(\varepsilon^{-3} \cdot \log^2 \varepsilon^{-1})$. A later work by Alon and Krivelevich (2002) showed that the original Algorithm 1 remains a property testing algorithm even for an appropriate $s = \Theta(\varepsilon^{-1} \cdot \log \varepsilon^{-1})$, which yields an improved query complexity of $O(\varepsilon^{-2} \cdot \log^2 \varepsilon^{-1})$.

Alon and Krivelevich (2002) showed that their algorithm is optimal in terms of the number of vertices whose edges it queries. However, it is not known whether it is also optimal in terms of the number of edges it queries. The best result known in this respect is a result of Bogdanov and Trevisan (2004) showing that any property testing algorithm for determining whether a graph is bipartite in the dense model must use $\Omega(\varepsilon^{-3/2})$ queries.

As a final comment, we would like to point out that the result of Goldreich *et al.* (1998) was originally presented in terms of both the distance ε from bipartiteness and the probability δ of error, and Exercise 6 is based on this presentation of the result.

N. Alon and M. Krivelevich. Testing k-colorability. *SIAM Journal on Discrete Mathematics*, 15(2): 211–227, 2002.

A. Bogdanov and L. Trevisan. Lower Bounds for Testing Bipartiteness in Dense Graphs. In *Proceedings of the 19th Annual IEEE Conference on Computational Complexity (CCC)*, 75–81, 2004.

O. Goldreich, S. Goldwasser and D. Ron. Property Testing and its Connection to Learning and Approximation. *Journal of the ACM*, 45(4): 653–750, 1998.

Exercise Solutions

Solution 1

Any graph over n vertices can be made connected by adding at most $n - 1$ new edges to it (for example, by fixing an arbitrary simple path going through all the vertices, and adding its edges to the graph if they are not already in it). Additionally, we observe that adding an edge to a graph corresponds to changing two entries in the adjacency matrix of this graph. Thus, any graph can be made connected by changing at most $2(n-1)$ entries in its adjacency matrix. By definition, the distance between the adjacency matrix of the original graph and the adjacency matrix of the connected graph obtained after the change of these up to $2(n - 1)$ entries is at most

$$\frac{2(n - 1)}{n^2} < 2n^{-1},$$

and thus, no graph is $2n^{-1}$-far from a connected graph.

Solution 2

It is easy to see that the claim we are requested to prove in this exercise follows from Lemma 5.

Lemma 5. *Given a bipartite graph G and a subset V' of its vertices whose size is at least 2, the induced subgraph $G[V']$ is also a bipartite graph.*

Proof. The fact that G is bipartite implies that its vertices can be partitioned into two disjoint subsets U and W, such that all edges of G connect a vertex of U with a vertex of W. Consider now an arbitrary edge e of $G[V']$. By the definition of $G[V']$, e is also an edge of G, and thus, it must connect a vertex of U with a vertex of W. Moreover, since $G[V']$ contains only vertices of V', we get that e must connect a vertex of $V' \cap U$ with a vertex of $V' \cap W$.

As e was chosen as a general edge of $G[V']$, we get that every edge of $G[V']$ connects a vertex of $V' \cap U$ with a vertex of $V' \cap W$. This already proves the lemma when both $V' \cap U$ and $V' \cap W$ are non-empty since $V' \cap U$ and $V' \cap W$ form a disjoint partition of the vertices of $G[V']$. Thus, only the case in which one of the sets $V' \cap U$ or $V' \cap W$ is empty remains to be considered. Since we already proved that every edge of $G[V']$ hits a vertex of each one of these sets, the graph $G[V']$ must contain no edges in this case. Thus, it is bipartite since it contains at least 2 vertices. $\qquad \square$

Solution 3

Assume first that there exists a partition of V into disjoint sets V_1 and V_2 such that the event $A(V_1, V_2)$ does not occur, and let us prove this implies that $G[V']$ is bipartite. The fact that $A(V_1, V_2)$ did not occur implies that $G[V']$ does not contain any edge within V_1 or V_2, and thus, it also does not contain any edge within the sets $V_1 \cap V'$ and $V_2 \cap V'$. If the last two sets are not empty, then they form a partition of the vertices of $G[V']$, and thus, we get that $G[V']$ is bipartite, as desired. Additionally, if one of the sets $V_1 \cap V'$ or $V_2 \cap V'$ is empty, then the observation that no edge is contained within these sets implies that $G[V']$ contains no edges, and thus, it is again bipartite since we assume $|V'| = s \geqslant 2$.

Assume now that $G[V']$ is bipartite, and let us prove that this implies the existence of a partition of V into disjoint sets V_1 and V_2 such that the event $A(V_1, V_2)$ does not occur. Since $G[V']$ is bipartite, there exists a partition (V_1', V_2') of V' such that no edge of $G[V']$ is within a set of this partition. Consider now the partition $(V \backslash V_2', V_2')$ of V, and consider an arbitrary edge e violating this partition. Since e violates this partition, it must be within one of the two sets of this partition, however, e cannot be within V_2' because we already know that no edge of $G[V']$ (and thus, also of G) is within $V_2' \subseteq V'$. Hence, e must be within the set $V \backslash V_2'$. Analogously, we can also get that the edge e cannot be an edge between two vertices of V_1', and thus, at least one of the endpoints of e must belong to the set $V \backslash (V_1' \cup V_2') = V \backslash V'$; which implies that e does not belong to $G[V']$. Since e was chosen as an arbitrary edge violating the partition $(V \backslash V_2', V_2')$, we get that no edge violating this partition belongs to $G[V']$, and thus, the event $A(V \backslash V_2', V_2')$ does not occur (by definition).

Solution 4

Let E' be the set of edges violating the partition $(U_1 \cup N(U_2), V \backslash (U_1 \cup N(U_2)))$. If there is an edge of E' that connects two vertices of U, then this edge is guaranteed to be in $G[V']$, and thus, the event $A(U_1 \cup N(U_2), V \backslash (U_1 \cup N(U_2)))$ happens with probability 1. Thus, we can safely assume from now on that this does not happen, which allows us to partition E' into two sets of edges E_1' and E_2', such that E_1' contains the edges of E' which hit a single vertex of $V \backslash U$, and E_2' contains the edges of E' which hit two vertices of $V \backslash U$. Note that, by Observation 1, the fact that G is ε-far from being bipartite guarantees that

$$|E_1'| + |E_2'| = |E'| \geqslant \frac{\varepsilon n^2}{2}.$$

We now pretend that the set W is selected by repeatedly picking a uniform vertex of $V \backslash U$ and adding it to W, until the set W contains $s - s_U$ vertices (which can require more than $s - s_U$ iterations if the same vertex is added to W multiple times). Let us denote the first $s - s_U$ vertices added to W according to this process by $u_1, u_2, \ldots, u_{s-s_U}$, and observe that these vertices are independent of each other. We also observe that the event $A(U_1 \cup N(U_2), V \backslash (U_1 \cup N(U_2)))$ is guaranteed to happen when the vertices $u_1, u_2, \ldots, u_{s-s_U}$ include the two endpoints of an edge of E_2' or the single vertex of an edge of E_1' that does not belong to U (because in these two cases the edge in question becomes a part of $G[V']$). Thus, if we denote by $U(e)$ the set of end points of an edge e that do not belong to U, then

$$1 - \Pr[A(U_1 \cup N(U_2), V \backslash (U_1 \cup N(U_2)))]$$

$$\leqslant \Pr\left[\forall_{1 \leqslant i,j \leqslant s-s_u} u_i u_j \notin E_2' \wedge \forall_{1 \leqslant i \leqslant s-s_u} u_i \notin \bigcup_{e \in E_1'} U(e)\right]$$

$$\leqslant \Pr\left[\forall_{1\leqslant i\leqslant \lfloor(s-s_u)/2\rfloor} u_{2i-1}u_{2i} \notin E_2' \wedge \forall_{1\leqslant i\leqslant \lfloor(s-s_u)/2\rfloor} u_{2i} \notin \bigcup_{e\in E_1'} U(e)\right]$$

$$= \prod_{i=1}^{\lfloor(s-s_u)/2\rfloor} \Pr\left[u_{2i-1}u_{2i} \notin E_2' \wedge u_{2i} \notin \bigcup_{e\in E_1'} U(e)\right]$$

$$\leqslant \prod_{i=1}^{\lfloor(s-s_u)/2\rfloor} \min\left\{\Pr[u_{2i-1}u_{2i} \notin E_2'], \Pr\left[u_{2i} \notin \bigcup_{e\in E_1'} U(e)\right]\right\},$$

where the equality holds since the vertices $u_1, u_2, \ldots, u_{s-s_U}$ are independent. We can now upper bound the two probabilities on the rightmost side as follows:

$$\Pr[u_{2i-1}u_{2i} \notin E_2'] = 1 - \frac{2|E_2'|}{|V\setminus U|^2} \leqslant 1 - \frac{2|E_2'|}{n^2}$$

and

$$\Pr\left[u_{2i} \notin \bigcup_{e\in E_1'} U(e)\right] = 1 - \frac{|\bigcup_{e\in E_1'} U(e)|}{|V\setminus U|} \leqslant 1 - \frac{|\bigcup_{e\in E_1'} U(e)|}{n} \leqslant 1 - \frac{|E_1'|}{n^2},$$

where the last inequality holds since a vertex can belong to at most $n-1$ edges. Combining all the inequalities we have proved so far, we get

$$1 - \Pr[A(U_1 \cup N(U_2), V\setminus(U_1 \cup N(U_2)))]$$

$$\leqslant \prod_{i=1}^{\lfloor(s-s_u)/2\rfloor} \min\left\{\Pr[u_{2i-1}u_{2i} \notin E_2'], \Pr\left[u_{2i} \notin \bigcup_{e\in E_1'} U(e)\right]\right\}$$

$$\leqslant \prod_{i=1}^{\lfloor(s-s_u)/2\rfloor} \min\left\{1 - \frac{2|E_2'|}{n^2}, 1 - \frac{|E_1'|}{n^2}\right\} \leqslant \prod_{i=1}^{\lfloor(s-s_u)/2\rfloor} \left(1 - \frac{|E_1'| + |E_2'|}{2n^2}\right)$$

$$\leqslant \prod_{i=1}^{\lfloor(s-s_u)/2\rfloor} \left(1 - \frac{\varepsilon}{4}\right) \leqslant e^{-\varepsilon\lfloor(s-s_u)/2\rfloor/4} \leqslant e^{-\varepsilon(s-s_u)/12},$$

where the second inequality holds since the minimum of two values is always upper bounded by their average and the last inequality follows from our assumption that $s - s_U \geqslant 2$.

Solution 5

Assume that the event $A(U_1 \cup N(U_2), V \backslash (U_1 \cup N(U_2) \cup R(U)))$ has happened. This implies that there is an edge e in $G[V']$ violating its partial partition. The edge e must be within one of the two sides of this partition, which gives us two cases to consider.

- The first case is that e connects two vertices of $U_1 \cup N(U_2)$. This case is analogous to the first three cases studied in the proof of Lemma 2, and the same proofs used in these three cases show that there must be an edge of $G[V']$ violating the partition $(U_1 \cup W_1, U_2 \cup W_2)$ of V' regardless of the chosen partition (W_1, W_2) of W.

- The second case we need to consider is the case that e connects two vertices of $V \backslash (U_1 \cup N(U_2) \cup R(U))$. One can observe that $V \backslash (U_1 \cup N(U_2) \cup R(U))$ contains only vertices of U_2 and vertices of $V \backslash U$ that have a neighbor in $U \backslash U_2 = U_1$, and thus, e connects two vertices of $U_2 \cup N(U_1)$. This property of e is symmetric to the property of e that we had in the first case (namely, $e \in U_1 \cup N(U_2)$), and thus, a symmetric proof can be used to show that also in this case there must be an edge of $G[V']$ violating the partition $(U_1 \cup W_1, U_2 \cup W_2)$ of V' regardless of the chosen partition (W_1, W_2) of W.

Solution 6

Let G be an ε-far graph for some $\varepsilon \in (0, 1)$, and consider the events I_1 and I_2 from the proof of Corollary 4. We recall that I_1 is the event that U has a good coverage and I_2 is the event that Algorithm 1 detects that G is not bipartite.

Repeating the proof of Lemma 3, we get that the event I_1 holds with probability at least $1 - \delta/2$ if $s_U \geqslant 8 \cdot \ln(16/(\delta\varepsilon))/\varepsilon$. Similarly, by repeating a part of the proof of Corollary 4, we get that $\Pr[I_2 | I_1] \geqslant 1 - \delta/2$ when $s \geqslant (c/\varepsilon + 1)s_U + 24 \ln(2/\delta)/\varepsilon$. Thus, by choosing

$$s_U = \left\lceil \frac{8 \cdot \ln(16/(\delta\varepsilon))}{\varepsilon} \right\rceil = \Theta(\varepsilon^{-1} \cdot (\ln \varepsilon^{-1} + \ln \delta^{-1}))$$

and

$$s = \min\left\{ \left\lceil \left(\frac{24 \cdot \ln 2}{\varepsilon} + 1 \right) s_U + \frac{24 \ln(2/\delta)}{\varepsilon} \right\rceil, n \right\}$$

$$= O[\varepsilon^{-1} \cdot (\varepsilon^{-1} \cdot (\ln \varepsilon^{-1} + \ln \delta^{-1})) + \varepsilon^{-1} \cdot \ln \delta^{-1}]$$

$$= O(\varepsilon^{-2} \cdot (\ln \varepsilon^{-1} + \ln \delta^{-1}))$$

we can guarantee that Algorithm 1 detects that G is not bipartite with probability at least

$$\Pr[I_2] \geqslant \Pr[I_1] \cdot \Pr[I_2|I_1] \geqslant \left(1 - \frac{\delta}{2}\right)^2 \geqslant 1 - \delta$$

(when $s \neq n$, this follows from what we proved above, otherwise, it follows from the fact that $G[V']$ is equal to the input graph of Algorithm 1 when $s = n$). This completes the solution for the exercise because we already know by Exercise 2 that Algorithm 1 always detects that a bipartite graph is bipartite, as long as $s \geqslant 2$.

Chapter 14

Algorithms for Boolean Functions

Boolean functions are functions which get (multiple) bits as their input and produce a (single) output bit based on these input bits. A few very simple examples of such functions are the standard logical gates of AND, OR and NOT, but the relationship between the study of Boolean functions and computer science is much deeper than the superficial relationship represented by these logical gates. In particular, results about Boolean functions have found applications in diverse fields of computer science such as coding theory and complexity.

The importance of Boolean functions has motivated the study of property testing algorithms that test various properties that such functions can have. In this chapter, we present algorithms for two such properties.

14.1 Model

We begin the chapter by presenting the *Boolean function model*, which is the property testing model that we assume throughout this chapter. Formally, a Boolean function is a function from $\{0,1\}^m$ to $\{0,1\}$, where $\{0,1\}^m$ is the set of all vectors of m bits (i.e., all vectors of m coordinates that have either 0 or 1 in each one of these coordinates). Thus, the set N of objects in the Boolean function model is the set of all possible functions $f\colon \{0,1\}^m \to \{0,1\}$. Since we consider arbitrary Boolean functions, it is natural to think of a function as a truth table (recall that the truth table of a function is a table that explicitly states the value of the function for every possible input — see Tables 14.1 and 14.2 for examples). This allows us to define the distance between two Boolean functions as the fraction of the

Table 14.1.   The truth table of the AND function.

Input 1	Input 2	Output
0	0	0
0	1	0
1	0	0
1	1	1

Table 14.2.   The truth table of the XOR function.

Input 1	Input 2	Output
0	0	0
0	1	1
1	0	1
1	1	0

entries in which their truth tables differ, i.e., the fraction of inputs on which the two functions produce different outputs. A more formal way to state this is that the distance between two Boolean functions $f \colon \{0,1\}^m \to \{0,1\}$ and $g \colon \{0,1\}^m \to \{0,1\}$ is

$$d(f, g) = \Pr_{x \in_R \{0,1\}^m} [f(x) \neq g(x)],$$

where the notation $x \in_R \{0,1\}^m$ indicates that x is a uniformly random vector out of $\{0,1\}^m$.

Exercise 1. Explain why the formal and informal definitions given above for the distance between f and g coincide. In other words, explain why the probability $\Pr_{x \in_R \{0,1\}^m} [f(x) \neq g(x)]$ is indeed equal to the fraction of inputs on which the functions f and g differ.

It is important to note that the representation of a Boolean function (for example, using its truth table) requires 2^m bits — one bit for every possible input. Thus, somewhat unintuitively, a linear time algorithm for such functions is an algorithm whose time complexity is $O(2^m)$, and a sublinear time algorithm for Boolean functions is only required to have a time complexity of $o(2^m)$. It is important to keep that in mind while reading the remainder of this chapter.

14.2 Testing Linearity

In this chapter, we often need to add bits modulo 2. To make the math we use more readable, we adopt throughout the chapter the convention that the addition of bits is always assumed to be modulo 2, unless we explicitly state otherwise. Using this convention, we can now define the property of Boolean functions that we study in this section.

A Boolean function $f: \{0,1\}^m \rightarrow \{0,1\}$ is *linear* if for every pair of vectors $x, y \in \{0,1\}^m$ it holds that $f(x)+f(y) = f(x+y)$.[1] To demonstrate this definition, let us consider the AND and XOR functions. As a reminder for the reader, we give the truth table of the AND function in Table 14.1 (note that $m = 2$ in this case).

Let x be the vector $(0,1)$ and y be the vector $(1,0)$. Observe that $AND(x) = AND(0,1) = 0$ and $AND(y) = AND(1,0) = 0$, but $AND(x + y) = AND(1,1) = 1$. Thus,

$$AND(x) + AND(y) = 0 + 0 = 0 \neq 1 = AND(x + y),$$

which shows that the AND function is not linear. Consider now the XOR function whose truth table is given in Table 14.2. One can verify using this table that for any vector $x \in \{0,1\}^m$ the XOR function obeys $XOR(x) = x_1 + x_2$.

This observation implies that for every two vectors $x, y \in \{0,1\}^2$, it holds that

$$XOR(x) + XOR(y) = (x_1 + x_2) + (y_1 + y_2) = (x_1 + y_1) + (x_2 + y_2)$$
$$= XOR(x + y).$$

Hence, the XOR function is an example of a linear Boolean function. A general characterization of the linear Boolean functions is given by Exercise 2.

Exercise 2. Prove that a Boolean function $f: \{0,1\}^m \rightarrow \{0,1\}$ is linear if and only if there exist m constants $a_1, a_2, \ldots, a_m \in \{0,1\}$ such that $f(x) = \sum_{i=1}^{m} a_i x_i$ for every vector $x \in \{0,1\}^m$.

In the remainder of this section, our objective is to find a property testing algorithm for determining whether a given Boolean function is linear. A very natural algorithm for this task is given as Algorithm 1. This algorithm picks random pairs of vectors (x, y) and then checks whether

---

[1] Given standard definitions of linearity for other objects, it is natural to require also that $f(c \cdot x) = c \cdot f(x)$ for every vector $x \in \{0,1\}^m$ and scalar $c \in \{0,1\}$. However, this is trivial for $c = 1$, and for $c = 0$ it becomes $f(\bar{0}) = 0$, which already follows from our definition of linearity because this definition implies $f(\bar{0}) + f(\bar{0}) = f(\bar{0} + \bar{0}) = f(\bar{0})$.

Algorithm 1: Testing Linearity (f, ε)

1. Let $s \leftarrow \lceil 12/\varepsilon \rceil$.
2. **repeat** *s times*:
3.   Pick uniformly at random and independently two vectors x and y from $\{0, 1\}^m$.
4.   **if** $f(x) + f(y) \neq f(x + y)$ **then return** "f is not linear".
5. **return** "f is linear".

---

f obeys the definition of linearity with respect to x, y and $x + y$. If the function fails to obey the definition of linearity for one of the pairs, then it is not linear, and the algorithm declares that this is the case. Otherwise, if the function obeys the definition of linearity for all the pairs checked, then the algorithm declares it to be linear.

It is clear from the description of the algorithm that it correctly detects that a linear Boolean function is indeed linear. Thus, to prove that Algorithm 1 is a property testing algorithm, we only need to prove that it detects with probability at least $2/3$ that a function f which is ε-far from being linear is not linear.

Given a non-linear Boolean function f, let us denote by $\eta(f)$ the probability that a single iteration of Algorithm 1 detects that it is not linear. More formally,

$$\eta(f) = \Pr_{x,y \in_R \{0,1\}^m} [f(x) + f(y) \neq f(x + y)].$$

Intuitively, it is natural to assume that $\eta(f)$ should be large when f is far from being linear. Exercise 3 shows that if we manage to show that $\eta(f)$ is at least $\varepsilon/6$ when f is ε-far from being linear, then this implies that Algorithm 1 is a property testing algorithm.

Exercise 3. Prove that if $\eta(f)$ is at least $\varepsilon/6$ whenever f is ε-far from being linear, then, given a function f which is ε-far from being linear, Algorithm 1 correctly detects that it is not linear with probability at least $2/3$.

Our next objective is of course to prove that $\eta(f)$ is indeed at least $\varepsilon/6$ whenever f is ε-far from being linear. Thus, let us assume by way of contradiction that this is not the case, and let f be a counterexample, i.e., f is ε-far from being linear but has $\eta(f) < \varepsilon/6$. Our plan is to establish a contradiction by showing that there is a linear function g whose distance from f is less than ε. In particular, we will show that this is the case for the function

$$g(x) = \arg\max_{b \in \{0,1\}} \Pr_{y \in_R \{0,1\}^m}[f(x+y) - f(y) = b].$$

Informally, the value of g for a vector x is obtained by calculating the difference $f(x+y) - f(y)$ for every vector y, and then assigning the more common value of this difference to be the value of $g(x)$. Before we begin to prove that g is linear and close to f, let us intuitively motivate its definition. Since we hope g to be linear, the value of g for a vector x should be equal to $g(x+y) - g(y)$ for every vector y. Moreover, since we hope g to be close to f, the difference $g(x+y) - g(y)$ should be equal to the difference $f(x+y) - f(y)$ most of the time. Thus, it is natural for a function g that is linear and close to f to obey the definition of g.

We now begin the formal analysis of the function g by showing that it is indeed close to f.

Lemma 1. *The distance between the functions f and g is at most $2\eta(f)$.*

Proof. Let U be the number of vectors in $\{0,1\}^m$ on which f and g disagree. By the definition of the distance between functions, the distance between f and g is

$$d(f,g) = \Pr_{x \in_R \{0,1\}^m}[f(x) \neq g(x)] = \frac{|U|}{2^m}.$$

Additionally, by the definition of g, for every vector $x \in U$ we have

$$f(x) \neq \arg\max_{b \in \{0,1\}} \Pr_{y \in_R \{0,1\}^m}[f(x+y) - f(y) = b],$$

which implies

$$\Pr_{y \in_R \{0,1\}^m}[f(x+y) - f(y) = f(x)] < 1/2.$$

This means that when x belongs to U, then a random y has a probability of more than $1/2$ to reveal that f is not linear. Thus, U should be small when $\eta(f)$ is small. More formally,

$$\eta(f) = \Pr_{x,y \in_R \{0,1\}^m}[f(x) + f(y) \neq f(x+y)]$$

$$= \mathbb{E}_{x \in_R \{0,1\}^m}[\Pr_{y \in_R \{0,1\}^m}[f(x) + f(y) \neq f(x+y)]]$$

$$\geq \mathbb{E}_{x \in_R \{0,1\}^m}[1_{x \in U} \cdot \tfrac{1}{2}] = \frac{|U|}{2^{m+1}} = \frac{d(f,g)}{2},$$

where $1_{x \in U}$ is an indicator for the event that x belongs to U. The lemma now follows by rearranging the last inequality. $\qquad\square$

Next, we need to show that g is linear. To prove this, we first need the helper Lemma 2. Note that the definition of g guarantees that $g(x)$ is equal to $f(x + y) - f(y)$ for at least half of the possible vectors y. The helper lemma shows that when $\eta(f)$ is not too large, $g(x)$ is in fact equal to $f(x + y) - f(y)$ for many more than half of the possible vectors y.

Lemma 2. *For every vector* $x \in \{0, 1\}^m$, $\Pr_{y \in_R \{0,1\}^m}[g(x) = f(x + y) - f(y)] \geq 1 - 2\eta(f)$.

Proof. Relating the probability $\Pr_{y \in_R \{0,1\}^m}[g(x) = f(x + y) - f(y)]$ to $\eta(f)$ is made more complicated by the fact that the definition of $\eta(f)$ is based on two random vectors, while the above probability includes only one such vector (note that x is deterministic). Thus, it should be easier to relate a probability such as $\Pr_{y,z \in_R \{0,1\}^m}[f(x + z) - f(z) = f(x + y) - f(y)]$ to $\eta(f)$. Fortunately, the two above probabilities are related. Intuitively, if the first probability is high, then both $f(x + y) - f(y)$ and $f(x + z) - f(z)$ are likely to be equal to $g(x)$, and thus, should likely be equal. More formally, if we denote by p the probability $\Pr_{y \in_R \{0,1\}^m}[g(x) = f(x + y) - f(y)]$, then we get

$$
\begin{aligned}
&\Pr_{y,z \in_R \{0,1\}^m}[f(x + z) - f(z) = f(x + y) - f(y)] \\
&= \Pr_{y,z \in_R \{0,1\}^m}[f(x + z) - f(z) = g(x) = f(x + y) - f(y)] \\
&\quad + \Pr_{y,z \in_R \{0,1\}^m}[f(x + z) - f(z) = 1 - g(x) = f(x + y) - f(y)] \\
&= p^2 + (1 - p)^2 = 1 - 2p(1 - p) \leq p,
\end{aligned}
$$

where the second equality is true since the vectors z and y are independent, and the inequality is true since the definition of g guarantees that p is at least $1/2$. To prove the lemma, it remains to show that the probability on the leftmost side is at least $1 - 2\eta(f)$. Since addition and subtraction of bits are equivalent operations (verify!), we get

$$
\begin{aligned}
&\Pr_{y,z \in_R \{0,1\}^m}[f(x + z) - f(z) = f(x + y) - f(y)] \\
&= \Pr_{y,z \in_R \{0,1\}^m}[f(x + z) + f(x + y) = f(y) + f(z)] \\
&\geq \Pr_{y,z \in_R \{0,1\}^m}[f(x + z) + f(x + y) = f(y + z) = f(y) + f(z)] \\
&\geq 1 - \Pr_{y,z \in_R \{0,1\}^m}[f(x + z) + f(x + y) \neq f(y + z)] \\
&\quad + \Pr_{y,z \in_R \{0,1\}^m}[f(z) + f(y) \neq f(y + z)] = 1 - 2\eta(f),
\end{aligned}
$$

where the second inequality follows from the union bound and the last equality holds since $x + z$ and $x + y$ are uniformly random vectors of $\{0, 1\}^m$ whose sum is $y + z$. □

We are now ready to prove that g is a linear function. Note that our assumption (by way of contradiction) that $\eta(f) < \varepsilon/6$, together with the observation that the distance of a function from linearity can be at most 1, implies $\eta(f) < 1/6$.

Corollary 1. *Since $\eta(f) < 1/6, g$ is linear.*

Proof. Consider any pair of vectors x and y. We need to show that $g(x) + g(y) = g(x + y)$. Naturally, this requirement is deterministic, which is problematic since all the guarantees we have on g are randomized. Thus, let us consider a uniformly random vector z in $\{0, 1\}^m$. Then, one can observe that the equality that we want to prove holds whenever the following three equalities hold.

(i) $g(x) = f(x + z) - f(z)$, (ii) $g(y) = f(y + x + z) - f(x + z)$ and (iii) $g(x + y) = f(x + y + z) - f(z)$.

Since z is a uniformly random vector, Lemma 2 implies that both Inequalities (i) and (iii), separately, hold with probability at least $1 - 2\eta(f)$. Moreover, since $x + z$ is also a uniformly random vector in $\{0, 1\}^m$, Inequality (ii) also holds with this probability. Thus, we get by the union bound that the probability that all three inequalities hold at the same time is at least $1 - 6\eta(f)$. Plugging in our knowledge that $\eta(f) < 1/6$, we get that there is a positive probability that Inequalities (i), (ii) and (iii) all hold at the same time, which implies that there must be some vector $z \in \{0, 1\}^m$ for which the three inequalities hold.[2] As discussed above, the existence of such a vector z implies that the equality $g(x) + g(y) = g(x + y)$, which we wanted to prove, is true. □

Lemma 1 and Corollary 1 imply together that the distance of f from the linear function g is at most $2\eta(f) < 2(\varepsilon/6) < \varepsilon$, which contradicts our assumption that f is a Boolean function that is ε-far from being linear while obeying $\eta(f) < \varepsilon/6$. Thus, as intended, we get that every Boolean function which is ε-far from being linear must obey $\eta(f) \geq \varepsilon/6$. Recall that, by Exercise 3, this implies that Algorithm 1 detects with probability at least $2/3$ that a Boolean function that is ε-far from being linear is not linear.

---

[2]Note that this is an application of the probabilistic method mentioned in Chapter 6.

Hence, Algorithm 1 is a property testing algorithm because we already observed above that it always detects that a linear function is linear.

Theorem 1. *Algorithm 1 is a property testing algorithm for determining whether a Boolean function is linear whose query complexity is $O(\varepsilon^{-1})$.*

An interesting additional property of g is given by Exercise 4.

Exercise 4. Prove that g is the closest linear Boolean function to f when f is ε-close to being linear for some $\varepsilon < 1/4$, which in particular implies that g is linear in this regime. **Hint:** Consider a linear Boolean function h that has the minimum distance to f among all such functions, and use the definition of g to prove that g is identical to h.

14.3 Testing Monotonicity

In this section, we are interested in testing an additional property of Boolean functions called monotonicity. A Boolean function $f\colon \{0,1\}^m \to \{0,1\}$ is *monotone* if for every pair of vectors $x, y \in \{0,1\}^m$ such that $x \leq y$ (where the comparison is done coordinate-wise) it holds that $f(x) \leq f(y)$. The following exercise is intended to help you get more familiar with the notion of the Boolean function monotonicity.

Exercise 5. Prove that the Boolean function $\text{AND}(x)$ presented in Section 2.5.2 is monotone, while the Boolean function $\text{XOR}(x)$ described in the same section is not.

In the study of Boolean functions, it is often very useful to refer to a concept known as the *Boolean hypercube*. Formally, the Boolean hypercube of dimension m is a graph whose vertices are the Boolean vectors of $\{0,1\}^m$, and two vertices $x, y \in \{0,1\}^m$ of the Boolean hypercube are connected by an edge if and only if they differ in exactly one coordinate. A graphical representation of the Boolean hypercubes of dimensions 1, 2 and 3 appear in Figure 14.1. Consider now an arbitrary edge (x, y) of the hypercube. By definition, the vectors x and y are identical in all coordinates except for one. Thus, either $x \leq y$ or $x \geq y$.[3] Definition 1 is made possible by this observation.

---

[3]This is not trivial for general vectors. For example, the vectors $x = (0, 1)$ and $y = (1, 0)$ obey neither $x \leq y$ nor $x \geq y$.

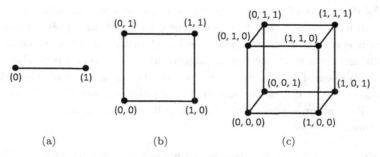

Figure 14.1. The Boolean hypercubes of dimensions 1(a), 2(b) and 3(c).

Definition 1. Consider an arbitrary edge (x, y) of the hypercube, and assume without loss of generality that $x \leq y$ (otherwise, we switch x and y). Then, we say that (x, y) is a *non-monotone edge* with respect to a Boolean function f if $f(x) > f(y)$.

Exercise 6. Prove that a Boolean function $f \colon \{0, 1\}^m \to \{0, 1\}$ is monotone if and only if there is no edge of the Boolean hypercube of dimension m that is non-monotone with respect to f.

The characterization of monotone functions given by the last exercise naturally suggests an algorithm for testing monotonicity of Boolean functions that given a Boolean function f picks a few random edges of the Boolean hypercube and checks whether they are monotone with respect to f. If one of the picked edges turns out to be non-monotone, then Exercise 6 implies that f is not monotone. Otherwise, if all the picked edges turn out to be monotone, then the algorithm declares f to be monotone. A more formal presentation of this algorithm is given as Algorithm 2.

Algorithm 2: Testing Monotonicity (f, ε)

1. Let $s \leftarrow \lceil 2m/\varepsilon \rceil$.
2. **repeat** s *times*:
3.   Pick a uniformly random edge (x, y) of the Boolean hypercube of dimension m.
4.   **if** $x \geq y$ **then** swap x and y.
5.   **if** $f(x) > f(y)$ **then return** "f is not monotone".
6. **return** "f is monotone".

As discussed above, f is guaranteed to be non-monotone whenever Algorithm 2 declares that this is the case, which implies that a monotone function is always declared monotone by Algorithm 2. Thus, to show that Algorithm 2 is a property testing algorithm, it only remains to show that given a Boolean function which is far from being monotone, Algorithm 2 detects that it is not monotone with a significant probability. To do this, we need the following property of Boolean functions that are far from being monotone.

Lemma 3. *If f is ε-far from being monotone, then at least $\varepsilon \cdot 2^{m-1}$ of the edges of the hypercube of dimension m are non-monotone with respect to f.*

We will prove Lemma 3 momentarily, but first let us show that it indeed implies that Algorithm 2 is a property testing algorithm.

Corollary 2. *Given a Boolean function $f: \{0,1\}^m \to \{0,1\}$ which is ε-far from being monotone, Algorithm 2 detects that it is non-monotone with probability at least $2/3$.*

Proof. By Lemma 3, every iteration of Algorithm 2 detects that f is non-monotone with probability at least

$$\frac{\varepsilon \cdot 2^{m-1}}{m \cdot 2^{m-1}} = \frac{\varepsilon}{m}$$

because the hypercube of dimension m contains $m \cdot 2^{m-1}$ edges (an edge of the hypercube is specified by the choice of the single coordinate in which the two endpoints of the edge differ and the values of the remaining $m - 1$ coordinates). Thus, the probability that no iteration of the algorithm detects that f is non-monotone is at most

$$\left(1 - \frac{\varepsilon}{m}\right)^s \le e^{-(\varepsilon/m)s} \le e^{-(\varepsilon/m)(2m/\varepsilon)} = e^{-2} < \frac{1}{3}. \qquad \square$$

It remains now to prove Lemma 3, which is equivalent to showing that if there are only a few edges of the Boolean hypercube that are non-monotone with respect to f, then f must be close to a monotone function. In order to prove this, we will describe a method for making a function monotone which makes only a small number of modifications when there are only a few edges of the Boolean hypercube that are non-monotone with respect to f.

The method we will describe considers the m dimensions of the Boolean hypercube sequentially, and "fixes" each direction separately. More formally, we say that an edge (x, y) of the Boolean hypercube belongs to dimension i if the single coordinate in which x and y differ is coordinate i. For example, in the Boolean hypercube of dimension 3, the edge between the vector $(0, 1, 0)$ and the vector $(0, 1, 1)$ belongs to dimension 3, while the edge between the vector $(1, 0, 1)$ and the vector $(1, 1, 1)$ belongs to dimension 2. Using this definition, we can now define $D_i(f)$ as the number of edges of the Boolean hypercube that belong to dimension i and are non-monotone with respect to the function f.

Note that, by Exercise 6, f is monotone if and only if $D_i(f)$ is 0 for all dimensions $1 \le i \le m$. Thus, "fixing" a dimension i of f means modifying f into a function g that obeys $D_i(g) = 0$. One natural way to do this is to simply flip the values assigned by f to the endpoints of every edge of dimension i that is non-monotone with respect to f. More formally, given a Boolean function f, $S_i(f)$ is a Boolean function whose value for every vector $x \in \{0,1\}^m$ is defined as follows. Let (x,y) be the single edge of the Boolean hypercube that involves x and belongs to dimension i, then

$$S_i(f)(x) = \begin{cases} 1 - f(x) & \text{if } (x, y) \text{ is non-monotone with respect to } f, \\ f(x) & \text{otherwise.} \end{cases}$$

A graphical example of the operation S_i is given in Figure 14.2. Lemma 4 gives a few properties of the operation S_i.

Lemma 4. *For every Boolean function $f : \{0,1\}^m \to \{0,1\}$ and dimension $1 \le i \le m$, the following hold.*

Figure 14.2. A graphical illustration of the S_i operation. The left side of this figure presents a Boolean function (with $m = 2$). The value of the Boolean function for every vector $x \in \{0,1\}^2$ appears in italics for clarity. The right side of the figures presents the function obtained by applying the operation S_2 to the function given on the left. Note that the original function has a single non-monotone edge in dimension 2 (the edge from $(0, 0)$ to $(0, 1)$), and thus, the function produced by the S_2 operation flips the values of f in the endpoints of this edge, while preserving the values of f for the two other vectors.

- $D_i(S_i(f)) = 0$.
- *For every other dimension* $1 \leq j \leq m$, $D_j(S_i(f)) \leq D_j(f)$. *In particular, if* $D_j(f) = 0$, *then* $D_j(S_i(f)) = 0$.

Proof.   Intuitively, the property $D_i(S_i(f)) = 0$ is equivalent to saying that the operation S_i "fixes" dimension i of f. The operation S_i was designed to achieve this goal, however, let us formally prove that this operation indeed manages to achieve it. Consider an arbitrary edge (x, y) of the Boolean hypercube, and let us assume (without loss of generality) that $x \leq y$. If $f(x) \leq f(y)$, then (x, y) is monotone with respect to f, and thus,

$$S_i(f)(x) = f(x) \leq f(y) = S_i(f)(y).$$

Otherwise, (x, y) is non-monotone with respect to f, which implies

$$S_i(f)(x) = 1 - f(x) < 1 - f(y) = S_i(f)(y).$$

Hence, in both cases (x, y) is monotone with respect to $S_i(f)$, which gives $D_i(S_i(f)) = 0$.

Intuitively, the other property that we need to prove (i.e., that $D_j(S_i(f)) \leq D_j(f)$ whenever j is a dimension other than i means that while "fixing" dimension i we do not make the situation worse in any other dimension. To prove this, let us partition the vectors of $\{0,1\}^m$ into sets of size 4, where the vectors of each set have identical values for all coordinates other than i and j. In other words, each set is determined by an assignment $\sigma\colon \{1, 2, \ldots, m\} \setminus \{i, j\} \to \{0, 1\}$ of values to every coordinate other than i and j, and the members of the set are the 4 vectors of $\{0,1\}^m$ that agree with σ on the coordinates other than i and j.

A useful property of the partition described above is that edges of the Boolean hypercube belonging to dimensions i and j always go between two vertices of the same set within the partition, which has two implications. The first implication is that the values of $S_i(f)$ for the vectors of a set in the partition are fully determined by the values assigned by f to these vectors; and the other implication is that to prove the lemma it is enough to show that $S_i(f)$ does not make the situation worse in dimension j within any given set of the partition because this will imply that it also does not make the situation worse in dimension j in general. The proof of the last claim (i.e., that $S_i(f)$ indeed does not make the situation worse in dimension j within any given set of the partition) is done through a case analysis in which we study every possible assignment of values by f to the four vectors of some set A of the partition. Specifically, we need to verify that for every such assignment the number of non-monotone edges of dimension j with respect to f between vectors of A is at least as large as the number of such edges with respect to $S_i(f)$. One can observe that out of the 16 possible assignments of values to A by the function f, 9 result in no non-monotone edges of dimension i with respect to f, and thus, make f and $S_i(f)$ identical within A. In the remaining 7 cases, the two functions differ within A, and these cases are studied in Figures 14.3 and 14.4.　　　　　　　□

Exercise 7. The operation $S_i(f)$ studied by Lemma 4 flips at the same time the values assigned by f to the two endpoints of every edge of dimension i which is non-monotone with respect to f. A natural alternative is to flip at each step the values assigned by f to the two endpoints of a single edge of dimension i which is non-monotone with respect to f. Show that unlike $S_i(f)$, such a flip of a single edge might increase the number of non-monotone edges in other dimensions.

Using Lemma 4, we are now ready to prove Lemma 3.

Proof of Lemma 3. Assume, by way of contradiction, that the lemma is not true, i.e., that there exists a Boolean function $f \colon \{0,1\}^m \to \{0,1\}$ which is ε-far from being monotone, but less than $\varepsilon \cdot 2^{m-1}$ of the edges of the Boolean hypercube of dimension m are non-monotone with respect to f. By definition, $D_i(f)$ is the number of edges belonging to dimension i

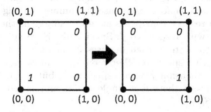

Figure 14.3. One of the cases in the proof of Lemma 4. The left rectangle represents one possible assignment of values by f to the vectors of the set A. More specifically, each vertex of this rectangle represents a single vector of A, where the two coordinates beside the vertex give the values of the coordinates i and j (in that order) of the vector in A that the vertex corresponds to, and the number in italics near the vertex gives the value assigned by f to this vector. In a similar way, the right rectangle represents the values assigned by $S_i(f)$ to the vectors of A. One can observe that the left rectangle includes a single non-monotone edge in dimension j, and so is the right rectangle. Hence, in the case described by this figure, $S_i(f)$ does not make the situation worse in dimension j compared to f.

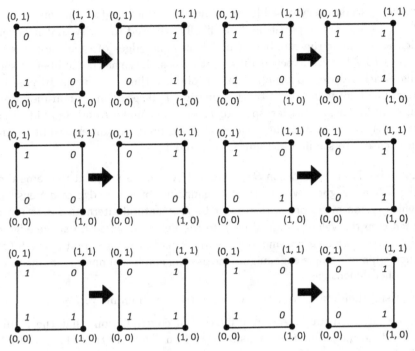

Figure 14.4. The cases of the proof of Lemma 4 which are not given in Figure 14.3. There are seven possible assignments of values by f to the four vertices of the set A that result in at least one non-monotone edge belonging to dimension i within the set. One of these assignments was depicted in Figure 14.3, and the other six cases are depicted in this figure (see Figure 14.3 for an explanation about the way in which each case is depicted). One can observe that in each case the number of edges of dimension j that are non-monotone with respect to $S_i(f)$ is at most as large as the number of such edges that are non-monotone with respect to f. Specifically, if we number the cases from left to right and from top to bottom, then in cases 2, 3 and 6 there are no non-monotone edges of dimension j with respect to either f or $S_i(f)$, in cases 1 and 4 there is a single non-monotone edge of dimension j with respect to f, but no such edge with respect to $S_i(f)$, and finally, in case 5 there is a single non-monotone edge of dimension j with respect to both f and $S_i(f)$.

that are non-monotone with respect to f. Since each edge of the Boolean hypercube belongs to exactly one dimension, the sum $\sum_{i=1}^{m} D_i(f)$ is exactly equal to the number of edges of the hypercube that are non-monotone with respect to f, which yields

$$\sum_{i=1}^{m} D_i(f) < \varepsilon \cdot 2^{m-1}.$$

Consider now the function $S_m(S_{m-1}(\cdots S_1(f)))$ — recall that S_i is the operation that "fixes" the edges of dimension i. Lemma 4 implies immediately that this function is monotone. To determine the number of vectors of $\{0, 1\}^m$ in which this function differs from f, we need to upper bound the number of values changed by each S_i operation. Since the operation S_i changes the two endpoints of every edge of dimension i that is non-monotone with respect to the function it gets, the number of modifications made by the operation S_i in the expression $S_m(S_{m-1}(\cdots S_1(f)))$ is upper bounded by

$$2D_i\left(S_{i-1}(S_{i-2}(\cdots S_1(f)))\right) \leq 2D_i(f),$$

where the inequality follows by a repeated application of Lemma 4. Summing up for every value of i the bound we got on the number of modifications made by each operation S_i in the expression $S_m(S_{m-1}(\cdots S_1(f)))$, we get that the monotone function given by this expression differs from f in at most

$$\sum_{i=1}^{m} 2D_i\left(f\right) = 2 \cdot \sum_{i=1}^{m} D_i\left(f\right) < 2\left(\varepsilon \cdot 2^{m-1}\right) = \varepsilon \cdot 2^m$$

values, which contradicts our assumption that f is ε-far from being monotone. □

Theorem 2 summarizes the properties of Algorithm 2. Recall that an algorithm on Boolean functions is sublinear if its time complexity is $o(2^m)$.

Theorem 2. *Algorithm 2 is a property testing algorithm for determining whether a function f is monotone whose time complexity is $O(m^2/\varepsilon)$.*

Proof. Exercise 6 and Corollary 2 prove together that Algorithm 2 is a property testing algorithm for determining whether its input function is monotone. Thus, the time complexity of Algorithm 2 remains to be analyzed. Algorithm 2 has at most $s = O(m/\varepsilon)$ iterations. We will prove that each one of these iterations can be executed in $O(m)$ time, which implies the theorem.

Each iteration of Algorithm 2 involves sampling a uniformly random edge of the Boolean hypercube and evaluating the input Boolean function on the two endpoints of this edge. Evaluating f on a point is equivalent to reading a value from an m-dimensional array, and thus, can be done in $O(m)$ time. Additionally, one can sample a uniformly random edge of the

Boolean hypercube of dimension m using the following procedure:

1. First, pick uniformly at random the dimension i to which the edge will belong.
2. Pick a uniformly random vector $x \in \{0, 1\}^m$, and let y be the vector obtained from x by flipping the value of coordinate i.
3. Output x and y as the two endpoints of the sampled edge.

Clearly, this procedure can be implemented in $O(m)$ time. Additionally, a symmetry argument shows that this procedure has an equal probability to pick every edge of the Boolean hypercube, which implies that it picks a uniformly random edge. $\qquad\square$

|| **Exercise 8.** Calculate the query complexity of Algorithm 2.

14.4 Bibliographic Notes

The algorithm described above for testing linearity (Algorithm 1) was suggested by Blum *et al.* (1993). Blum *et al.* studied their algorithm in the case of a function between general finite groups, and showed that even in this general case every single iteration of the algorithm detects correctly that a function which is ε-far from being linear is not linear with probability at least $2\varepsilon/9$. Improved probabilities were proved in a few later works (see, for example (Bellare *et al.*, 1993)), but we would like to mention here explicitly only the result of Bellare *et al.* (1996) who proved that, in the special case of the Boolean functions, a single iteration of Algorithm 1 detects that a function which is ε-far from being linear is not linear with probability at least ε. The last result is based on discrete Fourier analysis, and thus, we chose to present in this chapter a simpler and weaker analysis due to Ron (2010) which uses some of the ideas found in the original analysis due to Blum *et al.* (1993).

The algorithm described above for testing monotonicity of Boolean functions (Algorithm 2) and its analysis were originally given by Goldreich *et al.* (2000).

M. Bellare, D. Coppersmith, J. Håstad, M. A. Kiwi and M. Sudan. *IEEE Transactions on Information Theory*, 42(6): 1781–1795, 1996.

M. Bellare, S. Goldwasser, C. Lund and A. Russell. Efficient Probabilistically Checkable Proofs and Applications to Approximation. In *Proceedings* of the 25th Annual Symposium on Theory of Computing (STOC), May 1993.

M. Blum, M. Luby and R. Rubinfeld. Self-Testing/Correcting with Applications to Numerical Problems. *Journal of Computer and System Sciences*, 47(3): 549–595, 1993.

O. Goldreich, S. Goldwasser, E. Lehman, D. Ron and A. Samorodnitsky. Testing Monotonicity. *Combinatorica*, 20(3): 301–337, 2000.

D. Ron. Algorithmic and Analysis Techniques in Property Testing. *Foundations and Trends in Theoretical Computer Science*, 5(2): 73–205, 2010.

Exercise Solutions

Solution 1

When x is a uniformly random vector out of $\{0,1\}^m$, the probability $\Pr[f(x) \neq g(x)]$ is simply the fraction of the vectors $x \in \{0,1\}^m$ which obey the condition $f(x) \neq g(x)$, i.e., the fraction of the inputs which make f and g produce different outputs.

Solution 2

We begin by proving that if f is a Boolean function and $a_1, a_2, \ldots, a_m \in \{0,1\}$ are constants such that $f(x) = \sum_{i=1}^m a_i x_i$ for every vector $x \in \{0,1\}^m$, then f is linear. Let x and y be two arbitrary vectors in $\{0,1\}^m$. Then,

$$f(x) + f(y) = \sum_{i=1}^m a_i x_i + \sum_{i=1}^m a_i y_i = \sum_{i=1}^m a_i(x_i + y_i) = f(x + y),$$

which implies that f is indeed linear.

The more involved direction remains to be proved, namely that if f is a linear Boolean function, then there exist constants $a_1, a_2, \ldots, a_m \in \{0,1\}$ such that $f(x) = \sum_{i=1}^m a_i x_i$ for every vector $x \in \{0,1\}^m$. As a first step, observe that $f(\bar{0})$ must be 0 because the linearity of f guarantees that it obeys $f(\bar{0}) + f(\bar{0}) = f(\bar{0} + \bar{0}) = f(\bar{0})$. Let us denote now by $e^{(i)}$ a vector which takes the value 1 at coordinate i and the value 0 at the remaining coordinates. Using the equality of $f(\bar{0})$ to 0, we get for every vector $x \in \{0,1\}^m$ the equality

$$f\left(x_i \cdot e^{(i)}\right) = x_i \cdot f\left(e^{(i)}\right)$$

(verify the equality by plugging in the two possible values for x_i). The linearity of f now gives us

$$f(x) = f\left(\sum_{i=1}^{m} x_i \cdot e^{(i)}\right) = \sum_{i=1}^{m} f\left(x_i \cdot e^{(i)}\right) = \sum_{i=1}^{m} x_i \cdot f\left(e^{(i)}\right).$$

One can observe that the last equality completes the proof because x is a general vector in $\{0,1\}^m$ and $f(e^{(i)})$ is some constant in $\{0,1\}$ for every $1 \le i \le m$.

Solution 3

Consider a function f which is ε-far from being linear. By the assumption of the exercise, we get that $\eta(f) \ge \varepsilon/6$. In other words, every single iteration of Algorithm 1 has a probability of at least $\varepsilon/6$ to detect that f is not linear. Since the iterations are independent, and Algorithm 1 declares the function to be non-linear if a single iteration detects that it is not linear, we get that the probability that Algorithm 1 declares f to be linear is at most

$$\left(1 - \frac{\varepsilon}{6}\right)^{\text{number of iterations}} \le \left(1 - \frac{\varepsilon}{6}\right)^{\lceil 12/\varepsilon \rceil}$$

$$\le e^{-(\varepsilon/6)\lceil 12/\varepsilon \rceil} \le e^{-2} < \frac{1}{3},$$

where the second inequality holds due to the inequality $1 + x \le e^x$, which holds for every real value x.

Solution 4

Following the hint, let h be a linear Boolean function which has the minimum distance to f among all such functions. Since f is ε-close to being linear for some $\varepsilon < 1/4$, the set U of vectors on which f and h disagree contains less than $1/4$ of the vectors. Moreover, by the linearity of h, $h(x) = h(x + y) - h(y)$ for every two vectors $x, y \in \{0,1\}^m$. Hence, for every vector $x \in \{0,1\}^m$,

$$\Pr_{y \in \{0,1\}^m}[h(x) \ne f(x+y) - f(y)]$$

$$\le \Pr_{y \in \{0,1\}^m}[h(x+y) \ne f(x+y) \text{ or } h(y) \ne f(y)]$$

$$\leq \Pr_{y \in \{0,1\}^m} [h(x+y) \neq f(x+y)]$$

$$+ \Pr_{y \in \{0,1\}^m} [h(y) \neq f(y)] = 2 \cdot \frac{|U|}{2^m} < \frac{1}{2},$$

where the second inequality follows from the union bound. Observe now that the above calculation shows that $h(x)$ is the value in $\{0, 1\}$ that is equal to $f(x+y) - f(y)$ for more vectors $y \in \{0,1\}^m$, which makes it identical to $g(x)$ by definition.

Solution 5

We begin the solution by proving that $\text{AND}(x)$ is monotone. To do that, we need to verify that for every pair of vectors $x, y \in \{0, 1\}^2$ such that $x \leq y$, it holds that $\text{AND}(x) \leq \text{AND}(y)$. Since this trivially holds when $x = y$, we only need to verify it for the case that x and y are distinct vectors, which is done in Table 14.3. Note that indeed $\text{AND}(x) \leq \text{AND}(y)$ in every row of the table.

We now would like to prove that $\text{XOR}(x)$ is not monotone. Consider the vectors $x = \{0, 1\}$ and $y = \{1, 1\}$. Clearly, these are two vectors in $\{0, 1\}^2$ obeying $x \leq y$, however, one can verify that

$$\text{XOR}(x) = 1 > 0 = \text{XOR}(y).$$

Solution 6

We first prove that if $f : \{0, 1\}^m \to \{0, 1\}$ is a monotone Boolean function, then every edge of the Boolean hypercube of dimension m is monotone with respect to f. Fix an arbitrary edge (x, y) of this hypercube. As discussed above, we must have either $x \leq y$ or $y \leq x$, thus, we can assume without loss of generality that $x \leq y$. The monotonicity of f now implies that $f(x) \leq f(y)$, and therefore, by definition, the edge (x, y) is monotone with respect to f.

Table 14.3. The values of $\text{AND}(x)$ and $\text{AND}(y)$ for every pair of distinct vectors $x, y \in \{0, 1\}^2$ obeying $x \leq y$.

x	y	$\text{AND}(x)$	$\text{AND}(y)$
(0, 0)	(0, 1)	0	0
(0, 0)	(1, 0)	0	0
(0, 0)	(1, 1)	0	1
(0, 1)	(1, 1)	0	1
(1, 0)	(1, 1)	0	1

The other direction, namely that if $f\colon \{0,1\}^m \to \{0,1\}$ is a Boolean function such that every edge of the Boolean hypercube of dimension m is monotone with respect to f, then f is monotone, remains to be proved. Fix any two vectors $x, y \in \{0,1\}^m$ such that $x \le y$, and let us prove $f(x) \le f(y)$. For every $0 \le i \le m$, we define z_i as a vector which is equal to y on the first i coordinates and equal to x on the other coordinates. A useful observation about these vectors is as follows.

Observation 1. For every $1 \le i \le m$, $z_{i-1} \le z_i$.

Proof. The vectors z_{i-1} and z_i agree on all coordinates other than coordinate i. In coordinate i, the vector z_{i-1} takes the value of this coordinate in vector x, while the vector z_i takes the value of this coordinate in vector y. Since $x \le y$, the first value is at most the last value, which implies the observation.   □

If $z_{i-1} = z_i$, then $f(z_{i-1}) = f(z_i)$. Otherwise, the two vectors differ in exactly one coordinate (coordinate i), and thus, (z_{i-1}, z_i) is an edge of the hypercube of dimension m. Together with the last observation and the properties of f that we assumed, this implies $f(z_{i-1}) \le f(z_i)$. Note that together with our analysis of the case $z_{i-1} = z_i$, we get that the inequality $f(z_{i-1}) \le f(z_i)$ always holds.

It remains now to be observed that, by the definition of z_i, $z_0 = x$ and $z_m = y$, which implies

$$f(x) = f(z_0) \le f(z_1) \le \cdots \le f(z_m) = f(y).$$

Solution 7

Consider the function $f\colon \{0,1\}^2 \to \{0,1\}$ given on the left-hand side of Figure 14.5. One can observe that no edges of dimension 2 are non-monotone with respect to this function, but both edges of dimension 1 are. The right-hand side of the same figure gives the function obtained from f by flipping one of the two (non-monotone) edges of dimension 1. One can note that the edge between the vectors $(1, 0)$ and $(1, 1)$ is an edge of dimension 2 that is non-monotone with respect to the function resulting from the flip, despite the fact that no edges of dimension 2 were non-monotone with respect to the original function f.

Figure 14.5. A graphical illustration of a Boolean function (with $m = 2$), and the function obtained from it by flipping the values of the endpoints of a single edge. The left side of this figure presents the original function by specifying the value of this function for every vector $\{0, 1\}^2$ (the values appear in italics). The right side of the figure gives in a similar way the function obtained by flipping the values of the endpoints of the edge between the vectors $(0, 0)$ and $(1, 0)$.

Solution 8

Algorithm 2 has at most $s = O(m/\varepsilon)$ iterations, and in each one of these iterations, it evaluates the function f on two vectors. Thus, its query complexity is

$$2s = O(m/\varepsilon).$$

Note that this query complexity is smaller than the time complexity we have shown for the algorithm by a factor of m.

Part III: Map-Reduce

Chapter 15

Introduction to Map-Reduce

Up to this point in this book, we have seen algorithms that allow a single computer to handle big data problems by either using a very small amount of memory (streaming algorithms) or reading only a very small part of the data (sublinear time and local computation algorithms). A natural alternative approach for handling big data problems is to use *parallel algorithms*, i.e., algorithms that use multiple computers (or CPUs). The study of parallel algorithms dates back to the late 1970s, but their importance increased significantly over the last two decades because modern computer applications often necessitate processing of huge amounts of data in a relatively short timeframe, which is difficult to do with a single computer.

Using parallel algorithms requires the availability of multiple computers or CPUs for the algorithm to execute on, which can be achieved in one of two basic ways. One way is to create a specialized computer that hosts a large number of CPUs and allows these CPUs to interact with each other, and the other way is to build a cluster of simple computers that are connected by a communication network. Both ways have their advantages, but the latter one is used more often today because it requires only off-the-shelf hardware, and thus, tends to be much more economical. In particular, all the big modern Internet companies have constructed *computer clusters* of this kind whose computational power they either use for their own internal needs or rent to other companies.

The design of a parallel algorithm is a complicated task, which requires the designer to handle various issues that do not apply for *sequential algorithms*. One such issue is the need to identify the parts of the algorithm that are *parallelizable* and the parts of the algorithm that are inherently sequential. For example, multiplying matrices is an easily parallelizable task because calculating the value of every cell in the result matrix can be done independently. In contrast, predicting the change over time in a physical system (such as the weather) tends to be an inherently sequential task because it is very difficult to calculate the predicted state of the system at time $t + 1$ before the predicted state of the system at time t has been calculated.

Another issue appears when a parallel algorithm is intended to be executed on a computer cluster (rather than on a multi-CPU computer). Despite the very fast communication networks that are available today, the communication between computers inside the clusters is still significantly slower than the transfer of information between the components inside an individual computer. Thus, a parallel algorithm that is implemented on a computer cluster should strive to minimize the amount of information transferred between the computers of the cluster, even (to some extent) at the cost of performing more internal computations within the computers.

Implementing a parallel algorithm on a computer cluster also raises an additional issue, which, unlike the one discussed in the previous paragraph, is more relevant to the programmer implementing the algorithm than to the algorithm's designer. To understand this issue, we note that implementing a parallel algorithm on a computer cluster involves a large amount of "administrative" work that needs to be done in addition to the logic of the algorithm itself. For example, tasks should be assigned to the various computers of the cluster, and data has to be transferred accordingly and reliably between the computers. This administrative work is made more complicated by failures that often occur in components of the cluster (such as computers and communication links) during the algorithm's execution. While these components are usually reasonably reliable, their sheer number in the cluster makes a failure of some of them a likely event even within a relatively short time frame, which means that an algorithm implementation has to handle such failures on a regular basis.

In an attempt to alleviate the repetitive work of handling the above-mentioned administrative work, Google developed a framework known as *Map-Reduce* which handles this work, but requires the algorithm to have a given structure. A paper about the Map-Reduce framework was published by Google employees in 2004, which led to a rapid adoption of the framework by other organizations as well. Today, variants of the Map-Reduce framework are widely used for implementing parallel algorithms, and they are available on most computer clusters.[1]

The increasing importance of computer clusters in general, and the Map-Reduce framework in particular, has motivated research on algorithms designed for such clusters and the Map-Reduce framework. The current part of this book is devoted to the presentation of some examples of this research. The remaining parts of this chapter lay the foundations necessary for presenting these examples. In particular, they describe the Map-Reduce framework in some detail and present a stylized theoretical model of this framework. We note that the examples used in this chapter tend to be very simple, and their main objective is to help us present the framework and its theoretical model. The following chapters of the book include more sophisticated examples.

15.1 Some Details about Map-Reduce

Our objective in this section is to describe the main structure of the Map-Reduce framework. It is important, however, to stress that the Map-Reduce framework involves many additional details that we do not get into because they are less important for our purpose or differ between various Map-Reduce implementations. Thus, a reader who is interested in using a real-world Map-Reduce system should seek additional information about it rather than rely on the very general description given here.

To make our description of the Map-Reduce framework more substantial, it is useful to have a running example. Thus, assume that we are given some text, and that we would like to determine the frequency of the words in this text. In other words, we would like to determine the number of occurrences of each word in the text. In particular, consider the following paragraph from the story "Alice in Wonderland".

There seemed to be no use in waiting by the little door, so she went back to the table, half hoping she might find another key on it, or at any rate a book of rules for shutting people up like telescopes: this time she found a little bottle on it, ('which certainly was not here before,'

---

[1]One very popular open source implementation of Map-Reduce is available as a part of the Apache Hadoop open source software collection.

said Alice,) and round the neck of the bottle was a paper label, with the words 'DRINK ME' beautifully printed on it in large letters.

One can verify that this paragraph contains, for example, 5 occurrences of the word "the", 3 occurrences of the word "she" and a single occurrence of the word "drink".

Determining the frequency of the words in a text is a simple task, but if the text is long enough, then it makes sense to use a parallel algorithm for the job. Thus, we would like to design a Map-Reduce algorithm for it. The basic unit of information in the Map-Reduce framework is a pair of a key and a value. Hence, to process data using this framework, the data must be converted into a representation based on such pairs. The best way to do that depends of course on the exact data that we would like to process, but for the sake our example, let us assume that each word in the input text becomes a pair whose value is the word itself and whose key is the name of the text from which the word was taken. Thus, the first 18 words in the above text are represented using the following pairs (note that some of the pairs appear multiple times because the text contains repeating words).

(Alice in Wonderland, there)	(Alice in Wonderland, little)
(Alice in Wonderland, be)	(Alice in Wonderland, she)
(Alice in Wonderland, in)	(Alice in Wonderland, to)
(Alice in Wonderland, the)	(Alice in Wonderland, to)
(Alice in Wonderland, so)	(Alice in Wonderland, use)
(Alice in Wonderland, back)	(Alice in Wonderland, by)
(Alice in Wonderland, seemed)	(Alice in Wonderland, door)
(Alice in Wonderland, no)	(Alice in Wonderland, went)
(Alice in Wonderland, waiting)	(Alice in Wonderland, the)

Once the input data is represented as (key, value) pairs, the Map-Reduce framework can start processing it, which it does in three steps known as "map", "shuffle" and "reduce". In the map step (which is the first step), each one of the input pairs is mapped independently into a list of new pairs. To implement this step, the user of the system must specify a map procedure that gets a single input pair and produces a list of new pairs based on this input pair. The Map-Reduce system then takes care of applying this map procedure to every one of the input pairs.

In our word-frequency running example, we need a map procedure that gets an input pair and produces from it a single output pair that has the word of the input pair as its key and the number 1 as its value. Intuitively, the meaning of the value 1 is that the pair represents a single instance of the word that appears as its key.

Exercise 1. Write down a pseudocode representation for the map procedure described above. Additionally, list the pairs produced by applying this procedure to each one of the 18 input pairs listed above.

It is essential that the executions of the map procedure on the different input pairs will be independent, i.e., these executions should not attempt to pass information among themselves in any way (such as through a global variable). This independence allows the Map-Reduce framework to partition the mapping work between the computers of the cluster in an arbitrary way. In other words, the Map-Reduce framework sends some of the input pairs to each one of the computers of the cluster, and then these computers work in parallel and apply the map procedure to the input pairs that they have got.

Once the map procedure is applied to every one of the input pairs, the Map-Reduce framework advances to its second step (the shuffle step). In the *shuffle* step, the framework considers the set of distinct keys that appear in the pairs produced by the map step, and assigns for every such key a computer known as the *reducer* designated for this key. Then, every pair is transferred to the reducer designated for its key.

Going back to our word-frequency running example, recall that after the mapping step we have in this example a single pair for every word of the input text, and this pair contains the word as its key and the number 1 as its value. Thus, in the shuffle step, the Map-Reduce framework assigns a reducer computer for every distinct word in the text (key), and transfers to this reducer all the pairs having this key.[2]

---

[2]Observe that in a long text there are likely to be many distinct words, which will require the Map-Reduce framework to assign many reducers. As the number of available computers is limited, this might require the Map-Reduce framework to assign a single computer as the reducer of multiple keys. Fortunately, the framework hides this technical issue, and thus, we assume for simplicity in the description of the framework that there is a distinct reducer for each key.

Exercise 2. Consider the following pairs (these are the pairs produced by the map step based on the 18 input pairs listed above). Assuming that these pairs are the input for the shuffle step, determine how many reducers are assigned by the shuffle step and the list of pairs that are transferred to each one of these reducers.

(there, 1)	(seemed, 1)	(to, 1)	(be, 1)	(no, 1)	(use, 1)
(in, 1)	(waiting, 1)	(by, 1)	(the, 1)	(little, 1)	(door, 1)
(so, 1)	(she, 1)	(went, 1)	(back, 1)	(to, 1)	(the, 1)

After the shuffle step, all the pairs having a particular key are located on a single computer, namely the reducer designated for this key, and thus, can be processed as a group. This is done by the third and final step of the Map-Reduce framework — the reduce step. To implement this step, the user of the system specifies a reduce procedure that gets as input a key and the values of the pairs with this key, and based on this input produces a list of new pairs. The Map-Reduce system then executes this procedure, independently, on every key that appears in some pair. In other words, each reducer executes the reduce procedure once, and passes to it as parameters the key of the reducer and the values of the pairs with this key (which are exactly the pairs transferred to this reducer during the shuffle step).

In our running example, the keys of the pairs produced by the map step are the words of the original text. Thus, the reduce procedure is executed once for every distinct word in this text. Moreover, the execution corresponding to a word w gets as parameters the word w itself and the values of the pairs that have w as their key. These values are all 1 by construction, but by counting them, the reduce procedure can determine the number of appearances (or frequency) of the word w in the original text. The reduce procedure then outputs this information in the form of a new pair (w, c), where w is the word itself and c is its number of appearances.

Exercise 3. Write down a pseudocode representation for the reduce procedure described above.

Like in the case of the map procedure, it is important that the executions of the reduce procedure will also be independent, and will not try to communicate in any way. This independence allows all the reducers to execute the reduce procedure in parallel.

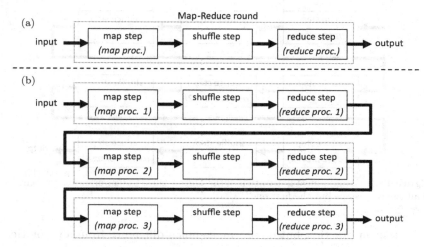

Figure 15.1. A graphical illustration of the different steps of the Map-Reduce framework. Part (a) presents a single Map-Reduce round, which consists of three steps: a map step, a shuffle step and a reduce step. Note that the map and reduce steps require the user of the system to provide a map procedure and a reduce procedure, respectively. Part (b) presents an execution involving three Map-Reduce rounds. The arrows present the flow of information during this execution. In particular, observe that the output of the reduce step of each round serves as the input for the map step of the next round. Also, note that the map and reduce procedures can differ between rounds.

The sequence of a map step, a shuffle step and a reduce step is called a *Map-Reduce round*. A graphical illustration of such a round can be found in Figure 15.1(a). In our running example, a single Map-Reduce round was sufficient for producing the output that we looked for (i.e., the frequency of every word in the text). However, in general it might be necessary to use multiple Map-Reduce rounds, where the output pairs of each round serve as the input pairs for the next round and each round has its own map and reduce procedures (see Figure 15.1(b) for a graphical illustration). We will see examples of such use later in this book.

15.2 Theoretical Model of Map-Reduce

The above description of the Map-Reduce framework can be transformed into a theoretical model in a straightforward way, but this will result in a model with quite a few "entities" such as (key, value) pairs, map procedures and reduce procedures, which is not desirable. To get a simpler model, we first need to remove some features of the Map-Reduce framework that are

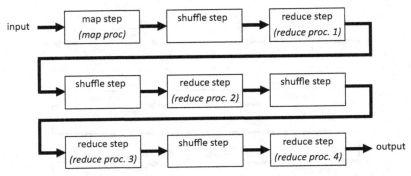

Figure 15.2. A graphical illustration of the Map-Reduce framework after the removal of all the map steps but the first one

important in practice, but do not make much difference from a theoretical point of view.

Consider a Map-Reduce execution involving multiple Map-Reduce rounds, and consider in particular a map step in this execution that belongs to an iteration other than the first one. Such a map step appears after a reduce step and processes independently each one of the output pairs of the reduce step. In principal, all the processing done by the map step could also be done by the reducers that generated the pairs, and thus, dropping it does not affect the computational power of the Map-Reduce execution. Using this argument, we can drop all the map steps of the Map-Reduce execution except for the map step of the first iteration, which results in a Map-Reduce execution consisting of a single map step followed by alternating reduce and shuffle steps (see Figure 15.2 for a graphical illustration).[3]

The next simplification that we would like to perform is more logical. Let us assume that there is a pre-assigned reducer for every possible key, and consider an arbitrary (key, value) pair produced by either the map procedure or one of the reduce procedures. Since all the reducers have been pre-assigned, the generation of such a pair is equivalent to sending the

---

[3]Despite the theoretical argument used above to justify the removal of all the map steps but the first one, practical Map-Reduce systems keep these steps because they have practical advantages. The map procedure is executed separately for every pair, while the reduce procedure is executed only once for all the pairs having the same key. Thus, work done by a map procedure tends to be partitioned into many small independent executions, while work done by a reduce procedure is usually partitioned into fewer and larger executions. Small executions can be better parallelized and also allow for an easier recovery in case of a fault in a hardware component, and thus, are preferable in practice.

value to the reducer of this key. Given this point of view, one can view the Map-Reduce execution after the dropping of the map steps as follows. Every piece of information (pair) of the input is processed independently by the map procedure, and while doing so, the map procedure can send arbitrary information to the reducers. The reducers then work in iterations. In the first iteration, every reducer processes the information it received from the executions of the map procedure, and can send information to other reducers and to itself. Similarly, in every other iteration every reducer processes the information sent to it from the reducers in the previous iteration, and can send information to the other reducers and to itself for processing in the next iteration.

Using the above intuitive view of the Map-Reduce execution, we are now ready to formulate it in a model, which we call in this book the *Map-Reduce model*. In this model, there is an infinite number of machines (or computers),[4] one machine associated with every possible "name". The computation in this model proceeds in iterations. In the first iteration, every piece of information is sent to a different machine, and this machine can process this piece of information in an arbitrary way. While processing the information, the machine can also send messages to other machines based on their names. In other words, while sending a message, the sending machine should specify the information of the message and the name of the destination machine for the message. In every one of the next iterations, every machine processes the messages that it received during the previous iteration, and while doing so can send messages to other machines to be processed in the next iteration (more formally, in iteration $i > 1$ every machine processes the messages sent to it during iteration $i - 1$ and can send messages to other machines — and these messages will be processed during iteration $i + 1$). In the last iteration, instead of sending messages, the machines are allowed to produce pieces of the output.

To exemplify the Map-Reduce model, let us explain how to convert to this model the algorithm described above for determining the frequency of words in a text. In this problem, the basic pieces of the input are the words of the text, and thus, we assume that every such word starts on

---

[4]The infinite number of machines in the Map-Reduce model might make it seem very far from any practical situation. However, one should keep in mind that only a finite set of these machines make any computation in algorithms that terminate in finite time, and that multiple such logical machines can be simulated on one real computer. Given these observations, there is no significant barrier for implementing the Map-Reduce model using a real-world system.

Algorithm 1: Algorithm for the First Iteration (*Word*)

1. Send the message "1" to the machine named *word*.

Algorithm 2: Algorithm for the Second Iteration (*Numbers*)

1. Let c be the sum of all the numbers received.
2. Output (name, c), where "name" is the name of this machine.

---

a different machine. Our plan is to use every machine for counting the number of instances of the word equal to its name. To do that, during the first iteration, every machine that received a word should send the number 1 to the machine whose name is equal to that word (intuitively, this 1 represents a single copy of the word). A more formal description of the procedure executed during the first iteration is given as Algorithm 1. To simplify the exposition, we use in this procedure (and in the rest of this book) the convention that only machines that got information execute the procedure; which means, for example, that a machine that did not get any input word does not execute the procedure of the first iteration.

In the second iteration, every machine whose name is a word that appeared in the original text gets the message "1" once for every appearance of this word. Thus, to calculate the frequency of this word, all that remains to be done is to add up these ones, and output this sum as the frequency of the word, which is formally done by Algorithm 2.

A *Map-Reduce algorithm* is an algorithm for the Map-Reduce model. Such an algorithm formally consists of a procedure for every iteration. For example, the procedures described by Algorithms 1 and 2 form together a Map-Reduce algorithm for the problem of calculating the frequency of words in a text.

Exercise 4. Describe a Map-Reduce algorithm that given the edges of a graph calculates the degree of every vertex in it.

We would like to conclude this section with two additional remarks.

(1) Note that at the beginning of an iteration of the Map-Reduce model, a machine has access only to messages that were sent to it during the previous iteration. In particular, the machine does not have access

to the information it had during this previous iteration. This is a convenient assumption for a stylized model, and it does not imply a strict restriction on Map-Reduce algorithms because a machine can send a message to itself with any information that it has now and might be useful in future iterations.

(2) We will occasionally make the useful assumption that all the machines have access to a small amount of common information such as the size of the input or a few common random bits. This assumption can be justified by observing that, in a real-world Map-Reduce system, if the common information is given as part of the value of every input (key, value) pair, then the map and reduce procedures can guarantee that this information is forwarded to every relevant machine by attaching them as part of the value to every (key, value) pair they generate.

15.3 Performance Measures

The study of Map-Reduce algorithms requires us to define performance measures for such algorithms that will allow us to evaluate algorithms and compare them to each other. The first such measure that we discuss here is the *machine space complexity*, i.e., the maximum space needed by any single machine. A Map-Reduce algorithm is usually of interest only when its machine space complexity is significantly smaller than the size of the input because otherwise the algorithm can use one iteration to forward all the input to a single machine and then process this input using a traditional sequential algorithm during the second iteration. Moreover, it is desirable to have algorithms with as low machine space complexity as possible because such algorithms can be executed using simple (and thus, cheap) computers even when the input size is very large.

Consider the Map-Reduce algorithm designed above for calculating the frequency of words. To determine its machine space complexity, we observe that during its first iteration every machine stores only a single word, while in the second iteration every machine stores the message "1" once for every appearance of its name in the original text. Thus, the machine space complexity of this algorithm is the maximum between two quantities: $O(\text{maximum word size})$ and $O(\text{maximum frequency of a word})$. The first quantity is usually not an issue because the maximum length of an English word is very moderate. In contrast, the second quantity is quite problematic since some common words such as "the" or "in" might appear very often in the text and make the machine space complexity as large (in order of magnitude) as the entire input. This is a significant disadvantage of the simple Map-Reduce algorithm we designed for calculating word frequencies, and we will see in Chapter 16 how to improve the algorithm and fix this issue.

Another performance measure, which is related to the machine space complexity, is the *total space complexity*. This performance measure is defined as the maximum space used by all the machines together in any single iteration. Clearly, the size of the input is a lower bound on the total space complexity of any Map-Reduce algorithm because when the algorithm begins, every piece of the input is stored on some machine. However, since Map-Reduce algorithms are typically used when the input is very large, it is undesirable for their total space complexity to be much larger than this lower bound. In particular, for a Map-Reduce algorithm to be considered reasonable, its total space complexity should not exceed the size of its input by more than a poly-logarithmic factor — i.e., a factor of $O(\log^c n)$, where n is the size of the input and c is a constant. It is important to observe that the total space complexity also upper bounds the amount of communication between machines done at every single iteration of the Map-Reduce algorithm. This is so because all the information communicated during an iteration is stored at the destination machines at the beginning of the next iteration.

It is not difficult to verify that the total space complexity of our algorithm for calculating word frequencies is on the same order of magnitude as the size of its input because (intuitively) the algorithm never duplicates a piece of information. Thus, this algorithm has an optimal total space complexity.

In contrast to the previous performance measures that were based on space, the next performance measures that we discuss are related to time. The first of these measures is the number of iterations performed by the algorithm. Perhaps surprisingly, this performance measure is usually considered the most important performance measure of a Map-Reduce algorithm. The reason for that is that the shuffle steps of the Map-Reduce framework tend to be very slow because they involve a lot of communication between machines. Thus, reducing the number of iterations (or equivalently, the number of shuffles) of a Map-Reduce algorithm often speeds it up even if the reduction in the number of iterations comes at the cost of a moderate increase in the amount of time used by the individual machines for computation. Usually, it is desirable for a Map-Reduce algorithm to use only a constant number of iterations, but a Map-Reduce algorithm is considered reasonable as long as its number of iterations is at most $O(\log n)$, where n is the size of its input.

The next performance measure we would like to discuss is the *machine time complexity*, which is the maximum running time used by any machine in a single iteration. Note that the product of the machine time complexity and the number of iterations provides, at least in theory, an upper bound on the time it takes for the Map-Reduce algorithm to terminate. In practice, however, this upper bound is not very accurate because the practical execution time also depends on factors such as hardware failures and the number of physical computers available. A related performance measure is the *work*, which is defined as the sum of the execution times used by all the machines in all the iterations. Since a Map-Reduce algorithm can be efficiently simulated by a sequential algorithm, its work cannot be significantly smaller than the time complexity of the best sequential algorithm. In contrast, the work of a good Map-Reduce algorithm should not be much larger than this lower bound. From a practical point of view, work is often important when the Map-Reduce algorithm is executed on a cloud service (i.e., on servers whose computational power is rented from someone else) because the cost of doing the computation often depends on the amount of computation done, which is exactly the work of the algorithm.

Going back to the algorithm described above for calculating word frequencies, we can observe that by definition it uses only two iterations (in its implementation in the Map-Reduce model). In the first iteration, every machine simply sends the message "1" to the machine whose name is equal to the input word received by this machine, and thus, it uses constant time. In the second iteration, every machine gets a single message for every appearance of its name in the original text, and it has to count these messages, which takes $O(\text{maximum frequency of a word})$ time. Thus, the machine time complexity of this algorithm is $O(\text{maximum frequency of a word})$, which is quite long because, as discussed above, the maximum frequency of a word tends to be on the same order of magnitude as the entire input length. In a subseqent chapter, we will see how to improve this performance measure as well.

Let us next calculate the work done by our algorithm. In the first iteration, every word of the input is processed by one machine for a constant amount of time, which results in a work proportional to the number of words in the input. In the second iteration, there is a single machine for each distinct word of the input, and this machine runs for a time proportional to the number of appearances of this word in the input, and thus, the total running time of all these machines is again proportional to the number of words in the input. Thus, the work of this algorithm is $O(\text{number of words}$ in the input), which is very good since one can verify that no sequential algorithm can (exactly) calculate the frequencies of all the words without reading the entire input at least once.

Exercise 5. In Exercise 4, you have described a Map-Reduce algorithm. Analyze its machine space complexity, total space complexity, number of iterations, machine time complexity and work.

15.4 A Different Theoretical Model

The real-world importance of the Map-Reduce framework has motivated the development of multiple theoretical models for it. In this book, we concentrate on the model that we named the "Map-Reduce model" because it is simpler than the original Map-Reduce framework, but still allows for easy conversation of Map-Reduce algorithms into programs for the Map-Reduce framework, and vice versa. Other theoretical models were developed with other objectives in mind. In particular, a model known as the *Massively Parallel Computation* (MPC) model became very popular in recent years. This model does not try to capture any particular framework (such as Map-Reduce) for computation using computer clusters. Instead, MPC strives to capture the basic nature of general computation using such clusters.

Despite the difference between the various theoretical models of Map-Reduce, most algorithms can be ported between them using a reasonable effort. Thus, in the rest of this book we exclusively concentrate on the Map-Reduce model. Nevertheless, for completeness, the current section is devoted to explaining the popular MPC model.

The MPC model consists of M machines each having S memory, where M and S are parameters of the model. Originally, the input is partitioned evenly between the M machines, and then the machines process it in iterations. In each iteration, each machine is allowed to make arbitrary calculations and send messages to the other machines. Like in the Map-Reduce model, messages sent during one iteration arrive at their destination machines on the next iteration. It is required that the total size of the messages sent or received by a single machine in a given iteration does not exceed its memory S. To understand this requirement, one should assume that the messages which a machine would like to send during a given iteration are stored in its memory until the end of the iteration. Once the iteration ends, these messages are transferred to the memory of their destination machines, where they can be accessed by these machines at the following iteration. Given this description, it is clear that the sizes of the messages sent or received by a machine should be counted toward its space complexity, and thus, their sum is restricted by S.

To substantiate the above description of the MPC model, let us consider a mock problem in which the input consist of n tokens, where every token has one of k colors for some constant k. The objective of the problem is to determine the number of tokens of each color. Let us now describe an algorithm for this problem in the MPC model. Originally, each one of the M machines is given up to $\lceil n/M \rceil$ tokens of the input. During the first iteration, each machine counts the number of tokens of each color that it was given and forwards these counts to machine number 1 (this is an arbitrary choice, any other fixed machine could be used instead). In the second iteration, machine number 1 gets the counts calculated by all the machines in iteration 1 and then combines them to produce the required output, i.e., the number of appearances of each one of the k colors in the input.

Exercise 6. Write down a pseudocode representation for the algorithm described above and determine how much memory S per machine is required for this algorithm.

Since the input is originally split evenly among the M machines, they should have enough memory together to store the entire input. Formally, this means that we must always have $S = \Omega(n/M)$, where n is the size of the input. It is desirable to design algorithms which do not require S to be much larger than this natural lower bound. For example, the solution of Exercise 6 shows that the algorithm we designed above for our mock problem can work with $S = \Theta(n/M)$ as long as $M = O(n^{0.5}/\log^{0.5} n)$.

15.5 Bibliographic Notes

The Map-Reduce framework was originally developed by Google and in 2004 it was published by Google employees in the paper by Dean and

Ghemawat (2004). Despite the huge practical success of the Map-Reduce framework, the first formal model for this framework was published by Karloff *et al.* (2010) only in 2010. Inspired by the work of Karloff *et al.* (2010), a few other theoretical models for Map-Reduce were developed by later papers. Of these, we mention here only two. The Map-Reduce model that we assume in this book is closely based on ideas developed by Lattanzi *et al.* (2011), and the more popular MPC model was suggested by Beame *et al.* (2017). The original motivation for the development of the MPC model by the last paper is that this model captures general computation using a computer cluster rather than a particular framework, which makes impossibility results proved for it more meaningful.

P. Beame, P. Koutris and D. Suciu. Communication Steps for Parallel Query Processing. *Journal of the ACM*, 64(6): 40:1–40:58, 2017.

J. Dean and S. Ghemawat. Map-Reduce: Simplified Data Processing on Large Clusters. In *Proceedings of the 6th Symposium on Operating Systems Design and Implementation (OSDI)*, 137–150, 2004.

H. J. Karloff, S. Suri and S. Vassilvitskii. A Model for Computation for Map-Reduce. In *Proceedings of the 21th ACM-SIAM Symposium on Discrete Algorithms (SODA)*, 938–948, 2010.

S. Lattanzi, B. Moseley, S. Suri and S. Vassilvitskii. Filtering: A Method for Solving Graph Problems in Map-Reduce. In *Proceedings of the 23rd Annual ACM Symposium on Parallelism in Algorithms and Architectures (SPAA)*, 85–94, 2011.

Exercise Solutions

Solution 1

A pseudocode for the map procedure described by the text before the exercise is given as Algorithm 3. Recall that the key in the pair that the procedure gets is the name of the text from which the word was taken, and the value in this pair is the word itself.

Applying this map procedure to each one of the pairs from the list appearing on page 3, independently, results in the following pairs. Observe that, like in the list from page 3, there are repetitions in this list.

Algorithm 3: Simple Map Procedure (*Key, Value*)

1. Output the pair (*value*, 1) and exit.

(there, 1)	(seemed, 1)	(to, 1)
(be, 1)	(no, 1)	(use, 1)
(in, 1)	(waiting, 1)	(by, 1)
(the, 1)	(little, 1)	(door, 1)
(so, 1)	(she, 1)	(went, 1)
(back, 1)	(to, 1)	(the, 1)

Solution 2

The 18 pairs listed have 16 distinct keys (because each one of the words "the" and "to" serves as the key of two pairs). Accordingly, 16 reducers are assigned, one for each one of the distinct keys. Each one of these reducers gets all the pairs whose key matches the key of the reducer. More specifically, the reducer of the key "the" gets the two identical (the, 1) pairs, the reducer of the key "to" gets the two identical (to, 1) pairs, and every one of the other reducers gets the single pair corresponding to its key.

Solution 3

A pseudocode for the reduce procedure described by the text before the exercise is given as Algorithm 4. Recall that the key which the procedure gets is a word of the original text and the values are the values of the pairs with this key. By construction, all these values are 1, but their number is the number of such pairs, i.e., the number of times that the key word appeared in the text.

Solution 4

The input for the problem we consider consists of the set of edges of the graph, and thus, every machine executing the procedure of the first iteration starts this iteration with a single such edge. We will make this machine send the message "1" to every one of the end points of this edge (we assume that the representation of the edge consists of its two end points, which makes

---

Algorithm 4: Simple Reduce Procedure (*Key, Values*)

1. Let c be the number of values received.
2. Output the pair (*key*, c) and exit.

Algorithm 5: Degrees Calculating — First Iteration (e)

1. Let u and v be the end points of e.
2. Send the message "1" to the machine named u and to the machine named v.

Algorithm 6: Degrees Calculating — Second Iteration (*Numbers*)

1. Let c be the sum of all the numbers received.
2. Output (name, c), where "name" is the name of this machine.

---

this step possible). Intuitively, this "1" represents a single edge hitting the end point. Formally, the procedure executed during the first iteration is given as Algorithm 5.

At the second iteration, every machine named after a vertex of the graph gets the message "1" once for every edge of the graph hitting this vertex, and thus, it can calculate the degree of this vertex by simply summing up these messages. This is formally done by Algorithm 6.

Algorithms 5 and 6 together form the Map-Reduce algorithm that we are requested to find by the exercise.

Solution 5

In this solution, we analyze the performance measures of the algorithm described in the solution for Exercise 4. By definition, this algorithm has two iterations. We continue the analysis of the algorithm by calculating its machine space and time complexities. Let us denote by n the number of vertices in the graph. In the first iteration of the algorithm, every machine stores one edge, which requires $O(\log n)$ space because every vertex can be represented using $O(\log n)$ bits. Additionally, the processing done by every machine consists of sending two messages, which requires $O(1)$ time. Consider now the second iteration of the algorithm. In this iteration, every machine associated with a vertex v gets a message of constant size for every edge hitting v, and has to count these messages. Thus, both the space used by the machine and its running time are O(the degree of v). Combining our findings for the two iterations of the algorithm, we get that the machine time complexity of the algorithm is $O(\max\{1, d\}) = O(d)$, where d is the maximum degree of any vertex; and the machine space complexity of the algorithm is $O(\max \{\log n, d\}) = O(\log n + d)$.

Our next step is to analyze the total space complexity of the algorithm. In the first iteration, every machine stores a different edge of the graph, and thus, the total space used by the machines is $O(m \log n)$, where m is the number of edges in the graph. In the second iteration, the machine named after each vertex v has to store a single message for every edge hitting this vertex, and additionally, it has to store its name (i.e., the vertex itself). Thus, the total space complexity of the machines in this iteration is

$$O(n \log n) + \sum_v O(\text{degree of } v) = O(n \log n + m).$$

Combining the bounds we got on the total space complexity used in every iteration, we get that the total space complexity of the algorithm is

$$O(\max\{m \log n, \ n \log n + m\}) = O(m \log n + n \log n).$$

To complete the solution, we also need to analyze the work done by the algorithm. In the first iteration, we have one machine for each edge, and this machine uses a constant processing time, and thus, the work done in this iteration is $O(m)$. In the second iteration, we have one machine for each vertex, and this machine does a work proportional to the degree of this vertex. Thus, the total work done by all the machines in the second iteration is

$$\sum_v O(\text{degree of } v) = O(m).$$

Hence, the work done by the algorithm, which is the sum of the work done by its two iterations, is $O(m)$.

Solution 6

Recall that in the first iteration of the algorithm, each machine counts the number of tokens it received of each color and forwards these counts to machine 1. A pseudocode representation for this is given as Algorithm 7. In this algorithm, we assume that the k colors are represented using the numbers 1 to k.

Algorithm 7: Color Counting — First Iteration (*Tokens*)

1. Let C be an array of size k initiated to zeros.
2. **for** every token t in *tokens* **do**
3.   Let i be the color of t.
4.   Increment by 1 the cell $C[i]$.
5. Send the array C to machine number 1.

Algorithm 8: Color Counting — Second Iteration $(C_1, C_2, \ldots, C_M)$

1. Let C be an array of size k initiated to zeros.
2. **for** $j = 1$ to M **do**
3.   **for** $i = 1$ to k **do**
4.   Update $C[i] = C[i] + C_j[i]$.
5. The array C represents the output. For every color i cell number i of the array stores the number of tokens of color i in the input.

In the second iteration, machine number 1 should combine all the counts it receives and produce the output. This is done by the pseudocode of Algorithm 8. In this pseudocode, we used C_j to denote the array C received from machine j.

Let us now calculate the minimum space per machine M necessary for this algorithm to work. In the first iteration, every machine stores up to $\lceil n/M \rceil$ tokens that it got plus the array C. If we assume that each token is represented by its color, then storing a token requires only constant space since we assumed that k is a constant. Additionally, observe that the array C can be represented using $O(k \log n) = O(\log n)$ bits because it consists of a constant number of cells and each one of these cells stores an integer value of at most n. Thus, the space complexity per machine required for the first iteration is at most $O(n/M + \log n)$. Note also that this memory is sufficient for storing the messages sent from the machine during the iteration because these messages consist of the array C alone.

Consider next the second iteration of the above algorithm. In this iteration, the algorithm keeps in memory $M + 1$ arrays, each requiring $O(\log n)$ space, and thus, its space complexity is $O(M \log n)$. Once again we observe that this memory is also large enough to store all the messages received by machine 1 at this iteration. Combining the space complexities we derived for the two iterations, we get that choosing $S = \Theta(n/M + M \log n)$ will allow the algorithm to work. For the discussion after the exercise, it is important to note that $S = \Theta(n/M)$ whenever $M \log n = O(n/M)$, which is true when $M = O(n^{0.5}/log^{0.5}n)$.

Chapter 16

Algorithms for Lists

Chapter 15 presented the Map-Reduce model and a few very simple algorithms for it. In this chapter, we will start to see more interesting Map-Reduce algorithms. All the algorithms that we will see in this chapter get either a list of words or a list of numbers as input.

16.1 Calculating Word Frequencies

We begin the chapter by revisiting a problem that we studied in Chapter 15. The input for this problem is a list of words, and the objective is to calculate the frequency of every word in the list, i.e., the number of appearances in the list of each distinct word. In Chapter 15, we saw a Map-Reduce algorithm for this problem that was very simple, but unfortunately had machine time and space complexities that could be as high as linear in the size of the input. Let us recall now the algorithm and the reason for its very large complexities. In the first iteration of the algorithm, every machine gets one word from the input list, and sends a message to the machine whose name matches this word. Then, in the second iteration of the algorithm, every machine whose name is a word gets one message for every appearance of this word in the original text, and can determine the frequency of the word by simply counting these messages. Since for every given word w there is a single machine of the second iteration which is responsible for counting

---

**Algorithm 1: Improved Algorithm for Word Frequencies —
First Iteration (Word)**

1. Pick a uniformly random integer r between 1 and $\lceil \sqrt{n} \rceil$.
2. Send 1 to the machine named $(word, r)$

---

all the messages resulting from the appearances of w, this single machine requires a lot of time and space when w is a frequent word, which results in the potentially very bad machine time and space complexities of the algorithm.

To improve the algorithm, we need to partition the work of counting the messages resulting from the appearances of a word w between multiple machines. Algorithm 1 does that by partitioning this work between $\lceil \sqrt{n} \rceil$ machines named $(w, 1), (w, 2), \ldots, (w, \lceil \sqrt{n} \rceil)$, where n is the number of words in the input. In the first iteration of this algorithm, which is formally given as Algorithm 1, every machine processes a single word of the input and sends the value 1 (which represents a single appearance) to a random machine out of the $\lceil \sqrt{n} \rceil$ machines assigned to this word.

Let us denote by $c_{w,r}$ the number of messages sent during the first iteration to machine (w, r). One can observe that the frequency of w is equal to the sum $\sum_{r=1}^{\lceil \sqrt{n} \rceil} c_{w,r}$ because every appearance of the word w in the original list results in a single message being sent to one of the machines $(w, 1), (w, 2), \ldots, (w, \lceil \sqrt{n} \rceil)$ during the first iteration. Thus, to calculate the frequency of w, we need to evaluate the above sum, which is done by the next two iterations of the algorithm. In the second iteration, each machine (w, r) counts the number $c_{w,r}$ of messages that it has got and forwards the count to the machine named after the word w. Then, in the third iteration, every machine named after a word w gets $\lceil \sqrt{n} \rceil$ counts from the machines $(w, 1), (w, 2), \ldots, (w, \lceil \sqrt{n} \rceil)$ and sums up these counts to get the frequency of the word w. A formal description of these two iterations appears as Algorithm 2.

The correctness of the algorithm follows from its description, so it remains to analyze its performance measures. In this analysis, we assume for simplicity that each individual word takes a constant amount of space.

Algorithm 2: Improved Algorithm for Word Frequencies

- **Second iteration (*numbers*)**
  1. Let us denote the name of this machine by (w, r).
  2. Sum up the numbers in the messages received (recall that every message sent during the first iteration contains the value 1, so this is equivalent to counting them). Let us denote the sum obtained by $c_{w,r}$.
  3. Send $c_{w,r}$ to the machine named w.

- **Third iteration (*numbers*)**
  1. Let us denote the name of this machine by w.
  2. Sum up the number in the messages received, and denote the sum by c_w.
  3. Output c_w as the frequency of w.

Exercise 1. Determine the number of iterations, total space complexity and work of the Map-Reduce algorithm described by Algorithms 1 and 2. **Hint:** Recall our assumption that the code of an iteration is performed only by machines which received messages during the previous iteration (in other words, a machine executes nothing if it got no input).

In addition to the three performance measures you were asked to determine in Exercise 1, there are two other performance measures that we would like to determine, namely the machine time and space complexities. Lemma 1 is a crucial step toward analyzing these complexities.

Lemma 1. *With high probability (i.e., with a probability that approaches 1 as n increases), no machine receives more than $2\sqrt{n}$ messages in the second iteration.*

Proof. Let us begin the proof by fixing some word w and an integer r' between 1 and $\lceil \sqrt{n} \rceil$. We would like to upper bound the probability that more than $2\sqrt{n}$ messages are sent to machine (w, r') during the first iteration. For this purpose, let us denote by r_i, for every integer $1 \leq i \leq n$, the random value r chosen during the first iteration by the machine processing word number i of the list. We also denote by X_i an indicator for the event that $r_i = r'$. Since r_i is a uniformly random integer out of the range $[1, \lceil \sqrt{n} \rceil]$,

$$\Pr[X_i = 1] = \Pr[r_i = r'] = \frac{1}{\lceil \sqrt{n} \rceil}.$$

We observe that the machine processing word number i (in the first iteration) can send a message to (w, r') only when $r_i = r'$, and thus, the sum $\sum_{i=1}^{n} X_i$ is an upper bound on the number of messages received by machine (w, r') in the second iteration. Moreover, this sum has a binomial distribution, which allows us to bound the probability that it is larger than $2\sqrt{n}$ using the Chernoff bound.

$$\Pr\left[\sum_{i=1}^{n} X_i > 2\sqrt{n}\right] = \Pr\left[\sum_{i=1}^{n} X_i > \frac{2\lceil \sqrt{n} \rceil}{\sqrt{n}} \cdot \mathrm{E}\left[\sum_{i=1}^{n} X_i\right]\right]$$

$$\leq e^{-\frac{\left(2n^{-0.5} \cdot \lceil \sqrt{n} \rceil - 1\right) \cdot \mathrm{E}[\sum_{i=1}^{n} X_i]}{3}}$$

$$= e^{-\frac{2\sqrt{n} - n/\lceil \sqrt{n} \rceil}{3}} \leq e^{-\frac{\sqrt{n}}{3}}.$$

So far we have proved that the probability of every single machine of the second iteration to receive more than $2\sqrt{n}$ messages is at most $e^{-\sqrt{n}/3}$. We also observe that there are only $n\lceil \sqrt{n} \rceil$ machines that might get messages in the second iteration (one for every word of the input and a value that r can get). Combining these facts using the union bound, we get that the probability that any machine of the second iteration gets more than $2\sqrt{n}$ messages is at most $n\lceil \sqrt{n} \rceil e^{-\sqrt{n}/3}$, which approaches 0 as n approaches infinity. $\square$

Corollary 1. *With high probability the machine time and space complexities of the Map-Reduce algorithm described by Algorithms 1 and 2 are $O(\sqrt{n})$ and $O(\sqrt{n} \cdot \log n)$, respectively.*

Proof. Let us denote by E the event that every machine of the second iteration receives only $O(\sqrt{n})$ messages. Lemma 1 shows that the event E occurs with high probability. Thus, it is enough to prove that the machine time and space complexities of the algorithm are as promised whenever E happens. The rest of the proof is devoted to showing that this is indeed the case.

In the first iteration, every machine stores only the word it processes and the random value r, and thus, requires only $O(\log n)$ space. Moreover, every such machine uses only constant time, and thus, both its running time and space usage are consistent with the machine time and space complexities that we would like to prove.

Consider now the second iteration of the algorithm. Since the time complexity of every machine in the second iteration is proportional to the number of messages it receives, we get that the machine time complexity in the second iteration is $O(\sqrt{n})$ as required whenever E happens. Additionally, we observe that in the second iteration every machine has to store the counts that it gets as messages and one additional counter. Thus, when E happens, the machine has to store $O(\sqrt{n})$ counters taking $O(\log n)$ space each, which leads to a machine space complexity of $O(\sqrt{n} \cdot \log n)$ as required.

Finally, let us consider the last iteration of the algorithm. In this iteration, every machine gets up to $\lceil \sqrt{n} \rceil = O(\sqrt{n})$ messages and adds them up, which requires $O(\sqrt{n})$ time. Moreover, since every message is an integer between 1 and n, storing all of them and their sum requires only $O(\sqrt{n} \cdot \log n)$ space. $\qquad\square$

Corollary 1 shows that the machine time and space complexities of the Map-Reduce algorithm we described for the problem of determining the frequencies of all the words in the list is roughly the square root of the length of the list (with high probability). This is of course a significant improvement over the roughly linear machine time and space complexities of the algorithm that was given for this problem in Chapter 15. However, when n is very large, one might want to further reduce the machine time and space complexities, which is the subject of Exercise 2.

Exercise 2. For every positive integer constant c, design a Map-Reduce algorithm with $c + 1$ iterations that given a list of words calculates the frequencies of all the words in the list and with high probability has machine time and space complexities of $O(n^{1/c})$ and $O(n^{1/c} \cdot \log n)$, respectively.

16.2 Prefix Sums

In this section, we consider a very natural problem called *All-Prefix-Sums*. The input for this problem is an array A of n numbers, and the objective is to calculate for every $1 \leq i \leq n$ the sum s_i of the first i numbers in A

(more formally, $s_i = \sum_{j=1}^{i} A[j]$). An easy sequential algorithm can calculate all the sums $s_1, s_2, \ldots, s_n$ in linear time (see Exercise 3), but the problem becomes more challenging in parallel computation settings such as the Map-Reduce model.

Exercise 3. Describe a linear time sequential algorithm for the All-Prefix-Sums problem.

There is no natural notion of arrays in the Map-Reduce model, and thus, to study the All-Prefix-Sums problem in this model we will assume that each cell of the array is encoded using an ordered pair of its index and value. More formally, the array A is encoded using the n pairs $(1, A[1]), (2, A[2]), \ldots, (n, A[n])$.

The algorithm we present for the All-Prefix-Sums problem is based on the use of a tree T of machines with n leaves. Each machine in T is identified by a pair (h, r), where h is the height of the machine in the tree and r is its index among the machines of T of height h. Since T has n leaves by definition, there are n machines on level 0 of it corresponding to the pairs $(0, 1), (0, 2), \ldots, (0, n)$. To construct the rest of the tree, let us now fix the maximum degree d of the nodes in the tree T. Then, we construct the next levels of the tree one after the other. Assume that we have already constructed level $h \geq 0$ of the tree and it has n_h machines $(h, 1), (h, 2), \ldots, (h, n_h)$, then there are two cases. If $n_h = 1$, then the single machine of level h is the root of T, and h is the top level of T. Otherwise, level $h+1$ consists of $\lceil n_h/d \rceil$ machines corresponding to the pairs $(h+1, 1)$, $(h+1, 2), \ldots, (h+1, \lceil n_h/d \rceil)$, where the parent of every machine (h, r) of level h is machine $(h+1, \lceil r/d \rceil)$ of level $h+1$. An example of a tree constructed this way can be found in Figure 16.1.

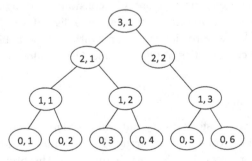

Figure 16.1. The tree T constructed for $d = 2$ and $n = 6$.

Our construction of T guarantees a few useful properties.

- Every machine has at most d children, and the height of the tree is the minimum height necessary for a tree with this property having n leafs, i.e., it is $\lceil \log_d n \rceil$.
- Each machine can calculate the pair of its parent machine.
- Each machine can calculate the pairs of its children machines. More specifically, the children of machine (h, r) of level $h > 0$ are the machines out of $(h-1, d(r-1)+1), (h-1, d(r-1)+2), \ldots, (h-1, dr)$ that exist.

We are now ready to describe a Map-Reduce algorithm for the All-Prefix-Sums problem. This algorithm consists of four stages. In the first stage, every machine that got an input pair $(i, A[i])$ transfers the value $A[i]$ to leaf number i of the tree T. In the second stage, every machine in the tree other than the root determines the sum of the values of the leaves in its subtree and sends this information to its parent. This is done in the following way, which essentially propagates information upwards in the tree from the leaves to the root.

- Every leaf $(0, r)$ forwards its value $A[r]$ to its parent. Note that this value is indeed equal to the sum of the values in the leaves in the subtree of $(0, r)$ since $(0, r)$ is the single leaf in this subtree.
- Each internal machine u with c children which is not the root waits until it receives a value from every one of these children. Let us denote these values by $v_1, v_2, \ldots, v_c$. Then, the machine forwards to its parent the sum $\sum_{i=1}^{c} v_i$. Note that since the subtrees of the children are disjoint and their union includes all the leaves in the subtree of u, this sum is indeed the sum of the values of the leaves in u's subtree given that $v_1, v_2, \ldots, v_c$ are the corresponding sums for the subtrees of u's children.

Given a machine u of the tree T, let us denote by $b(u)$ the number of leaves in T that appear before u in a pre-order traversal of T (i.e., leaves whose index is smaller than the index of every leaf in the subtree of u). In the third stage of the algorithm, every machine u determines $s_{b(u)}$. This is done by propagating information downward in the tree in the following way.

- Every machine u waits until it knows $s_{b(u)}$. The root knows $s_{b(u)}$ from the start because it is always 0. Other machines are given $s_{b(u)}$ by their parent at some point.

- Let us denote the children of u by $a_1, a_2, \ldots, a_c$ in the natural order, and let us denote by v_i the value sent by a_i in the second stage. Once u learns $s_{b(u)}$, it sends to every child a_i the sum $s_{b(u)} + \sum_{j=1}^{i-1} v_j$. Observe that $s_{b(u)}$ is the sum of the values of the leaves out of $1, 2, \ldots, b(a_i)$ that appear outside the subtree of u and $\sum_{j=1}^{i-1} v_j$ is the sum of the values of the leaves out of $1, 2, \ldots, b(a_i)$ that appear inside the subtree of u. Thus, the value forwarded to a_i is indeed the correct value for $s_{b(a_i)}$.

In the fourth and final stage of the algorithm, every leaf $(0, r)$ adds its value $A[r]$ to $s_{b((0,r))} = s_{r-1}$, which produces the value s_r that we have been looking for.

> **Exercise 4.** Describe the above algorithm for the All-Prefix-Sums problem in a more formal way. In particular, specify the messages that should be transferred in every given Map-Reduce iteration.

The correctness of the algorithm we described for All-Prefix-Sums was explained along with its description, and thus, we concentrate now on analyzing its performance. We remark that it is recommended to read the formal description of the algorithm given in the solution for Exercise 4 before going through the proofs of Lemmata 2 and 3.

Lemma 2. *The above algorithm for All-Prefix-Sums uses $O(\log_d n)$ Map-Reduce iterations.*

Proof. Stages 1 and 4 of the algorithm both involve only a single Map-Reduce iteration. Stages 2 and 3 require the algorithm to propagate information up and down the tree T. Since a single Map-Reduce iteration can be used for propagating the information over one level, and the height of the tree is $\lceil \log_d n \rceil$, $O(\log_d n)$ Map-Reduce iterations are sufficient for implementing each one of these stages. $\square$

Lemma 3. *The above algorithm for All-Prefix-Sums has machine space and total space complexities of $O(d \log n)$ and $O(n \log n)$, respectively, assuming that $2 \leq d \leq n$ and that every value in the input can be stored in constant space.*

Remark. Recall that the input for the All-Prefix-Sums problem consists of n pairs, and each such pair contains a value that can be stored in $O(1)$ space (by our assumption) and an index which requires $\Theta(\log n)$ space. Thus, even just storing the input for this problem requires $\Theta(n \log n)$ space, which implies that the total space complexity proved by Lemma 3 is optimal.

Proof. Storing the value received by a node from each one of its children requires $O(\log n)$ bits for the value itself, because the value is at most the sum of all the n input values, plus $O(\log d)$ bits for the identity of the son. Storing the value received by a node from its parent requires $O(\log n)$ bits again, and thus, the total space required for storing all this information (which is the machine space complexity of the algorithm) is only

$$d[O(\log n) + O(\log d)] + O(\log n) = O(d \log n).$$

Our next step is to upper bound the total space complexity of the algorithm. In the first iteration, only the input machines are active, and they use $O(n \log n)$ bits since they store n pairs and each pair requires $O(\log n)$ bits. In the other iterations, only the tree machines are active. Every one of the internal nodes of the tree requires $O(d \log n)$ bits as discussed above, and the number of such nodes is at most

$$\sum_{i=1}^{\lceil \log_d n \rceil} \lceil n/d^i \rceil \leq \log_d n + 1 + \sum_{i=1}^{\infty} n/d^i = \log_d n + 1 + \frac{n/d}{1 - 1/d}$$

$$\leq \log_d n + 1 + 2n/d = O(n/d).$$

Additionally, there are n leaves in T, and each one of these leaves requires only $O(\log n)$ bits of space (since they do not have d sons). Thus, the total space complexity required by the algorithm is

$$O(n/d) \cdot O(d \log n) + n \cdot O(\log n) = O(n \log n).$$

$\square$

Lemma 4. *Assuming that $2 \leq d \leq n$, the above algorithm for All-Prefix-Sums has machine time complexity and work of $O(d)$ and $O(n \log_d n)$, respectively.*

Proof. Machines that are not internal nodes of the tree T need only $O(1)$ time per iteration. In contrast, the internal nodes of the tree are often required to do some operations with respect to every one of their children, and thus, they require more time. Moreover, a naïve implementation of these nodes will require $\Theta(d^2)$ time per iteration because during the down propagation of information, each internal node is required to calculate up to d sums (the sum $\sum_{j=1}^{i-1} v_j$ for every $1 \leq i \leq c$, where c is the number of children of the node), and the calculation of each such individual sum might require up to $\Theta(d)$ time. However, it is not difficult to see that the calculation of all these sums together can also be done in $O(d)$ time because this calculation is an instance of the All-Prefix-Sums problem itself. Thus, no machine of the algorithm requires more than $O(d)$ time per iteration.

Recall that there are only $2n$ machines that are active in the algorithm and are not internal nodes of the tree T — the n input machines and the n leaves of the tree. As mentioned above, each one of these machines uses $O(1)$ time per iteration, and thus, their total work is at most

$$2n \cdot O(1) \cdot (\text{\# of iterations}) = O(n) \cdot O(\log_d n) = O(n \log_d n).$$

Next, we recall that in the proof of Lemma 3 we have seen that there are only $O(n/d)$ internal nodes in the tree T. Since each one of these nodes requires only $O(d)$ time per iteration, their total work is also at most

$$O(n/d) \cdot O(d) \cdot (\text{\# of iterations}) = O(n) \cdot O(\log_d n) = O(n \log_d n). \quad \square$$

Exercise 5. According to Lemma 4, the work done by our Map-Reduce algorithm for All-Prefix-Sums is larger than the $O(n)$ time required for the sequential algorithm for the problem. Show that the work of the Map-Reduce algorithm reduces to $O(n)$ if a machine is allowed access to information that it had in previous iterations (even if it did not forward this information to itself).

We can now summarize the properties of the Map-Reduce algorithm we have presented for the All-Prefix-Sums problem in Theorem 1.

Theorem 1. *For every integer $2 \leq d$, there is a Map-Reduce algorithm for the All-Prefix-Sums problem which uses $O(\log_d n)$ iterations and has a machine space complexity of $O(d \log n)$, a total space complexity of $O(n \log n)$, a machine time complexity of $O(d)$ and a work of $O(n \log_d n)$.*

To better understand the implications of Theorem 1, let us consider two possible choices for d. One option is to choose $d = 2$ (or any other constant value). This choice leads to Corollary 2, which exhibits very low machine space and time complexities but a super-constant number of iterations.

Corollary 2. *There is a Map-Reduce algorithm for the All-Prefix-Sums problem which uses $O(\log n)$ iterations and has a machine space complexity* of $O(\log n)$, a total space complexity of $O(n \log n)$, a machine time complexity of $O(1)$ and a work of $O(n \log n)$.

A different option is to choose $d = \lceil n^\varepsilon \rceil$ for some constant $\varepsilon \in (0, 1)$. This choice leads to larger machine space and time complexities, but only a constant number of iterations.

Corollary 3. *For every constant $\varepsilon \in (0, 1)$, there is a Map-Reduce algorithm for the All-Prefix-Sums problem which uses $O(\varepsilon^{-1})$ iterations and has a machine space complexity of $O(n^\varepsilon \log n)$, a total space complexity of $O(n \log n)$, a machine time complexity of $O(n^\varepsilon)$ and a work of $O(n\varepsilon^{-1})$.*

16.3 Indexing

In the description of the All-Prefix-Sums problem, we have assumed that every input value is accompanied by an index. Such an index is useful for many problems beside All-Prefix-Sums, but in many cases it is not supplied as part of the input. Thus, it is interesting to find a procedure that given a set of n input elements assigns a *unique index* between 1 and n to every one of these items. In this section, we will describe and analyze one such procedure, which is given as Algorithm 3.

The final line of Algorithm 3 makes sense only when every element is assigned a unique temporary index. Fortunately, Lemma 5 shows that this happens with high probability.

Lemma 5. *With probability $1 - O(n^{-1})$, every element is assigned a unique temporary index by Algorithm 3.*

Algorithm 3: Unique Indexing Finder

1. Every machine which received an input element e chooses a uniformly random integer between 1 and n^3 and assigns it as a *temporary index* for e.
2. Execute an algorithm for All-Prefix-Sums on an input generated as follows. For every $1 \leq i \leq n^3$, if there is an element whose temporary index was chosen to be i, include the pair $(i, 1)$ in the input; otherwise, include the pair $(i, 0)$.
3. If element e was assigned the temporary index i, assign s_i as its final index.

Proof. Fix an arbitrary order $e_1, e_2, \ldots, e_n$ over the elements, and let E_i be the event that the temporary index of element e_i coincides with the temporary index of some other element. One can observe that for any fixed choice of temporary indexes for the other elements, the event E_i happens with probability at most

$$\frac{(\# \text{ of other elements})}{n^3} = \frac{n-1}{n^3} < n^{-2}.$$

By the union bound, the probability that at least one of the events E_i happens is only

$$\Pr\left[\bigcup_{i=1}^{n} E_i\right] \leq \sum_{i=1}^{n} \Pr[E_i] \leq \sum_{i=1}^{n} n^{-2} = n^{-1},$$

which completes the proof of the lemma since the temporary indexes are unique when none of the events E_i happen. $\square$

Recall that the input fed by Algorithm 3 to the All-Prefix-Sums algorithm contains the value 1 for every one of the elements and the value 0 for non-elements. One consequence of this is that s_i is equal to the number of elements whose temporary indexes are at most i. Thus, when every element is assigned a unique temporary index, then the final index assigned by Algorithm 3 to every element e is equal to the location of this element in a list that contains all the elements and is sorted according to their temporary indexes. Since every element in a list of length n has a unique location between 1 and n, we get Observation 1.

Observation 1. With probability at least $1 - O(n^{-1})$, Algorithm 3 assigns a unique index between 1 and n to every input element.

Since Algorithm 3 simulates an instance of All-Prefix-Sums with n^3 input elements, simply plugging an implementation of our All-Prefix-Sums algorithm into it will result in an algorithm that (with high probability) has $O(\log_d n)$ iterations, a machine space complexity of $O(d)$, a total space complexity of $O(n^3 \log n)$, a machine time complexity of $O(d)$ and a work of $O(n^3 \log_d n)$. While some of these performance measures are very good, the total space complexity and the work are unacceptably high. Exercise 6 asks you to describe a more sophisticated implementation of Algorithm 3 that yields better total time complexity and work.

Exercise 6. Describe an implementation of Algorithm 3 that keeps the number of iterations, machine space complexity and machine time complexity stated above, but reduces the total space complexity and work to $O(n \log^2 n / \log d)$ and $O(n \log_d^2 n)$, respectively. **Hint:** Since the instance of All-Prefix-Sums generated by Algorithm 3 includes mostly zero values, the subtrees of many nodes of T include only such values, and thus, it is not necessary to explicitly execute the calculations done by such nodes.

16.4 Bibliographic Notes

The problem of determining the frequency of words is a canonical problem for the Map-Reduce framework since the introduction of this framework by Dean and Ghemawat (2004). The ideas behind the improved algorithm for this problem that we presented in this chapter can be traced back to the work of Karloff *et al.* (2010) on the first theoretical model for Map-Reduce.

The two other problems that we studied in this chapter, namely the All-Prefix-Sums and indexing problems, were first studied in the context of a theoretical Map-Reduce model by Goodrich *et al.* (2011). For the All-Prefix-Sums problem, the algorithm that we presented is identical to the algorithm of Goodrich *et al.* (2011). In contrast, for the indexing problem we presented an algorithm (Algorithm 3) which is based on an algorithm of Goodrich *et al.* (2011) but is simpler and less robust. In particular, the algorithm of Goodrich *et al.* (2011) successfully generates the unique final indexes even when the temporary indexes are not unique, and its performance measures remain good unless some temporary index is shared by many elements, which is an extremely unlikely event.

J. Dean and S. Ghemawat. MapReduce: Simplified Data Processing on Large Clusters. In *Proceedings of the 6th Symposium on Operating Systems Design and Implementation (OSDI)*, 137–150, December 2004.

M. T. Goodrich, N. Sitchinava and Q. Zhang. Sorting, Searching, and Simulation in the MapReduce Framework. In *Proceedings of the 22nd International Symposium on Algorithms and Computation (ISAAC)*, 374–383, December 2011.

H. J. Karloff, S. Suri and S. Vassilvitskii. A Model for Computation for MapReduce. In *Proceedings of the 21th ACM-SIAM Symposium on Discrete Algorithms (SODA)*, 938–948, January 2010.

Exercise Solutions

Solution 1

By definition, the Map-Reduce algorithm we consider has three iterations. Let us now determine its total space complexity. In the first iteration, each machine stores the word that it got and a number r that can be represented using $O(\log n)$ bits. Since there are n active machines in this iteration, the total space complexity of the machines in this iteration is $O(n \log n)$. In the second iteration, each machine stores three things: the messages that it got, the count of the number of these messages and its name. Both the count and the name of the machine are represented using $O(\log n)$ bits, and thus, the counts and the names of all the machines together contribute at most $O(n \log n)$ to the total space complexity of the second iteration (note that at most n machines were sent messages during the first iteration and these are the only machines that execute code in this iteration). To determine the space required for the messages received by the machines of the second iteration, we note that each such message takes $O(1)$ space because it always contains only the value 1 and that the number of such messages is exactly n because one message is generated for every word in the input. Thus, these messages contribute only $O(n)$ to the total space complexity of the second iteration, which is dominated by the $O(n \log n)$ required for the counts and names.

Consider now the third iteration of the Map-Reduce algorithm. In this iteration, each machine stores the counts that it got plus the frequency that it calculates. The total number of frequencies calculated is at most n because one frequency is calculated for every distinct word. To determine the number of counts received, we observe that every count that is received represents at least one word of the original text because a count is only generated by machines of the second iteration that received inputs. Thus, the number of counts received by the machines of the third iteration is also bounded by n, like the number of frequencies calculated by these machines. Since both the frequencies and the counts received are integers between 1 and n, each one of them can be stored using $O(\log n)$ space, which means that the total space complexity of the third iteration is $O(n \log n)$. Since this was also the total space complexity of the two previous iterations, it follows that the total space complexity of the entire algorithm is $O(n \log n)$.

To complete the solution, the work of the Map-Reduce algorithm remains to be determined. In the first iteration, we have n machines, and each one of them uses constant time; thus, this iteration contributes

$O(n)$ to the work. In the second iteration, the time complexity of each machine is proportional to the number of messages it receives. Since only n messages are sent during the first iteration (one for every word of the input), this means that the total contribution to the work by all the machines of the second iteration is $O(n)$. Similarly, in the third iteration, the time complexity of each machine is proportional to the number of counts that it receives. Above, we argued that the number of these counts is at most n, and thus, we get once more that the contribution of all the machines of the third iteration to the work is $O(n)$. Summing up the contributions to the work of all three iterations, we get that the work of the entire Map-Reduce algorithm is also $O(n)$.

Solution 2

Before describing the solution for the current exercise, let us discuss briefly the Map-Reduce algorithm represented by Algorithms 1 and 2. Specifically, let us fix an arbitrary word w from the input. Figure 16.2 graphically presents all the machines that process the appearances of this word, either directly or indirectly. The first row in the figure hosts the machines of the first round that process the individual occurrences of the word w in the input. The second row in the figure hosts the machines of the second iteration that are related to this word, i.e., the machines $(w, 1), (w, 2), \ldots, (w, \lceil \sqrt{n} \rceil)$. Finally, the third row in the figure hosts the single machine of the third iteration that is related to the word w, which is the machine named w. The figure also contains arrows representing the flow of messages between the above machines.

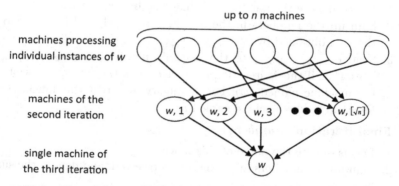

Figure 16.2. The machines related to the processing of a word w in the Map-Reduce algorithm described by Algorithms 1 and 2, and the flow of messages between them.

Let us now think of the machines and arrows of Figure 16.2 as a graph. Given this point of view, Lemma 1 is equivalent to saying that with high probability the degree of every vertex (machine) of this graph is only $O(\sqrt{n})$. Intuitively, this bound on the degree of the vertices in the graph is the key property that allowed us to show that the machine time and space complexities of the above Map-Reduce algorithm are both roughly on the order of $\sqrt{n}$. Thus, to get better machine time and space complexities, we need an algorithm which induces a graph with lower degrees, or in other words, an algorithm in which every machine gets less messages. Such an algorithm appears as Algorithm 4. Recall that c is a positive integer. It is also useful to observe that in every iteration i of this algorithm which is not the first or the last iteration there are $(\lceil n^{1/c} \rceil)^{c-i+1}$ machines that are involved in the processing of a word w. The names of these machines are $(w, r_1, r_2, \ldots, r_{c-i+1})$ for every possible assignment of integers between 1 and $\lceil n^{1/c} \rceil$ to the variables $r_1, r_2, \ldots, r_{c-i+1}$.

Algorithm 4: Improved Algorithm for Word Frequencies — $c + 1$ Iterations

- **First iteration (*word*)**

  1. Pick $c - 1$ independent random integers $r_1, r_2, \ldots, r_{c-1}$, where each r_i is chosen uniformly at random from the range 1 to $\lceil n^{1/c} \rceil$.
  2. Send 1 to the computer named $(word, r_1, r_2, \ldots, r_{c-1})$.

- **Iteration number i for $2 \leq i \leq c$ (*numbers*)**

  1. Let us denote the name of this machine by $(w, r_1, r_2, \ldots, r_{c-i+1})$.
  2. Sum up the numbers in the messages received, and let us denote the sum obtained by $c_{w,r_1,r_2,\ldots,r_{c-i+1}}$.
  3. Send $c_{w,r_1,r_2,\ldots,r_{c-i+1}}$ to the machine named $(w, r_1, r_2, \ldots, r_{c-i})$. Note that if this is iteration number c, then the message is sent to the machine named (w). For simplicity, we treat this machine as identical to the machine named w.

- **Final iteration (*numbers*)**

  1. Let us denote the name of this machine by w.
  2. Sum up the numbers in the messages received, and denote the sum by c_w.
  3. Output c_w as the frequency of w.

It is interesting to note that Algorithm 4 reduces to the Map-Reduce algorithm described by Algorithms 1 and 2 in the case of $c = 2$. However, we will analyze it now independently of this fact. We begin by proving its correctness.

Lemma 6. *Algorithm 4 determines correctly the frequencies of all the words in the input list.*

Proof. Fix a word w, and let A be the set of appearances of w in the input list. Additionally, for every appearance $a \in A$, we denote by $r(a)$ the vector $(r_1, r_2, \ldots, r_{c-1})$ of random values chosen by the machine that processed this appearance of w during the first iteration of Algorithm 4.

We will prove by induction on i that for every choice of integers $1 \leq r_1, r_2, \ldots, r_{c-i+1} \leq \lceil n^{1/c} \rceil$ the value $c_{w,r_1,r_2,\ldots,r_{c-i+1}}$ calculated by Algorithm 4 is exactly $|\{a \in A | \forall_{1 \leq j \leq c-i+1} r_j(a) = r_j\}|$ — here we use $r_j(a)$ to denote coordinate number j of the vector $r(a)$. We begin with the base case, which is the case of $i = 2$. Consider an arbitrary machine $(w, r_1, r_2, \ldots, r_{c-1})$. This machine got one message during the first iteration for every appearance $a \in A$ which had $r(a) = (r_1, r_2, \ldots, r_{c-1})$. Since all these messages contained the number 1, like all the other messages sent during the first iteration, their sum $c_{w,r_1,r_2,\ldots,r_{c-1}}$ is equal to

$$|\{a \in A | r(a) = (r_1, r_2, \ldots, r_{c-1})\}| = |\{a \in A | \forall_{1 \leq j \leq c-1} r_j(a) = r_j\}|,$$

which is what we wanted to prove.

Assume now that the claim we want to prove holds for some integer $2 \leq i - 1 \leq c$, and let us prove it for i. Consider an arbitrary machine $(w, r_1, r_2, \ldots, r_{c+i-1})$. This machine gets as a message the value $c_{w,r_1,r_2,\ldots,r_{c-i+2}}$ for every integer value of r_{c-i+2} between 1 and $\lceil n^{1/c} \rceil$. Thus, the sum $c_{w,r_1,r_2,\ldots,r_{c-i+1}}$ of these values obeys

$$c_{w,r_1,r_2,\ldots,r_{c-i+1}} = \sum_{i=1}^{\lceil n^{1/c} \rceil} c_{w,r_1,r_2,\ldots,r_{c-i+2}}$$

$$= \sum_{i=1}^{\lceil n^{1/c} \rceil} |\{a \in A | \forall_{1 \leq j \leq c-i+2} r_j(a) = r_j\}|$$

$$= |\{a \in A | \forall_{1 \leq j \leq c-i+1} r_j(a) = r_j\}|,$$

where the second equality holds by the induction hypothesis, and the last equality holds since i iterates over all the possible values for $r_{c-i+2}(a)$.

This completes the proof by induction. The lemma now follows since for $i = c + 1$, we got

$$c_w = |\{a \in A | \forall_{1 \leq j \leq 0} r_j(a) = r_j\}| = |A|.$$ $\qquad\square$

The performance of Algorithm 4 remains to be analyzed. By definition, this algorithm has $c + 1$ iterations as required. To analyze its machine time and space complexities, we first need to prove Lemma 7, which corresponds to Lemma 1 in the analysis of the Map-Reduce algorithm described by Algorithms 1 and 2.

Lemma 7. *With high probability no machine receives more than $2n^{1/c}$ messages in the second iteration of Algorithm 4.*

Proof. Let us begin the proof by fixing some word w and integers $r_1', r_2', \ldots r_{c-1}'$ between 1 and $\lceil n^{1/c} \rceil$. We would like to upper bound the probability that machine $(w, r_1', r_2', \ldots r_{c-1}')$ is sent more than $2n^{1/c}$ messages during the first iteration. For this purpose, let us denote by r_j^i, for every pair of integers $1 \leq i \leq n$ and $1 \leq j \leq c - 1$, the random value r_j chosen during the first iteration by the machine processing word number i of the list. We also denote by X_i an indicator for the event that $r_j^i = r_j'$ for every $1 \leq j \leq c - 1$. Since every value r_j^i is an independent uniformly random integer out of the range $[1, \lceil n^{1/c} \rceil]$, we get

$$\Pr[X_i = 1] = \Pr\left[\forall_{1 \leq j \leq c-1} r_j^i = r_j'\right] = \prod_{j=1}^{c-1} \Pr\left[r_j^i = r_j'\right]$$

$$= \prod_{j=1}^{c-1} \frac{1}{\lceil n^{1/c} \rceil} = \left(\lceil n^{1/c} \rceil\right)^{1-c}.$$

We observe that the machine processing word number i (in the first iteration) can send a message to $(w, r_1', r_2', \ldots, r_{c-1}')$ only when $X_i = 1$, and thus, the sum $\sum_{i=1}^{n} X_i$ is an upper bound on the number of messages received by machine $(w, r_1', r_2', \ldots, r_{c-1}')$ in the second iteration. Moreover, this sum has a binomial distribution, which allows us to bound the probability that it is larger than $2n^{1/c}$ using the Chernoff bound.

$$\Pr\left[\sum_{i=1}^{n} X_i > 2n^{1/c}\right] = \Pr\left[\sum_{i=1}^{n} X_i > \frac{2\left(\lceil n^{1/c} \rceil\right)^{c-1}}{n^{1-1/c}} \cdot \mathrm{E}\left[\sum_{i=1}^{n} X_i\right]\right]$$

$$\le e^{-\frac{\left(2n^{1/c-1}\cdot\left(\lceil n^{1/c}\rceil\right)^{c-1}-1\right)\cdot E[\sum_{i=1}^{n} X_i]}{3}}$$

$$= e^{-\frac{2n^{1/c}-n\left(\lceil n^{1/c}\rceil\right)^{1-c}}{3}} \le e^{-\frac{n^{1/c}}{3}}.$$

So far we have proved that the probability of every single machine of the second iteration receiving more than $2n^{1/c}$ messages is at most $e^{-\sqrt[c]{n}/3}$. We also observe that there are only $n \cdot (\lceil n^{1/c}\rceil)^c \le n \cdot (2n^{1/c})^c = 2^c n^2$ machines that might get messages in the second iteration (one for every pair of an input word w and a choice of values for $r_1, r_2, \ldots, r_{c-1}$). Combining these facts using the union bound, we get that the probability that any machine of the second iteration gets more than $2n^{1/c}$ messages is at most $2^c n^2 e^{-\sqrt[c]{n}/3}$, which approaches 0 as n approaches infinity because we treat c as a constant. $\qquad\square$

Corollary 4. *With high probability the machine time and space complexities of Algorithm 4 are $O(n^{1/c})$ and $O(n^{1/c} \cdot \log n)$, respectively.*

Proof. Let us denote by E the event that every machine of the second iteration receives only $O(n^{1/c})$ messages. Lemma 1 shows that the event E occurs with high probability. Thus, it is enough to prove that the machine time and space complexities of the algorithm are as promised whenever E happens. The rest of the proof is devoted to showing that this is indeed the case, and thus, implicitly assumes that E occurred.

In the first iteration, every machine stores only the word it processes and the random values $r_1, r_2, \ldots, r_{c-1}$, and thus, requires only $O(c \cdot \log n) = O(\log n)$ space, where the equality holds since we treat c as a constant. Moreover, every such machine uses only constant time, and thus, both its running time and space usage are consistent with the machine time and space complexities that we would like to prove.

Consider now another arbitrary iteration of the algorithm. Observe that the time complexity of every machine in this iteration is proportional to the number of messages it receives, thus, to show that the machine time complexity in this iteration is $O(n^{1/c})$, it is only required to prove that no machine of the iteration gets more than $O(n^{1/c})$ messages. For iteration number 2, that follows immediately from our assumption that the event E has occurred. For later iterations, we observe that every machine $(w, r_1, r_2, \ldots, r_{c-i+1})$ of iteration i gets a message only from machines $(w, r'_1, r'_2 \ldots r'_{c-i+2})$ of iteration $i-1$ whose name obeys $r'_j = r_j$ for every $1 \le j \le c - i + 1$. Since there are only $\lceil n^{1/c}\rceil$ values that

r'_{c-i+2} can take, there are only $\lceil n^{1/c} \rceil$ such machines, and therefore, there are also only that many messages that machine $(w, r_1, r_2, \ldots, r_{c-i+1})$ can receive.

Consider now the machine space complexity of iteration $i \geq 2$. Every machine in this iteration has to store its name, the counts that it gets as messages and one additional counter. As we argued before, each machine gets at most $\lceil n^{1/c} \rceil$ messages. We also observe that each value that it needs to store counts some of the appearances of a word w in the input list, and thus, is upper bounded by n. Thus, the space required for the counts stored by every single machine in iteration i is upper bounded by $(\lceil n^{1/c} \rceil + 1) \cdot O(\log n) = O(n^{1/c} \cdot \log n)$. Additionally, the name of the machine consists of the word w, which requires a constant space, and up to $c - 1$ additional values which require $O(\log n)$ space each, and thus, the name can be stored in $O(c \cdot \log n) = O(\log n)$ space, which is less than the machine space complexity that we need to prove. $\qquad\square$

Solution 3

The algorithm we suggest for the problem is given as Algorithm 5. It is not difficult to see that the time complexity of this algorithm is indeed $O(n)$. Moreover, one can prove by induction that the sums calculated by this algorithm obey $s_i = \sum_{j=1}^{i} A[j]$ for every $1 \leq i \leq n$.

Solution 4

The following is a formal presentation of the Map-Reduce algorithm described before the exercise. The first iteration corresponds to the first stage of the algorithm, iterations 2 up to $\lceil \log_d n \rceil + 1$ correspond to the second stage of the algorithm, iterations $\lceil \log_d n \rceil + 2$ up to $2\lceil \log_d n \rceil + 1$ correspond to the third stage of the algorithm, and finally, iteration number $2\lceil \log_d n \rceil + 2$ corresponds to the fourth stage of the algorithm.

Algorithm 5: Sequential Algorithm for All-Prefix-Sums (A)

1. Let $s_1 \leftarrow A[1]$.
2. **for** $i = 2$ to n **do**
3. $\quad$ Let $s_i \leftarrow s_{i-1} + A[i]$.

- **First iteration**

  Description: In this iteration, every machine that got an input pair of index and value forwards the value to the leaf machine of T corresponding to the index. Note that we use $T(h, r)$ to denote the machine of T corresponding to the pair (h, r).

  1. The input of the machine in this iteration is a pair $(index,\ value)$.
  2. Forward $value$ to the machine named $T(0, index)$.

- **Second iteration**

  Description: In this iteration we begin the upward propagation of information. Specifically, the leaf machines, which are the only machines that got messages (and thus, are active) in this iteration forward their values to their parents. Starting from this point, we use the convention that a machine keeps in a pair (i, v) the value v that it got from its zero-based ith son. The sole exception to this rule is the leaf machines which have no sons, and thus keep in $(0, v)$ their own value v as follows:

  1. Let $T(0, r)$ be the name of this leaf machine, and let us name the value it received by v.
  2. Forward the pair $(0, v)$ to myself (to keep it) and the pair $(r \bmod d, v)$ to my parent.

- **Iteration number i for $3 \leq i \leq \lceil \log_d n \rceil + 1$**

  Description: These iterations complete the upward propagation of information. In the beginning of iteration i only the machines in levels $0, 1, \ldots, i - 2$ of the tree have messages (and thus, are active). They all forward these messages to themselves to keep them for the next iteration, and the nodes at level $i - 2$ forward information also to their parents, which have not been active so far.

  1. Let $T(h, r)$ be the name of this machine.
  2. Let us denote by c the number of my children (or 1 if I am a leaf), then I received (either from myself or from my children) c pairs $(0, v_0), (1, v_1), \ldots, (c - 1, v_{c-1})$.
  3. Forward all the pairs $(0, v_0), (1, v_1), \ldots, (c - 1, v_{c-1})$ to myself, to keep them.
  4. **if** $h = i - 2$ **then**
  5.   Forward the pair $(r \bmod d, \sum_{i=0}^{c-1} v_i)$ to my parent machine $T(h + 1, \lceil r/d \rceil)$.

- **Iteration number** $\lceil \log_d n \rceil + 2$

  Description: This iteration begins the downward propagation of information. The root of the tree, which is the sole machine at level $\lceil \log_d n \rceil$, forwards to every child u of it the value $s_{b(u)}$. The other machines of the tree simply forward the information they have to themselves to keep it.

  1. Let $T(h, r)$ be the name of this machine.
  2. Let us denote by c the number of my children (or 1 if I am a leaf), then I received from myself c pairs $(0, v_0), (1, v_1), \ldots, (c - 1, v_{c-1})$.
  3. **if** $h = \lceil \log_d n \rceil$ **then**
  4.   Forward $\sum_{j=0}^{i-2} v_j$ to my ith son (machine $T(h - 1, d(r - 1) + i)$) for every $1 \le i \le c$.
  5. **else**
  6.   Forward the pairs $(0, v_0), (1, v_1), \ldots, (c - 1, v_{c-1})$ to myself, to keep them.

- **Iterations number** i **for** $\lceil \log_d n \rceil + 3 \le i \le 2\lceil \log_d n \rceil + 1$

  Description: These iterations complete the downward propagation of information. In the beginning of each such iteration, the machines at levels $0, 1, \ldots, 2\lceil \log_d n \rceil + 2 - i$ are active. Each one of these machines has the information that it got from its children (or their own value in case of leaves) and the machines at level $2\lceil \log_d n \rceil + 2 - i$ also have the value that they got from their parents. This allows the machines of level $2\lceil \log_d n \rceil + 2 - i$ to forward to every child u of theirs the value $s_{b(u)}$, while the machines of the lower levels simply forward to themselves the information that they have.

  1. Let $T(h, r)$ be the name of this machine.
  2. Let us denote by c the number of my children (or 1 if I am a leaf), then I received from myself c pairs $(0, v_0), (1, v_1), \ldots, (c - 1, v_{c-1})$.
  3. **if** $h = 2\lceil \log_d n \rceil + 2 - i$ **then**
  4.   I have received one value s from my parent.
  5.   Forward $s + \sum_{j=0}^{i-2} v_j$ to my ith son (machine $T(h - 1, d(r - 1) + i)$) for every $1 \le i \le c$.
  6. **else**
  7.   Forward the pairs $(0, v_0), (1, v_1), \ldots, (c - 1, v_{c-1})$ to myself, to keep them.

- **Iteration number** $2\lceil \log_d n \rceil + 2$

  Description: In this iteration, only the leaves are active. Each leaf $(0, r)$ has its own value stored in a pair $(0, v)$ and the value $s = s_{r-1}$ it got from its parent. By adding up these values, the leaf gets s_r.

1. Let $T(0, r)$ be the name of this leaf machine.
2. I received a value s from my parent and a pair $(0, v)$ from myself.
3. Output $s + v$ as the prefix sum s_r.

Solution 5

The term $\log_d n$ in the bound on the work proved by Lemma 4 follows from the fact that each machine of the Map-Reduce algorithm might operate during $O(\log_d n)$ iterations. However, one can note that only in a constant number out of these iterations a given machine does any job other than sending its information to itself in order to preserve it. Iterations in which a machine only sends information to itself become redundant if one allows a machine access to the information that it had in previous iterations. Thus, such access will allow us to reduce the number of iterations in which every given machine is active to $O(1)$; which will result in the removal of the $\log_d n$ term from the bound on the work done by the algorithm.

Solution 6

The algorithm we described in Section 16.2 for the All-Prefix-Sums problem was designed under the assumption that some value is given for every index between 1 and n. To lift this assumption, we modify the algorithm a bit. Specifically, in the stage in which the algorithm propagates information downwards, we make the nodes forward information only to the children from which they got information during the upward propagation phase of the algorithm (rather than sending a message to all their children as in the original algorithm). One can verify that after this change the algorithm still produces a value s_i for every index i for which a value was supplied as part of the input, and moreover, s_i is still correct in the sense that it is the sum of the values belonging to index i and lower indexes. Thus, the omission of pairs with zero values does not affect the s_i values produced by this algorithm for pairs that have not been omitted.

In particular, the above observation implies that, when using the above modified algorithm for All-Prefix-Sums in an implementation of Algorithm 3, the implementation can skip the generation of the zero valued pairs. Since only n out of the n^3 pairs generated by Algorithm 3 has a non-zero value (one pair for every input element of Algorithm 3), this greatly reduces the number of pairs generated by the algorithm. In the rest of this answer, we refer to the implementation of Algorithm 3 obtained this way as the "efficient implementation".

An additional useful property of our modified algorithm for All-Prefix-Sums is that the time and space resources used by every node of T depend on the number of active children it has (instead of d). Since the number of active children of a node u is upper bounded by the number of leaves in its subtree corresponding to indexes that were supplied with values (we denote the last number by d_u), we get that the machine space and time complexities of u in every given iteration are upper bounded by $O(d_u \log n)$ and $O(d_u)$, respectively. Since the efficient implementation of Algorithm 3 supplies only n values, the sum of d_u over all the nodes u of a given level of T is equal to n, and thus, the total space and time complexities of all the nodes of a given level of T in a single iteration are $O(n \log n)$ and $O(n)$, respectively. Multiplying the last space bound by the number of levels of the tree T (which is $O(\log_d n)$), we get the promised bound of

$$O(\log_d n) \cdot O(n \log n) = O(n \log^2 n / \log d)$$

on the total space complexity of the efficient implementation of Algorithm 3. To bound the work used by Algorithm 3, we recall that all the nodes of a given level of T use $O(n)$ computation in a single iteration. Multiplying this bound by the number of levels of the tree T and the number of iterations used by the algorithm (both of which are $O(\log_d n)$), we get also the promised bound on the work of the efficient implementation of Algorithm 3.

To complete the solution of the exercise, it remains to be observed that the modified algorithm for All-Prefix-Sums keeps the same bounds on the number of iterations, machine time complexity and machine space complexity as the original algorithm because the original analysis still applies to it. Intuitively, this is the case because the modification only decreases the amount of work that the algorithm does.

Chapter 17

Graph Algorithms

Up to this point in the book, all the Map-Reduce algorithms we have seen operated on inputs with very little combinatorial structure (essentially, all the algorithms operated on either sets or ordered lists of elements). To demonstrate that the Map-Reduce framework can also handle inputs with a significant combinatorial structure, we present in this chapter Map-Reduce algorithms for two graph problems.

17.1 Minimum Weight Spanning Tree

The first problem that we consider is the problem of computing a minimum weight spanning tree in an edge-weighted connected graph $G = (V, E)$ with n vertices and m edges. The algorithm we describe for this problem works as follows. Let us fix a target machine space complexity. If the graph G already has a small enough number of edges to fit this target machine space complexity, then the algorithm transmits all the edges of G to a single machine and computes a minimum weight spanning tree in a sequential manner. Otherwise, if G is too large to fit the target machine space complexity, then the algorithm filters (removes) a few edges of G and repeats the process. The filtering is done in two steps. In the first step, the edges of G are randomly split between multiple machines in a way that guarantees that each machine gets many edges, but not so many that its space usage will exceed the target machine space complexity. Then, in the second step, each machine computes a minimum weight spanning forest for the subgraph consisting of the edges that it received and filters out all the edges that do not belong to the forest obtained.

A pseudocode of this algorithm is given as Algorithm 1. The input parameter M of this algorithm roughly corresponds to the target machine space complexity from the above description of the algorithm, and we assume that its value is at least $3n$. Additionally, we recall that the minimum weight spanning forest of a graph G is a minimum weight subgraph of G that connects every pair of vertices that are connected by G itself. In particular, if G is connected, then its minimum weight spanning forests are exactly its minimum weight spanning trees.

It is not immediately clear how to implement Algorithm 1 as a Map-Reduce algorithm, and we will discuss this point in detail. However, before doing so, we first would like to prove that Algorithm 1 indeed outputs a minimum weight spanning tree of the graph G. To do so, we need to define some notation. Let k denote the number of iterations performed by Algorithm 1, and for every integer $0 \leqslant i \leqslant k$, let F_i denote an arbitrary minimum weight spanning forest of E_i. Additionally, given a set E of edges and a forest F, let us denote by $w(E)$ and $w(F)$ their weights, respectively. Lemma 1 uses this notation to show that the edges that are filtered in every given iteration of Algorithm 1 are not important, in some sense.

Lemma 1. *If Algorithm 1 terminates and (V, E_{i-1}) is connected for some integer $1 \leqslant i \leqslant k$, then (V, E_i) is also connected and $w(F_i) = w(F_{i-1})$.*

Remark: The condition that Algorithm 1 terminates is necessary in the lemma because the number of iterations k is not well-defined unless this condition holds.

Algorithm 1: (Minimum Weight Spanning Tree (V, E, M))

1. Let $E_0 \leftarrow E$ and $i \leftarrow 0$.
2. **while** $|E_i| > M$ **do**
3.   Update $i \leftarrow i + 1$.
4.   Let $p_i \leftarrow \lceil |E_{i-1}|/M \rceil$.
5.   Partition E_{i-1} into p_i sets $E_{i-1,1}, E_{i-1,2}, \ldots E_{i-1,p_i}$, where every edge $e \in E_{i-1}$ is assigned to one of the sets of the partition uniformly at random.
6.   For every $1 \leqslant j \leqslant p_i$, let $F_{i,j}$ be a minimum weight spanning forest of $(V, E_{i-1,j})$.
7.   Let $E_i \leftarrow \bigcup_{j=1}^{p_i} E(F_{i,j})$, where $E(F)$ denotes the set of edges of forest F.
8. **return** a minimum weight spanning forest of the graph (V, E_i).

Proof.   We begin the proof by showing that (V, E_i) is connected. Consider an arbitrary edge $e \in E_{i-1}$, and let us denote by $E_{i-1,j}$ the set that e arrives to in the partition computed during iteration i of Algorithm 1. Since the two end points of e are connected in $(V, E_{i-1,j})$ — for example, by e itself — the spanning forest $F_{i,j}$ must include a path between the end points of e, and so must the set E_i which includes all the edges of $F_{i,j}$ by definition. Since we chose e as an arbitrary edge of E_{i-1}, we get that the end points of every edge of E_{i-1} are connected in E_i. Thus, every path between two nodes in (V, E_{i-1}) can be converted into a path between the same two nodes in (V, E_i), which implies that (V, E_i) is connected because (V, E_{i-1}) is.

From this point on, we concentrate on proving the second part of the lemma, i.e., that $w(F_i) = w(F_{i-1})$. Recall that one way to find a minimum weight spanning forest is via Kruskal's algorithm, which considers the edges of the graph in an arbitrary non-decreasing weights order π, and adds every edge considered to the forest if and only if this addition does not create a cycle. Let us now assume that Kruskal's algorithm is applied to the graph (V, E_{i-1}), and that the order π used by the algorithm is chosen in such a way that guarantees that if e_1 and e_2 are edges of G of the same weight such that either $e_1 \in E_i$ and $e_2 \notin E_i$ or $e_1 \in F_i$ and $e_2 \notin F_i$, then e_1 appears before e_2 in π (such an order must exist since $F_i \subseteq E_i$). We denote by F'_{i-1} the minimum weight spanning forest of (V, E_{i-1}) produced by this execution of Kruskal's algorithm. Since both F_{i-1} and F'_{i-1} are minimum weight spanning forests of (V, E_{i-1}), we immediately get the equality $w(F_{i-1}) = w(F'_{i-1})$.

To complete the proof of the lemma, it still remains to show that the equality $w(F'_{i-1}) = w(F_i)$ holds as well, which we do by proving that $F'_{i-1} = F_i$. To prove this equality, let us assume by way of contradiction that $F'_{i-1} \neq F_i$, and let e be the first edge according to the order π that belongs either to $E(F_i) \backslash E(F'_{i-1})$ or to $E(F'_{i-1}) \backslash E(F_i)$. If $e \in E(F_i) \backslash E(F'_{i-1})$, then the construction of F'_{i-1} using Kruskal's algorithm guarantees that F'_{i-1} includes a path P between the end points of e consisting solely of edges that appear before e in the order π. However, the definition of e as the first edge according to π in which F'_{i-1} and F_i differ implies that all the edges of the path P belong also to F_i, and thus, close a cycle in F_i when combined with the edge e itself, which is a contradiction since F_i is a forest. This leaves us with the case of $e \in E(F'_{i-1}) \backslash E(F_i)$. Since $e \in E(F'_{i-1})$, the construction of F'_{i-1} by Kruskal's algorithm guarantees that there cannot exist a path in E_{i-1} between the end points of e which consists solely of edges that appear before e in the order π (because every edge e' of such a path would have been added to F'_{i-1} when considered by the algorithm unless F'_{i-1} had already contained at this point a path between the end points of e' consisting of edges that appear even earlier than e' in π). If $e \in E_i$, then from the facts that $e \notin E(F_i)$ and that F_i is a minimum weight spanning tree of (V, E_i), we get that F_i must contain a path between the end points of e consisting solely of edges which are at most as heavy as e. However, such edges must appear before e in the order π by the choice of this order, which contradicts our previous observation that the end points of e cannot be connected in E_{i-1} by a path of edges that appear before e in π. Similarly, if $e \notin E_i$, then we get that for some $1 \leqslant j \leqslant p_i$ we must have had $e \in E_{i-1,j}/F_{i,j}$, and since $F_{i,j}$ is a minimum weight spanning tree of $(V, E_{i-1,j})$, this implies that $F_{i-1,j}$ contains a path between the end points of e consisting solely of edges which are at most as heavy as e. Since all these edges belong to E_i, they all appear before e in the order π, and once again the existence of this path leads to a contradiction for the same reason as before. □

By combining the guarantee of Lemma 1 for every integer $1 \leqslant i \leqslant k$, we get Corollary 1.

Corollary 1. *If Algorithm 1 terminates and G is connected, then the output of the algorithm is a minimum weight spanning tree of G.*

Proof. Recall that $E = E_0$, and thus, (V, E_0) is connected. By repeatedly applying Lemma 1 for every integer $1 \leqslant i \leqslant k$, this implies that (V, E_k) is connected as well. Let us now denote the output of Algorithm 1 by T. The algorithm chooses T as a minimum weight spanning forest of (V, E_k). Since (V, E_k) is connected, this implies that T is a spanning tree. Moreover, since F_k is also a minimum weight spanning forest of (V, E_k), and thus, of the same weight as T, we get

$$w(T) = w(F_k) = w(F_{k-1}) = \cdots = w(F_0),$$

where all the equalities other than the first one hold due to Lemma 1. Thus, the spanning tree T is a minimum weight spanning tree of G because it has the same weight as the minimum weight spanning forest F_0. □

Our next objective in the analysis of Algorithm 1 is to bound the number of iterations it performs, and in particular, show that it terminates. This is done by Exercise 1, which shows that every iteration of Algorithm 1 makes progress by significantly decreasing the size of E_i (recall that we assume $M \geqslant 3n$).

Exercise 1. Show that for every $i \geqslant 1$, if Algorithm 1 performs at least i iterations, then $|E_i| \leqslant (2n/M) \cdot |E_{i-1}|$, and explain why this implies that Algorithm 1 performs less than $\log_{M/(2n)} m + 1$ iterations.

Note that Corollary 1 and Exercise 1 show together that Algorithm 1 always outputs a minimum weight spanning tree of G, which is what we wanted to show. As promised, we now discuss the implementation of Algorithm 1 as a Map-Reduce algorithm. Consider iteration i of the algorithm for some $1 \leqslant i \leqslant k$. In the beginning of this iteration, the edges are partitioned in some way between the machines. Let us denote by S_i the set of machines that has any edges at this point. The machines of S_i need to determine $|E_{i-1}|$ in order to calculate p_i. To do this, every machine of S_i forwards the number of edges that it has to a single "counter" machine which uses the next Map-Reduce iteration to calculate $|E_{i-1}|$ (by adding up all the values that it got) and sends back $|E_{i-1}|$ to all the machines of S_i. Once a machine of S_i gets to know $|E_{i-1}|$, it can calculate p_i and randomly partition its edges among the sets $E_{i-1,1}, E_{i-1,2}, \ldots, E_{i-1,p_i}$. Then, for every $1 \leqslant j \leqslant p_i$, all the edges of $E_{i-1,j}$ are forwarded to a single machine $L(i,j)$, which uses this set to calculate the minimum weight spanning forest $F_{i,j}$ through a sequential algorithm (such as Kruskal's algorithm). At this point, all the edges of $E_i = \cup_{j=1}^{p_i} F_{i,j}$ are available at the machines $L(i,1), L(i,2), \ldots, L(i,p_i)$, and thus, iteration number i of Algorithm 1 is done.

One can observe that the procedure described above for implementing an iteration of Algorithm 1 can also be used to detect whether such an iteration should start to begin with because every machine of S_i learns $|E_{i-1}|$ during the procedure, and thus, can compare it with M. If $|E_{i-1}|$ turns out to be no larger than M, which implies that we should actually compute the output of the algorithm rather than make another iteration, then all the edges of $|E_{i-1}|$ are forwarded to the single machine $L(i,1)$, which can then compute the output T of Algorithm 1 based on these edges.

Exercise 2. Write the details of the above implementation of the algorithm in a more formal way. In particular, specify the exact messages transmitted between the machines in each iteration.

The above implementation of Algorithm 1 is quite natural, but as is, it might result in a very high machine space and time complexities. To see why that is the case, note that in the first iteration of the algorithm every edge of the graph appears in its own input machine, and each one of these machines forwards a message to the counter machine. Thus, the counter machine has to store and process m messages, which may require $\Omega(n^2)$ space and time if the graph is dense. To solve this issue, we need to add to the algorithm a pre-processing step in which the edges of the graph are forwarded to a relatively small number of machines. More specifically, in the pre-processing step every input machine that has an edge (u, v) forwards this edge to the machine $L(u)$. It is easy to see that the addition of this pre-processing step does not break the above implementation of Algorithm 1. In the rest of this section, we will analyze the performance measures of the implementation with this pre-processing step, and we will see, in particular, that the addition of the pre-processing step allows us to guarantee good machine time and space complexities.

From the formal description of the implementation given in the solution of Exercise 2, one can observe that the number of Map-Reduce iterations required for the algorithm is only

$$3(k+1) + 2 = O(\log_{M/(2n)} m) = O(\log_{M/(2n)} n)$$

because the three Map-Reduce iterations of the implementation are repeated once for every iteration of Algorithm 1 and once more for detecting that the algorithm should terminate, and on top of that the algorithm uses only the two additional Map-Reduce iterations: one for pre-processing and one for calculating the output T. To study the other performance measures of Algorithm 1, we first need to bound the amount of information that each machine might receive. Besides the input machines, there are three kinds of machines in the implementation: machines whose name is $L(i, j)$ for some integers i and j, machines whose name is $L(u)$ for some vertex u and the counter machine. In the following, we treat machines of each one of these kinds separately.

Observation 1. For each vertex $u \in E$, the machine $L(u)$ gets at most n edges.

Proof. Only edges having u as one of their end points can be sent to $L(u)$ during the pre-processing step. The observation now follows because the degree of every node, including u, is upper bounded by $n - 1$. $\square$

Lemma 2. *Fix some iteration i of Algorithm 1, all the random decisions made by the algorithm before this iteration and an integer value $1 \leqslant j \leqslant p_i$. Then, even conditioned on all the random decisions we have fixed, with probability at least $1 - O(e^{-n})$ the machine $L(i, j)$ gets at most $2M$ edges.*

Proof. Intuitively, the lemma holds because the number p_i was chosen in a way that guarantees that each such machine gets at most M edges in expectation, and the number of edges the machine gets in practice should be very concentrated around its expectation because every edge is assigned independently.

More formally, recall that every edge of E_{i-1} is transmitted to the machine $L(i, j)$ with probability $1/p_i$, independently. Hence, if we denote by X the number of such edges that end up in $L(i, j)$, then X is distributed like $B(|E_{i-1}|, 1/p_i)$. Thus, by the Chernoff bound and the fact that $M \cdot p_i \geqslant |E_{i-1}|$, we get

$$\Pr[X > 2M] = \Pr\left[X > \frac{2M \cdot p_i}{|E_{i-1}|} \cdot \mathrm{E}[X]\right] \leqslant e^{-\left(\frac{2M \cdot p_i}{|E_{i-1}|} - 1\right) \cdot \frac{\mathrm{E}[X]}{3}}$$

$$= e^{-\left(2M - \frac{|E_{i-1}|}{p_i}\right)/3} \leqslant e^{-M/3} \leqslant e^{-n},$$

where the last two inequalities follow from our assumption that $M \geqslant 3n$. $\square$

Corollary 2. *With probability $1 - O(ne^{-n} \log n)$ all the machines whose name is of the form $L(i, j)$ get at most $2M$ edges each.*

Proof. Lemma 2 shows that for every iteration i of Algorithm 1, conditioned on the random decisions made in the previous iterations, every given machine $L(i, j)$ gets at most $2M$ edges with probability $1 - O(e^{-n})$. Thus, by the union bond, conditioned on the same assumption we get that the probability that some machine $L(i, j)$ gets more than $2M$ edges in iteration i is at most

$$p_i \cdot O(e^{-n}) = \left\lceil \frac{|E_{i-1}|}{M} \right\rceil \cdot O(e^{-n}) \leqslant \left\lceil \frac{n^2}{n} \right\rceil \cdot O(e^{-n}) = O(ne^{-n}),$$

where the inequality follows from our assumption that $M \geqslant 3n$ and the observation that the number m of edges in the graph G is upper bounded by n^2. We now note that since we obtained an upper bound on this probability that applies conditioned on any fixed choice of the random decisions in the previous iterations, the law of total probability allows us to remove the condition. Hence, the probability that for a fixed i any machine

$L(i, j)$ gets more than $2M$ edges is unconditionally at most $O(ne^{-n})$. Using the union bound again, we can now get from this that the probability that any machine whose name is of the form $L(i, j)$ gets more than $2M$ edges is at most

$$\left(\begin{array}{c} \text{maximum number of iterations} \\ \text{that the algorithm might have} \end{array}\right) \cdot O(ne^{-n}) = O(\log_{M/(2n)} n) \cdot O(ne^{-n})$$

$$= O(ne^{-n} \log n),$$

where the last equality follows again from the assumption that $M \geqslant 3n$. $\square$

Lemma 3. *In every iteration of Algorithm* 1, *the counter machine gets values from at most* $O(n)$ *machines.*

Proof. We begin the proof by observing that in the first iteration of Algorithm 1, the counter machine can get values only from the machines whose name is $L(u)$ for some vertex u. Since there are only n such machines, they send to the counter only n values during this iteration. Thus, in the rest of the proof we only need to consider the other iterations of Algorithm 1.

In the beginning of iteration $i \geqslant 2$ of Algorithm 1, the number of machines that have edges is p_{i-1} (specifically, these are the machines $L(i-1, 1)$, $L(i-1, 2), \ldots, L(i-1, p_{i-1})$). Since every one of these machines sends a single value to the counter machine during the iteration, the number of messages received by counter machine during the iteration is

$$p_{i-1} = \left\lceil \frac{|E_{i-2}|}{M} \right\rceil \leqslant \frac{n^2}{3n} + 1 = O(n). \qquad \square$$

Exercise 3. Use the above bounds on the amount of information received by each machine (i.e., the bounds given by Observation 1, Corollary 2 and Lemma 3) to show that with high probability (i.e., with a probability approaching 1 as n goes to infinity) the machine time and space complexities of Algorithm 1 are both at most $O(M \log n)$.

To bound the total space complexity of Algorithm 1, we note that this algorithm does not significantly replicate the data it gets. In other words, every edge is kept at every point of time only on a single machine. Thus, the space required for storing these edges is always upper bounded by $O(m \log n)$. In addition, Algorithm 1 uses space only for the counters sent to the counter machine and from it. There can be only $m + 1$ such counters in every iteration because only a machine that has at least one edge sends a counter to the counter machine, and each such counter is a number of value at most n^2, and thus, can be stored using $O(\log n)$ bits. Hence, the total space required for storing these counters is again $O(m \log n)$, and thus, the total space complexity of Algorithm 1 is bounded by this expression.

Let us now bound the work done by Algorithm 1. Observe that the time complexity of each machine used by Algorithm 1 is either linear in the number of edges and counters it gets or dominated by the time required to find a minimum spanning forest in the graph consisting of the edges it gets. Thus, if we use Kruskal's algorithm to find the minimum spanning forest, then a machine that gets m' edges has a time complexity of $O(m' \log m') = O(m' \log n)$. Together with the above observation that all the machines together get in a single iteration of Algorithm 1 only $O(m)$ edges and counters, this implies that Algorithm 1 does $O(m \log n)$ work in each iteration. Using now the bound we have proved above on the number of iterations that this algorithm makes, we get that the work it does throughout its execution is upper bounded by $O(m \log n \log_{M/(2n)} n) = O(m \log n \log_{M/n} n)$ iterations.

Theorem 1 summarizes the properties of Algorithm 1 that we have proved.

Theorem 1. *Algorithm 1 is a Map-Reduce algorithm for finding a minimum weight spanning tree which, with high probability, uses $O(\log_{M/n} n)$ iterations, $O(M \cdot \log n)$ machine time and space complexities, $O(m \log n \log_{M/n} n)$ work and $O(m \cdot \log n)$ total space complexity.*

We would like to draw the reader's attention to two remarks on Theorem 1.

- The analysis of the machine time complexity and work in Theorem 1 was based on the assumption that the algorithm uses Kruskal's algorithm to find minimum spanning forests. If faster algorithms are used for this purpose, then both the machine time complexity and work of Algorithm 1 can be somewhat improved.
- Recall that M was intuitively defined as our target machine space complexity. Theorem 1 shows that the machine space complexity of Algorithm 1 is indeed upper bounded by this target complexity up to an $O(\log n)$ factor. Varying the target machine space complexity M creates a tradeoff between the different performance measures of Algorithm 1. In particular, if M is set to be $3n$ (the minimum value allowed), then the algorithm uses only $O(n \log n)$ machine time and space but

requires $O(\log n)$ iterations and does $O(m \log^2 n)$ work. In contrast, if M is set to be $3n^{1+\varepsilon}$ for some constant $\varepsilon > 0$, then the number of iterations becomes a constant and the work reduces to $O(m \log n)$, but the machine time and space complexities increase to $O(n^{1+\varepsilon} \log n)$.

Exercise 4. Algorithm 1 is a randomized algorithm. Describe a way to derandomize it while keeping its performance measures unaffected. **Hint:** Randomness is used by Algorithm 1 only for efficiently redistributing the edges between the machines in a way that guarantees that with high probability every machine gets $O(M)$ edges. To solve the exercise, find an alternative deterministic redistribution scheme that has this property and is as efficient as the randomized scheme used by Algorithm 1.

17.2 Listing Triangles

The second problem that we consider in this chapter is the problem of *triangle listing*. An algorithm for this problem gets a graph and should list all the triangles in it. For example, based on the graph from Figure 17.1, the algorithm should output the 3 triangles appearing in this graph, which are $\{a, b, c\}$, $\{a, c, d\}$ and $\{c, d, e\}$. The problem of triangle listing is closely related to the problem of counting the triangles of a graph, which we studied in Chapter 8. Both problems have applications in the study of social networks, and it is usually possible to convert an algorithm for triangles listing into an algorithm for counting triangles by simply counting the number of triangles produced by the former algorithm.

A very simple and natural non-Map-Reduce algorithm for the problem of listing triangles is given as Algorithm 2. This algorithm simply enumerates every possible triplet of distinct vertices of the graph, and then outputs the triplets that happen to be triangles. One can verify that

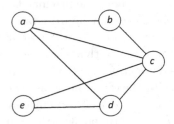

Figure 17.1. A graph with three triangles: $\{a, b, c\}$, $\{a, c, d\}$ and $\{c, d, e\}$.

Algorithm 2: (Simple Triangle Listing (V, E))

1. Assume that V is an array (if it is not, then an array containing all the vertices can be constructed in $O(n)$ time).
2. **for** $i = 1$ to n **do**
3.   **for** $j = i + 1$ to n **do**
4.   **for** $k = j + 1$ to n **do**
5.   **if** the three possible edges between $V[i]$, $V[j]$ and $V[k]$ all exist **then**
6.   Add the triangle $\{V[i], V[j], V[k]\}$ to the list of triangles in the graph.

---

this algorithm indeed outputs every triangle of the graph exactly once, and that it runs in $O(n^3)$ time because every one of its loops iterates at most n times.

Despite the simplicity of Algorithm 2, the dependence of its time complexity on n is optimal because a graph with n vertices might have $\Theta(n^3)$ triangles, and thus, this is the minimal amount of time necessary for listing them all. One can observe, however, that only very dense graphs can have so many triangles, which leaves open the possibility of faster algorithms for counting triangles in sparse graphs. Lemma 4 makes this intuitive observation more concrete by upper bounding the number of triangles that a graph with m edges might have.

Lemma 4. *A graph $G = (V, E)$ with m edges can contain at most $O(m^{3/2})$ triangles.*

Proof. In this proof, we say that a vertex of G is a *high-degree vertex* if its degree is $\sqrt{m}$ or more, otherwise, we say that it is a *low-degree vertex*. Using this definition, we can partition the triangles of G into two types. A triangle belongs to the first type if it contains only high-degree vertices, and to the second type otherwise.

We note that there can be only $2\sqrt{m}$ high-degree vertices in G since the total degree of all the vertices is $2m$. Thus, the number of triangles of the first type, which are triangles that include only such vertices, is upper bounded by

$$O((2\sqrt{m})^3) = O(m^{3/2}).$$

Let us now consider the triangles of the second type. We logically assign every such triangle to one of the low-degree vertices it includes (a triangle of the second type includes such a vertex by definition). One can observe that the number of triangles in which a vertex u participates is upper bounded by $(\deg(u))^2$ — because this expression upper bounds the number of ways in which we can group the neighbors of u into pairs — and thus, $(\deg(u))^2$ also upper bounds the number of triangles that are logically assigned to u. Since every triangle of the second type is logically assigned to some low-degree vertex, we can upper bound the number of triangles of this type by the expression

$$\sum_{\substack{v \in V \\ \deg(v) < \sqrt{m}}} (\deg(v))^2 \leqslant \sqrt{m} \cdot \sum_{\substack{v \in V \\ \deg(v) < \sqrt{m}}} \deg(v) \leqslant \sqrt{m} \cdot 2m = O(m^{3/2}).$$

This completes the proof of the lemma since we have shown that the number of triangles of the first type is also upper bounded by the same asymptotic expression. $\square$

Exercise 5. Show that Lemma 4 is tight by describing a graph with m edges and $\Omega(m^{3/2})$ triangles. Moreover, show that such a graph exists for any large enough number n of vertices.

Given the guarantee of Lemma 4, is it interesting to ask whether there exists an algorithm for listing triangles whose time complexity matches the guarantee of this lemma. It is clear that, as is, Algorithm 2 does not have this property since its time complexity is $\Theta(n^3)$ for every given input. However, this instance-independent time complexity is partially due to the naïve design of Algorithm 2. For example, even when there is no edge between $V[i]$ and $V[j]$, and thus, no triangle can include them both, Algorithm 2 will continue to enumerate many possible options for $V[k]$ and will check for each one of them whether $\{V[i], V[j], V[k]\}$ is a triangle. Algorithm 3 is an alternative implementation of Algorithm 2 that aims to get a speed up by taking advantage of situations of this kind.

The exact time complexity of Algorithm 3 depends on the method used to enumerate over all the neighbors of u that appear after it in the array V. However, let us assume here for simplicity that every vertex has a list of these neighbors. To get an intuitive understanding of the time complexity of Algorithm 3 given this assumption, we study it in the case in which the

---

Algorithm 3: (Faster Triangle Listing (V, E))

1. Assume that V is an array (if it is not, then an array containing all the vertices can be constructed in $O(n)$ time).
2. **for** every vertex $u \in V$ **do**
3.   **for** every neighbor v of u that appears after u in V **do**
4.   **for** every neighbor w of u that appears after v in V **do**
5.   if there is an edge between v and w **then**
6.   Add the triangle $\{u, v, w\}$ to the list of triangles in the graph.

---

input graph is a star. Recall that a *star* is a graph in which there is a single vertex (known as the *center* of the star) that is connected by edges to all the other vertices and there are no additional edges.

If the center of the star happens to be toward the end of the array V, then the time complexity of Algorithm 3 will be on the order of $\Theta(n) = \Theta(m)$ because every vertex has very few neighbors appearing after it in the array V. In contrast, if the center of the star appears toward the beginning of the array V, then the center of the star has $\Theta(n)$ neighbors appearing after it in the array, leading to a time complexity on the order of $\Theta(n^2)$, which is much larger than $O(m^{3/2}) = O(n^{3/2})$.

The above discussion shows that Algorithm 3 performs exceptionally well when the high-degree center of the star appears toward the end of the array V, but performs much worse when this high-degree vertex appears early in V. This intuitively suggests that it might be beneficial to sort the vertices in V according to their degrees because this will imply that the low-degree vertices will tend to appear at the beginning of V and the high-degree vertices will tend to appear at the end of V. In Exercise 6, you are asked to prove that this intuitive suggestion indeed works, and that it allows the time complexity of Algorithm 3 to roughly match the bound implied by Lemma 4.

Exercise 6. Prove that when V is sorted by the degree of its vertices, Algorithm 3 runs in $O(n + m^{3/2})$ time. **Hint:** Use ideas from the proof of Lemma 4.

At this point, we would like to use the ideas developed in the above discussion to get a good Map-Reduce algorithm for triangle listing. As usual, we assume that each edge of the graph is originally located in a different input machine. We also denote by $M(u)$, for every vertex u, a machine that is in charge of the iteration corresponding to u of the loop starting on Line 2 in Algorithm 3. In the first Map-Reduce iteration of the algorithm, every input machine that has an edge $e = (u, v)$ forwards this edge to the machines in charge of both its end points, i.e., the machines $M(u)$ and $M(v)$. Additionally, the input machine forwards e also to machines named $M(u, v)$ and $M(v, u)$ whose role will be explained later.

Note that at this point every machine $M(u)$ has access to all the edges hitting the vertex u. In the second iteration, every machine $M(u)$ uses this information to calculate the degree of u and forwards this information to every neighbor of u. One can observe that after the second iteration the machine $M(u)$ knows the degree of every neighbor of u, and thus, can order the set consisting of them and the vertex u itself according to their degrees. Ideally, we would like to use this order in the third iteration instead of the order of the array V that is used in Algorithm 3. However, to do so we need this order to be consistent across all the machines, i.e., if w and x are neighbors of both u and v, then the orders constructed by $M(u)$ and $M(v)$ should either both place w before x or both place x before w. To guarantee that this is the case, we need to define a more complex way to compare vertices than simply by their degree. Specifically, given two vertices u and v, we say that $u \prec v$ if

- if $\deg(u) < \deg(v)$,
- or $\deg(v) = \deg(w)$, and the label of u is smaller than the label of v (we assume that these labels are represented by numbers).

It is not difficult to see that the comparison operator $\prec$ is transitive, and moreover, for every two vertices $u \neq v$, we have either $u \prec v$ or $v \prec u$ (but not both). Thus, this operator defines an order over the vertices, and it is possible to use the order defined by this operator in place of the order of the array V in Algorithm 3. Accordingly, in the third Map-Reduce iteration, every machine $M(u)$ scans all the pairs of neighbors v and w of u such that $u \prec v \prec w$, and then sends to machine $M(v, w)$ a message indicating that $\{u, v, w\}$ is a suspected triangle. Note that at this point the machine $L(u)$ knows that the edges (u, v) and (u, w) both exist, so the suspected triangle $\{u, v, w\}$ is a real triangle whenever the edge (v, w) exists.

In the fourth, and last, Map-Reduce iteration of the algorithm, every machine $M(v, w)$ does the following. If this machine got an edge (v, w) from an input machine in the first iteration, then the edge (v, w) exists, and thus, every suspected triangle $\{u, v, w\}$ received by $M(v, w)$ is a real triangle, and should be reported as such. Otherwise, the edge (v, w) does not exist, and thus, any suspected triangle reaching $M(v, w)$ should be simply discarded.

Exercise 7. Explain in detail how the above algorithm can be implemented in the Map-Reduce model. In particular, explain the exact messages each machine should send in each iteration.

Let us now discuss the performance measures of the above Map-Reduce algorithm. First, it is clear that this algorithm uses four Map-Reduce iterations. Additionally, the solution of Exercise 6 can be easily adapted to show that the work done by this algorithm is $O(m^{3/2})$.[1] Exercise 8 asks you to analyze the other performance measures of the algorithm.

Exercise 8. Prove that the above Map-Reduce algorithm for triangle counting has machine time and space complexities of $O(m)$ and $O(n \log n)$, respectively, and a total space complexity of $O(m^{3/2} \log n)$.

Theorem 2 summarizes the properties of the Map-Reduce algorithm described above for triangle counting.

Theorem 2. *There exists a Map-Reduce algorithm for triangle counting which uses four iterations, does $O(m^{3/2})$ work, has machine time and space complexities of $O(m)$ and $O(n \log n)$, respectively, and a total space complexity of $O(m^{3/2} \log n)$.*

17.3 Bibliographic Notes

The Map-Reduce algorithm described in this chapter for the Minimum Weight Spanning Tree problem (Algorithm 1) was first presented by Lattanzi *et al.* (2011). This algorithm is based on a filtering technique that was suggested in that paper as a general technique for designing Map-Reduce algorithms for graph problems. In addition to the above algorithm, the paper includes algorithms based on the filtering technique for finding maximal matchings, approximate maximum weight matchings, approximate minimum vertex and edge covers and minimum cuts.

---

[1]Make sure that you understand why that is the case. In particular, note that unlike in Exercise 6, the work done by the Map-Reduce algorithm does not depend on n. This is a consequence of the fact that a vertex that does not appear in any edge is completely missing from the input of the Map-Reduce algorithm.

The offline (non-Map-Reduce) algorithm presented in this chapter for triangle listing (Algorithm 3) can be traced back to the work of Schank and Wagner (2005). This algorithm was adapted to the Map-Reduce framework by Suri and Vassilvitskii (2011) as part of a work that presented two algorithms for triangle listing in the Map-Reduce framework. As discussed above, Lemma 4 shows that the time complexity of Algorithm 3 is essentially optimal because it roughly matches the maximum number of triangles that a graph may have. It is interesting to note, however, that this is not the case for the simpler problem of triangle counting, for which faster algorithms are known (Alon *et al.* 1997).

N. Alon, R. Yuster and U. Zwick. Finding and Counting Given Length Cycles. *Algorithmica*, 17(3): 209–223, 1997.

S. Lattanzi, B. Moseley, S. Suri and S. Vassilvitskii. Filtering: A Method for Solving Graph Problems in MapReduce. In *Proceedings of the 23rd Annual ACM Symposium on Parallelism in Algorithms and Architectures (SPAA)*, 85–94, 2011.

T. Schank and D. Wagner. Finding, Counting and Listing All Triangles in Large Graphs, an Experimental Study. In *Proceedings on the 4th International Workshop on Experimental and Efficient Algorithms (WEA)*, 606–609, 2005.

S. Suri and S. Vassilvitskii. Counting Triangles and the Curse of the Last Reducer. In *Proceedings of the 20th International Conference on World Wide Web (WWW)*, 607–614, 2011.

Exercise Solutions

Solution 1

For every $1 \leqslant j \leqslant p_i$, the forest $F_{i,j}$ contains at most $n-1$ edges because it is a forest with n vertices. Thus,

$$|E_i| = \left| \bigcup_{j=1}^{p_i} E(F_{i,j}) \right| = \sum_{i=1}^{p_i} |E(F_{i,j})| \leqslant p_i n = \lceil |E_{i-1}|/M \rceil \cdot n$$

$$\leqslant 2(|E_{i-1}|/M) \cdot n = (2n/M) \cdot |E_{i-1}|, \tag{17.1}$$

where the second equality holds since the forests $F_{i,1}, F_{i,2}, \ldots, F_{i,p_i}$ are edge-disjoint and the second inequality holds since the fact that Algorithm 1 started the ith iteration implies that the size of E_{i-1} was at least M.

Let us now explain why Inequality (17.1) implies an upper bound on the number of iterations performed by Algorithm 1. Assume by way of contradiction that Algorithm 1 performs at least $\hat{\imath} = \lceil \log_{M/(2n)} m + 1 \rceil$ iterations. Then, by repeatedly applying Inequality (17.1) we get

$$|E_{\hat{\imath}-1}| \leqslant (2n/M)^{\hat{\imath}-1} \cdot |E_0| \leqslant (2n/M)^{\log_{M/(2n)} m} \cdot |E_0| = \frac{|E_0|}{m} = \frac{|E|}{m} = 1.$$

However, this implies $|E_{\hat{\imath}-1}| \leqslant M$ (since we assume $M \geqslant 3n$), and thus, contradicts our assumption that the algorithm started iteration number $\hat{\imath}$.

Solution 2

The Map-Reduce implementation of Algorithm 1 repeatedly applies the following three Map-Reduce iterations. Note that a machine executing the code of the first of these Map-Reduce iterations stops the algorithm and generates an output when it gets the message "terminate" from the previous Map-Reduce iteration. One can also verify that only a single machine (named $L(i, 1)$ for some i) gets the message "terminate", and thus, the algorithm always outputs a single forest.

Iteration 1. Calculate a minimum weight spanning forest F of the edges of G that this machine got at the end of the previous Map-Reduce iteration (if this is the first iteration, then this machine must be an input machine that got a single edge of G, in which case the calculated forest F contains exactly this edge). If the machine also got at the end of the previous iteration the message "terminate", then stop the algorithm at this point and output the forest F. Otherwise, forward the name of this machine and the number of edges of the forest F to the machine named "counter". Additionally, forward the edges of F to the current machine in order to keep them.

Iteration 2. In this iteration, every machine other than "counter" simply preserves the forest F that it calculated in the previous iteration by forwarding the edges of this forest to itself. The "counter" machine got a list of machines and a list of numbers. It then adds up all the numbers it got (to get the number edges in all the forests together), and forwards this sum to all the machines whose name it has got.

Iteration 3. Let t be the value obtained from the "counter" machine, and calculate $p = \lceil t/M \rceil$. Additionally, determine i as follows: if this machine has a name of the form $L(i, j)$, then use the value of i from this name. Otherwise, if this machine is an input machine, let $i = 0$. Then, for every edge $e \in E(F)$, choose uniformly and independently an integer value j_e between 1 and p and forward e to the machine named $L(i + 1, j_e)$. If $p = 1$, forward to $L(i + 1, 1)$ also the message "terminate" (note that in this case $L(i + 1, 1)$ receives all the edges that are still kept by the algorithm).

Solution 3

In this solution, we assume that every machine of the form $L(i, j)$ gets at most $2M$ edges, which happens with high probability by Corollary 2.

Observe that every input machine of Algorithm 1 receives a single edge, and then, it only needs to send this edge to the appropriate machines of the form $L(u)$. Hence, the space required by the input machine is the space required for storing a single edge, which is $O(\log n)$, and the time required for the machine is constant.

Consider now a machine whose name is of one of the forms $L(u)$ or $L(i, j)$. Such a machine gets at most $2M$ edges by Observation 1 and the assumption we have made above. Additionally, the machine gets the value p_i, which is a number of value at most n. Thus, all the information that the machine gets can be stored in $O(M \log n)$ space. Since the machine does not require significant additional space for its calculations, this is also the space complexity used by this machine. Finally, we observe that the time complexity of the machine is upper bounded by $O(M \log n)$ because the calculations done by the machine are dominated by the time required to compute a minimum spanning forest in the graph containing the edges of the machine, which can be done in $O(\min\{M, m\} \log \min\{M, m\}) = O(M \log n)$ time using Kruskal's algorithm.

The counter machine remains to be considered. Every time that this machine gets messages, it gets at most n messages by Lemma 3. Since each one of these messages is a count of edges, they are all numbers of value at most n^2. Hence, all the values this machine gets can be stored in $O(n \log n)$ space, and so can their sum, which is the value calculated by the counter machine. We also observe that the time complexity of the counter machine is linear in the number of messages it gets and, thus, is upper bounded by $O(n)$.

Combining all the above, we get that under our assumption the machine space and time complexities of Algorithm 1 are

$$\max\{O(\log n), O(M \log n), O(n \log n)\} = O(M \log n)$$

and

$$\max\{O(1), O(M \log n), O(n)\} = O(M \log n),$$

respectively.

Solution 4

Algorithm 1 uses randomness to partition in iteration i the set E_{i-1} into few subsets that contain $O(M)$ edges each. The use of randomness for that purpose is natural since the algorithm does not assume anything about the way in which the edges of E_{i-1} are partitioned between the machines before the iteration begins. However, one can observe that our implementation of Algorithm 1 gives a natural upper bound of n on the number of edges stored in each one of these machines. Thus, by grouping these machines into groups of a given size and then combining all the edges of the machines in a group, we can deterministically get a partition of E_{i-1} into few sets of size $O(M)$ each.

Following is a Map-Reduce algorithm based on the above idea. The algorithm starts with the pre-process iteration, which is similar to the pre-process iteration from the implementation of Algorithm 1, but sends the input edge (u, v) to machine $L(0, u)$ rather than $L(u)$. We assume here that every vertex u is represented by a number between 1 and n, and thus, the machines that get edges during this pre-process iteration are the machines $L(0, j)$ for every integer j between 1 and n.

Pre-process Iteration (performed by the input machines): Send the input edge (u, v) to the machine $L(0, u)$.

After the pre-process iteration, the algorithm performs repeatedly the next iteration until one of the machines stops the execution. Intuitively, this iteration corresponds to the three Map-Reduce iterations from the implementation of Algorithm 1. We note that we are able to combine here the three iterations into a single one because the current algorithm can calculate based on i a bound on the number of machines that have edges, which removes the need to calculate p_i.

Repeated Iteration: Let $L(i, j)$ be the name of this machine, and calculate a minimum weight spanning forest F of the edges of G that this machine got at the end of the previous iteration. If $i \geqslant \log_{M/(2n)} n$, stop the algorithm at this point and output the forest F. Otherwise, forward the edges of F to $L(i + 1, \lceil jn/M \rceil)$.

The analysis of the above Map-Reduce algorithm is very similar to the analysis of Algorithm 1. Thus, we only prove that every machine in it gets $O(M)$ edges and that it outputs a single forest F after at most $O(\log_{M/n} n)$ Map-Reduce iterations.

Lemma 5. *Every machine $L(i, j)$ gets $O(M)$ edges.*

Proof. For $i = 0$, the lemma holds since machine $L(0, u)$ gets only edges incident to u, and there can be at most n such edges. Consider now some integer $i \geqslant 1$, and consider an arbitrary machine $L(i, j)$. This machine gets edges only from machines $L(i - 1, j')$ such that

$$\lceil j'n/M \rceil = j.$$

One can observe that there can be only $\lceil M/n \rceil$ such machines. Moreover, the number of edges forwarded to $L(i, j)$ from each one of these machines is upper bounded by n since each machine forwards a forest. Thus, the number of edges $L(i, j)$ receives is at most $\lceil M/n \rceil \cdot n \leqslant M + n = O(M)$.
$\square$

Lemma 6. *The above Map-Reduce algorithm stops after $O(\log_{M/n} n)$ Map-Reduce iterations and outputs a single forest.*

Proof. It is clear that besides the pre-processing iteration, the Map-Reduce algorithm performs exactly $1 + \lceil \log_{M/2n} n \rceil = O(\log_{M/n} n)$ iterations. Thus, we concentrate on proving the other part of the lemma.

Consider an arbitrary machine $L(i, j)$ appearing during the execution of the algorithm. If this machine forwards edges, it forwards them to machine $L(i + 1, \lceil jn/M \rceil)$. We note that the number $\lceil jn/M \rceil$ is 1 when $j \leqslant M/n$ and is upper bounded by

$$jn/M + 1 = (j + M/n)/(M/n) \leqslant j/(M/(2n))$$

for larger values of j. Thus, the range of j values for which the machine $L(i, j)$ gets edges consists of the integers between 1 and n when $i = 0$ and reduces by a factor of $M/(2n)$ every time that i increases by 1 unless its size was already upper bounded by M/n, in which case it reduces to 1. Hence, for $i \geqslant \log_{M/(2n)} n$ (and thus, also when the algorithm stops) there is only a single machine $L(i, j)$ which has edges.
$\square$

Solution 5

Let n' be the largest integer such that $n'(n'-1)/2 \leqslant m$, and let us assume that m is large enough to guarantee that $n' \geqslant 3$ (since the exercise only asks us for a graph with $\Omega(m)$ triangles, it suffices to consider large enough values of m).

Consider now an arbitrary graph that contains a clique of n' vertices and m edges. Clearly, there is such a graph with any large enough number n of vertices (as long as we allow some vertices to have a degree of zero). Additionally, since the definition n' guarantees that $n'(n'+1) > 2m$, the number of triangles in the clique of this graph is

$$\frac{n'(n'-1)(n'-2)}{6} \geqslant \frac{n'(n'+1)^2}{48} \geqslant \frac{[n'(n'+1)]^{3/2}}{48} > \frac{m^{3/2}}{24} = O(m^{3/2}).$$

Solution 6

Given a vertex $u \in V$, let $N(u)$ be the set of neighbors of u that appear after u in the array V. Note that since we assume that V is sorted, the vertices in $N(u)$ must have a degree which is at least as high as the degree of u. Let us say, like in the proof of Lemma 4, that a vertex is a high-degree vertex if its degree is at least $\sqrt{m}$, and a low-degree vertex otherwise.

Our next objective is to prove the inequality

$$|N(u)| \leqslant \min\{2\deg(u), 2\sqrt{m}\}. \tag{17.2}$$

If u is a low-degree vertex, then this inequality holds because the fact that $N(u)$ contains only neighbors of u implies $|N(u)| \leqslant \deg(u) < \sqrt{m}$. Otherwise, if u is a high-degree vertex, then every vertex in $N(u)$ must have a degree of at least $\deg(u) \geqslant \sqrt{m}$. Since the total degree of all the vertices is $2m$, this implies $|N(u)| \leqslant 2\sqrt{m} \leqslant 2 \cdot \deg(u)$, and thus, Inequality (17.2) holds in this case as well.

At this point, we have completed the proof that Inequality (17.2) holds for every vertex $u \in V$, so it remains to be explained why it implies the lemma. For every vertex $u \in V$, Algorithm 3 does a work which is of the order of $1 + (|N(u)|)^2$ because it checks every pair v, w of vertices from $N(u)$. Hence, the total time complexity of the algorithm is on the order of

$$\sum_{u \in V}[1 + (|N(u)|)^2] \leqslant \sum_{u \in V}[1 + 4\sqrt{m} \cdot \deg(u)] = n + 4\sqrt{m} \cdot \sum_{u \in V} \deg(u)$$

$$= n + 4\sqrt{m} \cdot 2m = O(n + m^{3/2}).$$

Solution 7

Following is a detailed implementation in the Map-Reduce model of the algorithm described before the exercise.

Iteration 1. Every input machine that received an edge (u, v) forwards this edge to the machines $M(u, v)$ and $M(v, u)$. Additionally, it forwards the vertex u to $M(v)$ and the vertex v to $M(u)$.

Iteration 2. Every machine whose name is of the form $M(u, v)$ that received an edge during the previous iteration just forwards this information to itself. Consider now a machine whose name is of the form $M(u)$. Every such machine got from the previous iteration a list of the neighbors of the vertex u. In this iteration, this machine determines $\deg(u)$ by counting its neighbors, and forwards the pair $(u, \deg(u))$ to every neighbor of u and to itself — so that it will be available to $M(u)$ itself in the next iteration.

Iteration 3. Every machine whose name is of the form $M(u, v)$ that received an edge during the previous iteration forwards this information again to itself. Consider now a machine whose name is of the form $M(u)$. Every such machine got from the previous iteration pairs $(v, \deg(v))$ for every vertex v that is either u itself or a neighbor of u. In this iteration, this machine finds the set $N'(u)$ of the neighbors of u that appear after u itself according to the order defined by the operator $\prec$ (we note that this can be done since $M(u)$ has access to the degree of u and the degrees of all the neighbors of u). Then, for every distinct pair v, w of vertices from $N'(u)$, the machine forwards the node u to $M(v, w)$.

Iteration 4. For every machine whose name is of the form $M(u, v)$, if this machine got an edge from the previous iteration and at least one individual vertex, then for every individual vertex w that it received, it outputs the triangle $\{u, v, w\}$.

Solution 8

Let us consider the four iterations of the algorithm one after the other as follows:

- In the first iteration, every input machine forwards either the edge it got or a part of it to four machines. This requires $O(1)$ time and a space of $O(\log n)$, which is the space required for storing an edge (we assume here that a vertex can be stored using $O(\log n)$ space). The total space used by all the machines in this iteration is $O(m \log n)$ since there are m input machines, one for every edge of the input graph.

- In the second iteration, the machines whose name is of the form $M(u, v)$ simply forward to themselves the edge they got, which requires $O(1)$ time, $O(\log n)$ space per machine and $O(m \log n)$ space in total. The machines whose name is of the form $M(u)$ have to store all the neighbors of their vertex, count them and send the resulting degree to the machines in charge of these neighbors. This might require $O(n \log n)$ space and $O(m)$ time per machine — note that we bound here the degree of a vertex by n for the analysis of the space complexity and by m for the analysis of the time complexity. The total space complexity of all these machines is $O(\log n)$ times the sum of the degrees of all the vertices of the graph, which is $2m$, and thus, it is $O(m \log n)$. Adding up the numbers we got for the two kinds of machines, we get in this iteration machine time and space complexities of $O(m)$ and $O(n \log n)$, respectively, and a total space complexity of $O(m \log n)$.

- In the third iteration, the machines whose name is of the form $M(u, v)$ again simply forward to themselves the edge they got, which requires $O(1)$ time and $O(\log n)$ space per machine and $O(m \log n)$ space in total. The machines whose name is of the form $M(u)$ have to store the neighbors of u and the degrees of these neighbors, and then enumerate over all the pairs of these neighbors that are larger than u according to $\prec$. This requires $O(n \log n)$ space per machine, and $O(m \log n)$ space in total (because the sum of all the degrees of the vertices in the graph is $2m$).

  Determining the amount of time this requires per machine is slightly more involved. For a vertex u of degree at most $\sqrt{m}$, the time required is at most $O((\deg(u))^2) = O(m)$. Consider now a vertex u of degree at least $\sqrt{m}$. Since there can be at most $2\sqrt{m}$ vertices of the degree $\sqrt{m}$ or more, there can only be $2\sqrt{m}$ neighbors of u that appear after u according to $\prec$. Thus, the machine time complexity of $M(u)$ is upper bounded by $O((\sqrt{m})^2) = O(m)$.

  Adding up the numbers we got for the two kinds of machines, we get in this iteration machine time and space complexities of $O(m)$ and $O(n \log n)$, respectively, and a total space complexity of $O(m \log n)$.

- In the final iteration, each machine $M(u, v)$ might get a single message of size $O(\log n)$ from every machine $M(w)$. Thus, it uses $O(n \log n)$ space. For every such message, the machine has to output a single triangle, which requires $O(m)$ time because every machine $M(w)$

that sends a message to $M(u, v)$ must be associated with a vertex w with a non-zero degree. The total space complexity required by all the $M(u, v)$ machines is $O((m + t) \log n)$, where t is the number of suspected triangles because every machine $M(u, v)$ that gets t' suspected triangles requires $O((1 + t') \log n)$ space. It can be verified that the proof of Lemma 4 applies also to suspected triangles, and thus, $t = O(m^{3/2})$, which implies a total space complexity of $O(m^{3/2} \log n)$ for the iteration.

The above analysis solves the exercise because it shows that the algorithm obeys in every given iteration the machine time and space complexities and total space complexity specified by the exercise.

Chapter 18

Locality-Sensitive Hashing

An Internet search engine finds many results for a query. Often some of these results are near duplicates of other results.[1] Given this situation, most search engines will try to eliminate the near duplicate search results to avoid producing a very repetitive output. To do so, the search engine must be able to detect pairs of results that are similar. Consider now an online shopping service. Such services often try to recommend items to users, and one of the easiest ways to do this is to recommend an item that was bought by one user to other users that share a similar taste. However, to use this strategy, the online shopping service must be able to detect pairs of users that bought similar items in the past, and thus, can be assumed to have a similar taste.

The tasks that the search engine and the online shopping service need to perform in the above scenarios are just two examples of the more general problem of finding pairs of elements in a set that are similar based on a certain similarity measure. This general problem is very basic, and captures many additional practical problems besides the above two examples. Thus, a lot of research was done on non-trivial techniques to solve it. In this chapter, we will present one such interesting technique, which is known as *locality-sensitive hashing*.

---

[1]Two common examples for this phenomenon are a site which is hosted on multiple mirrors and sites corresponding to different semesters of the same course.

It should be noted that the subject of this chapter is not particularly related to Map-Reduce (despite the membership of this chapter in the Map-Reduce part of the book). Nevertheless, due to the usefulness of the locality-sensitive hashing technique in Big Data scenarios, it is often implemented in practice using Map-Reduce algorithms.

18.1 Main Idea

Given a set S, the easiest way to find pairs of elements of S that are similar is to simply compare every pair of elements of S. Unfortunately, this naïve strategy requires $\Theta(|S|^2)$ comparisons, and is thus, non-practical when the set S is large. To speed up the process of finding similar elements, we need some kind of *oracle* that can quickly find pairs that are likely to be similar. Then, we can compare only the elements within these likely pairs, and find out which of them are really similar.

An oracle for this purpose should have two (somewhat contradicting) properties. First, we would like it to output few *false-positive* pairs (a false-positive pair is a pair of far elements that the oracle marks as likely to be similar). This property is important because we make a comparison for every pair produced by the oracle, and thus, the use of the oracle is likely to lead to a significant speedup only if the oracle does not mark too many pairs as likely to be similar. The second property that we would like the oracle to have is that it should have few *false-negative* pairs (a false-negative is a pair of similar elements that is not marked as likely to be similar by the oracle). We need this property to guarantee that the speedup that we get by using the oracle does not come at the cost of missing too many similar pairs.

One way to get an oracle of the above kind is via a *locality-sensitive hash functions family*. Such a family is a set of hash functions from S to some range, which has the intuitive property that for any two given elements e_1, $e_2 \in S$ the probability of a hash function drawn uniformly at random from the family to map e_1 and e_2 to the same range item is related to the distance between e_1 and e_2. To make this definition more concrete, let us define for every real value c the function $f_c(x) = \lceil (x - c)/10 \rceil$. Then, the set of functions $F = \{f_c | c \in [0, 10)\}$ can be viewed as a family of hash functions mapping real numbers to integers. Exercise 1 shows that the probability of a hash function drawn uniformly at random from F to map two real numbers to the same integer diminishes as the distance between

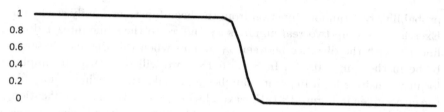

Figure 18.1. The ideal relationship between the distance of two elements e_1, $e_2 \in S$ and the probability that they are mapped to the same range item by a random function from a locality-sensitive hashing functions family. Elements that are close to each other are very likely to be mapped to the same range item, elements that are far from each other are very unlikely to be mapped to the same range item, and the "transition zone" between these two regimes is small.

the numbers increases, and thus, shows that F is a locality-sensitive hash functions family.[2]

Exercise 1. Prove that for any two given numbers x_1 and x_2, if f is a hash function drawn uniformly at random from F, then

$$\Pr[f(x_1) = f(x_2)] = \max\left\{0, 1 - \frac{|x_1 - x_2|}{10}\right\}.$$

Given a locality-sensitive family F of hash functions, one can construct an oracle of the kind described above by drawing a uniformly random function f from F and then applying it to all the elements of S. The oracle then reports a pair of S elements as likely to be similar if and only if both elements of the pair are mapped by f to the same range item. This procedure can often be done very efficiently, and moreover, it results in few false-positives and false-negatives when the probability of two elements e_1, $e_2 \in S$ to be mapped to the same range item by f depends on their distance from each other in a way resembling the S-shaped curve given by Figure 18.1.

Unfortunately, most natural constructions of locality-sensitive hash functions families do not produce such a nice dependence of the probability on the distance. In the typical case, there is a significant range of distances in which the probability is neither close to 0 nor to 1. For example, the

---

[2]We would like to stress that being "a locality-sensitive hash functions family" is an intuitive notion without a formal definition. However, there is a formal way to measure the quality of such a family, and we present it in Section 18.3.

probability of a random function from the hash functions family studied in Exercise 1 to map two real numbers x_1 and x_2 to the same integer drops linearly with the distance between x_1 and x_2 when this distance happens to be in the range $[0, 10]$. In Section 18.3, we will see a way to amplify locality-sensitive hash functions families and make them behave more like the curve given in Figure 18.1. However, before getting to this amplification, we present in Section 18.2 some examples of locality-sensitive hash functions families.

18.2 Examples of Locality-Sensitive Hash Functions Families

In this section, we consider a few *distance measures* (i.e., ways to measure distance between objects), and present appropriate locality-sensitive hash functions families for these measures. The first distance measure we consider is the *Hamming distance* between vectors. Given two vectors x, y with n coordinates, the Hamming distance between x and y — which we denote by $\text{dist}_H(x, y)$ — is defined as the number of coordinates in which x and y differ. For example, if $x = (0, 0, 1, 1, 0)$ and $y = (1, 0, 1, 0, 0)$, then the Hamming distance between x and y is 2 because the vectors $(0, 0, 1, 1, 0)$ and $(1, 0, 1, 0, 0)$ differ in two coordinates (the first and the fourth).

Let us denote by f_i the function which given a vector with n coordinates outputs the ith coordinate of this vector, and let $F_H = \{f_i | 1 \leqslant i \leqslant n\}$. Exercise 2 asks you to show that F_H is a locality-sensitive hash functions family with respect to the Hamming distance.

> **Exercise 2.** Show that for every two vectors x and y with n coordinates and a uniformly random function $f_i \in F_H$, it holds that $\Pr[f_i(x) = f_i(y)] = 1 - \text{dist}_H(x, y)/n$.

The Hamming distance measure is defined for any two vectors with the same number of coordinates. Another distance measure for vectors, known as the *angular distance*, is defined for non-zero vectors in vector spaces that have an inner product. To keep the presentation of this distance measure simple, we will restrict ourselves to non-zero vectors in $\mathbb{R}^n$ — recall that $\mathbb{R}^n$ consists of the vectors with n coordinates whose individual coordinates are real numbers. For such vectors, the angular distance between two vectors is simply the angle between them. Let us denote by $\text{dist}_\theta(x, y)$ the angular distance between vectors x and y.

Figure 18.2. Two vectors x and y with a low angle between them and a third vector z. Note that the angle between x and z is similar to the angle between y and z.

To design a locality-sensitive hashing functions family for the angular distance, we observe that for two vectors x and y with a small angle between them and an arbitrary third vector z, it is always true that the angle between x and z is close to the angle between y and z (see Figure 18.2). More formally, we have the following inequality:

$$|\text{dist}_\theta(x, z) - \text{dist}_\theta(y, z)| \leqslant \text{dist}_\theta(x, y).^3$$

This observation suggests an interesting way to check whether two vectors x and y have a small angle between them: pick a vector z with a uniformly random direction and check whether there is a correlation between the event that $\text{dist}_\theta(x, z)$ happens to be small and the event that $\text{dist}_\theta(y, z)$ happens to be small. One can implement this idea using a hash functions family as follows. For every vector z, we define

$$f_z(x) = \begin{cases} 1 & \text{if } \text{dist}_\theta(x, z) \geqslant 90°, \\ 0 & \text{otherwise.} \end{cases}$$

Then, the hash functions family is $F_\theta = \{f_z | z \text{ is a unit length vector in } \mathbb{R}^n\}$. This hash functions family is locality sensitive, and obeys

$$\Pr[f_z(x) = f_z(y)] = 1 - \frac{\text{dist}_\theta(x, y)}{180°} \tag{18.1}$$

for any two non-zero vectors $x, y \in \mathbb{R}^n$ and a function f_z drawn uniformly at random from F_θ. Exercise 3 asks you to prove this for $\mathbb{R}^2$.

Exercise 3. Prove that Equality (18.1) holds when x and y are arbitrary non-zero vectors in $\mathbb{R}^2$ and f_z is a uniformly random function from F_θ.

---

[3]Note that this inequality is equivalent to the triangle inequality.

Let us now consider a distance measure between sets which is known as the *Jaccard distance*. The Jaccard distance between two non-empty sets S_1 and S_2 is defined as the fraction of the elements of $S_1 \cup S_2$ that do not belong to both sets. More formally, the Jaccard distance $\text{dist}_J(S_1, S_2)$ between S_1 and S_2 is given by

$$\text{dist}_J(S_1, S_2) = 1 - \frac{|S_1 \cap S_2|}{|S_1 \cup S_2|}.$$

The Jaccard distance is very useful in practice because sets are a very general abstraction that can capture many practical objects. In particular, the Jaccard distance is often used to determine the distance between documents (but for this distance measure to make sense for this application, one has to carefully choose the method used to convert each document into a set).

From the definition of the Jaccard distance, it is easy to see that $1 - \text{dist}_J(S_1, S_2)$ is equal to the probability that a random element of $S_1 \cup S_2$ belongs to the intersection of these sets. A natural way to convert this observation into a hash function family is as follows. Let N be the ground set that contains all the possible elements. Then, for every element $e \in N$, we define a function

$$f_e(S) = \begin{cases} 1 & \text{if } e \in S, \\ 0 & \text{otherwise} \end{cases}.$$

Let $F_{J'} = \{f_e | e \in N\}$ be the hash functions family containing all these functions. Unfortunately, Exercise 4 shows that $F_{J'}$ is not a good locality-sensitive family because the probability $\Pr[f_e(S_1) = f_e(S_2)]$ strongly depends on the size of $S_1 \cup S_2$ (which makes this hash function family treat small sets as close to each other even when their Jaccard distance is quite large).

Exercise 4. Prove that for any two non-empty sets S_1 and S_2 and a uniformly random function $f_e \in F_{J'}$ it holds that

$$\Pr[f_e(S_1) = f_e(S_2)] = 1 - \frac{|S_1 \cup S_2| \cdot \text{dist}_J(S_1, S_2)}{|N|}.$$

Intuitively, the failure of the hash functions family $F_{J'}$ to be a good locality-sensitive family stems from the fact that the element e is a random element of N rather than a random element of $S_1 \cup S_2$, which makes a large difference for small sets. Thus, to get a better locality-sensitive hash functions family, we need each function in the family to behave as if it is defined by some element of $S_1 \cup S_2$. This might look like an impossible task because the functions of the family are not defined with respect to a particular pair of sets. However, it is possible to work around this difficulty by creating a hash function for every possible permutation π of N, and making the function f_π associated with the permutation π behave as if it is defined by the first element of $S_1 \cup S_2$ according to the permutation π. More concretely, we define for every permutation π the function $f_\pi(S)$ whose value is the first element of S according to the permutation π. Let us now define the hash functions family $F_J = \{f_\pi | \pi$ is a permutation of $N\}$. Exercise 5 shows that the functions of this family have the intuitive behavior described above, and that the family itself is locality sensitive.

Exercise 5. Observe that, for every two sets S_1 and S_2 and a permutation π of N, $f_\pi(S_1) = f_\pi(S_2)$ if and only if the first element of $S_1 \cup S_2$ according to the permutation π appears also in the intersection of the two sets. Then, use this observation to show that

$$\Pr[f_\pi(S_1) = f_\pi(S_2)] = 1 - \text{dist}_J(S_1, S_2)$$

when f_π is drawn uniformly at random from F_J.

18.3 Amplifying Locality-Sensitive Hash Functions Families

As noted above, in most natural examples of locality-sensitive hash functions families (including all the examples we have seen so far), the probability of two elements to be mapped to the same range item decreases in a moderate rate as the distance between the elements increases. This is very different from the ideal situation (depicted in Figure 18.1) in which this probability is close to 1 for close elements, and drops quickly to roughly 0 when the elements become slightly less close.

In this section, we present a way to amplify the locality-sensitive hash functions family and make their behavior closer to the ideal. To do so, we need a formal definition for the quality of such families. We say that a hash functions family F is (d_1, d_2, p_1, p_2)-*sensitive* for $d_1 < d_2$ and $p_1 > p_2$ if

- $\Pr[f(e_1) = f(e_2)] \geqslant p_1$ for any pair of elements e_1 and e_2 at distance at most d_1 from each other and a random hash function $f \in F$.
- $\Pr[f(e_1) = f(e_2)] \leqslant p_2$ for any pair of elements e_1 and e_2 at distance at least d_2 from each other and a random hash function $f \in F$.

Exercise 6. Prove that the hash functions family F_J defined in Section 18.2 is $(1/5, 2/5, 4/5, 3/5)$-sensitive.

We are now ready to describe two amplification operations that can be applied to a hash functions family in order to improve its parameters. The first of these operations is the *AND-construction*. Given a (d_1, d_2, p_1, p_2)-sensitive hash functions family F and an integer r, the r-AND-construction of F is a hash functions family G defined as follows. For every set of r (not necessarily distinct) functions $f_1, f_2, \ldots, f_r \in F$, the family G contains a function

$$g_{f_1, f_2, \ldots f_r}(x) = (f_1(x), f_2(x), \ldots, f_r(x)).$$

More intuitively, every function of G corresponds to r functions of F and it returns the same range item for two elements e_1 and e_2 if and only if all the r functions of F return the same range item for e_1 and e_2.

Exercise 7. Prove that G is (d_1, d_2, p_1^r, p_2^r)-sensitive.

The AND-construction reduces the probability of two elements to be mapped to the same range item regardless of their distance. However, the reduction is more substantial for elements that are far from each other. Mathematically, this is exhibited in Exercise 7 by the fact that the ratio p_1^r/p_2^r increases with r (recall that $p_1 \geq p_2$). Nevertheless, to get a close to ideal locality-sensitive hash functions family, we need a way to once again increase the probability of elements that are close to each other to be mapped to the same range item. The second augmentation operation, named *OR-construction*, is useful for this purpose.

Given a (d_1, d_2, p_1, p_2)-sensitive hash functions family F and an integer r, the r-OR-construction of F is a hash functions family G defined as follows. For every set of r (not necessarily distinct) functions $f_1, f_2, \ldots, f_r \in F$, the family G contains a function

$$g_{f_1, f_2, \ldots f_r}(x) = (f_1(x), f_2(x), \ldots, f_r(x)),$$

and two r-tuples produced by $g_{f_1, f_2, \ldots f_r}$ are considered equal if and only if they agree on at least one coordinate.[4] On an intuitive level, an

---

[4]Note that the equality operation defined here is unusual as it is not transitive. This is fine for the theoretical analysis done in this section, but makes the implementation of these ideas more involved. Some discussion of this issue appears in the solution of Exercise 9.

OR-construction is very similar to an AND-construction, with the sole difference being that now a function $g \in G$ corresponding to r functions $f_1, f_2, \ldots, f_r \in F$ outputs the same range item for two elements u and v if and only if at least one of the functions $f_1, f_2, \ldots, f_r$ outputs the same range item for both elements.

Exercise 8. Prove that the r-OR-construction G is $(d_1, d_2, 1 - (1 - p_1)^r, 1 - (1 - p_2)^r)$-sensitive.

As promised, the OR-construction increases the probability of any pair of elements to be mapped to the same range item. However, this increase is more prominent for close elements, as is mathematically demonstrated by the fact that $(1 - p_1)^r / (1 - p_2)^r$ is a decreasing function of r. Thus, the OR-construction can be used to counterbalance the effect of the AND-construction on close elements.

To make the use of the AND-construction and the OR-construction easier to understand, we now demonstrate it on a concrete example. Recall the locality-sensitive hash functions family F_J described in Section 18.2 for the Jaccard distance between sets. Exercise 5 showed that for a uniformly random function $f \in F_J$, the probability that f maps two sets S_1 and S_2 at distance d from each other to the same range item is $1 - d$. Figure 18.3(a) depicts this linear relationship between the distance and the probability of being mapped to the same range item. According to Exercise 6, the family F_J is $(1/5, 2/5, 4/5, 3/5)$-sensitive. Hence, if we consider sets at distance less than $1/5$ as "close" and sets at distance of more than $2/5$ as "far", then close sets are more likely than far sets to be mapped to the same range item, but not by much.

Let us now use the AND-construction and OR-construction to increase the gap between the probabilities of close and far sets to be mapped to the same range item. First, let us denote by F' the 20-AND-construction of F_J. Using Exercise 7, one can show that F' is $(1/5, 2/5, 0.0115, 0.0000366)$-sensitive (verify this!). Hence, the probability of close sets to be mapped to the same range item is now more than 300 times as large as the corresponding probability for far sets. However, even quite close sets are not very likely to be mapped to the same range item by F', as is demonstrated in Figure 18.3(b), which depicts the probability of a pair of sets to be mapped to the same range item by F' as a function of the distance between the sets. To fix that, we consider the 400-OR-construction of F'. Let us denote this 400-OR-construction by F''. Using Exercise 8, one can show that F'' is $(1/5, 2/5, 0.99, 0.015)$-sensitive (verify this also!), which means that close

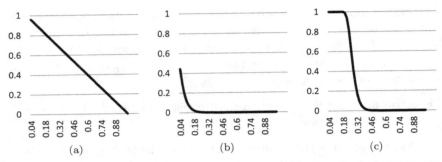

Figure 18.3. The probability of two sets to be mapped to the same range item, as a function of the distance between the sets, by a random hash function from (a) F_J, (b) F' and (c) F''.

sets have a probability of 0.99 to be mapped by F'' to the same range item, and for far sets this probability drops to as low as 0.015. A graphical demonstration of the nice properties of F'' is given by Figure 18.3(c), which depicts the probability of a pair of sets to be mapped to the same range item by a random function from F'' as a function of the distance between the sets. One can note that the shape of the graph in Figure 18.3(c) resembles the ideal shape described in Figure 18.1.

Exercise 9. The following is a natural Map-Reduce procedure that uses a locality-sensitive hash functions family F to find pairs of input elements that are suspected to be close to each other.

(1) A central machine draws a uniformly random function f from F, and this function is distributed to all the input machines.
(2) Every input machine applies f to the element e it got, and then forwards e to the machine named $f(e)$.
(3) Every non-input machine named M gets all the elements mapped by f to M. All these elements are reported as suspected to be close to each other (because they are all mapped by f to the same range item M).

The following parts of the exercise discuss some implementation details for the above procedure.

(a) Discuss the best way to distribute the random function f drawn by the central machine to all the input machines.
(b) The above procedure assumes that two outputs of f are considered equal if and only if they are identical. Unfortunately, this is not true for the OR-construction. Suggest a way to make the procedure work also for a hash functions family F obtained via an OR-construction.

18.4 Bibliographic Notes

The notion of the locality-sensitive hash functions family, and the formal way to quantify them using (d_1, d_2, p_1, p_2)-sensitivity, was first suggested by Indyk and Motwani (1998) and Gionis *et al.* (1999). The first of these works also noted that the hash functions family described in Section 3.4.2 for the Jaccard distance is locality sensitive. This hash functions family is often referred to as Min-Hashing, and it was first suggested by Broder *et al.* (1997, 1998). The locality-sensitive hash functions family described above for angular distance was suggested by Charkiar (2002). The same work also suggested such a family for another common distance measure known as the earth mover distance.

More information about locality-sensitive hashing, including the AND-construction and OR-construction described in Section 3.4.3, can be found in Leskovec (2014).

A. Z. Broder, M. Charikar, A. M. Frieze, and Michael Mitzenmacher. Min-wise Independent Permutations. In *Proceedings of the 30th ACM Symposium on Theory of Computing (STOC)*, 327–336, 1998.

A. Z. Broder, S. C. Glassman, M. S. Manasse and G. Zweig. Syntactic Clustering of the Web. *Computer Networks*, 29(8–13): 1157–1166, 1997.

M. S. Charikar. Similarity Estimation Techniques from Rounding Algorithms. In *Proceedings of the 34th ACM Symposium on Theory of Computing (STOC)*, 380–388, 2002.

A. Gionis, P. Indyk and R. Motwani. Similarity Search in high Dimensions via Hashing. In *Proceedings of the 25th International Conference on Very LargeData Bases (VLDB)*, 518–529, 1999.

P. Indyk and R. Motwani. Approximate Nearest Neighbor: Towards Removing the Curse of Dimensionality. In *Proceedings of the 30th ACM Symposium on Theory of Computing (STOC)*, 604–613, 1998.

J. Leskovec, A. Rajaraman and J. D. Ullman. Finding Similar Items. *Mining of Massive Datasets*, 73–130, 2014.

Exercise Solutions

Solution 1

Let c be a uniformly random value from the range $[0, 10)$, then the definition of the family F implies

$$\Pr[f(x_1) = f(x_2)] = \Pr[f_c(x_1) = f_c(x_2)] = \Pr\left[\left\lceil \frac{x_1 - c}{10} \right\rceil = \left\lceil \frac{x_2 - c}{10} \right\rceil\right].$$

To understand the event $\lceil (x_1 - c)/10 \rceil = \lceil (x_2 - c)/10 \rceil$, let us assume that the real line is partitioned into disjoint ranges $(10i, 10(i + 1)]$ for every integer i. Given this partition, the last event can be interpreted as the event that $x_1 - c$ and $x_2 - c$ end up in the same range. If $|x_1 - x_2| \geqslant 10$, then this can never happen because the distance between $x_1 - c$ and $x_2 - c$ is $|x_1 - x_2|$ and the length of each range is 10. Thus, the case of $|x_1 - x_2| < 10$ remains to be considered. In this case, the event $\lceil (x_1 - c)/10 \rceil = \lceil (x_2 - c)/10 \rceil$ happens if and only if the location of $x_1 - c$ within the range that includes it is at distance of at least $|x_1 - x_2|$ from the end of the range. Note that the distribution of c guarantees that the distance of $x_1 - c$ from the end of the range including it is a uniformly random number from the range $(0, 10]$, and thus, the probability that it is at least $|x_1 - x_2|$ is given by

$$1 - \frac{|x_1 - x_2|}{10 - 0} = 1 - \frac{|x_1 - x_2|}{10}.$$

Solution 2

Observe that $f_i(x) = f_i(y)$ if and only if the vectors x and y agree on their i-th coordinate. Thus, when f_i is drawn uniformly at random from F_H (which implies that i is drawn uniformly at random from the integers between 1 and n), we get

$$\Pr[f_i(x) = f_i(y)] = \frac{\text{\# of coordinates in which } x \text{ and } y \text{ agree}}{n}$$

$$= \frac{n - \text{dist}_H(x, y)}{n} = 1 - \frac{\text{dist}_H(x, y)}{n}.$$

Solution 3

Figure 18.4 depicts the vectors x and y and two regions, one around each one of these vectors, where the region around each vector z includes all the vectors whose angle with respect to z is at most $90°$. We denote the region around x by $N(x)$ and the region around y by $N(y)$. One can note that $f_z(x) = f_z(y)$ if and only if the vector z is in both these regions or in neither of them. Thus,

$$\Pr[f_z(x) = f_z(y)]$$

$$= \frac{\{\text{angular size of } N(x) \cap N(y)\} + \{\text{angular size of } \mathbb{R}^2 \setminus (N(x) \cap N(y))\}}{360°}.$$

Let us now relate the two angular sizes in the last equality to $\text{dist}_\theta(x, y)$. Since the angle between the vectors x and y is $\text{dist}_\theta(x, y)$, the angular size of the intersection between $N(x)$ and $N(y)$ is $180° - \text{dist}_\theta(x, y)$. Using the

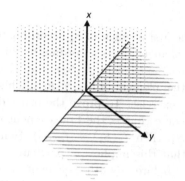

Figure 18.4. Vectors x and y in $\mathbb{R}^2$. Around the vector x there is a region marked with dots that includes all the vectors whose angle with respect to x is at most $90°$. Similarly, around y there is a region marked with lines that includes all the vectors whose angle with respect to y is at most $90°$.

inclusion and exclusion principal, this implies

$$\{\text{angular size of } \mathbb{R}^2 \backslash (N(x) \cup N(y))\}$$

$$= \{\text{angular size of } \mathbb{R}^2\} - \{\text{angular size of } N(x)\}$$

$$- \{\text{angular size of } N(y)\} + \{\text{angular size of } N(x) \cap N(y)\}$$

$$= 360° - 180° - 180° + (180° - \text{dist}_\theta(x, y)) = 180° - \text{dist}_\theta(x, y).$$

Combining all the above equations, we get

$$\Pr[f_z(x) = f_z(y)] = \frac{[180° - \text{dist}_\theta(x, y)] + [180° - \text{dist}_\theta(x, y)]}{360°}$$

$$= 1 - \frac{\text{dist}_\theta(x, y)}{180°}.$$

Solution 4

Note that $f_e(S_1) = f_e(S_2)$ if and only if e belongs to both these sets or to neither one of them. Thus,

$$\Pr[f_e(S_1) = f_e(S_2)] = \Pr[e \in S_1 \cap S_2] + \Pr[e \notin S_1 \cup S_2]$$

$$= \frac{|S_1 \cap S_2|}{|N|} + \left(1 - \frac{|S_1 \cup S_2|}{|N|}\right) = 1$$

$$- \frac{|S_1 \cup S_2| \cdot \text{dist}_J(S_1, S_2)}{|N|}.$$

To see that the last equality holds, plug in the definition of dist_J.

Solution 5

Recall that $f_\pi(S_1)$ is the first element of S_1 according to the permutation π, and $f_\pi(S_2)$ is the first element of S_2 according to this permutation. Thus, if $f_\pi(S_1) = f_\pi(S_2)$, then the element $f_\pi(S_1)$ is an element of $S_1 \cap S_2$ that appears before every other element of $S_1 \cup S_2$ in π. This proves one direction of the first part of the exercise. To prove the other direction, we need to show that if the element e that is the first element of $S_1 \cup S_2$ according to π belongs to $S_1 \cap S_2$, then $f_\pi(S_1) = f_\pi(S_2)$. Hence, assume that this is the case, and note that this implies, in particular, that e is an element of S_1 that appears in π before any other element of S_1. Thus, $f_\pi(S_1) = e$. Similarly, we also get $f_\pi(S_2) = e$, and consequently, $f_\pi(S_1) = e = f_\pi(S_2)$.

The second part of the exercise remains to be solved. Since π is a uniformly random permutation of N in this part of the exercise, a symmetry argument shows that the first element of $S_1 \cup S_2$ according to π (formally given by $f_\pi(S_1 \cup S_2)$) is a uniformly random element of $S_1 \cup S_2$. Thus,

$$\Pr[f_\pi(S_1) = f_\pi(S_2)] = \Pr[f_\pi(S_1 \cup S_2) \in S_1 \cap S_2]$$

$$= \frac{|S_1 \cap S_2|}{|S_1 \cup S_2|} = 1 - \operatorname{dist}_J(S_1, S_2).$$

Solution 6

Recall that by Exercise 5, for two sets S_1 and S_2 at Jaccard distance d from each other it holds that $\Pr[f(S_1) = f(S_2)] = 1 - d$ for a random hash function f from F_J. Thus, for $d \leqslant d_1 = 1/5$, we get

$$\Pr[f(S_1) = f(S_2)] = 1 - d \geqslant 1 - 1/5 = 4/5 = p_1.$$

Similarly, for $d \geqslant d_2 = 2/5$, we get

$$\Pr[f(S_1) = f(S_2)] = 1 - d \leqslant 1 - 2/5 = 3/5 = p_2.$$

Solution 7

Consider a pair e_1 and e_2 of elements at distance at most d_1. Since F is (d_1, d_2, p_1, p_2)-sensitive, $\Pr[f(e_1) = f(e_2)] \geqslant p_1$ for a uniformly random function $f \in F$. Consider now a uniformly random function $g \in G$. Since G contains a function for every choice of r (not necessarily distinct) functions from F, the uniformly random choice of g implies that it is associated with r

uniformly random functions $f_1, f_2, \ldots, f_r$ from F. Thus,

$$\Pr[g(e_1) = g(e_2)] = \Pr[\forall_{1 \leqslant i \leqslant r} f_i(e_1) = f_i(e_2)] = \prod_{i=1}^{r} \Pr[f(e_1) = f(e_2)]$$

$$\geqslant \prod_{i=1}^{r} p_1 = p_1^r. \tag{18.2}$$

It remains to be proved that $\Pr[g(e_1) = g(e_2)] \leqslant p_2^r$ when e_1 and e_2 are two elements at distance at least d_2 and g is a uniformly random function from G. However, the proof for this inequality is very similar to the proof of Inequality (18.2), and is thus, omitted.

Solution 8

The solution of this exercise is very similar to the solution of Exercise 7. However, for the sake of completeness, we repeat the following necessary arguments.

Consider a pair e_1 and e_2 of elements at distance at most d_1. Since F is (d_1, d_2, p_1, p_2)-sensitive, $\Pr[f(e_1) = f(e_2)] \geqslant p_1$ for a uniformly random function $f \in F$. Consider now a uniformly random function $g \in G$. Since G contains a function for every choice of r (not necessarily distinct) functions from F, the random choice of g implies that it is associated with r uniformly random functions $f_1, f_2, \ldots, f_r$ from F. Thus,

$$\Pr[g(e_1) = g(e_1)] = \Pr[\exists_{1 \leqslant i \leqslant r} f_i(e_1) = f_i(e_1)]$$

$$= 1 - \Pr[\forall_{1 \leqslant i \leqslant r} f_i(e_1) \neq f_i(e_1)]$$

$$= 1 - \prod_{i=1}^{r}(1 - \Pr[f_i(e_1) = f_i(e_2)])$$

$$\geqslant 1 - \prod_{i=1}^{r}(1 - p_1) = 1 - (1 - p_1)^r. \tag{18.3}$$

It remains to be proved that $\Pr[g(e_1) = g(e_2)] \leqslant 1 - (1 - p_2)^r$ when e_1 and e_2 are two elements at distance at least d_2 and g is a uniformly random function from G. However, the proof for this inequality is very similar to the proof of Inequality (18.3), and is thus, omitted.

Solution 9

(a) The most natural way to distribute the function f is via the following two Map-Reduce iterations method. In the first iteration, every input machine forwards its name to the pre-designed central machine. Then, in the second Map-Reduce iteration, the central machine forwards f to all the input machines. Unfortunately, using this natural method as is might result in large machine time and space complexities because it requires the central machine to store the names of all the input machines and send the function f to all of them. To solve this issue, it is necessary to split the work of the central machine between multiple machines. More specifically, we will use a tree T of machines with k levels and d children for every internal node. The root of the tree is the central machine, and then $k - 1$ Map-Reduce iterations are used to forward f along the tree T to the leaf machines. Once the function f gets to the leaves, all the input machines forward their names to random leaves of T, and each leaf that gets the names of input machines responds by forwarding to these machines the function f.

Observe that, under the above suggested solution, an internal node of the tree needs to forward f only to its children in T, and thus, has a small machine time complexity as long as d is kept moderate. Additionally, every leaf of the tree gets the names of roughly n/d^{k-1} input machines, where n is the number of elements, and thus, has a small machine time and space complexities when d^{k-1} is close to n. Combining these observations, we get that the suggested solution results in small machine time and space complexity whenever $d^{k-1} = \Theta(n)$ and d is small. While these requirements are somewhat contradictory, they can be made to hold together (even when we want d to be a constant) by setting $k = \Theta(\log n)$.

The above paragraphs were quite informal in the way they described the suggested solution and analyzed it. For the interested readers, we note that a more formal study of a very similar technique was done in the solution of Exercise 2 in Chapter 16.

(b) The procedure described by the exercise forwards every element e to the range item $f(e)$ it is mapped to by f, and then detects that two elements are mapped to the same range item by noting that they end up on the same machine. As noted by the exercise, this works only when range items are considered equal exactly when they are identical, which is not the case in the OR-construction.

The range of a hash functions family obtained as an r-OR-construction consists of r-tuples, where two tuples are considered equal if they agree on some coordinate. Thus, detecting that two tuples are equal is equivalent to detecting that their values for some coordinate are identical. This suggests the following modification to the procedure described by the exercise. Instead of forwarding the element e mapped to an r-tuple $(t_1, t_2, \ldots, t_r)$ to a machine named $(t_1, t_2, \ldots, t_r)$, we forward it to the r machines named (i, t_i) for every $1 \leqslant i \leqslant t$. Then, every machine (i, t) that gets multiple elements can know that the tuples corresponding to all these elements had the value t in the ith coordinate of their tuple, and thus, can declare all these elements as suspected to be close.

One drawback of this approach is that a pair of elements might be declared as suspected to be close multiple times if their tuples agree on multiple coordinates. If this is problematic, then one can solve it using the following trick. A machine (i, t) that detects that a pair of elements e_1 and e_2 might be close to each other should forward a message to a machine named (e_1, e_2). Then, in the next Map-Reduce iteration, each machine (e_1, e_2) that got one or more messages will report e_1 and e_2 as suspected to be close. This guarantees, at the cost of one additional Map-Reduce iteration, that every pair of elements is reported at most once as suspected to be close.

Index